ARISTOPHANES

was born in Athens about 445 B.C. His first play, produced when he was scarcely twenty years old, is nevertheless a mature work. Until his death about 388 B.C. he was the leading comic poet of Greece, towering above his rivals. Moses Hadas, in his introduction to this volume, writes: "If Aristophanes is without direct progeny his influence on subsequent satire and farce is very great. But valuable as he may be as a commentary on a uniquely valuable area of human experience or as a begetter of art in others, his true claim upon our attention is as the most brilliant and artistic and thoughtful wit our world has known."

MOSES HADAS, late Jay Professor of Greek at Columbia University, was the author of the authoritative **History of Greek Literature**, the companion **History of Latin Literature**, and **Hellenistic Culture: Fusion and Diffusion**. Bantam Books edited by Professor Hadas include **Greek Drama, Ten Plays by Euripides, The Aeneid**, and **The Essential Works of Stoicism**, in addition to his **Introduction to Classical Drama**.

BANTAM DRAMA

THE COMPLETE PLAYS OF ARISTOPHANES
edited by Moses Hadas
THE COMPLETE PLAYS OF SOPHOCLES edited by Moses Hadas
GREEK DRAMA edited by Moses Hadas
TRAGEDY: TEN MAJOR PLAYS edited by Robert O'Brien and
Bernard F. Dukore
TEN PLAYS BY EURIPIDES edited by Moses Hadas

THE COMPLETE PLAYS OF
ARISTOPHANES

EDITED AND
WITH AN INTRODUCTION
BY MOSES HADAS

BANTAM BOOKS · TORONTO · NEW YORK · LONDON

RL 8, IL 11+

THE COMPLETE PLAYS OF ARISTOPHANES
A Bantam Classic / July 1962

2nd printing .. December 1963   4th printing ..... August 1965
3rd printing .. December 1964   5th printing .... October 1966
6th printing ...... August 1967
Bantam World Drama edition / August 1968
8th printing .. November 1968   9th printing .... October 1969
Bantam edition / May 1971
11th printing .... March 1972   13th printing ... October 1974
12th printing .... August 1973   14th printing ...... May 1976
15th printing .... July 1978

Knights, Birds, Frogs: © Copyright, 1962, by the University of
Virginia Press; translated by Professor Robert H. Webb and in-
cluded in this volume by permission of the University of Virginia
Press, on behalf of Mrs. Webb.

Lysistrata, Ecclesiazusae: © Copyright, Jack Lindsay; translated
by Jack Lindsay. Reprinted by permission of Mr. Lindsay.

Acharnians, Peace, Thesmophoriazusae, Plutus: translated by
B. B. Rogers. Reprinted by permission of G. Bell and Sons, Ltd.,
London.

ISBN 0-553-12237-1

Published simultaneously in the United States and Canada

Bantam Books are published by Bantam Books, Inc. Its trade-
mark, consisting of the words "Bantam Books" and the por-
trayal of a bantam, is registered in the United States Patent
Office and in other countries. Marca Registrada. Bantam
Books, Inc., 666 Fifth Avenue, New York, New York 10019.

PRINTED IN THE UNITED STATES OF AMERICA

Contents

The Complete Plays
of Aristophanes

Introduction

The World Destroyed and Remade

Aristophanes is not the most profound or exalted of Greek poets, but he is the most creative. Others deal with the world as it is, glorifying it, perhaps, or justifying its flaws, discovering hidden values in it and suggesting how they may be realized; Aristophanes erases the world that is and constructs another. The tragedies we have are all based on traditional myths which the playwrights might interpret and embellish—provided the embellishment were appropriate and probable—but they could not significantly alter the ancient "history." Aristophanes abolishes history and all ordinary constraints of space and time, of gravity and physiology. If war has become tiresome he makes a private treaty with the enemy or goes to heaven to fetch down the goddess Peace. If Athens has become tiresome he builds a new city in the sky. If living poets are inadequate he goes to hell to fetch back an old one.

For their principal dramatis personae the tragic poets were limited to the traditional personages of myth. If Aristophanes wants a character he invents one. To us this does not seem remarkable, but we must remember that not only epic and tragedy and choral lyric but even the dialogues of Plato used only personages who were believed to be historical. And if characters are invented so are their doings. Aristophanes created his own world, and populated it with his own people, as a god might do.

The Universality of the Comic

And yet these invented people behave in ways consonant with our conceptions of human nature. Once we grant the validity of the new world which Aristophanes has created, what his people do in it seems perfectly normal. This involves another important difference between comedy and tragedy. The personages of tragedy do indeed grieve and rejoice as men everywhere and always have done, else their stories would be unprofitable and indeed meaningless to us. But sometimes we need to learn a particular code to understand that causes apparently inconsequential can generate intense emotional responses. Sometimes, similarly, we need to know a particular set of conventions to recognize that a thing is incongruous and therefore funny; but the incongruities which comedy invents are seldom so subtle as to require commentary. Laughter is more direct and more universal than the emotions of tragedy.

No Athenian of the fifth century B.C. (or indeed of any other) ever saw an Agamemnon or a Clytemnestra in the flesh; these stalking figures were deliberately built up by the poets, and their costumes and mode of speech, like their emotional intensity, were calculated to set them apart from ordinary humanity. The figures of comedy, historical (like Euripides or Plato) or invented, are familiar contemporary types, and their behavior is according to familiar norms. The figures of tragedy are sometimes little more than symbols to illustrate some permanent principle of morality; those of comedy have to do with simpler but more immediate problems of making peace, running a school, writing a play. In comedy alone do men drop the rigid poses they are given in graver kinds of writing and walk and talk on a level with their fellow citizens. When the tyrant of Syracuse asked how he could discover what Athenians were like, Plato advised him to read the comedies of Aristophanes.

Aristophanes should then be the most accessible of the fifth-century dramatists, and at many levels he is. He is not at all levels because preoccupation with the timely militates against timelessness. The tragic poets who deal with eternal problems write as if they knew they were addressing the ages. Aristophanes wrote for a specific audience and occasion, and would have laughed at the thought that remote generations might be fingering his plays. At the level of physiological jokes, therefore, and those that approach the physiological in universality, all who share our common physiology can understand him well enough. But allusions to contemporary persons, events, or usages, special connotations of words, and, in a more general view, the intellectual bent of Aristophanic wit sometimes leaves us in the dark—just as reflections of contemporary life in our comedy would be lost on a Greek audience. An old movie has Groucho Marx's secretary say, when two men are waiting to see him, "Epstein is waxing wroth," and Groucho replies, "Tell Roth to wax Epstein." How many volumes of commentary would a Greek require to understand all of the joke, and how unfunny it would be after he had studied the commentary! We do have helpful information to solve some puzzles in the compilations of scholia made in later antiquity, but much must remain only partially understood. But as in all classical literature so in Aristophanes also the specific merges with the general. From Aristophanes' contemporary Thucydides, for example, we learn the details of a particular war but we learn also about the nature of war generally. So in Aristophanes, if the details are not always clear the general principles are not only clear but instructive.

WIT AND HUMOR

More basic than the difficulty of forgotten allusions is the fact that Aristophanic comedy is intellectual rather than sentimental. What the essential nature of the comic is, is still an open question, but for assaying individual creators of comedy it is convenient and it may be instructive to distinguish between the sentimental kind, which engages the reader's sympathy for its personages as human beings, and the intellectual kind, which attacks the reader's head rather than his heart, or, if we may give the words these particular meanings, between humor and wit. In later European literature the outstanding protagonists of the two kinds are Cervantes and Rabelais. Cervantes engages our sympathy for Don Quixote until we wince for him when he is beaten or ridiculed; Gargantua and Pantagruel are bloodless figures of intellectual fun, and whatever befalls them our kibes are ungalled. Or, to look at the stage, the casts of Ben Jonson's *Volpone* or *Alchemist* can no more be hated than loved, for they are almost x's and y's in a mathematical demonstration; but we do come near loving Molière's Agnes just as we loathe his Tartuffe. If, in Aristophanes' *Clouds*, we feel kindly toward Socrates or Strepsiades, it is because we know Socrates from other sources and because we are sorry for old men we know who are bedeviled by wastrel sons; Aristophanes does nothing to waken our sympathy or play upon it. It is just where kindliness might be expected that we find him most heartless. He is notably cruel to old women, for example, as all writers of intellectual comedy tend to be: Gilbert and Sullivan, to cite one example, are.

Intellectual fun, needless to say, is not necessarily lofty. Pie-throwing and prat-falls are intellectual jokes, not humor. The basis of the intellectual joke is manifest incongruity.

Very often, as notably in Rabelais as in Aristophanes, the incongruity depends on kinds of word play: a pun is funny because it brings together two meanings of a word that are really incongruous. But puns are not the only kind of incongruity. It is incongruity, not sympathy for an impoverished gentleman, that makes us laugh at a top-hat that is dented or worn with patched shoes. If it were habitual with us to keep the queer members which flap at either side of our heads scrupulously swathed, nothing could be funnier than to see them unexpectedly exposed. That is why the phalluses and talk about them which are ordinarily discreetly covered are funny when exposed to an audience.

Obscenity Sacred and Profane

To use Aristophanes as a stick with which to belabor the Victorians and their progeny is false, for the Greeks too were Victorian; if they had not been, Aristophanes' bawdry would not have been incongruous and would not have amused the Greeks any more than it would have amused us. It is true that we are more reserved in these matters than were the Greeks, and hence the bawdry is to us more obtrusive; that is how "Aristophanic" has acquired its meaning. It is of course true that Aristophanes' plays are saturated with obscenity; excretory and sexual functions are explicit or implicit on every page, and dozens of seemingly innocent words apparently carried obscene connotations. But what should interest us is not that Aristophanes is so outspoken but that the rest of Greek literature is so pure, not that men seemed to relish obscenity (when have they not?) but that it was presented under the highest auspices of the state, to the entire population, at a religious festival under the presidency of a priest and on consecrated ground.

Obscenity was incongruous because Greek literature aside from comedy is one of the most decorous we know; it is more decorous, for example, than the literature of the Old Testament. It is as if dumping all bawdiness into one form served to keep the others pure, and that indeed is one implication of Euripides' *Bacchae*. The ferment which a man must exert himself to suppress if he would keep all the days of the year pure will nevertheless creep in to taint all 365 of them; but if he gives the ferment three days of carnival in which to boil itself away then he might hope to keep the other 362 untainted. The god who proved this arithmetic upon Pentheus in the *Bacchae* was of course the same Dionysus who was celebrated in the dramatic festivals.

If comedy is a wholesome purge we can understand how the enlightened authorities of a state might tolerate it, but the religious auspices must still seem odd to communicants of more austere religions. The explanation is that, as in the Greek art forms, a usage which originally had a religious rationale obvious to all came to be retained for aesthetic or other reasons after the religious burden had faded or disappeared. About the early history of comedy we know little—mainly because Aristotle did not like comedy and scanted it in his *Poetics*—but there can be no doubt that its origins are to be connected with a fertility cult, in which the element of sex would naturally be central. The beast mummery (as in the fantastic costuming and titles of the choruses) and the festive topsy-turvydom which gave inferiors license to make butts of their betters are surely integral to the cultic origins of comedy also. To what degree fifth-century audiences were conscious of the original significances of these elements of comedy we cannot be sure; but the sense of ritual surely remained, for the Greeks were extremely conservative in preserving established forms. Aristotle says that when an art form reaches its proper development it remains fixed. Euripides might revolutionize the spirit of tragedy, but he retained its form virtually unchanged.

THE FORM OF OLD COMEDY

It is because of its religious origins and associations, doubtless, and because Greek art is always observant of form that Aristophanes' plays fall into a regular pattern; the pattern is not so strict as tragedy's, but much more regular than in modern comedy. As in tragedy there is a *prologue;* the *parodos,* or entry of the chorus; the equivalent of *episodes,* separated from one another by fixed choral elements; and an *exodos,* or marching-away song. The chorus (usually numbering twenty-four) is much larger than the chorus of tragedy, and its apparently capricious arrangements accord to a strict pattern. In the *parabasis* the chorus comes forward to speak for the author in his own person. Here the author may justify his own work, defend himself against rivals or attack them, and here he may comment, like a columnist in a modern newspaper, on whatever abuses in the contemporary scene he may wish to animadvert upon. It is from the parabasis of

Old Comedy that the Roman genre of satire derived. At one point in the play the chorus divides into two, each half defending some point of view and abusing the other half, not only with words but sometimes even physically. Rowdy and uproarious as it may be, this contest or *agon* is usually a serious presentation of some contemporary problem. For each of the parts of the choral performance there was a prescribed meter; for example a patter song, called *pnigos* or "choker," was sung rapidly without drawing new breath.

The masks of comic actors, unlike those of tragedy, showed exaggeratedly coarse peasant types. The theory that there were a fixed set of masks—Old Man, Cook, Courtesan, etc.—somewhat as in the commedia dell'arte—does not apply to Old Comedy. Not only were the features of the masks coarse, but the actors were ridiculously padded on belly and buttocks, and had oversize phalluses appended. The padding allowed for all kinds of farcical business, as in the singeing of Mnesilochus in the *Thesmophoriazusae*. The prominent phalluses and the beast costumes of the chorus, as has been suggested, derived from early ritual associations of fertility cults. Providing the fanciful costumes for the chorus and training them in their intricate performances involved great expense; that is why the choral work is curtailed in Aristophanes' last plays, presented when Athens was impoverished.

The movement of an Aristophanic play is as regular as its form. The prologue, frequently a master-slave conversation, sets forth some fantastic scheme—a descent to hell, a sex strike, or the like—and the rest of the play is worked out on the assumption that the premises are the most commonplace in the world. In the agon the "good" side naturally wins and the bad is discomfited. The bad side goes off, often literally bruised, and the good goes to a riotous celebration, often accompanied by gay females. This is surely a relic of some sort of ritual "marriage" which was the culmination of a fertility celebration; psychologically it is the only acceptable solution of a comedy. The endings of tragedy, however grim they may be, are psychologically satisfying, but how else is a comedy to end?

THE TEACHING BRIEF

Aside from its creative fantasy and its purgative wit, what makes the comedy of Aristophanes memorable is its exquisite lyrics and its serious commentary—on politics, poetry, education, good citizenship. The qualities of lyric poetry are notoriously hard to communicate, in translation or description; all that can be said of Aristophanes' is that they are singularly graceful, with a sweetness that is more appealing because of the soil out of which they grow. Richest of all in this kind is the *Birds*, which the lyrics transform into an idyllic fairyland, but there are fine pieces in all the comedies. It is Aristophanes' lyricism, indeed, which lends his comedies wings, and that is why prose or inept verse translation is peculiarly unfortunate in his case. Without the lift of poetry much of his terrain is a malodorous and heavy bog in which people of certain tastes may take pleasure in wallowing, but which is a travesty of Aristophanes' scintillating artistry.

What is more surprising than lyricism or bawdiness to innocent readers who expect of farce only that it be rollicking is Aristophanes' mature commentary on perennial problems of political and social life. All the classic poets were looked upon and looked upon themselves as serious teachers—the doctrine of pure belles-lettres was invented by the precious Alexandrian court poets under the patronage of the Ptolemies—but none seems so conscious of a teaching mission as Aristophanes. For one thing his teaching was more explicit and immediate. The tragic poet might explore large questions of the ways of God to man; the comic poet told his audiences what was wrong with foreign policy or politicians, or how educationists were corrupting sound learning or neoteric poets corrupting good taste, and he invited immediate action, not merely a change in attitude. Outspoken criticism of what Euripides called "the statues in the market place" was a carnival privilege which probably originated in the revels of the fertility cult, but it has always been an element in serious comedy. We think of Rabelais' slashing criticism of state educational practices at the Sorbonne, or of war in the episode of the grape growers and cake bakers, of the entire antihumanist outlook upon life in his ideal Abbey of Thélème. "For children have tutors to guide them aright," Aristophanes makes Aeschylus say in the *Frogs*, "young manhood has poets for teachers."

So pervasive is the didactic in Aristophanes and so consistent the tenor of his criticism that many have thought that advocacy of a particular set of doctrines was his prime object and that he chose comedy as their most effective vehicle, and some have thought that he was actually in the pay of the conservative oligarchy. Nothing could be more mistaken. The proper description of Aristophanes is poet and comic genius. His object in writing plays was to amuse, and to do it so well that he would win the prize. But an intelligent man who is funny must be funny about something, and the traditions of the form in which Aristophanes worked involved comment on matters of public interest. In this respect the comic poet was something like a newspaper columnist, and as in the case of thoughtful columnists it happened that Aristophanes' comments on all questions followed a consistent direction.

The direction is at all points conservative. Aristophanes plainly does not like the relaxation of traditional standards which attended the rise of democratic power and looks back wistfully to the soberer ways of an earlier day. Like many upper-class Athenians he admired the Spartans and thought the war against them a regrettable mistake. This feeling is more or less under the surface in all the plays of the war period, but it is outspoken in the *Acharnians* and especially in the *Knights*. In the latter play he brushes aside the stunning victory of the Athenians at Sphacteria and exaggerates a minor success won by the knights at Corinth. He loathes Cleon (who took credit for the victory at Sphacteria), and thinks (in the *Wasps*) that the innovation of pay for jury duty, actually a measure to provide sustenance for the beleaguered and unemployed Athenians, was introduced by Cleon to strengthen his hold on the populace. And yet, as the *Lysistrata* shows, he is more moved by sympathy for the innocent sufferers of war than by anger against the warmongers. The amazing thing is that plays attacking the war policy when the state was at war could be given under state auspices and that Cleon could be most virulently attacked for bad morals and manners when he was himself in the audience.

Aristophanes is most bitter against the sophists, for it was their doctrine of man the measure which was the greatest solvent for traditional privilege and for traditional morality, and which encouraged the loquacious impertinence of sailors and artisans. In order to give force to his attack on the sophists he is willing to make Socrates, who was himself opposed to the sophists, a butt, because Socrates was a familiar figure and his appearance and manner invited ridicule. This does not mean, of course, that Aristophanes' shrewd attacks on the relaxed discipline and the criterion of expediency favored by the new education are without point. He strikes at Euripides in almost every play and makes him the chief butt of the *Frogs* and the *Thesmophoriazusae* because, following sophist doctrine, Euripides degraded tragedy from its lofty plane and vulgarized it by introducing commonplace characters and unseemly plots. And yet he pays Euripides the tacit compliment of imitating him, and for all his sympathy for Aeschylus, in the *Frogs*, he pronounces some unkind truths about Aeschylus' own faults of pomposity and turgidity. And the *Thesmophoriazusae* is a delightful piece of literary playfulness, wholly without malice. He dislikes innovations in music, and thinks the old tunes were better because they fostered manly discipline. He dislikes theories of social reform pointing to socialism or communism, mainly because people cannot in nature be equal, as these systems premise. Human nature, he holds, cannot be transformed by legislation: the exploiting officials whom communism was expected to re-form, in the *Ecclesiazusae*, promptly turn up as even more grasping commissars. He is thoroughly Athenian in making the interest of the state the gauge for all values: when Dionysus cannot decide between Euripides and Aeschylus on grounds of poetic merit (in the *Frogs*) the decision is reached by the soundness of the political advice which each offers. It is significant that the *Birds*, which is the most carefully wrought of all the plays, is also the most charming and utterly free from malice. It is the sad state of the human condition, and not a particular set of malefactors, that prompts the establishment of a utopia in a fanciful never-never land.

One final quality of the plays, which tells us more about the audience than the playwright, must be mentioned, and that is the volume of literary allusion which the audience was expected to recognize. There are allusions or intention-ally garbled quotations from tragedy (of which we owe the identification to the scholiasts) in all the plays; the *Thesmo-phoriazusae* and the *Frogs* turn on quotations, mainly from Euripides, and the *Frogs* expects of its audience a high de-gree of sophistication in literary criticism. All of this would be understandable in works directed to an esoteric audience of scholars; but these plays were addressed to the whole population, and were meant to win prizes, not be a *succès d'estime*. We have no better evidence than the plays of Aris-tophanes for the high level of general literary sophistication in Athens, as we have no better evidence than his plays for the effectiveness of Athenian *eleutheria* and *parrhesia*, liberty and freedom of speech.

The Man, His Rivals, His Successors

Except for the parabases of his own plays, in which he speaks of his own and his rivals' works, we know no more of Aristophanes than we do of the writers of tragedy. One distinction of Aristophanes is that whereas the surviving plays of Sophocles and Euripides were written in full maturity and most near the ends of their long lives, those of Aristophanes, except for the *Ecclesiazusae* and the *Plutus*, are a young man's work. Aristophanes was born about 445 B.C., and the *Acharnians*, produced in 425 when he was barely twenty, is a fully mature work. Details given in the ancient Lives from his plays or imaginary. His death cannot have occurred before 388 B.C.

In all, forty-four plays were attributed to Aristophanes, and of these some were produced under the names of other poets. The fact that the eleven plays of Aristophanes which we have are the only complete specimens of Old Comedy to survive is sufficient proof that his work was esteemed the best. Five of the eleven plays we have—*Acharnians*, *Knights*, *Clouds*, *Wasps*, and *Peace*—were produced one each year from 425 to 421. Then follow the *Birds*, Aristophanes' acknowledged masterpiece, 414; *Lysistrata* and *Thesmophoriazusae*, 411; and *Frogs*, 405. The fall of Athens in 404 was a blow to comedy as to other aspects of Attic creativity, and the two last plays of our corpus show spiritual as well as physical impoverishment. The *Ecclesiazusae*, produced in 392 B.C., shows a flagging of comic verve; the choral portions are perfunctory, and at one place our texts give merely the word "Chorus." *Plutus*, produced in 388 B.C., leaves the exuberant farce of the earlier Aristophanes almost entirely and makes a transition to the comedy of manners. There is no longer criticism of persons and policies but a travesty of the myth of the blind god of wealth to which no individual could take exception and which is applicable to any age or place. The *Plutus* was in fact far the most popular of Aristophanes' comedies in the Byzantine period.

There were, of course, many other masters of Old Comedy, a number of whom defeated Aristophanes in competitions, just as there were tragic poets who defeated Aeschylus, Sophocles, or Euripides. The Alexandrian scholars who constructed "canons" of poets in various genres joined Cratinus and Eupolis to Aristophanes in a triad to balance the Tragic

Three. It is clear that Aristophanes towered above his rivals by a greater interval than any tragic poet above his, but the work of the others, on the evidence of their fragments, is by no means negligible. Those whose loss is most regrettable are Epicharmus, the pioneer in the form, Crates, and Plato Comicus.

Greek Comedy after Old is traditionally classified as Middle and New. Of Middle Comedy little can be said, for although the volume was enormous we have no extant specimen of the genre and can only surmise its character from Aristophanes' *Plutus* and from such a play as Plautus' *Amphitryo*, which is also a travesty of myth and presumably drawn from a Middle Comedy model. In New Comedy, on the other hand, we have not only a complete play (the *Dyskolos*) and extensive fragments of the work of Menander but numerous adaptations of several other New Comedy playwrights in Plautus and Terence. It is New Comedy—which has affinities with the later work of Euripides—rather than tragedy or the farce of Aristophanes which is the ancestor of our European drama. The persons and plots of New Comedy are invented, as in Old Comedy, not drawn from ancient "history," but New Comedy represents the relationships and problems of Everyman, and is therefore the most exportable of all ancient dramatic forms.

If Aristophanes is without direct progeny his influence on subsequent satire and farce is very great. But valuable as he may be as a commentary on a uniquely valuable area of human experience or as a begetter of art in others, his true claim upon our attention is as the most brilliant and artistic and thoughtful wit our world has known.

THE TRANSLATIONS

Where a poet's doctrine is our chief concern a clear prose version may be better than mediocre verse; but for Aristophanes, though his teaching is significant, verse is mandatory. Without it the sparkle vanishes and the bawdiness is reduced to a noisome morass. Older verse translations have been antiquated by new standards of faithfulness and propriety. The first acceptable in English are those of Benjamin Bickley Rogers (1829-1919), which combine sparkle and melody with accuracy. Four of the Rogers versions are included in the present volume. Three others of similar quality but with an unmistakable American tang are from the hand of Robert

Henning Webb (1882-1952), late Professor of Greek in the University of Virginia. These are used with the generous permission of the University of Virginia Press, which plans to publish all of Webb's Aristophanes, with the translator's illuminating notes. Of the remaining four plays two have been translated, with his customary verve and felicity, by Jack Lindsay, the English scholar and poet, and two by the present editor.

Acharnians

The *Acharnians* was produced in 425 B.C., when Aristophanes was barely twenty, but in exuberant inventiveness, lyrical quality, serious political criticism, it is among Aristophanes' best plays. It won the first prize over Cratinus and Eupolis. The characteristic topsy-turvy fantasy upon which the play hinges is the notion that a man weary of an ill-considered war might make an individual peace with the enemy. Here Dicaeopolis makes such a peace with Sparta, but as he is about to celebrate the long-intermitted vintage festival he is attacked by a chorus of Acharnian charcoal burners who represent the war party and he wins a hearing by a parody of Euripides' *Telephus*. In a seriocomic speech he shows that the causes of the war were trifling, and wins over half the chorus, who are engaged in a violent agon by the other half. These call in the general Lamachus to assist them, but the general too is bested in argument, and the chorus, uniting on Dicaeopolis' side, deliver the poet's parabasis. Then Megarians and Boeotians bring in for sale the good things Athens has lacked. A herald summons Lamachus to a hard campaign, and another, Dicaeopolis to a wine party. Lamachus returns wounded, and Dicaeopolis reels in, having won the prize for drinking, on the arms of pretty flute girls, whom he leads out in procession. If we are astonished at the temerity of a poet who could say a word for the enemy and many words for pacifism amid the passions of war, we must be amazed at a democracy which permitted and sponsored such a play in time of war, and gave it first prize.

CHARACTERS

DICAEOPOLIS
CRIER
AMPHITHEUS
AMBASSADORS
PSEUDARTABAS
THEORUS
DAUGHTER OF DICAEOPOLIS
SLAVE OF EURIPIDES
EURIPIDES
LAMACHUS
A MEGARIAN

TWO YOUNG GIRLS, DAUGHTERS
OF THE MEGARIAN
AN INFORMER
A BOEOTIAN
NICARCHUS
SLAVE OF LAMACHUS
DERCETES, AN ATHENIAN
FARMER
A WEDDING GUEST
CHORUS OF ACHARNIAN
CHARCOAL BURNERS

Translated by B. B. Rogers

(DICAEOPOLIS *is discovered near the Pnyx, impatiently
awaiting the opening of the Assembly. His house, flanked
by those of* LAMACHUS *and* EURIPIDES, *is in the background.*)

DICAEOPOLIS. What heaps of things have bitten me to the
        heart!
A small few pleased me, very few, just four;
But those that vexed were sand-dune-hundredfold.
Let's see: what pleased me, worth my gladfulness?
I know a thing it cheered my heart to see;
The five-talent bribe vomited up by Cleon.
At that I brightened; and I love the Knights
For that performance; 'twas of price to Hellas.
Then I'd a tragic sorrow, when I looked
With open mouth for Aeschylus, and lo,
The Crier called, *Bring on your play, Theognis.*
Judge what an icy shock that gave my heart!
Next; pleased I was when Moschus left, and in
Dexitheus came with his Boeotian song.
But oh this year I nearly cracked my neck,
When in slipped Chaeris for the Orthian Chant.
But never yet since first I washed my face
Was I so bitten—in my brows with soap,
As now, when here's the fixed Assembly Day,
And morning come, and no one in the Pnyx.
They're in the Agora chattering, up and down
Scurrying to dodge the cord dripping red.
Why, even the Prytanes are not here! They'll come
Long after time, elbowing each other, jostling
For the front bench, streaming down all together
You can't think how. But as for making Peace
They do not care one jot. O City! City!
But I am always first of all to come,
And here I take my seat; then, all alone,
I pass the time complaining, yawning, stretching,
I fidget, write, twitch hairs out, do my sums,
Gaze fondly countryward, longing for Peace,
Loathing the town, sick for my village home,
Which never cried, *Come, buy my charcoal,* or
My vinegar, my oil, my anything;
But freely gave us all; no *buy*-word there.

So here I'm waiting, thoroughly prepared
To riot, wrangle, interrupt the speakers
Whene'er they speak of anything but Peace.
—But here they come, our noon-day Prytanes!
Aye, there they go! I told you how 'twould be;
Everyone jostling for the foremost place.

CRIER.   Move forward all,
Move up, within the consecrated line.
(AMPHITHEUS *enters in a violent hurry.*)

AMPHITHEUS. Speaking begun?

CRIER.   Who will address the meeting?

AMPHITHEUS. I.

CRIER. Who are *you?*

AMPHITHEUS.   Amphitheus.

CRIER.   Not a man?

AMPHITHEUS. No, an immortal. For the first Amphitheus
Was of Demeter and Triptolemus
The son: his son was Celeus; Celeus married
Phaenarete, who bore my sire Lycinus.
Hence I'm immortal; and the gods committed
To me alone the making peace with Sparta.
But, though immortal, I've no journey money;
The Prytanes won't provide it.

CRIER.   Constables, there!

AMPHITHEUS. O help me, Celeus! help, Triptolemus!

DICAEOPOLIS. Ye wrong the Assembly, Prytanes, ye do
    wrong it,
Dragging away a man who only wants
To give us Peace, and hanging up of shields.

CRIER. St! Take your seat.

DICAEOPOLIS.   By Apollo, no, not I,
Unless you prytanize about the Peace.

CRIER. Oyez! The Ambassadors from the Great King!
(*Enter, clad in gorgeous oriental apparel, the envoys sent
to the Persian court eleven years previously in the archon-
ship of Euthymenes,* 437-436 B.C.)

DICAEOPOLIS. What King! I'm sick to death of embassies,
And all their peacocks and their impositions.

CRIER. Keep silence!

DICAEOPOLIS.   Hey! Ecbatana, here's a show.

AMBASSADOR. You sent us, envoys to the Great King's Court,
Receiving each two drachmas daily, when
Euthymenes was Archon.

DICAEOPOLIS.   O me, the drachmas!

AMBASSADOR. And weary work we found it, sauntering on,
   Supinely stretched in our luxurious litters
   With awnings o'er us, through Caÿstrian plains.
   'Twas a bad time.

DICAEOPOLIS.   Aye, the good time was mine,
   Stretched in the litter on the ramparts here!

AMBASSADOR. And oft they feted us, and we perforce
   Out of their gold and crystal cups must drink
   The pure sweet wine.

DICAEOPOLIS.   O Cranaan city, mark you
   The insolent airs of these ambassadors?

AMBASSADOR. For only those are *there* accounted *men*
   Who drink the hardest, and who eat the most.

DICAEOPOLIS. As *here* the most debauched and dissolute.

AMBASSADOR. In the fourth year we reached the Great King's
   Court.
   But he, with all his troops, had gone to sit
   An eight-month session on the Golden Hills!

DICAEOPOLIS. Pray, at what time did he conclude his session?

AMBASSADOR. At the full moon; and so came home again.
   Then he too feted us, and set before us
   Whole pot-baked oxen—

DICAEOPOLIS.   And who ever heard
   Of pot-baked oxen? Out upon your lies!

AMBASSADOR. And an enormous bird, three times the size
   Of our Cleonymus: its name was—Gull.

DICAEOPOLIS. That's why you gulled us out of all those
   drachmas!

AMBASSADOR. And now we bring you Pseudo-Artabas
   The Great King's Eye.

DICAEOPOLIS.   O how I wish some raven
   Would come and strike out yours, the Ambassador's.

CRIER. Oyez! the Great King's Eye!

DICAEOPOLIS.   O Heracles!
   By Heaven, my man, you wear a warship look!
   What! Do you round the point, and spy the docks?
   Is that an oar pad underneath your eye?

AMBASSADOR. Now tell the Athenians, Pseudo-Artabas,
   What the Great King commissioned you to say.

PSEUDO-ARTABAS. Ijisti boutti furbiss upde rotti.[1]

AMBASSADOR. Do you understand?

DICAEOPOLIS.   By Apollo, no not I.

---

[1] This jumble is generally supposed to mean *I have just begun to repair
what is rotten.*

AMBASSADOR. He says the King is going to send you gold.
(*To* PSEUDO-ARTABAS.) Be more distinct and clear about
the gold.

PSEUDO-ARTABAS. No getti goldi, nincompoop Iawny.

DICAEOPOLIS. Wow, but that's clear enough!

AMBASSADOR. What does he say?

DICAEOPOLIS. He says the Ionians must be nincompoops
If they're expecting any gold from Persia.

AMBASSADOR. No, no: he spoke of golden income coupons.

DICAEOPOLIS. What income coupons? You're a great big liar!
You, get away; I'll test the man myself.
(*To* PSEUDO-ARTABAS.)
Now look at this (*Showing his fist.*): and answer Yes,
or No!
Or else I'll dye you with a Sardian dye.
Does the Great King intend to send us gold?
(PSEUDO-ARTABAS *nods dissent.*)
Then are our envoys here bamboozling us?
(*He nods assent.*)
These fellows nod in pure Hellenic style;
I do believe they come from hereabouts.
Aye, to be sure; why, one of these two eunuchs
Is Cleisthenes, Sibyrtius's son!
O you young shaver of the hot-souled rump,
With such a beard, you monkey, do you come
Tricked out among us in a eunuch's guise?
And who's this other chap? Not Straton, surely?

CRIER. St! Take your seat! Oyez!
The Council ask the Great King's Eye to dinner
At the Town Hall.

DICAEOPOLIS. Now is not that a throttler?
Here must I drudge at soldiering; while these rogues,
The Town-Hall door is never closed to *them.*
Now then, I'll do a great and startling deed.
Amphitheus! Where's Amphitheus?

AMBASSADOR. Here am I.

DICAEOPOLIS. Here be eight drachmas; take them; and with all
The Lacedaemonians make a private peace
For me, my wife and children: none besides.
(*To the Prytanes*[1] *and citizens.*)
Stick to your embassies and befoolings, you.

CRIER. Oyez! Theorus from Sitalces!

---

[1] Presiding officers.

THEORUS.   Here!

DICAEOPOLIS. O here's another humbug introduced.

THEORUS. We should not, sirs, have tarried long in Thrace—

DICAEOPOLIS. But for the salary you kept on drawing.

THEORUS. But for the storms, which covered Thrace with snow
  And froze the rivers. 'Twas about the season
  At which Theognis was performing here.
  I all that time was drinking with Sitalces;
  A most prodigious Athens lover he,
  So loyal an admirer, he would scribble
  On every wall *My beautiful Athenians!*
  His son, our newly made Athenian, longed
  To taste his Apaturian sausages,
  And bade his father help his fatherland.
  And *he*, with deep libations, vowed to help us
  With such a host that everyone would say
  Heavens! what a swarm of locusts comes this way!

DICAEOPOLIS. Hang me, if I believe a single word
  Of all that speech, except about the locusts.

THEORUS. And here he sends you the most warlike tribe
  Of all in Thrace.

DICAEOPOLIS.   Come, here's proof positive.

CRIER. The Thracians whom Theorus brought, come forward!

DICAEOPOLIS. What the plague's this?

THEORUS.   The Odomantian host.

DICAEOPOLIS. The Odomantians, phew! Hallo, look here.
  Are Odomantians all equipped like this?

THEORUS. Give them two drachmas each a day, and these
  Will targeteer Boeotia all to bits.

DICAEOPOLIS. Two drachmas for *these* scarecrows! Oh, our
  tars,
  Our noble tars, the safeguard of our state,
  Well may they groan at this. O! Murder! O!
  These Odomantian thieves have sacked my garlic.
  Put down the garlic! drop it!

THEORUS.   You rapscallion,
  How dare you touch them, when they're garlic-primed.

DICAEOPOLIS. O will you let them, Prytanes, use me thus,
  Barbarians too, in this my fatherland?
  But stop! I warn you not to hold the Assembly
  About the Thracians' pay. I tell you there's
  A portent come; I felt a drop of rain!

CRIER. The Thracians are to go, and two days hence
  Come here again. The Assembly is dissolved.

DICAEOPOLIS. O me, the salad I have lost this day!
But here's Amphitheus, back from Lacedaemon.
Well met, Amphitheus!

AMPHITHEUS.   Not till I've done running.
I have to flee the Acharnians, clean away.

DICAEOPOLIS. What mean you?

AMPHITHEUS.   I was bringing back in haste
The treaties, when some veterans smelt them out,
Acharnians, men of Marathon, hard in grain
As their own oak and maple, rough and tough;
And all at once they cried, O *villain, dare you
Bring treaties when our vineyards are cut down?*
Then in their lappets up they gathered stones;
I fled away: they followed roaring after.

DICAEOPOLIS. So let them roar. But have you got the treaties?

AMPHITHEUS. O yes, I have. Three samples; here they are.
These are the *five-year* treaties; take and taste them.

DICAEOPOLIS. Phew!

AMPHITHEUS.   What's the matter?

DICAEOPOLIS.   I don't like the things,
They smell of tar and naval preparations.

AMPHITHEUS. Then taste the *ten-year* samples; here they are.

DICAEOPOLIS. These smell of embassies to all the states,
Urgent, as if the Allies are hanging back.

AMPHITHEUS. Then here are treaties both by land and sea
For *thirty* years.

DICAEOPOLIS.   O Feast of Dionysus!
These have a smell of nectar and ambrosia,
And *never mind about the three days' rations,*
And in your mouth they say, *Go where you please.*
These do I welcome, these I pour, and drain,
Nor care a hang about your old Acharnians.
But I, released from War and War's alarms,
Will hold, within, the Rural Dionysia.

AMPHITHEUS. And I will flee those peppery old Acharnians.

CHORUS. Here's the trail; pursue, pursue him;
                     follow, follow, every man;
Question whosoever meets you
                     whitherward the fellow ran.
Much it boots the state to catch him!
          (*To the audience.*) O inform me, if ye know,
Where the man who bears the treaties
                     managed from my sight to go.

Fled and gone! Disappears!

            O this weary weight of years!

O were I   Now as spry

           As in youthful days gone by,

When I stuck   Like a man

            To Phaÿllus as he ran,

  And achieved   Second place

              In the race,

Though a great   Charcoal freight

          I was bearing on my head—

Not so light   From my sight

         Had this treaty bearer fled,

  Nor escaped   With such ease

            From the chase.

Now because my joints have stiffened,

         and my shins are young no more,

And the legs of Lacrateides

         by old age are burdened sore,

He's escaped us! But we'll follow:

        but he shall not boast that he

Got away from us Acharnians,

        howsoever old we be.

Who has dared   Father Zeus!

        Gods of heaven! to make a truce,

Who has pledged   Faith with those

       Who are evermore my foes;

Upon whom   War I make

       For my ruined vineyard's sake;

  And I ne'er   From the strife

         Will give o'er,

No, I ne'er   Will forbear,

       Till I pierce them in return,

Like a reed,   Sharply barbed

       Dagger-pointed, and they learn

  Not to tread   Down my vines

         Any more.

Now 'tis ours to seek the fellow,

        and Pelténe-ward to look,

And from land to land to chase him,

        till we bring the rogue to book.

Never shall I tire of pelting,

        pelting him to death with stones.

DICAEOPOLIS (*within*). Keep ye all the holy silence!

CHORUS. Hush! we've got him. Heard ye, comrades,
                              silence called in solemn tones?
 This is he, the man we're seeking.
                              Stand aside, and in a trice
 He, methinks, will stand before us,
                              coming out to sacrifice!

DICAEOPOLIS (*coming out*). Keep ye all the holy silence!
 Now, basket bearer, go you on in front,
 You, Xanthias, hold the phallus pole erect.

WIFE. Sit down the basket, girl: and we'll begin.

DAUGHTER. O mother, hand me here the gravy spoon,
 To ladle out the gravy on the cake.

DICAEOPOLIS. 'Tis well. Lord Dionysus, grant me now
 To show the show and make the sacrifice
 As thou would'st have me, I and all my house;
 Then keep with joy the Rural Dionysia;
 No more of soldiering now. And may this Peace
 Of thirty summers answer to my hopes.

WIFE. O daughter, bear the basket sweetly, sweet,
 With savory-eating look. Happy the man,
 Whoe'er he is, who weds you and begets
 Kittens as fair and saucy as yourself.
 Move on! but heed lest any in the crowd
 Should nibble off, unseen, your bits of gold.

DICAEOPOLIS. O Xanthias, walk behind the basket bearer,
 Holding, you two, the phallus pole erect.
 And I'll bring up the rear, and sing the hymn:
 Wife, watch me from the roof. Now then, proceed.

 (*Singing.*) O Phales, comrade revel-roaming
 Of Bacchus, wanderer of the gloaming,
 Of wives and boys the naughty lover,
 Here in my home I gladly greet you,
 Six weary years of absence over;
 For I have made a private treaty
 And said good-by to toils and fusses,
 And fights, and fighting Lamachuses.

 Far happier 'tis to me and sweeter,
 O Phales, Phales, some soft glade in,
 To woo the saucy, arch, deceiving,
 Young Thratta (Strymodore his maiden),
 As from my woodland fells I meet her

Descending with my fagots laden,
And catch her up, and ill entreat her,
And make her pay the fine for thieving.

O Phales, Phales, come and sup,
And in the morn, to brave you up,
Of Peace you'll quaff a jovial cup;
And mid the chimney sparks our useless shield we'll hang.
CHORUS. That's the man who made the treaty;
   There he stands   Full in view;
Pelt him, pelt him, pelt him, pelt him,
   Pelt him you!   Pelt him you!
DICAEOPOLIS. Heracles! what ails the fellows?
                    Hang it all, you'll smash the pot!
CHORUS. It is *you* we will smash with our
                  stones, you detestable head.
DICAEOPOLIS. O most worshipful Acharnians,
                why? what reason have you got?
CHORUS. Dare you ask?   Traitor base!
                Dare you look me in the face?
You who make,   You alone,
            Private treaties of your own!
Shameless heart!   Shameless hand!
            Traitor to your fatherland!
DICAEOPOLIS. But you know not why I did it:
           hear me now the facts declare.
CHORUS. Hear you? No!   You're to die;
           Beneath a stony cairn to lie!
DICAEOPOLIS. Not, O not until you've heard me;
         worthy sirs, forbear, forbear!
CHORUS. No delay!   You to slay
           We'll immediately begin.
No debate!   You we hate
         Worse than Cleon's self, whose skin
I'll ere long   Cut to shoes
         For the worthy Knights to use.
But from *you*, who made a treaty
         with the false Laconian crew,
I will hear no long orations,
         I will surely punish you.
DICAEOPOLIS. Worthy fellows, for the moment
        those Laconians pretermit;
'Tis a question of my treaty,
        was I right in making it?

CHORUS. Right to make it! when with Sparta
                 no engagement sacred stands,
Not the altar, not the oath pledge,
                 not the faith of clasped right hands!
DICAEOPOLIS. Yet I know that these our foemen,
                 who our bitter wrath excite,
Were not always wrong entirely,
                 nor ourselves entirely right.
CHORUS. Not entirely, shameless rascal?
                 Do you such opinions dare
Openly to flaunt before me?
                 Shall I then a traitor spare?
DICAEOPOLIS. Not entirely, not entirely!
                 I can prove by reasons strong
That in many points the Spartans
                 at our hands have suffered wrong.
CHORUS. This is quite a heart-perplexing,
                 terrible affair indeed,
If you mean that you will venture
                 for our enemies to plead.
DICAEOPOLIS. Aye, and if I plead not truly,
                 or the people doubt display,
On a chopping-block I'm willing,
                 whilst I speak, my head to lay.
CHORUS. Why so slack, my fellow burghers?
                 Let us stone the naughty varlet,
Let us scarify and shred him
                 to a uniform of scarlet.
DICAEOPOLIS. What a red and dangerous ember
                 sparkled up within you then!
Won't you hear me, won't you hear me,
                 good Acharnians, worthy men?
CHORUS. Never, never, will we hear you.
DICAEOPOLIS.   That will cause me bitter woe.
CHORUS. If I do, perdition seize me!
DICAEOPOLIS.   O Acharnians, say not so.
CHORUS. Know that you must die this instant.
DICAEOPOLIS.   Then I'll make you suffer too.
For my safety I've a hostage,
                 one that's very dear to you.
Now I'll bring him out and slay him;
                 you shall see your darling's end.
CHORUS. O Acharnian fellow burghers,
                 what can words like these portend

To our noble band of brethren?

               Think you that the man can hold
Any child of ours in durance?

                  What can make him wax so bold?
DICAEOPOLIS. Now then pelt me; here's the hostage!

                   I will slay and will not spare.
I shall speedily discover

               which of you for charcoal care.
CHORUS. Heaven preserve us! 'tis a scuttle,

               'tis my fellow burgher true!
Never do the thing you mention:

               never do, O never do!
DICAEOPOLIS. Cry aloud! I'm going to slay him;

               I shall neither hear nor heed.
CHORUS. You will slay then this charcoal adorer,

               its equal in years!
DICAEOPOLIS. Aye, for when I craved a hearing

               you refused to hear me plead.
CHORUS. Ah! but now! Now you may!

               Whatsoever suits you say.
Say you love, Say you prize,

               Our detested enemies.
Ne'er will I Faithless prove

               To the scuttle which I love.
DICAEOPOLIS. Well then first, the stones you gathered,

               throw them out upon the ground.
CHORUS. Out they go! All my hoard!

               Please to lay aside the sword.
DICAEOPOLIS. But I fear that in your pockets

               other missiles may be found.
CHORUS. All are gone! Every one!

               See my garment shaken wide!
Don't evade Promise made.

               Lay, O lay the sword aside.
Here's my robe Shaken out,

               As I twist and twirl about.
DICAEOPOLIS. You would then, would you, shake your cries
   aloft,
And this Parnesian charcoal all but died,
Slain by the madness of its fellow burghers.
And in its fright this scuttle, cuttlewise,
Voided its inky blackness on my clothes.
Alas that men should carry hearts as sour

As unripe grapes, to pelt and roar, nor hear
A tempered statement mingled half and half;
Not though I'm willing o'er a chopping block
To say my say for Lacedaemon's folk.
And yet I love, be sure, my own dear life.

CHORUS. O why not bring the block

out of doors without delay,

And speak the mighty speech

which you think will win the day?

For really I've a longing

to hear what you will say!

So in the fashion you yourself prescribed,
Place here the chopping block and start your speech.

DICAEOPOLIS. Well look and see, the chopping block is here,
And I'm to speak, poor little friendless I.
Still never mind; I won't protect myself,
I'll speak my mind for Lacedaemon's folk.
And yet I fear; for well I know the moods
Of our good country people, how they love
To hear the City and themselves bepraised
By some intriguing humbug, right or wrong,
Nor ever dream they are being bought and sold.
And well I know the minds of those old men
Looking for nothing but a verdict bite.
Aye and I know what I myself endured
At Cleon's hands for last year's Comedy.
How to the Council house he dragged me off,
And slanged, and lied, and slandered, and betongued me,
Roaring Cycloborus-wise; till I well nigh
Was done to death, bemiryslushified.
Now therefore suffer me, before I start,
To dress me up the loathliest way I can.

CHORUS. O why keep putting off with that shilly-shally air?
Hieronymus may lend you, for anything I care,
The shaggy "Cap of Darkness" from his tangle-matted hair.
Then open all the wiles of Sisyphus,
Since this encounter will not brook delay.

DICAEOPOLIS. Now must my heart be strong, and I depart
To find Euripides. Boy! Ho there, boy!

CEPHISOPHON. Who calls me?

DICAEOPOLIS.   Is Euripides within?

CEPHISOPHON. Within and not within, if you conceive me.

DICAEOPOLIS. Within and not within?

CEPHISOPHON. 'Tis even so.
   His mind, without, is culling flowers of song,
   But he, within, is sitting up aloft
   Writing a play.

DICAEOPOLIS. O lucky, lucky poet,
   Whose very servant says such clever things!
   But call him.

CEPHISOPHON. But it can't be done.

DICAEOPOLIS. But still . . . !
   For go I won't. I'll hammer at the door.
   Euripides, my sweet one!
   O if you ever hearkened, hearken now.
   'Tis I, Cholleidian Dicaeopolis.

EURIPIDES. But I've no time.

DICAEOPOLIS. But pivot.

EURIPIDES. But it can't be done.

DICAEOPOLIS. But still . . . !

EURIPIDES. Well then, I'll pivot, but I can't come down.

DICAEOPOLIS. Euripides!

EURIPIDES. Aye.

DICAEOPOLIS. Why do you write up there,
   And not down here? That's why you make lame heroes.
   And wherefore sit you robed in tragic rags,
   A pitiful garb? That's why you make them beggars.
   But by your knees, Euripides, I pray,
   Lend me some rags from that old play of yours;
   For to the Chorus I today must speak
   A lengthy speech; and if I fail, 'tis *death*.

EURIPIDES. Rags! Rags! what rags? Mean you the rags wherein
   This poor old Oeneus came upon the stage?

DICAEOPOLIS. Not Oeneus, no; a wretcheder man than he.

EURIPIDES. Those that blind Phoenix wore?

DICAEOPOLIS. Not Phoenix, no;
   Some other man still wretcheder than Phoenix.

EURIPIDES. What shreds of raiment can the fellow mean?
   Can it be those of beggarly Philoctetes?

DICAEOPOLIS. One far, far, far, more beggarly than he.

EURIPIDES. Can it be then the loathly gaberdine
   Wherein the lame Bellerophon was clad?

DICAEOPOLIS. Bellerophon? no; yet mine too limped and begged,
   A terrible chap to talk.

EURIPIDES. I know the man.
   The Mysian Telephus.

DICAEOPOLIS.   Telephus it is!
   Lend me, I pray, that hero's swaddling clothes.
EURIPIDES. Boy, fetch him out the rags of Telephus.
   They lie above the Thyesteian rags,
   'Twixt those and Ino's.
CEPHISOPHON (to DICAEOPOLIS). Take them; here they are.
DICAEOPOLIS (holding up the tattered garment against the
      light).
   Lord Zeus, whose eyes can pierce through everywhere,
   Let me be dressed the loathliest way I can.
   Euripides, you have freely given the rags,
   Now give, I pray you, what pertains to these,
   The Mysian cap to set upon my head.
   For I've today to act a beggar's part,
   To be myself, yet not to seem myself;
   The audience there will know me who I am,
   Whilst all the Chorus stand like idiots by,
   The while I fillip them with cunning words.
EURIPIDES. Take it; you subtly plan ingenious schemes.
DICAEOPOLIS. To you, good luck; to Telephus—what I wish
      him!
   Yah! why I'm full of cunning words already.
   But now, I think I need a beggar's staff.
EURIPIDES. Take this, and get you from the marble halls.
DICAEOPOLIS. O Soul, thou seest me from the mansion thrust,
   Still wanting many a boon. Now in thy prayer
   Be close and instant. Give, Euripides,
   A little basket with a hole burnt through it.
EURIPIDES. What need you, hapless one, of this poor wicker?
DICAEOPOLIS. No need perchance; but O I want it so.
EURIPIDES. Know that you're wearisome, and get you gone.
DICAEOPOLIS. Alas! Heaven bless you, as it blessed your
      mother.
EURIPIDES. Leave me in peace.
DICAEOPOLIS.   Just one thing more, but one,
   A little tankard with a broken rim.
EURIPIDES. Here. Now be off. You trouble us; begone.
DICAEOPOLIS. You know not yet what ill you do yourself.
   Sweet, dear Euripides, but one thing more,
   Give me a little pitcher, plugged with sponge.
EURIPIDES. Fellow, you're taking the whole tragedy.
   Here, take it and begone.
DICAEOPOLIS.   I'm going now.
   And yet! there's one thing more, which if I get not

I'm ruined. Sweetest, best Euripides,
With this I'll go, and never come again;
Give me some withered leaves to fill my basket.

EURIPIDES. You'll slay me! Here! My plays are disappearing.

DICAEOPOLIS. Enough! I go. Too troublesome by far
Am I, not knowing that the chieftains hate me!
Good Heavens! I'm ruined. I had clean forgotten
The thing whereon my whole success depends.
My own Euripides, my best and sweetest,
Perdition seize me if I ask aught else
Save this one thing, this only, only this,
Give me some chervil, borrowing from your mother.

EURIPIDES. The man insults us. Shut the palace up.

DICAEOPOLIS. O Soul, without our chervil we must go.
Knowest thou the perilous strife thou hast to strive,
Speaking in favor of Laconian men?
On, on, my Soul! Here is the line. How? What?
Swallow Euripides, and yet not budge?
Oh, good! Advance, O long-enduring heart,
Go thither, lay thine head upon the block,
And say whatever to thyself seems good.
Take courage! Forward! March! O well done, heart!

CHORUS. What will you say? What will you do?
    Man, is it true
You are made up of iron and of shamelessness too?
You who will, one against us all, debate,
Offering your neck a hostage to the State!
    Nought does he fear.
Since you will have it so, speak, we will hear.

DICAEOPOLIS. Bear me no grudge, spectators, if, a beggar,
I dare to speak before the Athenian people
About the city in a comic play.
For what is true even comedy can tell.
And I shall utter startling things but true.
Nor now can Cleon slander me because,
With strangers present, I defame the State.
'Tis the Lenaea, and we're all alone;
No strangers yet have come; nor from the states
Have yet arrived the tribute and allies.
We're quite alone clean-winnowed; for I count
Our alien residents the civic bran.
    The Lacedaemonians I detest entirely;
And may Poseidon, Lord of Taenarum,
Shake all their houses down about their ears;

For I, like you, have had my vines cut down.
But after all—for none but friends are here—
Why the Laconians do we blame for this?
For men of ours, I do not say the State,
Remember this, I do not say the State,
But worthless fellows of a worthless stamp,
Ill-coined, ill-minted, spurious little chaps,
Kept on denouncing Megara's little coats.
And if a cucumber or hare they saw,
Or sucking pig, or garlic, or lump salt,
All were Megarian, and were sold offhand.
Still these were trifles, and our country's way.
But some young tipsy cottabus players went
And stole from Megara-town the fair Simaetha.
Then the Megarians, garlicked with the smart,
Stole, in return, two of Aspasia's hussies.
From these three Wantons o'er the Hellenic race
Burst forth the first beginnings of the War.
For then, in wrath, the Olympian Pericles
Thundered and lightened, and confounded Hellas,
Enacting laws which ran like drinking-songs,
That the Megarians presently depart
From earth and sea, the mainland, and the mart.
Then the Megarians, slowly famishing,
Besought their Spartan friends to get the Law
Of the three Wantons canceled and withdrawn.
And oft they asked us, but we yielded not.
Then followed instantly the clash of shields.
Ye'll say *They should not;* but what should they, then?
Come now, had some Laconian, sailing out,
Denounced and sold a small Seriphian dog,
Would you have sat unmoved? Far, far from that!
Ye would have launched three hundred ships of war,
And all the City had at once been full
Of shouting troops, of fuss with trierarchs,
Of paying wages, gilding Pallases,
Of rations measured, roaring colonnades,
Of wineskins, oarloops, bargaining for casks,
Of nets of onions, olives, garlic heads,
Of chaplets, pilchards, flute girls, and black eyes.
And all the arsenal had rung with noise
Of oar spars planed, pegs hammered, oar loops fitted,
Of boatswains' calls, and flutes, and trills, and whistles.

This had ye done; and shall not Telephus,
Think we, do this? we've got no brains at all.

SEMICHORUS I. Aye, say you so, you rascally villain you?
And this from you, a beggar? Dare you blame us
Because, perchance, we've got informers here?

SEMICHORUS II. Aye, by Poseidon, every word he says
Is true and right; he tells no lies at all.

SEMICHORUS I. True or untrue, is he the man to say it?
I'll pay him out, though, for his insolent speech.

SEMICHORUS II. Whither away? I pray you stay. If him you hurt,
You'll find your own self hoisted up directly.

(*A scuffle takes place in the orchestra, in which the leader
of the first semichorus is worsted.*)

SEMICHORUS I. Lamachus! Help! with thy glances of lightning;
Terrible-crested, appear in thy pride,
Come, O Lamachus, tribesman and friend to us;
Is there a stormer of cities beside?
Is there a captain? O come ye in haste,
Help me, O help! I am caught by the waist.

LAMACHUS. Whence came the cry of battle to my ears?
Where shall I charge? where cast the battle din?
Who roused the sleeping Gorgon from its case?

DICAEOPOLIS. O Lamachus hero, O those crests and cohorts!

SEMICHORUS I. O Lamachus, here has this fellow been
With frothy words abusing all the State.

LAMACHUS. You dare, you beggar, say such things as those?

DICAEOPOLIS. O Lamachus hero, grant me pardon true
If I, a beggar, spake or chattered aught.

LAMACHUS. What said you? Hey?

DICAEOPOLIS.   I can't remember yet.
I get so dizzy at the sight of arms.
I pray you lay that terrible shield aside.

LAMACHUS. There then.

DICAEOPOLIS.   Now set it upside down before me.

LAMACHUS. 'Tis done.

DICAEOPOLIS.   Now give me from your crest that plume.

LAMACHUS. Here; take the feather.

DICAEOPOLIS.   Now then, hold my head,
And let me vomit. I so loathe those crests.

LAMACHUS. What! use my feather, rogue, to make you vomit?

DICAEOPOLIS. A feather is it, Lamachus? Pray what bird
Produced it? Is it a Great Boastard's plume?

LAMACHUS. Death and Destruction!

DICAEOPOLIS. No, no, Lamachus.
That's not for strength like yours. If strong you are
Why don't you circumcise me? You're well armed.

LAMACHUS. What! you, a beggar, beard the general so?

DICAEOPOLIS. A beggar am I, Lamachus?

LAMACHUS. What else?

DICAEOPOLIS. An honest townsman, not an office-seekrian,
Since war began, an active-service-seekrian,
But you're, since war began, a full-pay-seekrian.

LAMACHUS. The people chose me—

DICAEOPOLIS. Aye, three cuckoo-birds.
That's what I loathe; that's why I made my treaty,
When gray-haired veterans in the ranks I saw,
And boys like you, paltry malingering boys,
Off, some to Thrace—their daily pay three drachmas—
Phaenippuses, Hipparchidreprobatians,
And some with Chares, to Chaonia some,
Geretotheodores, Diomirogues, and some
To Camarina, Gela, and Grineela.

LAMACHUS. The people chose them—

DICAEOPOLIS. And how comes it, pray,
That you are always in receipt of pay,
And these are *never*? Come, Marilades,
You are old and gray; when have you served as envoy?
Never! Yet he's a steady, active man.
Well then, Euphorides, Prinides, Dracyllus,
Have *you* Ecbatana or Chaonia seen?
Never! But Coesyra's son and Lamachus,
They have; to whom, for debts and calls unpaid,
Their friends but now, like people throwing out
Their slops at eve, were crying *Stand away!*

LAMACHUS. O me! Democracy! can this be borne?

DICAEOPOLIS. No, not if Lamachus receive no pay.

LAMACHUS. But I with all the Peloponnesian folk
Will always fight, and vex them everyway,
By land, by sea, with all my might and main.

(*Exit.*)

DICAEOPOLIS. And I to all the Peloponnesian folk,
Megarians and Boeotians, give full leave
To trade with me; but not to Lamachus.

(*Exit.*)

CHORUS. The man has the best of the wordy debate, and the
hearts of the people is winning

To his plea for the truce. Now doff we our robes,
  our own anapaestics beginning.

Since first to exhibit his plays he began,
                our chorus instructor has never
Come forth to confess in this public address
                how tactful he is and how clever.
But now that he knows he is slandered by foes
                before Athens so quick to assent,
Pretending he jeers our City and sneers
                at the people with evil intent,
He is ready and fain his cause to maintain
                before Athens so quick to repent.
Let honor and praise be the guerdon, he says,
                of the poet whose satire has stayed you
From believing the orators' novel conceits
                wherewith they cajoled and betrayed you;
Who bids you despise adulation and lies
                nor be citizens Vacant and Vain.
For before, when an embassy came from the states
                intriguing your favor to gain,
And called you the town of the *violet crown*,
                so grand and exalted ye grew,
That at once on your tiptails erect ye would sit,
                those *crowns* were so pleasant to you.
And then, if they added the *shiny*, they got
                whatever they asked for their praises,
Though apter, I ween, for an oily sardine
                than for you and your City the phrase is.
By this he's a true benefactor to you,
                and by showing with humor dramatic
The way that our wise democratic allies
                are ruled by our State democratic.
And therefore their people will come oversea,
                their tribute to bring to the City,
Consumed with desire to behold and admire
                the poet so fearless and witty,
Who dared in the presence of Athens to speak
                the thing that is rightful and true.
And truly the fame of his prowess, by this,
                has been bruited the universe through,
When the Sovereign of Persia, desiring to test
                what the end of our warfare will be,

Inquired of the Spartan ambassadors, first,
>which nation is queen of the sea,
And next, which the wonderful Poet has got,
>as its stern and unsparing adviser;
For those who are lashed by his satire, he said,
>must surely be better and wiser,
And they'll in the war be the stronger by far,
>enjoying his counsel and skill.
And therefore the Spartans approach you today
>with proffers of Peace and Goodwill,
Just asking indeed that Aegina ye cede;
>and nought do they care for the isle,
But you of the Poet who serves you so well
>they fain would despoil and beguile.
But be *you* on your guard nor surrender the bard;
>for his Art shall be righteous and true.
Rare blessings and great will he work for the State,
>rare happiness shower upon you;
Not fawning, or bribing, or striving to cheat
>with an empty unprincipled jest;
Not seeking your favor to curry or nurse,
>but teaching the things that are best.

And therefore I say to the people today,
Let Cleon the worst of his villainies try,
His anger I fear not, his threats I defy!
For Honor and Right beside me will fight,
>And never shall I
In ought that relates to the city be found
Such a craven as he, such a profligate hound.

O Muse, fiery-flashing, with temper of flame,
>energetic, Acharnian, come to my gaze,
Like the wild spark that leaps from the evergreen oak,
>when its red-glowing charcoal is fanned to a blaze,
And the small fish are lying all in order for the frying:
And some are mixing Thasian, richly dight, shiny bright,
>And some dip the small fish therein;
Come, fiery-flashing Maid, to thy fellow burgher's aid,
With exactly such a song, so glowing and so strong,
>To our old rustic melodies akin.

We the veterans blame the City.
>Is it meet and right that we,

Who of old, in manhood's vigor,

> fought your battles on the sea,

Should in age be left untended,

> yea exposed to shame and ill?

Is it right to let the youngsters

> air their pert forensic skill,

Grappling us with writs and warrants,

> holding up our age to scorn?

We who now have lost our music,

> feeble nothings, dull, forlorn,

We whose only "Safe Poseidon"

> is the staff we lean upon,

There we stand, decayed and muttering,

> hard beside the Courthouse Stone,

Nought discerning all around us

> save the darkness of our case.

Comes the youngster, who has compassed

> for himself the accuser's place,

Slings his tight and nipping phrases,

> tackling us with legal scraps,

Pulls us up and cross-examines,

> setting little verbal traps,

Rends and rattles old Tithonus

> till the man is dazed and blind;

Till with toothless gums he mumbles,

> then departs condemned and fined;

Sobbing, weeping, as he passes,

> to his friends he murmurs low,

All I've saved to buy a coffin

> *now to pay the fine must go.*

How can it be seemly a gray-headed man by the Water-
clock's stream to decoy and to slay,

Who of old, young and bold, labored hard for the State,
who would wipe off his sweat and return to the fray?

At Marathon arrayed, to the battle shock we ran,

And our mettle we displayed, foot to foot, man to man,
And our name and our fame shall not die.

Aye in youth we were Pursuers on the Marathonian
plain,

But in age Pursuers vex us, and our best defense is vain.
To this what can Marpsias reply?

Oh, Thucydides to witness,

> bowed with age, in sore distress,

Feebly struggling in the clutches
of that Scythian wilderness
Fluent glib Cephisodemus—
Oh the sorrowful display!
I myself was moved with pity,
yea and wiped a tear away,
Grieved at heart the gallant veteran
by an archer mauled to view;
Him who, were he, by Demeter,
that Thucydides we knew,
Would have stood no airs or nonsense
from the Goddess Travel-sore,
Would have thrown, the mighty wrestler,
ten Evathluses or more,
Shouted down three thousand archers
with his accents of command,
Shot his own accuser's kinsmen
in their Scythian fatherland.
Nay, but if ye will not leave us
to our hardly earned repose,
Sort the writs, divide the actions,
separating these from those;
Who assails the old and toothless
should be old and toothless too;
For a youngster, wantons, gabblers,
Cleinias' son the trick may do.
So for future fines and exiles,
fair and square the balance hold,
Let the youngster sue the youngster,
and the old man sue the old.

DICAEOPOLIS. These are the boundaries of my market place;
And here may all the Peloponnesian folk,
Megarians and Boeotians, freely trade
Selling to me, but Lamachus may not.
And these three thongs, of Leprous make, I set
As market clerks, elected by the lot.
Within these bounds may not informer come,
Or any other syco-Phasian man.
But I'll go fetch the Treaty Pillar here,
And set it up in some conspicuous place.

MEGARIAN. Guid day, Athanian market, Megara's luve!
By Frien'ly Zeus, I've miss't ye like my mither.
But ye, puir bairnies o' a warefu' father,

Speed up, ye'll aiblins fin' a barley-bannock.
Now listen, bairns; atten' wi' a' yere—painch;
Whilk wad ye liefer, to be sellt or clemmed?

GIRLS. Liefer be sellt! Liefer be sellt!

MEGARIAN. An' sae say I mysel'! But wha sae doited
As to gie aught for *you*, a sicker skaith?
Aweel, I ken a pawkie Megara-trick,
I'se busk ye up, an' say I'm bringin' piggies.
Here, slip these wee bit clooties on yere nieves,
An' shaw yeresells a decent grumphie's weans.
For gin' I tak' ye hame unsellt, by Hairmes
Ye'll thole the warst extremities o' clemmin'.
Ne'est, pit thir lang pig-snowties owre yere nebs,
An' stech yere bodies in this sackie. Sae.
An' min' ye grunt an' grane an' g-r-r awa',
An' mak' the skirls o' little Mystery piggies.
Mysel' will ca' for Dicaeopolis.
Hae! Dicaeopolis!
Are ye for buyin' onie pigs the day?

DICAEOPOLIS. How now, Megarian?

MEGARIAN.   Come to niffer, guidman.

DICAEOPOLIS. How fare ye all?

MEGARIAN.   A' greetin' by the fire.

DICAEOPOLIS. And very jolly too if there's a piper.
What do your people do besides?

MEGARIAN.   Sae sae.
For when I cam' frae Megara toun the morn,
Our Lairds o' Council were in gran' debate
How we might quickliest perish, but an' ben.

DICAEOPOLIS. So ye'll lose all your troubles.

MEGARIAN.   What for no?

DICAEOPOLIS. What else at Megara? What's the price of wheat?

MEGARIAN. Och! high eneugh: high as the Gudes, an' higher.

DICAEOPOLIS. Got any salt?

MEGARIAN.   Ye're maisters o' our saut.

DICAEOPOLIS. Or garlic?

MEGARIAN.   Garlic, quotha! when yeresells,
Makin' yere raids like onie swarm o' mice,
Howkit up a' the rooties wi' a stak'.

DICAEOPOLIS. What *have* you got then?

MEGARIAN.   Mystery piggies, I.

DICAEOPOLIS. That's good; let's see them.

MEGARIAN.   Hae! They're bonnie piggies.
  Lift it, an't please you; 'tis sae sleek an' bonnie.

DICAEOPOLIS. What on earth's this?

MEGARIAN.   A piggie that, by Zeus.

DICAEOPOLIS. A pig! What sort of pig?

MEGARIAN.   A Megara piggie.
  What! no a piggie that?

DICAEOPOLIS.   It doesn't seem so.

MEGARIAN. 'Tis awfu'! Och the disbelievin' carle!
  Uphaudin' she's na piggie! Will ye wad,
  My cantie frien', a pinch o' thymy saut
  She's no piggie in the Hellanian use?

DICAEOPOLIS. A human being's—

MEGARIAN.   Weel, by Diocles,
  She's mine; wha's piggie did ye think she was?
  Mon? wad ye hear them skirlin'?

DICAEOPOLIS.   By the Powers,
  I would indeed.

MEGARIAN.   Now piggies, skirl awa'.
  Ye winna? winna skirl, ye graceless hizzies?
  By Hairmes then I'se tak' ye hame again.

GIRLS. Weel! weel! weel!

MEGARIAN. This no a piggie?

DICAEOPOLIS.   Faith, it seems so now,
  But 'twont remain so for five years I'm thinking.

MEGARIAN. Trowth, tak' my word for't, she'll be like her
  mither.

DICAEOPOLIS. But she's no good for offerings.

MEGARIAN.   What for no?
  What for nae guid for offerins?

DICAEOPOLIS.   She's no tail.

MEGARIAN. Aweel, the puir wee thing, she's owre young yet.
  But when she's auld, she'll have a gawcie tail.
  Bud wad ye rear them, here's a bonnie piggie!

DICAEOPOLIS. Why she's the staring image of the other.

MEGARIAN. They're o' ane father an' ane mither, baith.
  But bide a wee, an' when she's fat an' curlie
  She'll be an offerin' gran' for Aphrodite.

DICAEOPOLIS. A pig's no sacrifice for Aphrodite.

MEGARIAN. What, no for Her! Mon, for hirsel' the lane.
  Why there's nae flesh sae tastie as the flesh
  O' thae sma piggies, roastit on a spit.

DICAEOPOLIS. But can they feed without their mother yet?

MEGARIAN. Poteidan, yes! withouten father too.

DICAEOPOLIS. What will they eat most freely?

MEGARIAN.   Aught ye gie them.
  But spier yoursel'.

DICAEOPOLIS.   Hey, piggy, piggy!

FIRST GIRL.   Weel

DICAEOPOLIS. Do you like peas, you piggy?

FIRST GIRL.   Wee, wee, weel

DICAEOPOLIS. What, and Phibalean figs as well?

FIRST GIRL.   Wee, weel

DICAEOPOLIS. What, and you other piggy?

SECOND GIRL.   Wee, wee, weel

DICAEOPOLIS. Eh, but ye're squealing bravely for the figs.
  Bring out some figs here, one of you within,
  For these small piggies. Will they eat them? Yah!
  Worshipful Heracles! how they are gobbling now.
  Whence come the pigs? They seem to me Aetallian.

MEGARIAN. Na, na; they haena eaten a' thae figs.
  See here; here's ane I pickit up mysel'.

DICAEOPOLIS. Upon my word, they are jolly little beasts.
  What shall I give you for the pair? let's hear.

MEGARIAN. Gie me for ane a tie o' garlic, will ye,
  An' for the tither half a peck o' saut.

DICAEOPOLIS. I'll buy them: stay you here awhile.

MEGARIAN.   Aye, aye.
  Traffickin' Hairmes, wad that I could swap
  Baith' wife an' mither on sic terms as thae.

INFORMER. Man! who are *you*?

MEGARIAN.   Ane Megara piggie-seller.

INFORMER. Then I'll denounce your goods and you yourself
  As enemies!

MEGARIAN.   Hech, here it comes again,
  The vera primal source of a' our wae.

INFORMER. You'll Megarize to your cost. Let go the sack.

MEGARIAN. Dicaeopolis! Dicaeopolis! Here's a chiel
  Denouncin' me.

DICAEOPOLIS (*re-entering*). Where is he? Market clerks,
  Why don't you keep these sycophants away?
  What! show him up without a lantern wick?

INFORMER. Not show our enemies up?

DICAEOPOLIS.   You had better not.
  Get out, and do your showing otherwhere.

MEGARIAN. The pest thae birkies are in Athans toun!

DICAEOPOLIS. Well never mind, Megarian, take the things,

Garlic and salt, for which you sold the pigs.
Farewell!

MEGARIAN.   That's na our way in Megara toun.

DICAEOPOLIS. Then on my head the officious wish return!

MEGARIAN. O piggies, try withouten father now
To eat wi' saut yere bannock, an' ye git ane.

CHORUS. A happy lot the man has got:
                    his scheme devised with wondrous art
Proceeds and prospers as you see;
                and now he'll sit in his private Mart
  The fruit of his bold design to reap.
  And O if a Ctesias come this way,
  Or other informers vex us, they
  Will soon for their trespass weep.

No sneak shall grieve you buying first
                  the fish you wanted to possess,
No Prepis on your dainty robes
                wipe off his utter loathsomeness.
  You'll no Cleonymus jostle there;
  But all unsoiled through the Mart you'll go,
  And no Hyperbolus work you woe
  With writs enough and to spare.

Never within these bounds shall walk
                  the little fop we all despise,
The young Cratinus neatly shorn
                with single razor wanton-wise,
  That Artemon-engineer of ill,
  Whose father sprang from an old he goat,
  And father and son, as ye all may note,
  Are rank with its fragrance still.

No Pauson, scurvy knave, shall here
                  insult you in the market place,
No vile Lysistratus, to all
                Cholargian folk a dire disgrace,
  That deep-dyed sinner, that low buffoon,
  Who always shivers and hungers sore
  Full thirty days, or it may be more,
  In every course of the moon.

BOEOTIAN. Hech sirs, my shouther's sair, wat Heracles!
Ismeny lad, pit doon thae pennyroyal

Wi' tentie care. Pipers wha cam' frae Thaibes
Blaw oop the auld tyke's hurdies wi' the banes.

DICAEOPOLIS. Hang you! shut up! Off from my doors, you wasps!

Whence flew these curst Chaeridian bumble-drones
Here, to my door? Get to the ravens? Hence!

BOEOTIAN. An' recht ye are, by Iolaus, stranger.
They've blawn behint me a' the wa' frae Thaibes,
An' danged the blossom aff my pennyroyal.
But buy, an't please you, onie thing I've got,
Some o' thae cleckin' or thae four-winged gear.

DICAEOPOLIS. O welcome, dear Boeotian muffin-eater,
What have you there?

BOEOTIAN. A' that Boeoty gies us.
Mats, dittany, pennyroyal, lantern wicks,
An' dooks, an' kaes, an' francolins, an' coots,
Plivers an' divers.

DICAEOPOLIS. Eh? Why then, I think,
You've brought fowl weather to my market place.

BOEOTIAN. Aye, an' I'm bringin' maukins, geese, an' tods
Easels an' weasels, urchins, moles, an' cats,
An' otters too, an' eels frae Loch Copaïs.

DICAEOPOLIS. O man, to men their daintiest morsel bringing.
Let me salute the eels, if eels you bring.

BOEOTIAN. Primest o' Loch Copaïs' fifty dochters
Come oot o' that; and' mak' the stranger welcome.

O loved, and lost, and longed for, thou art come,
A presence grateful to the Comic choirs,
And dear to Morychus. Bring me out at once,
O kitchen-knaves, the brazier and the fan.
Behold, my lads, this best of all the eels,
Six years a truant, scarce returning now.
O children, welcome her; to you I'll give
A charcoal fire for this sweet stranger's sake.
Out with her! Never may I lose again,
Not even in death, my darling dressed in—beet.

BOEOTIAN. Whaur sall I get the siller for the feesh?

DICAEOPOLIS. This you shall give me as a market toll.
But tell me, are these other things for sale?

BOEOTIAN. Aye are they, a' thae goods.

DICAEOPOLIS. And at what price?
Or would you swap for something else?

BOEOTIAN. I'se swap
For gear we haena, but ye Attics hae.

DICAEOPOLIS. Well then, what say you to Phaleric sprats,
  Or earthenware?
BOEOTIAN.   Sprats! ware! we've thae at hame.
  Gie us some gear we lack, an' ye've a rowth o'.
DICAEOPOLIS. I'll tell you what; pack an *informer* up,
  Like ware for exportation.
BOEOTIAN.   Mon! that's guid.
  By the Twa Gudes, an' unco gain I'se mak'.
  Takin' a monkey fu' o' plaguy tricks.
DICAEOPOLIS. And here's Nicarchus coming to denounce you!
BOEOTIAN. He's sma' in bouk.
DICAEOPOLIS.   But every inch is bad.
NICARCHUS. Whose is this merchandise?
BOEOTIAN. ·   'Tis a' mine here.
  Frae Thaibes, wat Zeus, I bure it.
NICARCHUS.   Then I here
  Denounce it all as enemies!
BOEOTIAN.   Hout awa!
  Do ye mak' war an' enmity wi' the burdies?
NICARCHUS. Them and you too.
BOEOTIAN.   What hae I dune ye wrang?
NICARCHUS. That will I say for the bystanders' sake.
  A lantern wick you are bringing from the foe.
DICAEOPOLIS. Show him up, would you, for a lantern wick?
NICARCHUS. Aye, for that lantern wick will fire the docks.
DICAEOPOLIS. A lantern wick the docks! O dear, and how?
NICARCHUS. If a Boeotian stuck it in a beetle,
  And sent it, lighted, down a watercourse
  Straight to the docks, watching when Boreas blew
  His stiffest breeze, then if the ships caught fire,
  They'd blaze up in an instant.
DICAEOPOLIS.   Blaze, you rascal!
  What, with a beetle and a lantern wick?
NICARCHUS. Bear witness!
DICAEOPOLIS.   Stop his mouth, and bring me litter.
  I'll pack him up, like earthenware, for carriage,
  So they mayn't crack him on their journey home.
CHORUS. Tie up, O best of men, with care
  The honest stranger's piece of ware,
    For fear they break it,
  As homeward on their backs they take it.
DICAEOPOLIS. To that, be sure, I'll have regard;
  Indeed it creaks as though 'twere charred,

By cracks molested,
And altogether God-detested.

CHORUS. How shall he deal with it?

DICAEOPOLIS. For every use 'tis fit,
A cup of ills, a lawsuit can,
For audits an informing pan,
A poisoned chalice
Full filled with every kind of malice.

CHORUS. But who can safely use, I pray,
A thing like this from day to day
In household matters,
A thing that always creaks and clatters?

DICAEOPOLIS. He's strong, my worthy friend, and tough:
He will not break for usage rough,
Not though you shove him
Head foremost down, his heels above him.

CHORUS (to BOEOTIAN). You've got a lovely pack.

BOEOTIAN. A bonnie hairst I'se mak'.

CHORUS. Aye, best of friends, your harvest make,
And whereso'er it please you take
This artful, knowing
And best-equipped informer going.

DICAEOPOLIS. 'Twas a tough business, but I've packed the scamp.
Lift up and take your piece of ware, Boeotian.

BOEOTIAN. Gae, pit your shouther underneath, Ismeny.

DICAEOPOLIS. And pray be careful as you take him home.
You've got a rotten bale of goods, but stilll
And if you make a harvest out of *him*,
You'll be in luck's way, as regards informers.

SERVANT. Dicaeopolis!

DICAEOPOLIS.   Well? why are you shouting?

SERVANT.   Why?
Lamachus bids you, toward the Pitcher feast,
Give him some thrushes for this drachma here,
And for three drachmas one Copaïc eel.

DICAEOPOLIS. Who is this Lamachus that wants the eel?

SERVANT. The dread, the tough, the terrible, who wields
The Gorgon shield, and shakes three shadowy plumes.

DICAEOPOLIS. An eel for *him?* Not though his shield he gave me!
Let him go shake his plumes at his salt fish.
If he demur, I'll call the Market clerks.

Now for myself I'll carry all these things
Indoors, to the tune *o' merles an' mavises wings.*
CHORUS. Have ye seen him, all ye people,
seen the man of matchless art,
Seen him, by his private treaty,
traffic gain from every mart,
   Goods from every neighbor;
Some required for household uses;
some 'twere pleasant warm to eat;
All the wealth of all the cities
lavished here before his feet,
   Free from toil and labor.

War I'll never welcome in
to share my hospitality,
Never shall the fellow sing
Harmodius in my company,
Always in his cups he acts
so rudely and offensively.
Tipsily he burst upon
our happy quiet family,
Breaking this, upsetting that,
and brawling most pugnaciously.
Yea when we entreated him
with hospitable courtesy,
Sit you down, and drink a cup,
a Cup of Love and Harmony,
All the more he burnt the poles
we wanted for our husbandry,
Aye and spilt perforce the liquor
treasured up within our vines.

Proudly he prepares to banquet.
Did ye mark him, all elate,
As a sample of his living
cast these plumes before his gate?
   Grand his ostentation!
O of Cypris foster-sister,
and of every heavenly Grace,
Never knew I till this moment
all the glory of thy face,
   Reconciliation!

O that Love would you and me
unite in endless harmony,

Love as he is pictured with

> the wreath of roses smilingly.

Maybe you regard me as

> a fragment of antiquity:

Ah, but if I get you, dear,

> I'll show my triple husbandry.

First a row of vinelets will I

> plant prolonged and orderly,

Next the little fig-tree shoots

> beside them, growing lustily,

Thirdly the domestic vine;

> although I am so elderly.

Round them all shall olives grow,

> to form a pleasant boundary.

Thence will you and I anoint us,

> darling, when the New Moon shines.

CRIER. Oyez! Oyez!
Come, drain your pitchers to the trumpet's sound,
In our old fashion. Whoso drains *his* first,
Shall have, for prize, a skin of—Ctesiphon.

DICAEOPOLIS. Lads! Lassies! heard ye not the words he said?
What are ye at? Do ye not hear the Crier?
Quick! stew and roast, and turn the roasting flesh,
Unspit the haremeat, weave the coronals,
Bring the spits here, and I'll impale the thrushes.

CHORUS. I envy much your happy plan,
I envy more, you lucky man,
The joys you're now possessing.

DICAEOPOLIS. What, when around the spits you see

> the thrushes roasting gloriously?

CHORUS. And that's a saying I admire.

DICAEOPOLIS. Boy, poke me up the charcoal fire.

CHORUS. O listen with what cookly art
And gracious care, so trim and smart,
His own repast he's dressing.

(*Enter* DERCETES, *an Athenian farmer.*)

DERCETES. Alas! Alas!

DICAEOPOLIS. O Heracles, who's there?

DERCETES. An ill-starred man.

DICAEOPOLIS. Then keep it to yourself.

DERCETES. O—for you only hold the truces, dear—
Measure me out though but five years of Peace.

DICAEOPOLIS. What ails you?

DERCETES. Ruined! Lost my oxen twain.

DICAEOPOLIS. Where from?

DERCETES. From Phyle. The Boeotians stole them.

DICAEOPOLIS. And yet you are clad in white, you ill-starred
loon!

DERCETES. They twain maintained me in the very lap
Of affluent muckery.

DICAEOPOLIS. Well, what want you now?

DERCETES. Lost my two eyes, weeping my oxen twain.
Come, if you care for Dercetes of Phyle,
Rub some Peace ointment, do, on my two eyes.

DICAEOPOLIS. Why, bless the fool, I'm not a public surgeon.

DERCETES. *Do* now; I'll maybe find my oxen twain.

DICAEOPOLIS. No, go and weep at Pittalus's door.

DERCETES. Do, just one single drop. Just drop me here
Into this quill one little drop of Peace.

DICAEOPOLIS. No, not one twitterlet; take your tears else-
where.

DERCETES. Alas! Alas! my darling yoke of oxen.

CHORUS. He loves the Treaty's pleasant taste;
He will not be, methinks, in haste
To let another share it.

DICAEOPOLIS. Pour on the tripe the honey, you!
And you, the cuttle richly stew!

CHORUS. How trumpetlike his orders sound.

DICAEOPOLIS. Be sure the bits of eel are browned.

CHORUS. The words you speak, your savory rites,
Keep sharpening so our appetites
That we can hardly bear it.

DICAEOPOLIS. Now roast these other things and brown them
nicely.

GROOMSMAN. O Dicaeopolis!

DICAEOPOLIS. Who's there! who's there?

GROOMSMAN. A bridegroom sends you from his wedding banquet
These bits of meat.

DICAEOPOLIS. Well done, whoe'er he is.

GROOMSMAN. And in return he bids you pour him out,
To keep him safely with his bride at home,
Into this ointment pot one dram of Peace.

DICAEOPOLIS. Take, take your meat away; I can't abide it.
Not for ten thousand drachmas would I give him
One drop of Peace. Hey, who comes here?

GROOMSMAN. The bridesmaid
Bringing a private message from the bride.

DICAEOPOLIS. Well, what have *you* to say? Who wants the
  bride?
  (*Affects to listen.*)
  O heaven, the laughable request she makes
  To keep her bridegroom safely by her side.
  I'll do it; bring the truces; she's a woman,
  Unfit to bear the burdens of the war.
  Now, hold the myrrh box underneath, my girl.
  Know you the way to use it? Tell the bride,
  When they're enrolling soldiers for the war,
  To rub the bridegroom every night with this.
  Now take the truces back, and bring the ladle.
  I'll fill the winecups for the Pitcher feast.

CHORUS. But here runs one with eyebrows puckered up.
  Methinks he comes a messenger of woe.

CRIER. O toils, and fights, and fighting Lamachuses!

LAMACHUS. Who clangs around my bronze-accoutered halls?

CRIER. The generals bid you take your crests and cohorts,
  And hurry off this instant; to keep watch
  Amongst the mountain passes in the snow.
  For news has come that at this Pitcher feast
  Boeotian bandits mean to raid our lands.

LAMACHUS. O generals, great in numbers, small in worth!
  Shame that I may not even enjoy the feast.

DICAEOPOLIS. O expedition battle-Lamachaean!

LAMACHUS. O dear, what *you!* Do *you* insult me too?

DICAEOPOLIS. What would you fight with Geryon, the four-
  winged?

LAMACHUS. O woe!
  O what a message has this Crier brought me!

DICAEOPOLIS. Oho! what message will this runner bring me?

MESSENGER. Dicaeopolis!

DICAEOPOLIS.   Well?

MESSENGER.   Come at once to supper,
  And bring your pitcher, and your supper chest.
  The priest of Bacchus sends to fetch you thither.
  And do be quick: you keep the supper waiting.
  For all things else are ready and prepared,
  The couches, tables, sofa cushions, rugs,
  Wreaths, sweetmeats, myrrh, the harlotry are there,
  Whole-meal cakes, cheese-cakes, sesame-honey-cakes,
  And dancing girls, *Harmodius' dearest* ones.
  So pray make haste.

LAMACHUS.   O wretched, wretched me!

DICAEOPOLIS. Aye the great Gorgon 'twas you chose for
    patron.
    Now close the house, and pack the supper up.
LAMACHUS. Boy, bring me out my soldier's knapsack here.
DICAEOPOLIS. Boy, bring me out my supper basket here.
LAMACHUS. Boy, bring me onions, with some thymy salt.
DICAEOPOLIS. For me, fish fillets: onions I detest.
LAMACHUS. Boy, bring me here a leaf of rotten fish.
DICAEOPOLIS. A tit-bit leaf for me; I'll toast it there.
LAMACHUS. Now bring me here my helmet's double plume.
DICAEOPOLIS. And bring me here my thrushes and ring doves.
LAMACHUS. How nice and white this ostrich plume to view.
DICAEOPOLIS. How nice and brown this pigeon's flesh to eat.
LAMACHUS. Man, don't keep jeering at my armor so.
DICAEOPOLIS. Man, don't keep peering at my thrushes so.
LAMACHUS. Bring me the casket with the three crests in it.
DICAEOPOLIS. Bring me the basket with the hare's flesh in it.
LAMACHUS. Surely the moths my crest have eaten up.
DICAEOPOLIS. Sure this hare soup I'll eat before I sup.
LAMACHUS. Fellow, I'll thank you not to talk to *me*.
DICAEOPOLIS. Nay, but the boy and I, we can't agree.
    Come will you bet, and Lamachus decide,
    Locusts or thrushes, which the daintier are?
LAMACHUS. Insolent knave!
DICAEOPOLIS.   (*to the boy*). Locusts, he says, by far.
LAMACHUS. Boy, boy, take down the spear, and bring it here.
DICAEOPOLIS. Boy, take the sweetbread off and bring it here.
LAMACHUS. Hold firmly to the spear while I pull off
    The case.
DICAEOPOLIS.   And you, hold firmly to the spit.
LAMACHUS. Boy, bring the framework to support my shield.
DICAEOPOLIS. Boy, bring the bakemeats to support my frame.
LAMACHUS. Bring here the grim-backed circle of the shield.
DICAEOPOLIS. And here the cheese-backed circle of the cake.
LAMACHUS. Is not this—mockery, plain for men to see?
DICAEOPOLIS. Is not this—cheese-cake, sweet for men to eat?
LAMACHUS. Pour on the oil, boy. Gazing on my shield,
    I see an old man tried for cowardliness.
DICAEOPOLIS. Pour on the honey. Gazing on my cake,
    I see an old man mocking Lamachus.
LAMACHUS. Bring me a casque, to arm the outer man.
DICAEOPOLIS. Bring me a cask to warm the inner man.
LAMACHUS. With this I'll arm myself against the foe.
DICAEOPOLIS. With this I'll warm myself against the feast.

LAMACHUS. Boy, lash the blankets up against the shield.
DICAEOPOLIS. Boy, lash the supper up against the chest.
LAMACHUS. Myself will bear my knapsack for myself.
DICAEOPOLIS. Myself will wear my wraps, and haste away.
LAMACHUS. Take up the shield, my boy, and bring it on.
  Snowing! good lack, a wintry prospect mine.
DICAEOPOLIS. Take up the chest; a suppery prospect mine.
CHORUS. Off to your duties, my heroes bold.
  Different truly the paths ye tread;
  One to drink with wreaths on his head;
  One to watch, and shiver with cold,
  Lonely, the while his antagonist passes
  The sweetest of hours with the sweetest of lasses.

Pray we that Zeus calmly reduce
          to destruction emphatic and utter
That meanest of poets and meanest of men,
          Antimachus, offspring of Sputter;
  The Choregus who sent me away
          without any supper at all
  At the feast of Lenaea; I pray,
          two Woes that Choregus befall.
  May he hanker for a dish
          of the subtle cuttlefish;
  May he see the cuttle sailing
          through its brine and through its oil,
  On its little table lying,
          hot and hissing from the frying,
  Till it anchor close beside him,
          when alas! and woe betide him!
  As he reaches forth his hand
          for the meal the Gods provide him,
  May a dog snatch and carry off the spoil, off the spoil,
  May a dog snatch and carry off the spoil.
Duly the first Woe is rehearsed;
          attend while the other I'm telling.
It is night, and our gentleman, after a ride,
          is returning on foot to his dwelling;
  With ague he's sorely bested,
          and he's feeling uncommonly ill,
  When suddenly down on his head
          comes Orestes's club with a will.
  'Tis Orestes, hero mad,
          'tis the drunkard and the pad.

Then stooping in the darkness
let him grope about the place,
If his hand can find a brickbat
at Orestes to be flung;
But instead of any brickbat
may he grasp a podge of dung,
And rushing on with this, Orestes may he miss,
And hit young Cratinus in the face, in the face,
And hit young Cratinus in the face.

ATTENDANT. Varlets who dwell in Lamachus's halls,
Heat water, knaves, heat water in a pot.
Make ready lint, and salves, and greasy wool,
And ankle bandages. Your lord is hurt,
Pierced by a stake whilst leaping o'er a trench.
Then, twisting round, he wrenched his ankle out,
And, falling, cracked his skull upon a stone;
And shocked the sleeping Gorgon from his shield.
Then the Great Boastard's plume being cast away
Prone on the rocks, a dolorous cry he raised,
O glorious Eye, with this my last fond look
The heavenly light I leave; my day is done.
He spake, and straightway falls into a ditch:
Jumps up again: confronts the runaways,
And prods the fleeing bandits with his spear.
But here he enters. Open wide the door.

LAMACHUS. O lack-a-day! O lack-a-day!
I'm hacked, I'm killed, by hostile lances!
But worse than wound or lance 'twill grieve me
If Dicaeopolis perceive me
And mock, and mock at my mischances.
DICAEOPOLIS. O lucky day! O lucky day!
What mortal ever can be richer,
Than he who feels, my golden misses,
Your softest, closest, loveliest kisses.
'Twas I, 'twas I, first drained the pitcher.
LAMACHUS. O me, my woeful dolorous lot!
O me, the gruesome wounds I've got!
DICAEOPOLIS. My darling Lamachippus, is it not?
LAMACHUS. O doleful chance!
DICAEOPOLIS.   O cursed spite!
LAMACHUS. Why give me a kiss?
DICAEOPOLIS.   Why give me a bite?
LAMACHUS. O me the heavy, heavy charge they tried.

DICAEOPOLIS. Who makes a charge this happy Pitcher-tide?

LAMACHUS. O Paean, Healer! heal me, Paean, pray.

DICAEOPOLIS. 'Tis not the Healer's festival today.

LAMACHUS. O lift me gently round the hips,
My comrades true!

DICAEOPOLIS. O kiss me warmly on the lips,
My darlings, do!

LAMACHUS. My brain is dizzy with the blow
Of hostile stone.

DICAEOPOLIS. Mine's dizzy too: to bed I'll go,
And not alone.

LAMACHUS. O take me in your healing hands, and bring
To Pittalus this battered frame of mine.

DICAEOPOLIS. O take me to the judges. Where's the King
That rules the feast? hand me my skin of wine.

LAMACHUS. A lance has struck me through the bone
So piteously! so piteously!
(*He is helped off the stage.*)

DICAEOPOLIS. I've drained the pitcher all alone;
Sing ho! Sing ho! for Victory.

CHORUS. Sing ho! Sing ho! for Victory then,
If so you bid, if so you bid.

DICAEOPOLIS. I filled it with neat wine, my men,
And quaffed it at a gulp, I did.

CHORUS. Sing ho! brave heart, the wineskin take,
And onward go, and onward go.

DICAEOPOLIS. And ye must follow in my wake,
And sing for Victory ho! sing ho!

CHORUS. O yes, we'll follow for your sake
Your wineskin and yourself, I trow.
Sing ho! for Victory won, sing ho!

(*Exeunt.*)

Knights

The *Knights*, produced in 424 B.C., is an outspoken attack upon Cleon, the democratic leader, who came into control of Athenian policy after the death of Pericles. A few months before the play was presented Demosthenes had initiated but Cleon had brought to a successful conclusion the brilliant exploit at Sphacteria which caused the Spartans to propose peace (Thucydides 4.1–41). In the play (54 ff.) Demosthenes says: "The other day I kneaded a Laconian cake at Pylos, but the Paphlagonian with rascally effrontery dodged in and snatched it up and himself served up the cake I had kneaded." The play starts with a transparent allegory as two slaves of crotchety old Demos ("the people"), got up to resemble the generals Nicias and Demosthenes (the older editions so name the characters), complain of the bullying of Demos' new favorite, a Paphlagonian leather seller, who represents Cleon. Among the oracles they steal from Cleon (Paphlagon) is one which foretells that Cleon shall be supplanted by a sausage seller. The Sausageman appears, and is persuaded that his rascality and impudence qualify him; Cleon accuses his slaves of treason, and the chorus of knights, possibly riding pickaback, rush to their assistance. Cleon dashes out to complain to the senate; but the Sausageman has outdone Cleon in brazenness, and when both seek to win over Demos, the Sausageman (now named Agoracritus) succeeds. During a second parabasis the Sausageman (who had apparently assumed his earlier character only to out-Cleon Cleon) has rejuvenated Demos by stewing him in a pot; Demos comes forth determined to abolish innovations and restore the old-fashioned ways. It is said that the maskmakers refused to provide a mask for Cleon and that Aristophanes played the part himself. But that the play could be presented at all, with Cleon himself in the audience, is another evidence of Athenian freedom of speech.

CHARACTERS

DEMOS ("PEOPLE OF ATHENS")

PAPHLAGON
NICIAS   } SLAVES OF DEMOS
DEMOSTHENES

SAUSAGEMAN
CHORUS OF KNIGHTS

Translated by R. H. Webb

(The foreground shows a sketchy representation of the Pnyx. Behind is the house of DEMOS, *flanked by those of* PAPHLAGON *(Cleon) and the* SAUSAGEMAN. *Two slaves, whose masks show them to be the Athenian generals* DEMOSTHENES *and* NICIAS, *emerge from* DEMOS' *house, wailing.)*

DEMOSTHENES. Ouch! How I hurt! . . . Oh Lordy! Goodness me!
    That Paphlagon our master lately bought . . .
    Confound him anyway, and all his tricks!
    For, since the day he got into this house,
    There's been a perfect itch of beatings here.

NICIAS. Yes, damn the peerless Paphlagonian . . .
    Him and his lies!

DEMOSTHENES. How do you feel, my boy?

NICIAS. No worse than you, I'm sure.

DEMOSTHENES.   Well then, come on.
    Let's sing a sob duet to Olympus' tune.

BOTH. *Boohoo boohoo boohoo boohoo boohoo!*

DEMOSTHENES. What are we wailing for? No use to whine.
    We'd best be thinking how to save our lives.

NICIAS. How *can* we?

DEMOSTHENES.   *You* tell!

NICIAS.   Me? Oh no, you first.
    Now don't let's quarrel.

DEMOSTHENES.   I refuse. So there!

NICIAS. *Wilt thou not say for me what I should say?*

DEMOSTHENES. Buck up and *say* it! Then it's my turn next.

NICIAS. There's no buck *in* me. Oh to speak my thought
    As daintily as dear Euripides!

DEMOSTHENES. No more of that. . . . No spinach! . . . What's your *plan?*
    We've got to wiggle out of this somehow.

NICIAS. All right. Say *daddle,* just like that. . . . Go on.

DEMOSTHENES. *Daddle.*

NICIAS.   And now say *let's ske.*

DEMOSTHENES.   *Let's ske.*

NICIAS.   Good!
    Now say them in succession . . . *daddle, let's ske* . . .
    Slowly at first, then speeding up a bit—
    Exactly as in bedtime solitaire.

DEMOSTHENES. Well, *daddle . . . let's ske, daddle, let's ske-daddle!*

NICIAS. Isn't it fun?

DEMOSTHENES.   Oh yes, but dangerous—
A game that I'm afraid to play.

NICIAS.   How so?

DEMOSTHENES. Because it puts my skin in jeopardy!

NICIAS. Nothing remains then, but to throw ourselves
Upon the tender mercy of the gods.

DEMOSTHENES. The gods! Don't tell me you believe in *them!*

NICIAS. Of course I do.

DEMOSTHENES.   And on what evidence?

NICIAS. Because they hate me so! That's proof enough.

DEMOSTHENES. Quite plausible! But think of something else.—
Suppose we lay the facts before the house?

NICIAS. Not bad. . . . And make this one request of them—
To show us clearly, by their smiles or frowns,
Whether or not they like our comedy.

DEMOSTHENES. Our boss is Demos, farmer born and bred,
Business address, the Pnyx; a chronic grouch,
High-tempered, sixtyish, a trifle deaf,
But knows his beans. Last market day he bought
A slave—a tanner, name of Paphlagon,
The biggest rogue and liar hereabouts.
He learned in no time what the old man likes . . .
Not only *made* his boots but licked them too.
He toadied, flattered, wheedled him for fair,
And oiled him up with soothing saddle soap:
Just try one case, sir. Here's your fee in full.
An early bath, then dinner—soup to nuts.
And, later on, a bite of supper, eh?
What's more, the tidbits *we* prepare he steals
And gets the credit for. The other day,
When I'd cooked up a Spartan mess at Pylos,
The scamp slipped by me, grabbed the dish and ran
And brought it to the master as his own!
No one's allowed to do a thing but *him* . . .
Stands with a leather duster, while he eats,
And shoos away political bugaboos.
He knows the old boy dotes on oracles,
And reads them to him till he's pleased as Punch,
Filling him full of lies about us all.
And when the beatings start, this Paphlagon

Goes round among the servants dropping hints
That they'd be wise to purchase his protection:
You saw the whaling that young Hylas got?
You want to live? Then make it worth my while.
And we, of course, pay up. For otherwise
The boss would kick the stuffing out of us.—
So now, my friend, we must decide at once
What line to take, and who can help us take it.

NICIAS. Couldn't do better than my *daddle* line!

DEMOSTHENES. He'd never let us get away with it. . . .
Sees all, knows all—Colossus-Paphlagon—
Right foot in Pylos, left foot on the Pnyx;
His bottom in Chaonia's fairyland,
His fingers in the pies of Hungery,
His head upon sweet Grafton's tempting banks!

NICIAS. *Then naught, methinks, can serve us, save to die.*

DEMOSTHENES. Too true! But we must die a noble death.

NICIAS. Oh for a noble death, a hero's death!
'Tis best that we should drink the blood of bulls.
How fine to die like great Themistocles!

DEMOSTHENES. Nay, rather, drink a toast to Lady Luck,
Who might inspire us with a happy thought.

NICIAS. Drink, is it? Drink! It's always drink with you!
How can a drunkard offer sound advice?

DEMOSTHENES. Indeed? . . . You and your wishy-washy pap!
You dare to scoff at wine as *un*inspiring?
What could be more conducive to success?
When people drink, 'tis then they prosper most;
They're rich, their deals go through, they win their suits,
They're generous and helpful to their friends.
Draw me a flagon of the precious stuff,
To wet my wits and show how smart I am!

NICIAS. This drinking . . . it will be our ruin yet.

DEMOSTHENES. Salvation, rather! . . . Go.—I'll take it easy.
Once I am tight, I'll spray the premises
With showers of tricky schemes and stratagems.

NICIAS. Good thing for me I wasn't caught at this!

DEMOSTHENES. And what's old tittle-tattle up to?

NICIAS.   Drunk,
And snoozing, sprawled upon a stack of hides,
His belly full of confiscated buns.

DEMOSTHENES. Pour me a bubbling big libation, now.

NICIAS. Well, here you are. Pray to Good Fortune, first.

DEMOSTHENES. Good Fortune! Ha! Good Pramnian! . . . Drink
    her down!—

    O Blessed Spirit, thine is the thought, not mine!

NICIAS. What thought? What *is* it, man?

DEMOSTHENES.   The oracles!

    Go steal those oracles of Paphlagon's,

    And bring them out before he wakes.

NICIAS.   Uh-huh.

    I fear my fortune doesn't look so good!

DEMOSTHENES. Myself, methinks I'll take a swig, meanwhile,

    To wet my wits, and show how smart I am!

NICIAS. Still snoring . . . deuce of a racket . . . fore and aft.

    He never even saw me get the one

    That he's been guarding specially.

DEMOSTHENES.   Bright lad!

    Here, let me read it. Pour me out a drink.

    Now we shall see what this is all about.

    O wondrous wisdom! Quick! I need a drink!

NICIAS. There! Tell me what it says.

DEMOSTHENES. Another, please.

NICIAS. That's funny talk from any oracle!

DEMOSTHENES. O Mighty Prophet!

NICIAS.   What's he *say?*

DEMOSTHENES.   A drink!

NICIAS. The prophet surely liked his liquor, what?

DEMOSTHENES. You wretch! No wonder you were on your
    guard.

    You lived in mortal fear of *this.*

NICIAS.   Of what?

DEMOSTHENES. It's here foretold how he shall meet his end.

NICIAS. Well, how?

DEMOSTHENES.   The oracle expressly says

    The first Big Boss of Athens is to be

    A man whose business is to peddle ropes.

NICIAS. That's Peddler No. 1. Go on. Who's next?

DEMOSTHENES. Then comes another man who peddles sheep.

NICIAS. And what's the fate of Peddler No. 2?

DEMOSTHENES. To boss until a bigger knave appears.

    Then *he* is out, succeeded by a chap

    Who peddles hides—a thief, and with a voice

    To drown a mountain torrent in the spring.

NICIAS. That nice sheep peddler had to be done in

    By this hide peddler?

DEMOSTHENES.   Yes.

NICIAS. Oh goodness me,
If only we could find one peddler more!

DEMOSTHENES. There *is* another . . . with a monstrous trade.

NICIAS. Who is he?

DEMOSTHENES. Sure you want to know?

NICIAS. Oh please!

DEMOSTHENES. Well, sheep are doomed to yield to . . . sausages!

NICIAS. A *sausage* peddler? God! That *is* a business!
Where shall we ever find a man like that?

DEMOSTHENES. We've got to search.

NICIAS. A miracle! . . . Look there!
He comes, he comes! Headed for market. See?
(*Enter* SAUSAGEMAN.)

DEMOSTHENES. Immortal Sausageman! My dearest friend!
Incarnate Savior of the Land, and us!

SAUSAGEMAN. What *is* this? Why . . . ?

DEMOSTHENES. Approach, and you shall learn
How great and glorious is your destiny!

NICIAS. You make him put his table down right here,
And tell him all about the oracle.
I'll go inside and shadow Paphlagon.

DEMOSTHENES. Now set your stock-in-trade upon the ground,
And then salute the gods and Mother Earth.

SAUSAGEMAN. All right. . . . So what?

DEMOSTHENES. O rich, O blessed one,
Today's stepchild, tomorrow's superman,
Master of smiling Athens, Prince and Chief!

SAUSAGEMAN. Quit mocking me, and let me go to work.
I've guts to wash and sausages to sell.

DEMOSTHENES. Sausages? Guts? Why you're an ass! . . . Come,
look.
Thou seest yonder serried ranks?

SAUSAGEMAN. I do.

DEMOSTHENES. You shall be lord of all that you survey—
Markets and harbors, Senate, Pnyx, and courts.
You'll wipe your feet upon the High Command,
And keep your wenches in the City Hall!

SAUSAGEMAN. Who? Me?

DEMOSTHENES. Yes, you! And more than that, my friend.
Just climb up on your table, won't you please? . . .
You see those islands scattered round about?

SAUSAGEMAN. I do.

DEMOSTHENES. The towns, the ports, the shipping?

SAUSAGEMAN.   Yes.

DEMOSTHENES. Then don't you think your future's pretty
    grand?

  Now cast your right eye east, to Caria,

  And turn the left to Carthage, in the west.

SAUSAGEMAN. My future will be *cockeyed*, sure as fate!

DEMOSTHENES. All you behold is yours, to buy and sell.

  You'll be, according to this oracle,

  The greatest man on earth.

SAUSAGEMAN.   But *look* at me—

  A sausage peddler, not a gentleman!

DEMOSTHENES. That is precisely why it's possible.

  You've got the brass, you're common, you're a bum!

SAUSAGEMAN. But I'm not fit. The job's too big for me.

DEMOSTHENES. Oh mercy! Why? Why don't you think you're
    fit?

  You're conscious of some fatal decency!

  Your parents weren't *respectable?*

SAUSAGEMAN.   Hell, no!

  I'm just a guttersnipe.

DEMOSTHENES.   Heaven be praised!

  A most propitious start for politics!

SAUSAGEMAN. But, my dear sir, I've got no education.

  Oh, I can read and write a little bit.

DEMOSTHENES. Your only handicap—that "little bit"!

  No educated man can be a boss,

  These days, nor yet a man of character. . . .

  Only an ignoramus and a rogue!

  So don't reject the largesse of the gods.

SAUSAGEMAN. What does the oracle say?

DEMOSTHENES.   Oh, splendid things,

  In most profoundly enigmatic style:

  Verily, when, in his hunger, the great hook-clawed tanner-
    eagle

  Seizes for prey in his beak the serpent, the blood-drinking
    booby,

  Then shall be spilled, of a surety, the best Paphlagonian
    pickle.

  God will endue the sellers of guts with eminent power,

  Aye, with glory, unless they prefer to peddle their sausage.

SAUSAGEMAN. And where do *I* come in? Just tell me that.

DEMOSTHENES. The "tanner-eagle," of course, is Paphlagon.

SAUSAGEMAN. And why is he "hook-clawed"?

DEMOSTHENES. Because, forsooth,
He *hooks* whtaever he gets his *claws* upon!

SAUSAGEMAN. But what's the "serpent" for?

DEMOSTHENES. Quite obvious.
Serpents are long, and so are sausages;
And both "drink blood." . . . Well, don't you see it yet?
The prophet says the snake will beat the bird,
Provided he's not wheedled out of it.

SAUSAGEMAN. He'd have "provided" for me better still,
If he had told me how to run the country!

DEMOSTHENES. Easy enough. Do what you're doing now—
Making a hash of things in general,
Sweetening up the mess to the public taste
With a dash of oratorical applesauce!
The other requisites are clearly yours—
A raucous voice, you're cockney to the core . . .
Yes, everything you need for statesmanship.
Apollo and the prophets all agree.
But pray, my lad, pray hard, to Billiken . . .
And never take your eye off Paphlagon!

SAUSAGEMAN. Who will support me, eh? The plutocrats
Are in a funk; the poor are jittery.

DEMOSTHENES. Ah, but a thousand Knights, good men and true,
Despise him. They will back you to the end;
And so will every decent man in town.
These clever people in the audience,
And I, and God, can all be counted on.
Don't be afraid. His likeness isn't good.
Our mask-designers were so scared of him
They wouldn't reproduce the fellow's face.
But he'll be known. This public is no fool.

NICIAS. Lord help us, Paphlagon is coming out!
(*Enter* PAPHLAGON.)

PAPHLAGON. By the Twelve Gods you two shall pay for it—
Conspiring years and years against the State!
Chalcidean goblet, what? . . . Aha! I see!
You're plotting a Chalcidean revolt!
You'll die for this, you brace of miscreants!

DEMOSTHENES. O noble Sausageman, I pray you, pause.
Come back! Stand firm! Be loyal to the Cause!—
Ho, ye horseman! Hither! Hither! 'Tis the crisis of the fight.
Double-quick! Panaetius, Simon, march your troopers
column right!

There they are!—Now turn, confront him. You have nothing
    more to fear.
See the dust ascending yonder? Your allies are very near.
Stand and face him. Run and chase him. Lick him. Kick
    him in the rear!
(Enter CHORUS.*)*

CHORUS. Smite the villain, the confounder of our goodly
    cavalry,
Publican and bottomless Charybdis of rapacity,
And a villain . . . yes, a villain—let me say it just once
    more—
Who, on every day that passes, plays the villain o'er and
    o'er!
With your blows demoralize him. Drive him into utter rout.
Hate him bitterly, as I do. Set upon him with a shout.
But be cautious. He'll evade you. For he has the artful skill
By which Eucrates succeeded in escaping to his mill.

PAPHLAGON. Ho, ye jurors, long my brothers in the fee fra-
    ternity,
Whom my lusty voice defendeth—right or wrong, it's one
    to me—
Bring your forces. Quell the sources of this dark conspiracy!

CHORUS. We conspire to stop your eating in our orchard every
    peach,
And by premature impeachment pinching all that you can
    reach—
Not alone the juicy fellows, soft, and quick to show a
    bruise,
But the green ones too you manage quite effectively to use;
And from off the highest branches of our master's spread-
    ing tree
Down by hook or crook you pull them, gulping them with
    gruesome glee.
Yes, your game is lamblike victims, meek, impractical and
    mild,
Innocent and rich, as helpless in the courtroom as a child.

PAPHLAGON. *You* attack me? What injustice? It's beauty I said
    'twas right
That a statue be erected on Athena's lofty height
To commemorate your valor, that I'm *in* this nasty plight.

CHORUS. What a liar! What a slick one, with his knavish com-
    pliments!
Does he think that we are dotards? Does he think we
    have no sense?

Now then, if we fail on this side, we shall wallop him on
    that;

Should he underpass my punches, I shall boot him to the
    mat!

PAPHLAGON. Save me, wardsmen, fellow tribesmen! I am
    gored by savage foes!

CHORUS. Yelling? That is how you always floor the people
    you oppose.

SAUSAGEMAN. Not today! If yelling does it, let me at him!
    Down he goes!

CHORUS. Good! If you outyell this person, you're the cham-
    pion, no mistake.

But if he's the shameless victor, then it's we that take the
    cake!

PAPHLAGON. I indict him as a traitor, and shall now proceed
    to tell

How he ships the Spartan navy precious soup matériel.

SAUSAGEMAN. But when *you* with empty belly breeze to City
    Hall to dine,

Home you sail at evening laden with a cargo superfine!

DEMOSTHENES. Yes, by God, illegal traffic . . . fish fillet and
    bread and meat—

Better fare than, at those dinners, Pericles did ever eat!

PAPHLAGON. Tough on you when I start howling.

SAUSAGEMAN. You'll be dead when I stop yowling.

PAPHLAGON. I shall shout till I outyell you.

SAUSAGEMAN. I shall screech until I fell you.

PAPHLAGON. As Commander I'll confound you.

SAUSAGEMAN. Then I'll beat your back, you hound, you.

PAPHLAGON. But my lies will soon outstrip you.

SAUSAGEMAN. By a short cut I shall trip you.

PAPHLAGON. Look me in the face, unblinking.

SAUSAGEMAN. Ever find a gamin shrinking?

PAPHLAGON. I'll dissect you, if you mutter . . .

SAUSAGEMAN. They'll collect *you* from the gutter!

PAPHLAGON. I'm a crook. Confess that you're one.

SAUSAGEMAN. So I do . . . a simon-pure one.

PAPHLAGON. I can swear down any witness.

SAUSAGEMAN. That's another's special fitness.

PAPHLAGON. When the senate learns, my beauty,
    That you never paid the duty
      On this stuff, too bad for you!

CHORUS.   O you brash, horrid fellow,
          How you bawl, how you bellow

Through the whole realm of nature,
Through the whole Legislature!
    Courts are stricken,
    Judges sicken;
  Revenue Collectors all
  Tremble at your trumpet call.
  Sling the mud, rake the muck!
  See them dive, see them duck!
When you sight the tribute moneys,
  From our lofty Citadel,
Sailing in like schools of tunnies,
  Ears are deafened at your yell.

PAPHLAGON. I know who designed this business, and who sewed it up so neat.

SAUSAGEMAN. Yes, if you don't know your stitching, I don't know my sausage meat—

Selling soles of rotten leather to a country customer,

Bevel-edged, and so appearing thicker than they really were;

But, before the chap had worn them for a single day, they grew

Easily ten inches wider than they'd been when they were new.

DEMOSTHENES. That's the trick he played on *me*, sir. How my neighbors laughed, the rogues!

Short of Pergasae, I tell you, I was swimming in those brogues!

CHORUS.   You displayed, from the first,
          Sheer audacity, the true
        Patron saint of the worst
          Of the politician crew;
        And employed it to defame us,
          Milking our dominion herds,
        While the son of Hippodamus
          Wept for all his wasted words.
  Ah, but a Savior to Athens is granted,
Meaner than you, sir. The town is enchanted.
          He will check you,
          He will wreck you.
            His fine talents
            Will outbalance,
          Foxy bluffer,
          All your brass.

> You're a duffer;
> He has class!

Thou who wert born and reared like all the leaders of this nation,

Prove to the world how useless is a decent education!

SAUSAGEMAN. Then hear me test his character, and force him to a showdown.

PAPHLAGON. Me first!

SAUSAGEMAN.   Oh no! I'm bumptious too, and every bit as lowdown!

CHORUS. If that one doesn't lay him out, declare your *folks* were *lower!*

PAPHLAGON. I *will* speak first!

SAUSAGEMAN.   You'll not!

PAPHLAGON.   Says who?

SAUSAGEMAN.   You'll not, say I, once more!

We'll argue, first, who'll *be* the first. And you'll be last, I vow it.

PAPHLAGON. I *must* be first, or I shall burst!

SAUSAGEMAN.   You shan't! I won't allow it!

CHORUS. Oh let him burst, for heaven's sake! 'Twould be a fine solution.

PAPHLAGON. How dare you challenge face to face my skill in elocution?

SAUSAGEMAN. I can concoct an argument as well as mustard dressing.

PAPHLAGON. Concoct an argument, indeed! Don't tell me you're professing

To serve from raw materials a solid feast of reason?

Your malady is common here, *in* season, *out* of season.

Having contrived to win a suit against a foreign victim,

Rehearsing day and night the speech by which at last you tricked 'im,

Abjuring wine, and showing off before your friends, by golly

You think yourself an orator. Unmitigated folly!

SAUSAGEMAN. And *you* drink what, that you alone can speak 'mid perfect quiet?

The town's reduced to silence. Is it something in your diet?

PAPHLAGON. You hope to find a match for me? Hot herrings I'll devour,

Washing them down with quarts of grog; and then display
  my power

In fishwife language that will make the Pylos captains
  cower!

SAUSAGEMAN. Give *me* a slug of chitt'lin's and a mug of good
  pot licker,

And watch these greasy hands of mine without an eyelid's
  flicker

Throttle the gang of demagogues and Nicias outbicker!

CHORUS. I like the rest of what you've said, but find it rather
  rummy

That *all* the gravy should descend to *your* capacious
  tummy!

PAPHLAGON. Bolting a big-mouth bass, I'll drive Miletus to
  distraction.

SAUSAGEMAN. Polishing off a roast, I'll lease the Mines in one
  transaction.

PAPHLAGON. I'll pounce upon the Senators and let them have
  a lacing.

SAUSAGEMAN. I'll rip the lining from your rear to use for
  sausage casing!

PAPHLAGON. I'll grab you by your lordly rump and drag you
  off, bent double.

CHORUS. You'll have to drag me too, my boy, if *he* gets into
  trouble!

PAPHLAGON. You shall be tortured on the rack.

SAUSAGEMAN. For cowardice you'll get the sack.

PAPHLAGON. Your hide upon my bench I'll pin . . .

SAUSAGEMAN. I'll make a thief's purse from your skin . . .

PAPHLAGON. Spread-eagle you upon the ground.

SAUSAGEMAN. And you'll be scrap meat by the pound.

PAPHLAGON. Your lashes, one by one, I'll pluck.

SAUSAGEMAN. I'll snatch your gizzard, just for luck.

DEMOSTHENES. What's more, by God, we'll gag the lout
And pull his lying tongue way out;
    And then look through,
    As butchers do,
      That yawning throat
From stem to stern,
Until we learn
    If he's a big
  And healthy shoat
    Or measly pig
      At bottom!

CHORUS.   Fire is hot; but a hotter
                 Thing is here, in a plotter
                   Blest with gall that is the pride
                   Of a town well supplied!
                     Go and get him!
                     Never let him
                 Doubt your skill. Knock him giddy!
                 Thought it would be easy, did 'e?
                   Tarry not. Work with haste,
                   While you have him round the waist.
                 Don't I know the ugly blighter?
                 Soften up the leatherjack.
                 He will prove a craven fighter,
                   In the very first attack!

SAUSAGEMAN. Nothing but a tradesman, spending all his life-
      time in a shop.
   But we held him quite a hero when he reaped another's
      crop.
   And the many sheaves he garnered, though they weren't
      his own at all,
   He has kept in stock for drying, hoping thus to make a
      haul.

PAPHLAGON. I've no fear of you whatever, while the Senate
      House is there,
   And the People sit assembled with that same old stupid
      stare!

CHORUS.   What a bold, brazen beak!
                      Not a flicker, not a flush!
                        What a front, what a cheek!
                        Doesn't blench, doesn't blush!
                        If I love you, let me be a
                        Blanket on Cratinus' bed,
                          Or, as choric volunteer,
                          Sing for Morsimus, instead!
                 Flitting from bower to blossoming bower,
                 Sipping the sweets of the briberry-flower,
                          May your dining
                          And your wining,
                          Won by cheating,
                          Prove but fleeting.
                          Then my sole
                          Song would be:
                            Quaff a bowl
                            To Victory!

And Julius' son, old beagle-eye, would greet, methinks, the
    New Year

In joyful tones, with "God be praised!" and "Glory Hal-
    lelujah!"

PAPHLAGON. To primacy in shamelessness indulge no false
    pretension—

Or may I never hear the prayer that opens a Convention!

SAUSAGEMAN. By all the buffets I received when I was but a
    laddie,

And all the smacks with butcher knives delivered by my
    daddy,

I'll prove myself superior. For, otherwise, quite vainly

Would I have grown to be so great on scraps and refuse,
    mainly.

PAPHLAGON. On refuse, like an alley cat? And now, sir, more's
    the pity,

You dare confront this Catamount that terrifies the city?

SAUSAGEMAN. Why not? I mastered trickery before I left the
    cradle!

I'd fool the scullions in the kitchen, pointing with the ladle:
*Look yonder, boys, you see that bird? . . . A swallow.
    Spring is here!*

And *when* they looked, I stole some meat—just made it
    disappear!

CHORUS. A clever ruse! A meaty brain! You saw 'twas bound
    to follow

That thievery and nettles both are best before the swallow!

SAUSAGEMAN. Besides, I got away with it. For if one *did*
    detect me,

I'd swear—the steak between my hams—'twas wicked to
    suspect me!

Indeed a politician said, who saw me act so smarty,

This boy will surely some day lead the Democratic Party!

CHORUS. A good surmise, and evidently this is how he
    guessed it:

You lied about the meat you pinched, the while your rump
    caressed it!

PAPHLAGON. I'll take you down a peg or two. You both shall
    soon be drooping.

I'll burst upon you like a storm, tempestuously swooping

Upon the land and sea at once, o'er field and billow
    whooping.

SAUSAGEMAN. Then I shall reef my sausages and send myself
    a-skidding

Across the waves, to you bad luck and plenty of it bidding!

DEMOSTHENES. I'll mind the bilge in case she leaks, and be on hand to bale 'er.

PAPHLAGON. For stealing thousands from the State, *you'll* visit with the jailer.

CHORUS. Watch out! Ease off the sheet a bit! The wind's about to veer—

A spanking, persecuting gale that whistles in my ear.

SAUSAGEMAN. And fifty grand I know you got in bribes from Potidaea.

PAPHLAGON. Keep mum, and ten per cent is yours, in this and other cases.

CHORUS. He'll take it gladly, that he will! Go loosen up the braces.

The wind has dropped like anything!

PAPHLAGON. Suit upon suit 'gainst you I'll bring,
At half a million bucks a fling.

SAUSAGEMAN. For slacking, *you* shall face a score;
For theft, a thousand . . . maybe more.

PAPHLAGON. You bear the curse, I here proclaim,
Of the Goddess who gave this town her name.

SAUSAGEMAN. Your Grandpapa, say I, was one
Of the bodyguard . . .

PAPHLAGON. Of whom, old son?

SAUSAGEMAN. Of Princess *Hida*, Hippias' mate.

PAPHLAGON. You lying scamp!

SAUSAGEMAN. You reprobate!

CHORUS. Pommel him well!

PAPHLAGON. My goodness me!
Why, this is a conspiracy!

CHORUS. Now wield your guts and swing your tripe,
And lash with many a manful swipe
That spacious maw
And bloated cor-
Poration!

Most noble youth of brain and brawn, of courage quite transcendent,

Revealed as Savior of the State and all on her dependent,

You met the foe in skilled debate, and subtle past all measure.

Oh, would that we might sing you praise in words to match our pleasure!

PAPHLAGON. By all that's holy, I have not been blind;
I know precisely how this plot was framed,

And nailed and glued together, piece by piece.

SAUSAGEMAN. And *I'm* not blind to your intrigues at Argos—
Working for Argive friendship, so he *says*,
But meeting certain Spartans privately . . .

CHORUS. Good gracious! Don't *you* know some metaphors?

SAUSAGEMAN. And forging, while the fires of war are hot,
A chain of graft for handling prisoners.

CHORUS. Hooray for blacksmith versus carpenter!

SAUSAGEMAN. They're hammering out the matter in cahoots.
And don't you think your money or your friends
Can bribe or talk me into silence . . . No!
The People shall be told of this affair.

PAPHLAGON. And I shall go before the Senators
To make report of this conspiracy—
Your secret conclaves in the dark of night,
Your understandings with the Persian Court,
And in Boeotia with Big Cheeses there!

SAUSAGEMAN. I wish I had some. . . . How's it selling now?

PAPHLAGON. I'll pin you to the plank, by Hercules!

(Exit.)

CHORUS. And what will *you* do? How's your pulse, old man?
For now or never will you prove your boast
Of having hid that meat between your legs.
So hurry, hurry! On to the Senate House!
He'll crash the meeting, smear us all with lies,
And raise an everlasting hullabaloo.

SAUSAGEMAN. Why, to be sure I'll go, right straight from here,
Leaving with you my sausages and things.

DEMOSTHENES. Take this and grease your neck and shoulders
well.
Then, if he backbites, wriggle out of it.

SAUSAGEMAN. Oh, good! You should have been a wrestling
coach.

DEMOSTHENES. Now chew this stalk of garlic. . . . Here.

SAUSAGEMAN.   But why?

DEMOSTHENES. A cocktail for a gamy bantam, sir!
Well, off you go!

SAUSAGEMAN.   Aye aye!

DEMOSTHENES.   Remember now
To peck him, heckle him, gobble up his comb
And eat his wattles, ere you head for home!

(Exeunt.)

CHORUS.   *Farewell on thy quest;*
            Thy mission fulfill

At my eager behest.
God save thee until
By the end of the day,
Bold champion mine,
Thou hast come from the fray
With victory thine,
Thy head in a ha-
Lo of laurell

Ye folk in whose hearts
There is love for the Arts,
Who never refuse
To solicit the Muse,
Attend. We digress
In a thoughtful address
Anapaestic.

If any old-timer, some comedy rhymer whose verses un-
doubtedly bore you,
Had hopefully thought we could ever be brought to deliver
his speeches before you,
Just wager upon it we wouldn't have done it. But this is a
poet worth hearing.
His hates are the same as our own; his aim is the truth and
frankness unfearing;
He'll meet undismayed typhoons, tornadoes, from any
direction appearing.
Now numerous people are coming to see him, inquiring in
puzzled confusion
Why still he delays to acknowledge his plays, and prefers
to remain in seclusion.
He wants to reply to this query, and I have agreed to en-
deavor to do it.
It isn't stupidity . . . no, nor timidity. Here is what forces
him to it:
Full well does he know that staging a show is a business
harder than any;
Our Muse is a Miss who has lavished her kisses on merely
a few among many.
And you, one finds, have annual minds—you grow fresh
whims every summer,
First greeting with cheers, then treating to jeers, the works
of a veteran mummer.

Take Magnes. Recall his deplorable fall when the snows of
old were descending.

And yet he had vanquished his foes to a man, in a series
of triumphs unending.

A very magician, superb technician, his choruses brightened the scenery;

His *Birds* and his *Flies* had enraptured your eyes, and his
Frogs in the bravest of greenery;

His *Harpists* had danced, his *Lydians* pranced, to the zenith
of popular favor.

But forth he was cast, when his heyday was past and his
wit was bereft of its savor.

Remember Cratinus, colleague of mine. Swept on by a
flood of ovation,

Through plains, through meadows, he dizzily sped, wrought
havoc of all vegetation;

Each oak, each elm, each rival o'erwhelming, he left in his
wake desolation.

'Twas ever the thing, at a party, to sing "Lady Graft, of
the slippery sandal,"

"Ye builders of song both shapely and strong." In short, his
success was a scandal.

You look at him now with indifference. How can you fail to
be stirred by compunction?

A harp unstrung, joints gaping and sprung, completely
unable to function,

He's all played out, but dodders about, a babbling dotard,
a Connas.

His laurels are yellow, and thirst, poor fellow, is killing
him. Why, mercy on us,

He ought to be drinking in state, I should think, adorned
with the trophies of battle,

And have a front seat with the Drama's elite, not striding
the boards with his prattle.

Even Crates was hated and roundly berated. Your critics
assailed him with truncheons,

Whose menu, while thin, to be sure, for a dinner, provided
delectable luncheons.

He carefully wrought every nice little thought with a taste
that was neat and selective;

And held his own to the end—he alone—now stumbling,
now quite effective.

Recalling these three, you'll doubtless agree that our poet
had reason to shudder.

He says, furthermore, you must master the oar in advance
of attempting the rudder,
And likewise serve on deck, and observe the vagaries of
wind and of weather;
Naught else can equip you to captain a ship. So, all things
taken together—
Since, too well-bred to go barging ahead, he showed sound
sense in this matter—
Come, raise a salute for our poet, en route for the goal of
your famous regatta;

That, cheered by the thrill
Of Lenaean good will,
He may merit the prize,
And depart with the light
Of success in his eyes,
And a brow that is bright-
Ly resplendent!

Lord of the Horse, Poseidon, who
Lovest the ring of iron shoe,
Lovest the neigh of noble steed,
Lovest the dark triremes that speed
Onward to win the races;
Lovest the chariot's bright array
Filling the track, while joy, dismay
Vie upon youthful faces;

Thou whom dolphins delight,
Dancing before thee
Far 'neath Sunium's height,
Come, we implore thee!

Son of Cronus, Geraestus' King,
Praise for victories won we bring,
Praise to Phormio's Friend we sing.
God of gods, we adore thee!

Now we wish to laud our fathers and exalt them high in
fame,
Who were men of Athens worthy, and of great Athena's
name.
On the land forever fighting, fighting in the ship-fenced
host,

All-victorious, ever glorious, they have been our nation's
    boast.
Not a man of them, confronted by the foe upon the field,
Counted heads; their hearts were ringing with the watch-
    word *Never yield!*
If perchance in thick of battle one was thrown upon the
    ground,
Up he'd leap and dust his tunic, swearing he had not been
    downed.
Yes, they fought until the finish, and they never made a fuss
For a bid to public dinners, working through Cleaenetus.
Nowadays they get a front seat and a Prytaneum meal,
Or refuse to lead your armies. We, the Knights, however,
    feel
Proud to serve the State for nothing, and the gods to whom
    we pray.
But, as guerdon of our valor, we would ask you, if we may,
When this weary war is over and we're free from toil and
    care,
Not to criticize our manners, or the way we cut our hair!

> Pallas Athena, thou whose hand
> Guardeth in safety this our land—
> Noblest of lands in art, in war,
> Noblest in power flung afar,
>
> And of all lands most pious—
> Bring us again thy Victory,
> Ready to fight on land, on sea,
> Should to shoulder by us.
>
> Come, O Victory, dear
>   Comrade of showmen.
> Thou'rt my champion here,
>   Foe of my foemen!
>
> Come, O Pallas, to greet our gaze,
> Grant us trophies of might to raise.
> Now, if ever in bygone days,
>   Be thou victory's omen!

Next we wish to praise our horses and express to them our
    thanks.

Well they merit commendation for their service in the ranks,

Where they bore the brunt of battle, in attack and in defense.

What they've done on land, however, isn't nearly so immense

As the time they jumped on shipboard—finest sight you've ever seen . . .

Garlic, onions, in each knapsack; water, too, in each canteen.

Took their seats upon the benches quite as any sailor would,

Gripping tight the oars and neighing, *Heave ho, gee whoa, make it good!*

Speed her up! What ails us? You, there—pull away, you yearling scamp!

Bounding off the boat at Corinth, how the youngsters pitched their camp,

Searching far and wide for cover, digging beds with great dispatch.

And their food, instead of clover, was the shellfish they would catch

Crawling forth into the open; or, if not, they gouged them out.

Why, according to Theorus, one Corinthian crab did shout,

Lord Poseidon, is there no place deep enough for me to hide,

Where I may, on land or water, from these Knights in peace abide?

(*Enter* SAUSAGEMAN.)

CHORUS. O dearest fellow! O you gallant lad!

What grave anxiety we felt for you!

But now you're back, thank goodness, safe and sound.

Report the issue of your daring game.

SAUSAGEMAN. I won it. Victor is my middle name!

CHORUS.   In a glad Te Deum ringing

          Let us lift our voice. . . . Ah,

     Lovely is the word you're bringing,

          And your deed is fairer far.

     Tell me all. Feast my ear.

          For I know

          That I would go

     Miles and miles, this to hear.

     So relate the wondrous story;

     Venture to reveal your glory.

How you thrill me,
How you fill me,
Noble sir, with heartening cheer!
SAUSAGEMAN. It is indeed a tale *worth* hearing.—Well,
I followed after him, close on his heels.
Once he had passed the doors, his thunders rolled.
Portentous, mountainous, volcanic words
He hurled against those dark Conspirators,
The odious Knights. The Senate sat entranced,
Letting the humbug stuff them full of prunes.
They scowled and frowned; quite peppery they got.
And when I saw that they believed his talk . . .
Were taken in by all his ballyhoo,
I breathed a prayer: *Guardian angels mine,*
Ye lying, thieving, frisky, wanton Imps,
Gutters of Athens where I got my start,
Grant me today a shameless tongue and glib,
A brazen throat! And, as I prayed, I heard
A rumble from some jackass on my right.
This omen I saluted. Then I banged
The wicket gate wide open with my butt,
And stretched my jaws prodigiously and howled,
I bring you happy tidings, Senators.
For never have I seen, since war broke out,
Anchovies cheaper than they are today!
Forthwith that stormy sea of faces smiled—
Nay, beamed—and passed a rising vote of thanks.
I then suggested, as an inside tip,
That, if they wished to make them cheaper still,
They go and corner every jar in town.
Prolonged applause, and open-mouthed delight!
But Paphlagon was on to me, of course.
He knows his Senate . . . what it wants to hear.
So he said, *Gentlemen, I move that we,*
In gratitude for this most welcome news,
Offer Her Ladyship one hundred bulls.
All eyes and ears were turned to *him* again.
But I can play a bullish market too:
Double your bid! I cried . . . *Two hundred bulls!*
And furthermore I move we make a vow
To slay for Artemis a thousand goats,
If sardines sell a dozen for a cent!
Lo, back to me our statesmen pivoted,
And he was paralyzed, but spluttered on

Until the sergeants hauled him off the floor.
Then, bedlam! All stood up and yelled like mad.
Paphlagon pled with them: *One moment! Wait!*
Hear what the Spartan envoy has to say.
He comes proposing terms of peace, says he.
But with one voice your Solons hollered back,
To hell with peace! Today's no time for that.
It isn't peace they want, but cheap sardines.
They know we've got 'em! Let the war go on!
And then they shouted motions to adjourn,
And helter-skelter hopped the balustrade.
I took a short cut to the Agora,
And bought up all the seasoning in sight,
Which, when they came to buy it for their fish,
I gave them, gratis. *Was* I popular!
Hurrah! they screamed, and praised me to the skies.
So here I am, the Senate in my mitts.
What did it cost me? Just about two bits!

CHORUS. Everything that you have done, sir,
            Marks a coming man. . . . Yes,
         He has found another one, sir,
            Better trained in trickiness,
         More adroit, too, than he
                  In the craft
                  Of subtle graft,
         Wily words, repartee.
         But be careful of the sinner,
         If you hope to prove the winner.
                  I'll befriend you,
                  And defend you.
         You may count, you know, on me!

SAUSAGEMAN. Ah, there he comes, a tidal wave of wrath,
   Ready to spread confusion in his path,
And swallow *me*. But am I trembling? Pooh!
   (*Enter* PAPHLAGON.)

PAPHLAGON. If there is left in me a single lie,
   I'll finish you this very day, or bust!

SAUSAGEMAN. Delighted, Signor Braggadocio!
   Me rump to you, sir! . . . *Cock-a-doodle-doo!*

PAPHLAGON. I'll eat you up. I'll wipe you off the earth,
   Or else, by heaven, I'm not fit to live!

SAUSAGEMAN. Same here, if I don't down you in one gulp . . .
   And give myself an awful stomachache!

PAPHLAGON. Now by that Seat of Honor which I won . . .

SAUSAGEMAN. And lost. For I'll be sitting there instead,
And you'll be watching from the balcony!

PAPHLAGON. I'll clap you in the stocks, so help me God!

SAUSAGEMAN. How savage! Br-r-rh! . . . What can I soothe
him with? . . .
Maybe you'd like a bunch of long green kale!

PAPHLAGON. I'll sink my hooks in you and snatch . . .

SAUSAGEMAN.   Me too—
The bellyful *you* hooked from City Hall!

PAPHLAGON. I'll drag you right before the People, where . . .

SAUSAGEMAN. *My* drag is better, due to bigger lies!

PAPHLAGON. They'll never listen—not to you, my man.
To me, why they are nothing but a joke.

SAUSAGEMAN. Jolly well *own* the People, don't you, now?

PAPHLAGON. Because I know the pap to feed them on.

SAUSAGEMAN. And cheat them on, exactly like a nurse
Who chews the baby's food up nice and fine
And bolts a good three-fourths of it herself!

PAPHLAGON. The People are as putty in my hands,
To push and pull, open and shut, at will.

SAUSAGEMAN. Why, that's no trick at all for my behind!

PAPHLAGON. Wait till I'm through, and no one will believe
That in the Senate you insulted me.
On to the People!

SAUSAGEMAN.   Surely. *I* don't mind.

PAPHLAGON. O Demos, won't you please come out?

SAUSAGEMAN.   Yes, do.
Come out, sir.

PAPHLAGON.   Demos, dearest friend I have,
Please come and see how they're abusing me.

DEMOS. What's all the rumpus? . . . Get away from here!
You're messing up my nice Thanksgiving wreath.
(*Noticing* PAPHLAGON.) Why, what's the matter, son?

PAPHLAGON.   They're mauling me—
This fellow and these fancy dudes.

DEMOS.   But why?

PAPHLAGON. From jealousy, because I love you so.
(*To* SAUSAGEMAN.) And who are you?

SAUSAGEMAN.   His rival for your hand!
Long have I wished to prove my love for you,
And so have many worthy citizens;
But this chap here is always in the way.
You are precisely like flirtatious boys:
A gentlemanly suitor you reject,

And throw yourself away on common trash—
Cobblers and tanners, peddlers of lamps, and such.

PAPHLAGON. Well, don't I give him service?

SAUSAGEMAN.   Tell me how?

PAPHLAGON. I cut in on the Pylos generals,
And brought their blooming Spartans home in chains.

SAUSAGEMAN. I sneaked behind the cooks in Papa's shop,
And stole the stew that someone else had boiled!

PAPHLAGON. Call your Assembly, then, why don't you, sir,
And put our friendship to the acid test,
So you can choose between the two of us.

SAUSAGEMAN. Yes, do decide . . . but not upon the Pnyx.

DEMOS. Refuse to sit in any other place.
Aye, Pnyx or nothing! Come on. Forward march!

SAUSAGEMAN. Oh Lordy me! I'm done for now, I fear.
At home, the old man's quite intelligent;
But, once he takes his seat upon that rock,
He goggles like a peasant packing figs!

CHORUS.   Now give your canvas all the rope
            You have aboard the vessel,
       And ship an ever dauntless hope.
            Show him you can wrestle.
       With logic bring him to his knees;
            Down the desperado.
       From tightest corners he can squeeze,
            Resourceful renegade.
       Go out to meet him like a breeze,
            A genuine tornado!

But watch him. Before he can launch an attack, you first,
     in the finest of fettle,
Maneuver your galley alongside his, and threaten his decks
     with your metal.

PAPHLAGON. To mighty Athena, Guardian Goddess, I utter
     this bold imprecation:
Unless I have been the supreme benefactor of all the
     Athenian nation—
Save Lysicles' self, and his girls-about-town, the fair
     Salabaccho and Cynna—
May I never again, in payment for nothing, he asked to a
     City Hall dinner!
If, ceasing to battle your foes singlehanded, I show that my
     love for you falters,

Then murder me, butcher me, saw me in half, to be cut
  into bridles and halters!

SAUSAGEMAN. If *I* do not love you and cherish you, Demos,
  grind me into boloney

And cook me along with the rest of the scraps; or, if still
  you desire testimony,

I wish you would grate me with cheese into a salad; or,
  what may be less sanguinary,

Insert this fork in my tenderest parts, and pull for the State
  Cemetery!

PAPHLAGON. What subject of yours, dear Master, could possibly hold you in deeper affection?

Your Treasury balance has never been larger than after my
  Senate election.

I strangled, I choked them, demanding your share—and my
  own—in every transaction;

Not caring a hoot for the citizens' feelings provided you
  got satisfaction.

SAUSAGEMAN. There's nothing so wonderful, Demos, in that.
  I'll do no less for your pleasure:

Purloining the loaves that another has baked, I'll set them
  before you, full measure.

Why, *he* doesn't love you. *He* isn't your friend. I can prove
  it, or else I'm a liar:

'Tis only because he enjoys the sensation of toasting his
  shins at your fire!

For though you at Marathon fought for your country and
  utterly routed the Persians—

Bestowing a boon upon subsequent orators fond of stylistic
  diversions—

It troubles him not that you sit upon stone while you listen
  to lengthy discursions;

But here is a pillow I made you, to comfort that dear
  Salaminian bottom.

Pray rise. . . . There now! And, speaking of friends, here-
  after you'll know how to spot 'em!

DEMOS. Who *are* you, my boy? Don't tell me you're one of
  Harmodius' many descendants!

Be that as it may, you have done me a service of true
  patriotic resplendence.

PAPHLAGON. How little it cost you to earn his good will—a
  trivial, childish attention!

SAUSAGEMAN. And *you* have assuredly snared him with bait
  far *less* deserving of mention.

PAPHLAGON. That never a champion, sir, have you had, displaying my eminent talents,

I'm willing to wager, placing my head, my life itself, in the balance.

SAUSAGEMAN. His champion? Bah! Eight years you have seen him unbearably jammed in the city—

In tubs, in turrets, in cubbyholes quartered—without one vestige of pity.

In fact, you've *kept* him confined as he is, to improve your chances to bleed him.

When Archeptolemus brought us a truce, you scorned it. No one would heed him;

An envoy offering peace you rebuff, with a kick in the fanny to speed him.

PAPHLAGON. The war must go on till he's sov'reign of Greece. For the oracles say, if he'll stick it,

He's destined to judge in Arcadian courts, a dollar a day on his ticket.

Meantime, I promise to tend him with care and to make things easy and pleasant,

But somehow or other, by fair or by foul, to provide him his fee as a present.

SAUSAGEMAN. We fight to secure him a place on the Bench in the heart of the Peloponnesus?

No, rather to boost your imperial bribes, those millions of which you would fleece us:

While he, as he gropes in the fog of the war, may be blind to your vicious behavior,

And, needing the dole from necessity dire, look upon you as his savior.

If ever he gets back home to his farm, and can live where it's peaceful and sunny,

And tone up his nerve with a saucer of porridge, and say how-de-do to some honey,

He'll learn that you cheated him out of his rights with your pittance of government money,

And grimly this rustic will reach for his blackball, to check your degraded ambitions.

You know this is true. That's why you deceive him with oracles, dreams, apparitions.

PAPHLAGON. Atrocious, to utter against me a charge that is naught but the rankest of slander,

And prejudice me with the people of Athens by totally false propaganda!

I've done for them more than Themistocles did, as states-
man *or* as commander.

SAUSAGEMAN. *O City of Argos, ye hear what he saith?* With
him you compete? On what showing?

Our larder he found at a very low ebb; he left us with
cup overflowing.

To a slim table d' hôte he appended Piraeus, the cream of
suburban side dishes,

Enhancing our national fare by importing a line of delectable fishes.

You sought to divide our people asunder by walling them
off into classes,

You oracle-mongering peer of a hero spurned by ignorant
asses,

While you at your banquetings crumble the bread that was
bought by the toil of the masses!

PAPHLAGON. What right has he, Demos, to speak of me so—
this vulgar political ringer—
Because of my love for you?

DEMOS.   Stop it! No more will I hear
from a chronic mud slinger!

Today you're exposed, after years at my hearth, a scone hid
deep in the ashes!

SAUSAGEMAN. Quite true, dear Demos, the fellow's a knave, a
villain whom nothing abashes.

Whenever you nod, he cunningly nips
The tender and toothsome *salary* tips:
And washes them down with the gravy he got
By dipping his spoon in the Treasury pot.

PAPHLAGON. To pay you for this, I shall cause you to rue
The thousands and thousands embezzled by you.

SAUSAGEMAN. What lashing and splashing and beating about!
You're a thug, and a traitor, beyond any doubt.
                    The proof of the facts,
                    Will be found in your acts
                    (And I hope I may die
                    If I'm telling a lie):
                    Mytilene, as balm
                    For the itch in your arm,
                    Once tickled your palm
                    Good and plenty!

CHORUS.   *From Heaven thou art come to us*
                As Man's consummate blessing.
          How glib of tongue! Miraculous!

> Ever onward pressing,
> You'll be the first Hellenic mind,
> Here, abroad, unshaken.
> Go wield the trident, rouse the wind,
> The mighty seas awaken,
> Stirring the whole of humankind ...
> And bringing home the bacon!

Don't loose your grip. You have him now. He's ready for the slaughter.

You'll pin him to the mat. Indeed, with flanks like yours, you ought ter!

PAPHLAGON. Good sirs, it has not come to that. The fight is mine, believe me.

I've done a deed so wondrous great, that, if I don't deceive me,

'Twill muzzle all my enemies. They will not dare revile us

So long as anything remains of the shields I brought from Pylos.

SAUSAGEMAN. Aha! Those shields! Now there you make a dangerous admission.

For if you loved your country, should you, of your own volition,

Have left them hanging in the Porch with handles in position?

I tell you, Demos, 'twas a plot, by which, in case you needed

To discipline this rascal, you would find yourself impeded.

Behold in market there his gang of husky tanner fellows,

And next to them the crowded booths of cheese and honey sellers.

They're all in one conspiracy of secret anarchism,

If you get mad and start to play the game of ostracism,

In depth of night they'll take those shields and occupy the passes

Through which you get your daily bread, and starve your helpless masses.

DEMOS. He left the handles on, you say? How very hypocritical!—

You've swindled me for years and years with petty schemes political.

PAPHLAGON. Come, come, dear sir! To argument so easily surrender?

You can't suppose you'll ever find a more secure defender

Than one who checks conspiracies and makes them die
a-borning;

Who, unassisted, spies them out and bawls a timely warning.

SAUSAGEMAN. You emulate eel fishermen. In water clear and
quiet

They never catch a thing; but when they've made a muddy
riot

By stirring it this way and that, the sport is very pretty.

So *you* do *your* best fishing when you've shaken up the
city!—

I say, you've sold a lot of hides. I wish you'd tell me
whether

You ever gave your precious pal a single piece of leather

To mend his ancient brogues.

DEMOS.   Not once, in all his life
together!

SAUSAGEMAN. You see, then, what he really is—a pennypinch-
ing peasant!

But here's a pair of shoes I bought you. Wear them, sir ...
my present!

DEMOS. Of all the men I know, you most deserve a string of
medals.

There's none more loyal to the State, more friendly to my
pedals!

PAPHLAGON. To think that one old pair of shoes should have
so great a power

That you forget the services I render you each hour,

Like robbing Gryttus of his vote, when pansies were in
flower!

SAUSAGEMAN. How horrid, to inaugurate these privy inquisi-
tions!

And as to why you hate the pansies, I've my own suspicions:

Plain jealousy, because they make unequaled politicians!—

But look at Demos shivering without a shirt to bless him.

You never saw he needed something woolly to caress him,

Nor in this winter underwear have you been moved to
dress him.

DEMOS. Now that's a thing Themistocles, I grant you, never
thought of—

Though I admit Piraeus *was* a clever notion, sort of!

But here's a wrinkle quite as smart, and closer than a
brother.

PAPHLAGON. You always circumvent me with some monkey-shine or other!

SAUSAGEMAN. My tricks are yours, sir . . . like the slippers borrowed in a flurry.

When at a party, taken short, a fellow has to hurry!

PAPHLAGON. My skill in flattery is such that you can not excel it:

This handsome cloak around him.... There! ... *You're* out of luck!

DEMOS. Phew! Smell it!

Get off my back and go to hell! You stink of hides; I hate you!

SAUSAGEMAN. That's why he put it on your shoulders—to asphyxiate you!

The selfsame plot he tried before—that silphium. Remember How cheap it got to be?

DEMOS. I do. 'Twas only last November.

SAUSAGEMAN. He rigged the market . . . *made* it cheap, that you folks, all unwitting,

Might buy and eat such quantities that, when the court was sitting,

You'd raise an odor fit to gas your colleagues on the jury!

DEMOS. I know. My johnny said as much. It made me mad as fury.

SAUSAGEMAN. And did you not that very morning turn a sickly yellow?

DEMOS. I did; and 'twas the doing of this carrot-headed fellow!

PAPHLAGON. Obsequious buffoonery! A blatant bullyragger!

SAUSAGEMAN. Because our Goddess ordered me to vanquish you in swagger!

PAPHLAGON. Impossible! For I'm the man, good Demos, who engages

To give you, for no work at all, a tasty bowl of wages.

SAUSAGEMAN. Accept from me a little jar of soothing embrocation,

To rub the chilblains on your legs. . . . Delightful preparation.

PAPHLAGON. And I will pluck your graying hairs and make you young and cheery.

SAUSAGEMAN. And here's a rabbit tail, to wipe your eyes when they are bleery.

PAPHLAGON. And here's a *head* for you to wipe your *nose* upon, my dearie!

SAUSAGEMAN. On mine! On mine!

PAPHLAGON. You stand in line!
I'll make you captain of a ship
Too old to take another trip.
Repairing her will never end;
You'll have to spend and spend and spend;
And I'll arrange it so that they'll
Be giving you a rotten sail.

CHORUS. The man is bubbling! Stop it! Stop!
You're boiling over. Soon you'll pop!
We really ought to draw the fire,
And with this spoon skim off his ire.

PAPHLAGON. I'll squeeze the villain till he cracks
Beneath a heavy income tax:
To pay him for his lordly airs,
I'll bracket him with millionaires.

SAUSAGEMAN. Your threats I'll answer not in kind;
But here's a wish that comes to mind:
A tempting dish
Of cuttlefish
Is steaming right before your eyes;
And you, proposing to revise
Milesian quotas, and rake in
A pocketful if you should win,
Are all agog to eat your fill,
And make the blessed meeting still;
But while you munch
This tasty lunch,
They send for you, and in your greed
For both the money and the feed,
I hope you choke
Until you croak,
Heartbroken!

CHORUS. Bravo! Well done, my boy! Oh, beautifully done,
indeed!

DEMOS. Aye aye! A worthy citizen, that's clear . . .
The worthiest I've seen for many a day—
Friend of the commoner . . . and common*est*!—
I want no steward who displays his "love"
By serving me a fare confined to *war*fare!
Give me my seal. You're fired.

PAPHLAGON. Take it, then.
But just remember that if I'm discharged,
You'll get a far worse scoundrel in my place!

DEMOS. Why, this is positively not my ring!
 The seal is altogether different,
 Or else I'm blind.

SAUSAGEMAN.   I say, what *is* your crest?

DEMOS. A fat hamburger, toasted to a turn.

SAUSAGEMAN. Hamburger? Not a sign of one.

DEMOS.   What's there?

SAUSAGEMAN. A bloated buzzard, ranting on a rock!

DEMOS. Oh mercy!

SAUSAGEMAN.   What's the matter?

DEMOS.   Throw it away!
 The rascal had *Cleonymus's* crest!—
 Take this, and be my butler from now on.

PAPHLAGON. Don't do it, Master, *please*, until you hear
 The oracles I have.

SAUSAGEMAN.   Then hear mine too!

PAPHLAGON. And *stem the tide as a goatskin* once again!

SAUSAGEMAN. Listen to *him*, and you will *be* the goat,
 And furthermore he'll *skin* you to the hilt!

PAPHLAGON. My prophets say that you shall rule the world,
 A monarch in *a rosy coronet*.

SAUSAGEMAN. Mine say that in a gilded chariot,
 Wearing *a spangled robe and diadem*,

CHORUS. You shall pursue Queen Smicythe and spouse!
 Well, go at once and get your oracles,
 For him to hear.

DEMOS. (*to* PAPHLAGON). And you get yours. . . . Proceed.

PAPHLAGON. I'm ready.

SAUSAGEMAN.   So am I. Why not, indeed?

                                        (*Exeunt.*)

CHORUS. Oh the joy of that blessed morn—
     Joy for us who are native born,
     Joy for all who our streets adorn—
         When Sir Cleon is buried!

     Yet some grumpy old men I saw
     In the shops where they sit and paw
     Idly over the suits-at-law,
         Held the contrary, saying:

     Had our Cleon not grown so great,
     Two things handy in halls of state—

Spoon and pestle, to stir up hate—
Now would surely be lacking.

I confess it is strange to me
That his knowledge of Harmony
Is confined to a single key.
    But his cronies inform us

That in school he had one concern—
A Sharp Major alone he'd learn . . .
Played naught else when it came his turn,
    Till his teacher, despairing,

Sent him home in a huff, and said,
Son, for music you have no head,
But I swear that before you're dead
    You'll be A Major Sharper!

(*Enter* PAPHLAGON *with an armful of oracles. Almost simultaneously* SAUSAGEMAN *appears with a still larger bundle.*)

PAPHLAGON. Well, there you are, and that's not all I've got!
SAUSAGEMAN. Whew! Am I pooped! And that's not all, by half!
DEMOS. What are they?
PAPHLAGON.   Oracles.
DEMOS.   So many?
PAPHLAGON.   Pshaw!
    I have another boxful yet.
SAUSAGEMAN.   So've I . . .
    An attic full, and two apartment houses!
DEMOS. Who is the author of these prophecies?
PAPHLAGON. Bakis, of mine.
DEMOS.   And who delivered yours?
SAUSAGEMAN. Fakis! You know him? Bakis' elder brother!
DEMOS. What are they all about?
PAPHLAGON.   Athens, and Pylos,
    And you, and me, and pretty much everything.
DEMOS. Well, what are yours about?
SAUSAGEMAN.   Athens, and porridge,
    And Sparta, and fresh mackerel for sale,
    And grocers who short-weight you if they can,
    And you, and me, and pretty much everything!
DEMOS. Go on and read them to me, both of you . . .
    Especially that one I like so much—
    How I shall be *an eagle in the clouds.*

PAPHLAGON. *Then hearken, pray, and give me close attention.*
Ponder, son of Erechtheus, the "trend of the words" that Apollo
Trumpeted forth from his shrine, "'mid holy and worshipful tripods."
Care doth he bid thee maintain for the sharp-toothed, consecrate watch dog,
Who, to defend thee from bane, ever barketh and splitteth his gullet.
He will provide thee with wages; for, if he doth not, he will perish:
Flocks of inimical ravens are spitefully cawing against him.

DEMOS. Don't understand a single word of it!
Erechtheus, dogs and ravens . . . What's it *mean?*

PAPHLAGON. Well, I'm the watch dog, barking at your door.
Phoebus is warning you to keep me safe.

SAUSAGEMAN. That isn't what the oracle says at all.
Your dog has gnawed away whole chunks of it!—
Here's one that tells the truth about this dog.

DEMOS. Go on . . . but not until I find a stone;
Your doggy oracle may snap at me!

SAUSAGEMAN. *Ponder, son of Erechtheus, thy Cerberus, cruel enslaver,*
Who, though he waggeth his tail, doth watch thee while thou art dining,
Quick to devour the meat, when apart thou art vacantly gazing.
Creeping alone to the kitchen with doglike stealth in the nightime,
Clean will he lick thy platters, and feed on the sweets of the Islands.

DEMOS. Hurrah for Fakis! He's the lad for me!

PAPHLAGON. Wait, Master! Hear one more, and then decide.
Soon shall a woman in holiest Athens "give birth to a lion,"
Who for the People will fight great swarms of political midges,
"Standing, as 'twere, in defense of his cubs." So guard him securely,
Building about him a high "wooden wall" with turrets of iron.
You know what *that* means?

DEMOS.   No, by God, I don't!

PAPHLAGON. That *I* should be protected . . . Plain as day:
To you I've been *a lion* of defense.

DEMOS. You've been *a-lyin'* to me long enough!

SAUSAGEMAN. Ah, but he's careful not to tell you, sir,
What *kind* of wood-and-iron wall it is,
In which Apollo gave you strict command
To *guard him securely.*

DEMOS. What do *you* think, eh?

SAUSAGEMAN. The pillory!

DEMOS. Now *there's* an oracle
I have a hunch will shortly be fulfilled!

PAPHLAGON. Hearken thou not; 'tis merely the spiteful cawing of ravens.
But do thou cherish the hawk in grateful and loving remembrance—
He then ensnared and imprisoned the Lacedaemonian rookies.

SAUSAGEMAN. That was a gamble, made in a spirit of drunken bravado.
Why dost thou judge it of moment, thou witless scion of Cecrops?
Even a woman can carry a load that a man puts upon her;
Fight she could not; in her *fright*, she'd exhibit a streak of pale yellow!

PAPHLAGON. Nay, but I pray thee consider how Pylos is sung by the prophet:
Pylos doth lie beyond Pylos . . .

DEMOS. What does it mean—
beyond Pylos?

SAUSAGEMAN. Only that soon you'll be having a case of . . .
ahem . . . *Pyelitis!*

DEMOS. Then I had better start the water cure.

SAUSAGEMAN. This Knight of the Bath has cornered all the tubs!—
Now here's an oracle about the navy,
Calling for your particular regard.

DEMOS. Read it. I hope and trust it will explain
How I shall find the money to pay the gobs!

SAUSAGEMAN. *'Ware of the Canine Fox, son of Aegeus, lest he beguile thee:*
Treacherous, crafty and swift, withal a redoubtable Reynard.
Know who it is?

DEMOS. Of course—Philostratus, foxy old *Fido!*

SAUSAGEMAN. You're wrong. Paphlagon's always asking you

For ships to go around collecting tribute?
Loxias warns you not to let him have them.

DEMOS. A *trireme* is a *Canine Fox?* How come?

SAUSAGEMAN. Isn't a trireme fast? . . . So is a dog!

DEMOS. But what's the point of tacking on the *fox?*

SAUSAGEMAN. A very clever hint at your marines—
The little foxes that despoil the vines!

DEMOS. All right. . . .
But where's the cash to *feed* the little foxes?

SAUSAGEMAN. Leave it to me. It's yours within three days.
Hearken again, I implore, to the ominous words of Apollo:
Guard thee, my son, he commandeth, *against the wiles of
Cyllene.*

DEMOS. Who is Cyllene, I ask you?

SAUSAGEMAN. Why, Paphlagon, sir. Can
you doubt it?
Silly he is, to be sure, and *lean* as the hungriest beggar!

PAPHLAGON. Falsely interpreted, Master. The oracle meant by
Cyllene
None but the good Diopeithes, because he resembles
Silenus!
Nay, but I have a response in words that are wingèd, fore-
telling
How you shall *soar as the eagle*, ruling the world in one
kingdom.

SAUSAGEMAN. I have another, sir, naming the world *and* the
Indian Ocean. . . .
How you shall judge in the courts of Ecbatana, munching
your pretzels!

PAPHLAGON. Ah, but a vision I had: I beheld our national
Goddess
Pouring a bountiful stream of prosperity over her people.

SAUSAGEMAN. Strange . . . I too had a vision: I dreamt that
Mistress Athena
Down from her Citadel came to us, bearing an owl on her
shoulder.
Then she lifted a cruse and anointed your head with
ambrosia,
While upon *him* she decanted a cruet of vinegar dressing!

DEMOS. Hooray, hooray!
Old Fakis is the sharpest of the lot!
I put myself entirely in your hands,
To tend my age and train me all anew.

PAPHLAGON. Not yet, I beg you. Give me one more chance,
    And you shall have fresh barley every day.
DEMOS. Sick of your "barley"! You and Thuphanes
    Have fooled me long enough with promises.
PAPHLAGON. This time I'll pass out meal, already ground.
SAUSAGEMAN. And I'll distribute bread, already baked,
    And prime roast beef. All *you* need do is *eat!*
DEMOS. Well, hurry up, whatever you have in mind.
    For I shall give the reins of government
    To him who offers me the best ragout!
PAPHLAGON. I'll beat you to it!
SAUSAGEMAN. No you won't. . . . Not you!
CHORUS.   Ah Demos, you hold a sway
          The fairest on earth today.
          You speak, and mankind obey
             In sheer trepidation.
          Yet, gullible as a boy
          Beguiled by a stupid toy,
          To flattery insincere
          You lend a delighted ear,
          Allowing your *mind*, I fear,
             To take a vacation!
DEMOS.   You've nothing beneath your hair!
          You think I am not all there?
          It's only that I've a flair
             For living in clover.
          I love to be bottle-fed,
          And cry for my daily bread,
          So keep me a scalawag
          And let him collect his swag;
          And when he has filled his bag,
             I topple him over!
CHORUS.   If such is your wily plan—
          So smart that you really can
          Thus make of your servantman
             A useful breadwinner,
          It might be as well to fix
          A pen for him on the Pnyx,
          And fatten him for a treat
          Sometime when you're short of meat;
          Then sacrifice him, and eat
             Fresh mutton for dinner.
DEMOS.   You'll find me astute enough
          To call every time their bluff

Who think they are up to snuff,
  And I am a greenhorn.
Whenever they rob me, I
  Am watching them on the sly.
They fancy they fool Brer Fox,
Till, probed by the ballot box,
They're forced to disgorge the rocks
  That they are so keen on!

PAPHLAGON. You go to grass!

SAUSAGEMAN.   You blighter! Same to you!

PAPHLAGON. Well, Master, here I've sat a couple of ages,
  Ready to serve you when you say the word.

SAUSAGEMAN. Me too, all set for ten or a dozen ages . . .
  A thousand ages, and ages and ages more.

DEMOS. And I've been waiting thirty thousand ages,
  Hating you both, and ages and ages more!

SAUSAGEMAN. Know what?

DEMOS.   And if I don't, you do, of course!

SAUSAGEMAN. Just draw a starting line for him and me,
  That each of us may have an equal chance.

DEMOS. Aye. . . . Are you ready?

PAPHLAGON. }
SAUSAGEMAN. }   Yes, sir.

DEMOS.   Go!

SAUSAGEMAN.   No fair!
  Move over!

DEMOS.   Lucky day for Demos, what?
  I'm quite a belle, with two devoted swains!

PAPHLAGON. This easy chair puts me one lap ahead.

SAUSAGEMAN. One lap behind this table, my good friend!

PAPHLAGON. Here is a barley scone I made you, sir,
  Of hallowed grain that grew in Pylos field.

SAUSAGEMAN. These croissants our dear Goddess shaped for
    you
  Around the finger of her ivory hand.

DEMOS. A finger truly elephantine, eh?

PAPHLAGON. And now a bowl of beautiful pea soup,
  Dished up for you by Pallas, the Sup . . . reme.

SAUSAGEMAN. Your Guardian she is, no doubt of that;
  And crowns you with this mighty pot of broth.

DEMOS. Ah, were it not for her pot . . . ential might,
  This wouldn't be a *city* any more!

PAPHLAGON. The Mistress of Panic sends this pan of fish.

SAUSAGEMAN. The Daughter of a Puissant Sire presents
    This fine boiled meat and tripe and sausages.

DEMOS. Full of boloney is the Blessed Saint!

PAPHLAGON. The Queen of the Awesome Crest would have
      you eat
    This roe, the better to row your ships, my dear!

SAUSAGEMAN. Then you must eat these spareribs too.

DEMOS.   What for?

SAUSAGEMAN. Athena sent them with express intent:
    She wants your triremes to have *ribs* to *spare!*
    The navy is her pet, as she has shown.
    And here's a drink for you, mixed half-and-half.

DEMOS. *M-m-m.* Good, with plenty of authority!

SAUSAGEMAN. Of course. Its *author* was the Triton-born!

PAPHLAGON. Accept from me a luscious slice of cake.

SAUSAGEMAN. Don't bother with it. Here's the cake itself!

PAPHLAGON. But not a mess of hare, his favorite!

SAUSAGEMAN. God! To be beaten by a rabbit leg!
    Come, come, my heart, we need diplomacy.

PAPHLAGON. Too bad! Look at it!

SAUSAGEMAN.   Doesn't worry *me,*
    For yonder come important people . . .

PAPHLAGON.   Who?

SAUSAGEMAN. Ambassadors, with pockets full of gold!

PAPHLAGON. Where? Where?

SAUSAGEMAN.   What's that to you? Let them alone!
    Here, Master, is a rabbit stew from me!

PAPHLAGON. Damn it, what right had you to steal my stuff?

SAUSAGEMAN. The same *you* had to steal those Pylos boys!

DEMOS. Now tell me, how did you think up that trick?

SAUSAGEMAN. The Goddess gave the thought; the theft was
    mine!

PAPHLAGON. 'Twas I that ran the risk!

SAUSAGEMAN.   Who cooked it? I!

DEMOS. Get out! The credit's his who *serves* the meal!

PAPHLAGON. A shameless scoundrel! I have met my match!

SAUSAGEMAN. Why not decide, dear Demos, which of us
    Has done the most for your imperial . . . belly?

DEMOS. How shall I choose between you in a way
    To win the approbation of the house?

SAUSAGEMAN. I'll tell you. Confiscate that box of mine
    And see what's in it. Likewise, Paphlagon's.
    And don't you worry, you'll decide all right.

DEMOS. Well, what's in this one?

SAUSAGEMAN.   Nothing! Empty, see?
   I gave you everything on earth I had.
DEMOS. That's what I call a democratic box!
SAUSAGEMAN. Now just step over here and peep in his . . .
   Look there!
DEMOS.   My Lord, chock full of goodies still!
   Oh what a sight of cake he held out on me,
   Giving to me one teeny-weeny slice!
SAUSAGEMAN. Exactly what he always did to you.
   Doling you out a fraction of his take,
   The bulk of it he hoarded for himself.
DEMOS. You rogue, you thief, is that the way you fooled me?
   Yet upon thee I lavished gifts and crowns!
PAPHLAGON. I did my stealing for the public good.
DEMOS. Off with that garland. *He's* to wear it now.
   I'll put it on him . . .
SAUSAGEMAN.   Jailbird, do as you're told!
PAPHLAGON. Nay nay, I have an oracle foretelling
   Who is to vanquish me, and who alone.
SAUSAGEMAN. The name it gives, I doubt not, is my own!
PAPHLAGON. Hold! I would prove thee on the evidence,
   To learn if thou dost fit the Word of God.
   And first I would apply to thee this test:
   What school didst thou attend, sir, as a boy?
SAUSAGEMAN. The school of hard knocks, in a cook's employ.
PAPHLAGON. How sayst? The oracle doth grip my soul! . . .
   Ah well! . . .
   What type of wrestling wert thou taught?
SAUSAGEMAN.   To lie,
   Forswearing theft, and never blink an eye!
PAPHLAGON. *Phoebus Apollo, what wouldst thou do to me?*
   And, as a youth, what calling hadst thou then?
SAUSAGEMAN. Sold sausages . . . and pleased the gentlemen!
PAPHLAGON. Ah, misery! I am no more, no more!
   One fragile hope to bring me safe to shore:
   Was 't in the Agora, or at the gates,
   That thou didst sell thy sausages, in sooth?
SAUSAGEMAN. Beside the gates, fast by the herring booth.
PAPHLAGON. Alas! The prophecy hath been fulfilled!
   Come, wheel within his house this man of doom!
   Garland, farewell! I leave thee sorrowful.
   Another man will now possess thee . . . oh,
   No truer thief, but happier, I trow!
SAUSAGEMAN. Zeus of the Hellenes, thine the victory!

CHORUS. *Hail to the victor glorious!* Don't forget
　　You owe success to me. I ask but this—
　　That I may be your Phanus—press your suits!
DEMOS. What is your name, my friend?
SAUSAGEMAN. 　　　　　　　　　　　　Agoracritus—
　　A *critter* of the Agora, that is!
DEMOS. Agoracritus may now take charge of me,
　　And do as he wishes with this Paphlagon.
SAUSAGEMAN. Yes, sir. And I'll look after you so well,
　　That you'll admit no person of my parts
　　Has ever come to cheer Ass . . . enian hearts!

　　　　　　　　　　　　　　　　　　　　(*Exeunt.*)

CHORUS. 　　　*Beginning or ending our lays,*
　　　　　　　What fairer to sing than the praises
　　　　　　　　　　Sung by fleeting
　　　　　　Horsemen, who yearn to be greeting . . .
　　　　　　　　Not Lysistratus, for one!
　　　　　　And Thumantis, Poverty's son,
　　　　　　　　　Would we sadly—
　　　　　　　　　Far from gladly—
　　　　　　　　　Hit and run!
　　　　　　　　　　Lord Apollo,
　　　　　　　　　How he doth whine,
　　　　　　　　　　And doth wallow
　　　　　　　　　There at thy Shrine,
　　　　　　　　　　And doth pray—
　　　　　　Lean, hungry, forever and aye
　　　　　　　　A homeless gamin—
　　　　　　　　　For a stay
　　　　　　　　　　Of famine!

In abusing the unworthy there is surely no disgrace;
'Tis an honor to the decent, when you look it in the face.
If a certain man deserving of the lowest of ill fame
Were himself renowned, I wouldn't be obliged to use a
　　name
Loved by me and known wherever human wits are not too
　　dim
To be able to distinguish white from . . . well, the Orthian
　　Hymn!
Arignotus has a brother, though in traits they're not akin;
For Ariphrades, the other, prides himself upon his sin.
Now if he were merely sinful, I'd not mention him to you;

But in lecherous abandon he has thought up something
    new—
For the lips that *he* caresses never have been heard to
    speak!
And the nasty little verses that he writes are nauseous—
Patterned after Polymnestus and the lewd Oeonichus.
Now unless you loathe this creature, I advise you not to
    think
That in my house you will ever have a chance to take a
    drink!

> *The watches of night I bemuse*
> *With thoughts that are prone to confuse me,*
> *Oft I wonder*
> How, with such ease—how in thunder—
> Does Cleonymus get fed?
> For he grazes, so it is said,
> With the wealthy,
> Like a healthy
> Quadruped!
> From the manger
> Never will go,
> Though the granger
> Voices his woe
> In a prayer:
> *I beg you, sir, rise from your chair*
> *While you're able.*
> *Spare, do spare*
> *The table!*

At a meeting of our triremes here in port the other day,
Rumor has it that the eldest of the group was heard to say,
"Have they told you, dearest maidens, what hath now be-
    fallen us?"
We are asked to go to Carthage, five score strong. . . .
    Preposterous!
Who demands it? Why, that vapid demagogue, Hyperbolus!
All were shocked, and thought it frightful—more than they
    could tolerate.
Then another spoke, a youngster who had never shipped a
    mate:
Lord preserve us! I'll not do it. I had rather, if I must,
To escape from such a captain, stay in dry dock till I rust!
So will I, remarked a third one. *By the gods, I shall decline,*

*As my name is Shipman's Gracie and my flesh is healthy
      pine!*
If it passes the Assembly, we should hie us to the haunt
Of the Holy Ones for refuge, and deprive him of the vaunt
That he made a fool of Athens when he led us on that jaunt.
Let him sail, if set upon it, by himself from here to Hell,
*In the trays in which he peddled those fine lamps he used
      to sell!*

SAUSAGEMAN. I call you to silence, a seal on your lips, a pause
      in the life of the nation.

The courts you adore must adjourn forthwith, completely
      suspend litigation;

And the house unite in a paean of praise to our gods for
      this new dispensation.

CHORUS. Bright Day-Star of Athens, her islands and peoples,
      our bravest defender now living,

Make known the glad tidings at which we should darken
      our streets with the smoke of thanksgiving.

SAUSAGEMAN. In caldrons of magic I've boiled good Demos.
      Once more he is handsome and gallant.

CHORUS. And where is he now, O marvelous man, of truly
      original talent?

SAUSAGEMAN. At home in his Athens, *the violet-crowned*, fair
      Queen of the cities of Hellas.

CHORUS. I'm longing to see him. What is he like? Is he dressed
      in state? Will you tell us?

SAUSAGEMAN. The same as he was when Miltiades knew him,
      and just Aristides.—But hear!

Full soon shall you know. The hinges are creaking that
      open his grand Propylaea.—

Now greet the appearance of Athens the ancient with
      eulogies such as beseem us—

Yon city of wonder in story, in song, the abode of illustrious
      Demos!

CHORUS. *Hail, Athens the gleaming, the violet-crowned,* the
      object of earth's emulation,

Reveal to thy people the Monarch of Hellas, for all man-
      kind's adoration!

SAUSAGEMAN. Behold him, refulgent in pristine garb, with
      grasshopper brooch ornamented,

And redolent now not of ballots. . . . No, but with perfume
      and peace he is scented.

CHORUS. All hail unto thee, great Prince of the Hellenes! Our
      homage we happily render.

Today you are worthy of Athens herself, and the trophy of
    Marathon's splendor!

DEMOS. Agoracritus, my best of friends, come here.
    A good job, that—to boil me back to youth!

SAUSAGEMAN. If you but knew in what a state you were,
    And what you did, you'd think I was a god!

DEMOS. What *did* I do? Be frank. What *was* my state?

SAUSAGEMAN. Well, in Assembly meetings, when one said,
    My love is yours, dear Demos, yours alone;
    My constant care, and counsel too, you have—
    Whenever one began a speech that way,
    You flapped your wings and tossed your horns!

DEMOS.   I *did?*

SAUSAGEMAN. And then he had you snugly in the bag.

DEMOS. You mean it? . . .
    That was their game, and I so innocent?

SAUSAGEMAN. Your ears were theirs, to open or to shut
    As easily as any parasol!

DEMOS. Was I so big a fool, so doddering?

SAUSAGEMAN. Oh yes. And if there was an argument
    Between two speakers—one for building ships,
    The other chap for doles and bonuses—
    The dole proponent ran away with it.—
    I say, why hang your head? Sit up again.

DEMOS. I'm so ashamed of how I used to act.

SAUSAGEMAN. Don't worry. You are not so much at fault
    As those who duped you. But from this time on,
    If any smarty lawyer says to you,
    No juryman will get his meat and bread,
    Unless he finds in favor of the plaintiff!
    What will you do to such a fellow, eh?

DEMOS. I'll snatch him up and pitch him into limbo,
    Tying around his neck . . . Hyperbolus!

SAUSAGEMAN. That's right. That's talking sense! And, on the
    whole,
    Please tell me, how will you run the government?

DEMOS. Well, first of all, the sailors of my fleet
    Shall get their pay in full each time they dock!

SAUSAGEMAN. Good news that is for many a bobtail rump!

DEMOS. And once a man is on the muster roll,
    He'll stay there—influential friends or not.
    The list, as posted, will remain unchanged.

SAUSAGEMAN. That puts a crimp in poor Cleonymus!

DEMOS. And no more smoothies loafing on the street.

SAUSAGEMAN. Then what will Cleisthenes and Strato do?

DEMOS. I mean those drugstore intellectuals
    Who sit around and drawl such stuff as this:
    A shrewd lad, Phaeax! . . . Got acquitted, too.
    What style! How practical, synthetical,
    Epigrammatical, dynamical,
    Polemical toward the hypercritical!

SAUSAGEMAN. So you're sardonical toward the finical?

DEMOS. I'm going to make these softies ride to hounds,
    And work some other muscle than their tongues!

SAUSAGEMAN. Then I present you with this shooting stick;
    And, for a caddie, here's a buck cadet—
    Or, if you like it otherwise, a *doe!*

DEMOS. Splendid! The good old days are back again!

SAUSAGEMAN. But wait! . . . Treaties of peace I have for you—
    Fifteen-year-olds . . . two of them.—This way, girls!

DEMOS. Two prettier pieces I have never seen.
    And I can *treat* 'em *right*, if I'm allowed!
    Where did you find them?

SAUSAGEMAN.   There inside your house,
    Where Paphlagon had hidden them away.
    But now they're yours, to take back to the farm.

DEMOS. What about Paphlagon? What punishment
    Is he to suffer for his knavery?

SAUSAGEMAN. He'll just take on my business, nothing more—
    A one-horse sausage stand outside the gates—
    Hot dogs and donkey hash his specialties—
    In drunken brawls, the whoreson, with the whores,
    Quenching his thirst with water from the baths!

DEMOS. Now that's precisely what the scamp deserves—
    To whoop it up with gutter rats and cats!
    And you shall have his front seat at the show,
    And be my guest today in the City Hall.
    Here, take this dinner coat and follow me.—
    Hustle him off, before our foreign friends
    Who suffered from him. That will make amends.

                                        (*Exeunt.*)

Clouds

Clouds is an examination of the teaching of the sophists, whose moral position is stated most succinctly in Pheidippides' justification for beating his own father. Law and its moral imperatives, the sophists held, are man-made, for reasons of expediency, and have no other authority; if they can be shown to be no longer expedient they may properly be revised. The doctrine is potentially subversive of all tradition, and inevitably aroused the indignation of such conservatives as Aristophanes. The issue is epitomized in rival theories of education, and it is a contest between the new and old in education that Aristophanes here presents. The treatment of Socrates is unfair, for he did not study natural science, did not charge fees, was not a sophist. But a caricaturist who wished to attack sophists could scarcely avoid making Socrates his butt; not only was he the best-known teacher (but without the aura of sanctity which time has given him), but his physical idiosyncrasies invited caricature. It is said that when the maskmaker's art was applauded on his double's first appearance, Socrates stood up in his seat to show the likeness. Our text of the play is a revision, which was never officially presented; the original play ran third.

CHARACTERS

STREPSIADES

PHEIDIPPIDES

SERVANT OF STREPSIADES

STUDENTS OF SOCRATES

SOCRATES

RIGHT LOGIC

WRONG LOGIC

PASIAS, A CREDITOR

AMYNIAS, ANOTHER

CHORUS OF CLOUDS

Translated by Moses Hadas

(STREPSIADES *is discovered in his bed awake, and* PHEIDIP-
PIDES *in his asleep.*)

STREPSIADES. Zeus almighty! How endless the nights!
Will day never come? Way back I heard the rooster,
But my household snores. How times have changed!
Curses on war, for many reasons: I may not punish
My own servants. And there, snug under five blankets,
Lies my young hopeful, snoring fore and aft.
I'll snuggle in, if that's the thing, and snore too.
    But I can't. I'm pricked awake by debts and duns
And stable bills—through this fine son of mine.
He curls his long hair, rides, drives, even dreams horses;
And I am ruined. The moon is in her last quarter,
And interest is mounting. Boy! Light a lamp
And bring my ledger. I'll con my creditors and reckon the
    interest.
Let me see, *Two hundred dollars to Pasias.*
Why two hundred to Pasias? What were they for?
Oh, yes! The cob; I should have got me a cobblestone
To smash my eye out.

PHEIDIPPIDES (*in his sleep*). You're cheating, Philo! Keep to
    your own track!

STREPSIADES. That's it; that's the plague that's ruining me.
He's racing horses even in his sleep.

PHEIDIPPIDES (*in his sleep*). How many turns do the war
    chariots drive?

STREPSIADES. Plenty of turns have you driven your father.
What disaster comes after the Pasias entry?
To Amynias, fifty dollars for a sulky with wheels.

PHEIDIPPIDES (*still asleep*). Dismount, unharness, and away!

STREPSIADES. You have unharnessed me. I am dismounted
And with a vengeance—all my goods in pawn,
Fines, forfeitures, interest upon interest.

PHEIDIPPIDES. Why so upset, Father? Why twist and turn
The whole night through?

STREPSIADES. Some bailiff out of the mattress is biting me.

PHEIDIPPIDES. Be a good chap and let me sleep.

STREPSIADES. Sleep away, but these debts will fall on your
    own head.
Ah, well. Damn that matchmaker who egged me on
To marry that precious mother of yours.

My life on the farm was the sweetest ever,
Untidy, unswept, unbuttoned, brimming with
Honey and sheep and oil, and then I married—
A niece of Megacles son of Megacles, a town lady,
Proud, luxurious, extravagant. Rare bedfellows!
I reeking of wine vat, figs, and fleeces,
She of perfume and saffron and wanton kisses.
I'll not say she was idle, for she drove hard;
I used to tell her, pointing to this cloak,
Threadbare and worn, *Wife, you drive too hard*.

BOY. We've no more oil in the lamp.

STREPSIADES. Why did you light such a sot of a lamp?
Come and be beaten.

BOY. Why should I be beaten?

STREPSIADES. For cramming such a fat wick.
Then when this son of ours was born, my good wife and I
Wrangled over the name we'd call him. She wanted
Some knightly thing—Xanthippus, Charippus, Callipides.
I wanted a frugal name—Pheidonides, for his grandpa.
After long bickering we compromised on Pheidippides.
She took the boy and spoiled him: *When you are big
You'll wear a cape like a Megacles and drive to town.*
I'd say: *You'll wear a poncho like your dad's,
And drive the goats from pasture.* But to what I said
He paid no mind, and infected my fortune with horse fever.
Now after cogitating all night I have found one way,
A superb and stunning way, and if I persuade him to it
I shall be saved. But first I must wake him.
How can I wake him most soothingly? Pheidippides,
Pheidippides darling!

PHEIDIPPIDES. What's up?

STREPSIADES. Kiss me and give me your hand.

PHEIDIPPIDES. There. Now what?

STREPSIADES. Tell me, do you love me?

PHEIDIPPIDES. Yes, by Poseidon of Horses.

STREPSIADES. No, never by that horsey god; it's he who is to blame
For all my troubles. But if you love me truly and sincerely,
Son, do as I say.

PHEIDIPPIDES. What must I do?

STREPSIADES. Change your habits at once; go and learn what I
prescribe.

PHEIDIPPIDES. Speak out. What would you have me do?

STREPSIADES. Will you assent?

PHEIDIPPIDES. I will, by Dionysus.

STREPSIADES. Look this way. See that little gate and the shanty
    beyond?

PHEIDIPPIDES. I do; what's it for, Father?

STREPSIADES. That is the Think-shop of sage souls. There dwell
    men
  Who maintain the heaven's a snuffer and we men coals.
  They teach (if you pay them) how to win any case,
  Right or wrong.

PHEIDIPPIDES. Who are they?

STREPSIADES. I don't rightly know the name, but they are deep
    thinkers
  And fine gentlemen.

PHEIDIPPIDES. They're scoundrels, I know them. You mean
    those impostors,
  Pale and barefoot. That miserable Socrates is one,
  Chaerephon another.

STREPSIADES. Hush, hush! Don't talk like a baby! Be one of
    them,
  If the family's dear to you at all, and give up horses.

PHEIDIPPIDES. No, by Dionysus, even if you'd give me
  Leogoras' blooded beasts.

STREPSIADES. Do go, I implore you, darling lad. Go and learn.

PHEIDIPPIDES. And what would you have me learn?

STREPSIADES. They have, people say, two Logics, the Better,
    whatever that is,
  And the Worse. That latter teaches a man to speak unjustly
  And win. If you learn that Unjust Logic, not a penny
  Of what I owe on your account would I have to pay.

PHEIDIPPIDES. I will not. I could not face the knights
  With my complexion scraped away.

STREPSIADES. Then, by Demeter, you'll eat no more of mine,
  You nor your trotters or pacers. Out of my house,
  To the crows with you!

PHEIDIPPIDES. Uncle Megacles won't see me horseless.
  To him I'll go; you I ignore.

                                     (*Exit.*)

STREPSIADES. I'm thrown, but I'll not stay down. *I'll* get the
    schooling.
  I'll say a prayer and go to the Think-shop myself.
  —But I'm old, forgetful, slow; how can I learn
  Their sharp subtleties? But go I must. Why dawdle here?
  Why not knock at the door? Boy! Hi, boy!

STUDENT (*within*). Damn it! Who's knocking?

STREPSIADES. Pheidon's son, Strepsiades, of Cicynna.

STUDENT. A dolt, by Zeus, for kicking the door so very un-
subtly

And causing my mental conception to miscarry!

STREPSIADES. Forgive me; I'm only a country yokel. But

Tell me what your conception was.

STUDENT. Against the rule, except to students.

STREPSIADES. It's all right to tell me. I've come to the Think-
shop

To be a student.

STUDENT. I will tell you, but you must treat it as a mystery.

Socrates asked Chaerephon how many of its own feet

A flea could jump—one had bitten Chaerephon's brow

And then jumped to Socrates' head.

STREPSIADES. And how did he measure the jump?

STUDENT. Most ingeniously. He melted wax, caught the flea,
dipped its feet,

And the hardened wax made Persian slippers. Unfastening
these,

He found their size.

STREPSIADES. Royal Zeus! What an acute intellect!

STUDENT. What would you say if you heard another Socratic
ingenuity?

STREPSIADES. What was it? Tell me, I beg you.

STUDENT. Chaerephon asked him whether gnats, in his
opinion,

Hummed through the mouth, or through their tails.

STREPSIADES. And what did he say about the gnats?

STUDENT. He declared that the gnat's entrail is small; the
breath

Therefore proceeds through it with violence toward the tail.

Hence the rump resounds with the force of the blast.

STREPSIADES. So the rump of the gnat is a trumpet! Thrice-
blessed

For his entrail analysis! Easily can he evade a judgment

Who understands the gnat's anatomy.

STUDENT. But yesterday a high thought was lost through a
lizard.

STREPSIADES. How so? Tell me.

STUDENT. As he gaped up at the moon, investigating her paths

And turnings, from off the roof a lizard befouled him.

STREPSIADES. The lizard befouling Socrates tickles me.

STUDENT. Yesterday there was no supper for us.

STREPSIADES. So? What did he think up for barley?

STUDENT. He strewed mathematical sand on the table, bent a spit

    To make a compass—and with it filched a cloak from school.

STREPSIADES. Why admire Thales? Open, open the Think-shop door,

    Quickly show me Socrates. I hunger to learn. Open!

    (*The interior is revealed, showing students in grotesque postures.*)

    Heracles! What manner of beasts are these?

STUDENT. Why surprised? What do they look like?

STREPSIADES. Like the Spartans captured at Pylos. Why are their eyes

    Riveted to the ground?

STUDENT. They are investigating what's under it.

STREPSIADES. Onions, of course. Don't bother, you fellows.

    I know where there are big fine ones. But those stooping over—

    What are they after?

STUDENT. They are researching sub-Tartarean darkness.

STREPSIADES. Then why does the rump gaze heavenward?

STUDENT. His secondary interest is astronomy. —In with you all;

    He may find us here.

STREPSIADES. No, please, let them stay. I've a little thing

    To communicate to them.

STUDENT. But they mustn't stay out in the open so long.

STREPSIADES (*pointing to various maps and instruments*). In heaven's name, what are these things? Tell me.

STUDENT. This is used in astronomy.

STREPSIADES. And this?

STUDENT. Geometry.

STREPSIADES. What's it for?

STUDENT. To measure land.

STREPSIADES. For allotments?

STUDENT. No, the whole thing.

STREPSIADES. Shrewd. A democratic and profitable notion.

STUDENT. Here you have a map of the whole world. See? This is Athens.

STREPSIADES. You don't say! But it can't be: there are no juries sitting.

STUDENT. But this area is really Attica.

STREPSIADES. Then where are my neighbors of Cicynna?

STUDENT. There; and this, as you see is Euboea, stretching along our shore.

STREPSIADES. We did the stretching, we and Pericles. But where's Sparta?

STUDENT. Where? Right here.

STREPSIADES. How near! Do try to move it farther away.

STUDENT. Can't by Zeus.

STREPSIADES. You'll be sorry. But tell me, who's the fellow up in the basket?

STUDENT. Himself.

STREPSIADES. What's Himself?

STUDENT. Socrates.

STREPSIADES. Socrates! —You call him for me, loud!

(*Exit* STUDENT.)

STUDENT. You call him yourself; I've no time.

STREPSIADES. Socrates! Dear Socrates!

SOCRATES. Why do you call me, creature of a day?

STREPSIADES. Tell me first, please, what it is you are doing.

SOCRATES. I tread on air and contemplate the sun.

STREPSIADES. 'Tis from a basket then you look down on gods, not from earth.

SOCRATES. Never could I have rightly discerned matters celestial

Did I not suspend my judgment and mingle my intellect

With its kindred air. If I gazed upward from below, nothing

Could I find. Earth's force draws intellect's sap to itself.

And so it is with watercress too.

STREPSIADES. How's that? Intellect draws sap into watercress?

But come down, dear Socrates, down to me, and teach me

The things I came for.

SOCRATES. What did you come for?

STREPSIADES. To learn to speak. I am wracked and ruined and dispossessed

By most malignant debts and usury.

SOCRATES. How could you fall into debt without knowing it?

STREPSIADES. It was the galloping consumption, a voracious plague.

But teach me the other of your Logics, the nonpaying one.

Whatever your fee is, I swear by the gods I'll pay it.

SOCRATES. What gods? With us, gods are not legal tender.

STREPSIADES. Then how do you swear? By iron cartwheels like the Byzantines?

SOCRATES. Would you like clear knowledge of matters celestial?

The truth about them?

STREPSIADES. Yes, if there is any.

SOCRATES. And to associate with the Lady Clouds, our own patronesses?

STREPSIADES. Very much!

SOCRATES. Then sit down on that sacred pallet.

STREPSIADES. Done.

SOCRATES. Take this chaplet.

STREPSIADES. What for? Dear me, Socrates, are you going to sacrifice me,
  Like Athamas?

SOCRATES. No; this is our ritual for initiates.

STREPSIADES. What's the advantage?

SOCRATES (*pouring meal over* STREPSIADES). You'll be a powdery prattler, eloquence bolted fine.

STREPSIADES. You're not fooling. I'm being pounded to dust.

SOCRATES. The graybeard must in silence now attend unto my prayer.—
  Thou who holdest the world aloft, all-powerful measureless Air,
  Ether bright and brilliant Clouds who make the thunder roll,
  Arise and shine, ladies divine, uplift this thinker's soul.

STREPSIADES. Not yet! I must wrap up in my cloak;
  Luckless me, I brought no rain cap.

SOCRATES. Come forth, come forth, ye worshipful Clouds, present yourselves to sight,
  Whether ye sit snow-crowned on Olympus' sacred height,
  Or in your father Ocean's glade make holy Nymphs to dance,
  Or from outpourings of River Nile dip waters that entrance,
  Or whether you Lake Maeotis keep or Mimas' snowy tor:
  Receive our offering, heed our prayer, 'tis you we all adore.
  (*The* CHORUS OF CLOUDS *is heard from a distance before they appear on the scene.*)

CHORUS. Ascend we, Clouds eternal, display we our dewy nature,
  From resounding Father Ocean rise to mountain's lofty stature,
  Where from misty treetops far gazing we may espy
  Earth well-watered and all its fruits, boisterous rivers high,
  And lordly sea deep-roaring. Unwearied Ether's beaming eyes
  Illuminate the prospect distant: put we on our deathless guise.

socrates. Clearly have you heard my call, ye sacred Clouds
    and wondrous.—

    Heard you not their speech to me in mantic roar and
    thunderous?

strepsiades. I too revere your Cloudships, but your wondrous
    howls

    I must trump with my own thunder. Fright has colicked my
    bowels:

    I must treat your holy nostrils with sacrifice unsavory.

socrates. Clowning forbear; this is no time for low buffoonish
    knavery.

    Keep the holy silence! Hark! The stirrings of their melody!

chorus.   Maiden bearers of rain and dew,
           Come we Pallas' land to view,
           The land of Cecrops' manly brood,
           Beloved land where long has stood
           The holy Mysteries' sacred shrine
           Where are vouchsafed rites divine.
           To the heavenly gods here gifts are brought,
           Their lofty fanes by pilgrims sought;
           Here are brilliant festivals to cheer
           And holiday joyous throughout the year;
           And when new springtime comes again.
           Bromius gathers his graceful train.
           Echoing flutes give forth their song;
           Dance and sing the choral throng.

strepsiades. 'Fore Zeus, Socrates, I beg you, who are these
    beings?

    Who so solemnly resound? Can they be Lady Heroes?

socrates. No; heavenly Clouds are they, potent deities for the
    shiftless.

    'Tis they who supply acumen and casuistry, verbal sleights,
    circumlocutions,

    Quick repartee and knockout arguments.

strepsiades. That's why, when I heard them, my heart gave
    a bound,

    Yearning for hair-splitting logic, for debate about smoke,

    To meet argument with subtler argument, to contradict and
    refute.

    If such a thing may be, I crave to see them face to face.

socrates. Then look toward Parnes. They are descending I
    see.

strepsiades. Where, where? Point them out.

SOCRATES. They are marching along in a regular throng
through vale and dale.

STREPSIADES. What can the matter be? I cannot see them.

SOCRATES. Look there, by the stage door.

STREPSIADES. Now I do glimpse them, but barely.

SOCRATES. Now surely you must see them, if you are not
pumpkin-blind.

STREPSIADES. By Zeus I do. Awesome creatures! They occupy
every inch.

(Enter the CHORUS.)

SOCRATES. Did you never know or imagine they were goddesses?

STREPSIADES. Not I, so help me! I'd a notion they were fog
and smoke.

SOCRATES. Look you, man, these are the nursing mothers of
sophists,

Fakers, quacks, bejeweled longhairs, bards bombastical,

Chorus projectors and star interpreters; these idlers they
support

For flattering them in oracular mouthings.

STREPSIADES. It's these then who write of "the ravaging onset

Of the moist glittering clouds," "the hair of the hurricane

Hundred-headed," "tempestuous typhoons," "birds crook-
clawed

Loftily soaring," or "the clouds' outpouring of dewy floods";

In return they wolf down slabs of mullet and dainty
thrushes.

SOCRATES. Surely for value received.

STREPSIADES. Tell me then please, if they are truly Clouds,
why

Do they look like women? Clouds are not women!

SOCRATES. What are they then?

STREPSIADES. I don't rightly know; spread fleeces, perhaps, but
not a bit

Like women; these have noses.

SOCRATES. I'll put you a question.

STREPSIADES. Quick, let's have it.

SOCRATES. Have you never noticed a cloud resembling a
centaur, a leopard, a wolf, a bull?

STREPSIADES. Of course. So what?

SOCRATES. They turn into what they like. If ever they see a
brute

Shaggy-haired, Jerome say, centaurs they become to jeer his
fad.

STREPSIADES. And if they see that treasury-rifler Simon, what then?

SOCRATES. To show his character they turn suddenly to wolves.

STREPSIADES. 'Twas the sight of chicken-hearted Cleonymus yesterday, then,

That turned them into timorous deer.

SOCRATES. Just so. And because they spied Cleisthenes they are now turned to women.

STREPSIADES. Then welcome, ladies! Your celestial voices, right royal queens,

Suffer me too to hearken.

CHORUS. Greetings, old man, who seek the science of subtle speech!

And you too, priest of cobweb folly; say what you wish.

No sophist high-flown would we rather oblige, Prodicus excepted;

He for his mind and wit, but you because you strut in the streets

And roll your eyes and go barefoot and take abuse and walk in pride

Confident in our patronage.

STREPSIADES. O Earth! what an awesome and portentous sound!

SOCRATES. They alone are deities, all the others nonsense.

STREPSIADES. But Zeus on Olympus, by Earth, is he no god?

SOCRATES. What Zeus? Don't be silly; there is no Zeus.

STREPSIADES. No? Then who rains? First tell me that.

SOCRATES. These clouds, of course, and I'll prove it by evidence plain.

Come, did you ever see rain without clouds? But Zeus should bring rain

From a clear sky, when clouds are vacationing.

STREPSIADES. By Apollo, yes; that suits your argument perfectly, and I thought

'Twas Zeus making water through a sieve. But tell me who thunders?

Thunder is what makes me tremble.

SOCRATES. It's the rolling of the clouds that makes thunder.

STREPSIADES. But how, you boldest of men?

SOCRATES. When they are saturated with much water they toss about perforce,

And of necessity bump into each other waterlogged; they burst

With the heavy clash and so produce their roar.

STREPSIADES. But the power that forces them to toss about, is
it not Zeus?

SOCRATES. Not at all; it's the aerial Vortex.

STREPSIADES. Vortex? I was not aware Zeus was no more and
Vortex,

King in his place. But the roar of the thunder you have not
yet expounded.

SOCRATES. Did you not hear me say the full clouds' clashing
One against the other by reason of their density emit
thunder?

STREPSIADES. But how am I to believe this?

SOCRATES. I'll use yourself to demonstrate. At the Panathenaea when you've gorged

And your belly wambles, does it not resound with rum-
bling?

STREPSIADES. By Apollo yes! First it roils me and churns, and
then like thunder

It rumbles and roars, gently at first, *pappax, pappax*,
crescendo

Then, *papapappax*, and when I have eased myself *papapa-
papappax*, until

It thunders for fair like those clouds.

SOCRATES. Is it not likely, then, when your tiny tummy so loud
can roar

That infinite ether roar louder? Both alike are breaking of
wind.

STREPSIADES. But the lightning—tell me whence come its blazing flashes

Which char or singe us. Surely Zeus firing at perjurers?

SOCRATES. Fool, you reek of antediluvian ignorance. If perjurers

Are the target why has Simon never been struck, or
Cleonymus,

Or Theorus, perjurers all? But Zeus' own temple he strikes,
And *Sunium, Athens' headland*, and the mighty oaks. Why?
Oaks are no perjurers.

STREPSIADES. Can't say; your point seems sound. What then *is*
thunder?

SOCRATES. When a dry wind in its rise is locked into the
clouds, bladderlike

It inflates them; so compressed they burst forth with violence

And ignite in their volatile flight.

STREPSIADES. Precisely what I suffered, by Zeus, at Zeus' festival.

I cooked a paunch for my clan and forgot to slit it. It blew up

And burst, spattered my eyes, singed my whiskers, scorched my face.

CHORUS. Man who craves high wisdom of us, in Athens, in Greece: enviable

Shall you be if your mind is retentive and acute and industrious,

If you weary not standing or walking or freezing, if you care not

For food and abstain from wine, from gymnastics, from trifling,

And what befits a proper man esteem as best—to prevail in doing and scheming,

To campaign with whetted tongue.

STREPSIADES. For toughness of spirit, for worrisome care, for a belly

Frugal and pinched and starvation fare, rest assured; pound away

As hard as you like—I am ready.

SOCRATES. You do further engage to believe in no god save only

Our trinity—Chaos, Clouds, Tongue?

STREPSIADES. I'll not give them the time of day; no more sacrifice,

No libations, no incense.

CHORUS. Tell us boldly what you'd have us do; you'll not be disappointed

If you honor and adore us and strive for suppleness.

STREPSIADES. It's very little I want, Ladies, only to outdistance

All Greek chatterers by a hundred furlongs.

CHORUS. So be it. From this time forth no public proposals shall succeed like yours.

STREPSIADES. No public proposals, please. For myself only I want to twist

Lawsuits and slip from creditors' clutches.

CHORUS. Your wish you'll obtain; 'tis a trifle. Commit yourself now

To our clerks.

STREPSIADES. Trusting in you I will do so, for I am crushed by Necessity.

Blooded nags and a nagging wife have worn me down.

—My body use as you will. I yield it to blows, to hunger and thirst,

To heat and to cold. Flay me alive if so my debts I evade

And be regarded of men as bold, smooth-tongued, impudent, insistent,

A sneak, a liar, a contriver, a shuffler, a rasp for laws,

A prater, perjurer, pettifogger, a brazen braggart and boaster,

Slippery and slithy, a guzzler of garbage. If so I am called

By the man in the street, your people may deal with me however they like—

Mince my guts, by Demeter, and serve me up to the Thinkers.

CHORUS. That's the spirit, fearless and bold. When you have learned

What we teach, be sure your fame among mortals will tower heaven-high.

STREPSIADES. And how shall I fare?

CHORUS. All your life you will spend with us, the most enviable of mortals.

STREPSIADES. Shall I really see such felicity?

CHORUS. Always crowds shall be thronging at your door hoping

To consult you in cases involving millions, and you'll collect as you choose.

—Take the old fellow in hand, try your curriculum on him;

Stir his mind up, examine his intellect.

SOCRATES. Come now, tell me your study habits. So I will know

What novel artillery I should bring to bear upon you.

STREPSIADES. Is it under siege you'll put me, in heaven's name?

SOCRATES. No. Just some short questions. Is your memory good?

STREPSIADES. It depends. Very good if someone owes me, very bad,

Alas, if I owe someone.

SOCRATES. Have you a gift for speaking?

STREPSIADES. For speaking, no; for cheating, yes.

SOCRATES. How good are you at learning?

STREPSIADES. Pretty good.

SOCRATES. Quick now, when I toss you some soaring notion snag it at once.

STREPSIADES. What? Must I snap up cleverness like a dog?

SOCRATES. The man is a stupid oaf. I'm afraid, old chap,
    you'll require the rod.
  Let's see; what do you do if a man strikes you?
STREPSIADES. I am struck, I wait a bit and get witnesses, and
    after a time
  I bring suit.
SOCRATES. Take your coat off.
STREPSIADES. Have I done something wrong?
SOCRATES. No, the custom is to come in naked.
STREPSIADES. But I'm not coming to search for stolen articles.
SOCRATES. No nonsense! Take it off!
STREPSIADES. Tell me this. If I attend to my studies and am
    diligent
  Which of your students shall I be most like?
SOCRATES. You'll be spit and image of Chaerephon.
STREPSIADES. Why then, my damnable luck, I'll be half dead.
SOCRATES. Enough of your lip and follow me. This way!
STREPSIADES. First give me a honey cake to hold. I'm as scared
    of that den
  As of stepping into Trophonimus' cave.
SOCRATES. In with you! Stop fiddling with the door!
(STREPSIADES *and* SOCRATES *retire into the Think-shop.*)
CHORUS.   Fare you well for your courage: march on!
         —Though far advanced in life's last stage
         He braves the toils of a greener age
         And labors hard to become a sage.

Dear spectators, freely shall I speak to you, yes and truly,
So help me Dionysus, whose ward I am. So surely may I
    win,
So surely be deemed a poet, as I reckon you a clever
    audience
And this the best of my plays. Much labor has it cost me,
And I thought you'd approve it, but I retired defeated,
Most unfairly, by clumsy rivals. 'Tis you I blame, the
    clever,
For whose sake I took such pains. Even so, men right-
    minded
I'll never willingly betray. Those discerning critics
Who spoke well of my *Wastrel and Sage* 'tis pleasure to
    address.
Yet a maid, I could not bring that play forth; 'twas shel-
    tered
By another, and you supported and provided its breeding.
Secure thenceforth I counted the pledges of your good will.

Now comes this new play searching for spectators acute
Like those, like Electra seeking her brother's curl.
A glimpse will suffice. Observe her purity: no appendage
Of leather, red-tipped and gross, to arouse adolescent
Laughter; no jeering of baldheads or obscene dancing;
No pantaloon punctuating his lines by poking his neighbor
To cover bad jokes; no flying torch-bearer shouting *iou*.
Its libretto gives my play trust. Poet though I am,
I do not wear my hair long or try the cheat of repeating
Myself time and again. Always I contrive novel notions,
None like its fellows, all ingenious. Mighty Cleon I whacked
In the belly, but forebore to trample him when he was
 down;
Whereas my rivals, once Hyperbolus lent a foothold, never
 ceased
Pounding that poltroon, and his mother to boot. First
 Eupolis
Dragging his *Maricas* on, villainously distorting my
 Knights,
Dragging on a drunken crone just to do a dirty dance—
The crone that Phrynichus invented, to be swallowed by a
 whale.
Hermippus too assailed Hyperbolus; upon Hyperbolus
 poetasters all
Their sallies aimed, aping even my eely figures. Whoso is
 amused
By such stuff, let him take no pleasure in me or in mine.
But in my inventions if you find delight, your reputation
For cleverness will forever abide.

> Zeus king of gods who rules on high,
> Thee first to our dance do I summon;
> Then thee, mighty wielder of the trident,
> Untamed upheaver of the briny deep;
> And thee, our father of great name,
> Revered Ether, nurturer of all;
> And thee, driver of horses, who floods
> Earth's plain with shining rays, divinity great
> Among gods and mortals alike.

Wisest of spectators, your attention if you please!
We have been wronged. More than all gods
Have we helped your city, yet on us alone you bestow
No sacrifice or libation. We watch over you ever:
At enterprises unreasonable we thunder and hail;

When Paphlagon, tanner abhorred, for General you chose
Our brows we knitted and we made a fearful show
Of thunder and lightning. Moon forsook her orbit,
And Sun drew his wick in; he'd no more shine,
He declared, if Cleon commanded your armies.
But choose him you did. In this city, they say,
Folly is endemic, but your mistakes the gods
Transform to advantage. How this folly can profit
I'll readily show. Convict that cormorant Cleon
Of bribery and theft, muzzle and pillory him,
And then as of old your mistakes to profit
Will turn and your city fare the better.

      Come Phoebus, Delian king,
      Who holds the lofty Cynthian tor;
      And blessed Artemis in whose golden hall
      Lydian maidens their orisons pour;
      And thou Athena, wielder of the aegis,
      Our own city's mighty stay;
      And comely Dionysus, Parnassus' master,
      Whose torches illumine the Delphian revels.

Moon accosted us, when we were ready packed for our
    trip here,
And gave us a message for you: cordial greetings first
To Athenians and allies, and then complaint of shabby
    treatment.
All of you she has benefited, she said, not obscurely but
    visibly.
First, a drachma worth of light she saves you monthly.
Buy no torch, a man out for the evening tells his servant,
Moon is bright and clear. Other benefits she mentions,
But you subvert the calendar and fail to observe her days.
When sacred days go unobserved and defrauded gods go
    hungry
It's Moon they threaten. At the hour of sacrifice you are
    busy
With lawsuits; and when gods observe a fast, mourning for
    Memnon
Or Sarpedon, you feast and frolic. For such neglect we gods
Deprived Hyperbolus of last year's award; now he'll know
To mark his days by Lady Moon.
(SOCRATES *and then* STREPSIADES *emerge from the Think-
shop.*)

SOCRATES. Respiration, Chaos, Air! Never so stupid
   A dolt have I seen, so witless, awkward, forgetful!
   Before he learns them he forgets the quibbles I teach.
   Still, I'll call him outdoors here to the light.
   Where's Strepsiades? Come and bring your cot!

STREPSIADES. The bedbugs won't let me.

SOCRATES. Hurry, put it down, pay attention.

STREPSIADES. Here I am.

SOCRATES. Tell me, what do you want to learn first
   That you were never taught before—measures, words,
     rhythms?

STREPSIADES. Measures for mine. Lately a grocer cheated me
   of two quarts.

SOCRATES. Not that at all. Do you prefer trimeter or tetra-
   meter?

STREPSIADES. Make mine a fifth.

SOCRATES. You're talking rot, fellow.

STREPSIADES. Don't five fifths make a gallon?

SOCRATES. Damn you for a stupid yokel. We'll try rhythm.

STREPSIADES. How can rhythm help with barley meal?

SOCRATES. You'll shine in society if you know what rhythm
   Fits the sword dance and what suits finger play.

STREPSIADES. Finger play, by Zeus, I do know.

SOCRATES. Then tell me.

STREPSIADES. This finger here, but when I was a shaver this
   one.

SOCRATES. Vulgar oaf!

STREPSIADES. But none of this stuff interests me, ninny.

SOCRATES. What does?

STREPSIADES. It's that unjust Logic I'm after.

SOCRATES. But there are necessary preliminaries. Among
   quadrupeds,
   Which are male?

STREPSIADES. I should be queer not to know that: Ram, Goat,
   Bull, Dog, Fowl.

SOCRATES. See your mistake? Same word for male and female
   fowl.

STREPSIADES. What do you mean?

SOCRATES. What? "Fowl" and "fowl."

STREPSIADES. Sure; but what ought I say?

SOCRATES. "Fowl" and "fowlette."

STREPSIADES. "Fowlette"? Good, by Air! For that one lesson
   I'll fill you a trough of barley.

SOCRATES. Another howler. You made "trough" masculine: it's
      feminine.

STREPSIADES. How did I make it masculine?

SOCRATES. By making its ending like Cleonymus'.

STREPSIADES. But Cleonymus has no trough; he does his
      kneading
   In a doughnut-shaped vessel. What should I say?

SOCRATES. What? Call it "she," as you call Sostrate "she."

STREPSIADES. Is trough a woman?

SOCRATES. Right.

STREPSIADES. Miss Trough, then, and Miss Cleonymus.

SOCRATES. There's more about names that you must learn.
   Which are male and which female?

STREPSIADES. The female I know well enough.

SOCRATES. Let's hear.

STREPSIADES. Lysilla, Philinna, Cleitagora, Demetria.

SOCRATES. And now male names?

STREPSIADES. Ten thousand. Philoxenus, Melesias, Amynias.

SOCRATES. But those are not male, fool.

STREPSIADES. Not male?

SOCRATES. No. How would you greet Amynias if you met him?

STREPSIADES. How? "Hi there, Amynia!"

SOCRATES. See? When you call you make the name feminine.

STREPSIADES. Right and proper for a draft dodger. But why
      study
   What everyone knows?

SOCRATES. Why indeed? Here, lie down.

STREPSIADES. What must I do?

SOCRATES. Ponder your problem.

STREPSIADES. Not on that bed, please. If ponder I must
   Let me do it on the ground.

SOCRATES. The bed's the only way.

STREPSIADES. Worse luck; The bugs will certainly collect this
      day.

SOCRATES. Ponder well, on your problem brood,
   Put on your woolly thinking hood.
   If at first you are stumped, jump to a new device;
   Sweet sleep be absent from your vigilant eyes.

STREPSIADES. Ouch! ouch! ouch!

CHORUS. What's the trouble? What ails you?

STREPSIADES. I'm murdered! From that sack
   Fierce Corinthians creep to attack.
      My flanks they chaw,
      My ribs they gnaw,

My blood they suck,
My genitals pluck,
My rump they excavate,
They'll leave me inanimate.

CHORUS. Less fuss, please!

STREPSIADES. How can I? My hide is gone, gone my cash,
My shoes are gone, I'm pulped to hash.
To top it all, as I hummed a tune to banish
Sleep, I myself came near to vanish.

SOCRATES. You, there! What are you doing? Pondering?

STREPSIADES. Me? Poseidon, yes.

SOCRATES. And what have you pondered?

STREPSIADES. Whether these bugs will leave a scrap of me.

SOCRATES. Drop dead, fool.

STREPSIADES. So I have.

SOCRATES. Don't be a softy. Cover up. You've got to find some notion
Circumventory and deprivatory.

STREPSIADES. Ah, how conjecture a notion deprivatory out of a blanket?

SOCRATES. Let's see what our chap's about. Hey, you! Asleep?

STREPSIADES. Not me, by Apollo.

SOCRATES. Got hold of something?

STREPSIADES. Not a thing, by Zeus.

SOCRATES. Nothing at all?

STREPSIADES. Only my rod in my right.

SOCRATES. Cover up quick and ponder!

STREPSIADES. About what? You tell me, Socrates.

SOCRATES. Find what you want first, and tell me.

STREPSIADES. I've told you what I want a thousand times.
It's the interest. I don't want to pay anyone a cent.

SOCRATES. Come on, cover up. Splinter your thoughts fine and consider
Your business in detail. Make your divisions exact.

STREPSIADES. What a mess!

SOCRATES. Keep still. If you are baffled by some thought leave it
And then stir it up and balance it.

STREPSIADES. Darling Socrates!

SOCRATES. What is it, old fellow?

STREPSIADES. I've got a deprivatory notion for my duns.

SOCRATES. Explain, please.

STREPSIADES. What would you say if—

SOCRATES. If what?

STREPSIADES. If I hired a Thessalian witch, pulled the moon down,

Shut it up in a round helmet box like a mirror,

And kept it there.

SOCRATES. What good would that do you?

STREPSIADES. What good? If the moon never rose I'd not pay interest.

SOCRATES. And why not?

STREPSIADES. Because bills fall due at new moon.

SOCRATES. Good. Here's another problem for you. Suppose you lost

A suit for five talents: how evade payment?

STREPSIADES. How? I don't know, but let me think.

SOCRATES. Don't always hunch your mind around yourself;

Let your speculations range through the air, like a June bug

On a string.

STREPSIADES. I've found a clever evasion of the suit, as you'll agree.

SOCRATES. What is it?

STREPSIADES. You must have seen at the druggist's the stone,

Pretty, transparent, to kindle fire with?

SOCRATES. You mean crystal?

STREPSIADES. Yes. I'd get one; when the clerk was entering sentence

I'd stand a way off, in the sun, and melt the writing away.

SOCRATES. Neat, by the Graces!

STREPSIADES. What fun to have a verdict erased for five talents!

SOCRATES. Quick, now. Snap this one up.

STREPSIADES. Which?

SOCRATES. How forestall opponents in a suit you're bound to lose?

STREPSIADES. Simple and easy.

SOCRATES. Tell me.

STREPSIADES. I will. At the case before mine I'd hang myself.

SOCRATES. Ridiculous!

STREPSIADES. It isn't. Nobody could try me if I were dead.

SOCRATES. Absurd. Be off. I'll teach you no more.

STREPSIADES. Why not? Please, Socrates.

SOCRATES. Whatever you learn you forget at once. Tell me:

What was it you learned first?

STREPSIADES. Let's see. What was it now? What was first? The thing

We knead barley in, what was it now? Dear me, what?

SOCRATES. Devil take you, brainless and lumpish Methuselah!

STREPSIADES. What'll happen to me now? If I don't learn tonguetwisting

I'm done for. Come on, Clouds, give me good advice!

CHORUS. Our advice, codger, is this: Send your son,
If you have one, to study in your place.

STREPSIADES. I do have a son, quite a gentleman, but he won't study.

Now what will become of me?

CHORUS. You give in to him?

STREPSIADES. He's headstrong you see, and robust, a sprig
Of the high-flying Coesyra ladies. Still, I'll go to him,
And if he refuses I'll turn him out of the house.
Wait for me a minute; I'll be back.

(SOCRATES *retires to the Think-shop,* STREPSIADES *to his house.*)

CHORUS. Observe now if you please
What abundant blessings to you fall
Through us alone of deities;
Ready is your dupe whenever you call.
Whatever you bid him do he'll heed;
While he's elated and glassy-eyed,
Strike fast, finish all your deed;
He won't forever stay mesmerized.

(*Enter* STREPSIADES *with* PHEIDIPPIDES.)

STREPSIADES. You'll not stay here, by Mist! Go to Megacles,
Feed on his columns.

PHEIDIPPIDES. What's ailing you, Pater, you're not in your senses;
By Olympian Zeus you're not.

STREPSIADES. Olympian Zeus, forsooth; What a simpleton!
A fellow your age to believe in Zeus!

PHEIDIPPIDES. What's there to laugh at, pray?

STREPSIADES. The thought that a squirt like you has fuddy-fuddy notions.
Come here and I'll enlighten you. I'll tell you something
To make you a man. But don't tell a soul.

PHEIDIPPIDES. Very well. What is it?

STREPSIADES. You swore by Zeus.

PHEIDIPPIDES. So I did.

STREPSIADES. See what a fine thing education is. Pheidippides,
There is no Zeus.

PHEIDIPPIDES. Who is there then?

STREPSIADES. Vortex is king; he booted Zeus out.

PHEIDIPPIDES. What drivel!

STREPSIADES. But it's a fact.

PHEIDIPPIDES. Who says so?

STREPSIADES. Socrates the Melian and Chaerephon the flea-
track expert.

PHEIDIPPIDES. Are you so far gone as to believe such loonies?

STREPSIADES. Hold your tongue! Speak no ill of men so clever
and sage.
They're so frugal they never shave or use oil or go to the
bath
For a wash. But you've scrubbed me clean, like a corpse.
Now do go at once and be educated for me.

PHEIDIPPIDES. Can a man learn anything good from *them*?

STREPSIADES. Is that so? All that men regard as culture. You'll
realize
How ignorant you are and how stupid. But wait a minute.
(STREPSIADES *steps aside to fetch two birds.*)

PHEIDIPPIDES. Dear me, what'll I do with my crazy father?
Shall I bring suit
To prove incompetence? Speak to the undertakers?

STREPSIADES. Look here now. What do you think this is?

PHEIDIPPIDES. A fowl.

STREPSIADES. Good enough. And this?

PHEIDIPPIDES. A fowl.

STREPSIADES. Both the same? Ridiculous. Don't do it again.
Call this fowl, this fowlette.

PHEIDIPPIDES. Fowlette? Is this the cleverness you learned
From the earth-born inside?

STREPSIADES. And much else. But each time I learn something
I forget it at once. I'm too old.

PHEIDIPPIDES. Is this why you lost your coat?

STREPSIADES. I didn't lose it; I pondered it away.

PHEIDIPPIDES. And your shoes? How did you dispose of them,
silly?

STREPSIADES. Like Pericles, "as requisite." But come on,
Let's go. Humor your father and then do as you like.
I humored you, I know, when you were six and lisping.
With the first jury-money I received, I bought you
A little cart at Zeus' festival.

PHEIDIPPIDES. You'll be sorry for all this, you know.

STREPSIADES. Thank you for minding me. Come here, Socrates,
come!
I bring you this son of mine. He didn't want to, but I
persuaded him.

(*Enter* SOCRATES.)

SOCRATES. What a babe it is, all innocent of our hanging baskets.

PHEIDIPPIDES. You'd look innocent if you were hangèd.

STREPSIADES. Blast you! Insulting your teacher!

SOCRATES. Look, "hangèd." What a naïve pronunciation, what pouting lips!

How could this booby learn to dodge a summons, frame an indictment,

Win over the wide-eyed. Hyperbolus learned—for a talent.

STREPSIADES. Don't worry, teach him; he's naturally quick. When he was a toddler

He used to build mud-houses, scoop out ships, make carts out of leather,

And the loveliest frogs out of pomegranate rind. He'll surely learn

Both Logics—the Better, whatever that is, and the Worse,

To overturn the Better by crooked speech. If he can't learn both,

He must by all means learn the Wrong.

SOCRATES. He shall learn from the Logics in person. I must go.

STREPSIADES. But remember, he must be able to argue all justice down.

(SOCRATES *withdraws. Enter* RIGHT LOGIC *and* WRONG LOGIC, *quarreling.*)

RIGHT LOGIC. Out here! Brazen as you are, will you flaunt yourself before these spectators?

WRONG LOGIC. Choose your ground. I can ruin you better before a crowd.

RIGHT LOGIC. You ruin me? And who are you?

WRONG LOGIC. A Logic.

RIGHT LOGIC. But the worse.

WRONG LOGIC. Still I'll beat you, who claim to be my better.

RIGHT LOGIC. What device will you use?

WRONG LOGIC. New notions I invent.

RIGHT LOGIC. Such stuff succeeds with the fools out there.

WRONG LOGIC. No, the wise.

RIGHT LOGIC. I'll lay you out.

WRONG LOGIC. Tell me, doing what?

RIGHT LOGIC. Speaking what's just.

WRONG LOGIC. And I'll smother it by speaking the contrary. There's no such thing

As justice, say I.

RIGHT LOGIC. You say there's not?

WRONG LOGIC. Where is it, tell me.

RIGHT LOGIC. With the gods.

WRONG LOGIC. Then why, if there's justice, was Zeus not ruined
For tying his father up?

RIGHT LOGIC. Faugh, I'm getting nauseous; give me a basin.

WRONG LOGIC. You're a broken down spastic driveler.

RIGHT LOGIC. You're a shameless bunghole.

WRONG LOGIC. Roses—coming from you.

RIGHT LOGIC. And a clown.

WRONG LOGIC. A crown of violets.

RIGHT LOGIC. A parricide.

WRONG LOGIC. You spangle me with gold and don't know it.

RIGHT LOGIC. It used to be lead.

WRONG LOGIC. But now it's an ornament for me.

RIGHT LOGIC. You're very brazen.

WRONG LOGIC. And you're a fogy.

RIGHT LOGIC. It's because of you the young fellows won't go to school. One day
Athens will know the sort of thing you teach fools.

WRONG LOGIC. You are meager and bare.

RIGHT LOGIC. And you are fat and saucy. But you used to be a pauper,
Call yourself Mysian Telephus, and out of your scrap bag
Munch maxims of Pandeletus.

WRONG LOGIC. Ah, the cleverness you recall!

RIGHT LOGIC. Ah, the folly, yours and the city's which keeps you
To be a pest to its lads.

WRONG LOGIC. This one you'll never teach, Methuselah.

RIGHT LOGIC. If he's to be saved, I will, and he'll learn something besides chatter.

WRONG LOGIC. Come this way. Let the man rave.

RIGHT LOGIC. You'll be sorry if you lay hand on him.

CHORUS. Stop bickering and squabbling. *You* show what you taught
In times gone by, and *you* the new education. Your arguments
He'll hear and choose his school.

RIGHT LOGIC. I'm willing.

WRONG LOGIC. I too.

CHORUS. Which of you will speak first?

WRONG LOGIC. I yield to him. Whatever he may say I'll shout down

With my novel formulations and fancies. Then if he's
    still able
To mumble, my arguments like hornets will sting his face
    and eyes
Till he's ruined utterly.

CHORUS. Confident in eloquence, in argument polemical,
    In devices disputatious, in formulae fantastical,
    See now which the better proves. Critical the position:
    Will devoted friends of mine prevail in competition?

        O thou who didst our sires address
        With maxims many and choice,
        Set forth the character you profess,
        Sound forth your stately voice.

RIGHT LOGIC. Education is my theme. I'll tell how it was in
    days gone by
When Sobriety was its goal, and truth like mine was rated
    high.
Children then had no license to chatter; gravely they
    marched to school,
The boys of a village all in a body, simplicity was the rule,
Not muffled in wraps though it snowed a blizzard, striding
    with legs apart,
Singing some old and martial strain just as their elders had
    taught.
If anyone ventured to corrupt the tune with trills or synco-
    pations,
As Phrynis' followers are wont to do with freakish in-
    novations,
His hide would be trounced on the Muses' account as
    crassly irreverent.
Before the master they modestly sat, not sprawlingly im-
    pudent.
No part unseemly could ever be seen; when they rose
    they smoothed the soil,
Their bodies' impress to erase and drooling lovers to foil.
No lad was anointed below the belt, but like the velvety
    peach
Free and unconstricted bloomed the natural furze of the
    breech.
They did not modulate the voice a lecherous ear to entice,
Nor sway their hips and flaunt themselves to attract
    lecherous eyes.

From radish heads they all abstained and such fare aphro-
disiac
Anise and parsley left untouched to supply the old men's lack.
No sea-food dainties and no guzzling, or twining legs behind one's back.

WRONG LOGIC. Chewing tobacco, revival meetings, chatau-
quas,
Hoopskirts, fascinators, antimacassars!

RIGHT LOGIC. Yet 'twas that antique discipline which Mara-
thon heroes did nurture:
In long warm cloaks those softies go to whom you teach
your culture.
When in the Panathenaic dances they are called on to
perform,
Behind their shields they huddle close and insult the
Triton-born;
Choked am I with indignation at the spectacle so tragic.
Wherefore choose me, my brave young friend, choose me,
the better Logic.
The market place you'll learn to hate, from hot baths to
abstain,
Of shameful deeds to be ashamed, flouting scorners to
disdain;
To yield your seat to honored elders, your parents never
to vex,
No disgrace to perpetrate, to mold in yourself as in wax
The image chaste of modesty, not to loiter and not to stare
At the naked dancing girls—you'd shatter reputation fair
By accepting their invitation; nor show your father im-
pertinence,
Reviling as a fogy the very source of youthful sustenance.

WRONG LOGIC. If you follow such advice my lad, so give me
Dionysus joy,
You'll live a piglet's kind of life, and they'll call you Mama's
boy.

RIGHT LOGIC. But all aglow with bloom of health in gymnasia you'll while your day,
Not to the market place for trifling quibbles as is the
current way,
Not dragged to court for some piddling suit by fans of
litigious sport;
But down to the Academy you will go with some friend of
your own sort,

With white reed crowned races to run down by the olive
    trees,
Fragrant with woodbine, with no carking care, amid falling
    poplar leaves,
Delighting in the spring-time rustle of plane and elm in
    the playful breeze.
        If these precepts you will heed
        And to them your mind apply,
        A stalwart chest shall be your meed,
        Complexion bright, shoulders high,
        A tiny tongue, a stout behind,
        And a diminutive masculine member.
        If to the new-fangled you give your mind
        Your complexion will be a shade of umber,
        Shoulders puny, a chest like a flea's,
        Tongue enormous, bottom weak,
        Full of whereases and wordy decrees,
        Your only art gibberish to speak.
        He'll teach you to think foul is fair,
        And fair, he'll tell you, is foul reckoned;
        He'll put you in Antimachus' chair,
        And steep you in slops in half a second.
CHORUS. Glorious wisdom's advocate, how loftily you tower,
  How sweet the aroma of your utterance delectable!
  Blessed those who lived when you were in your flower!
  Now you whose Muse is seductive and pliable,
  Some novelty you'll need, some contrivances cunning,
  To counter the esteem your rival has won.
  To outstrip the master, produce arguments stunning,
  Or you'll slink from the lists a figure of fun.
WRONG LOGIC. His arguments all to overthrow my vitals seethe
    and glow.
  The Lesser Logic am I? Your sages call me so
  Because the pioneer was I in devising refutations
  Of laws that on conventions rest and codified traditions.
  To win a case for the weaker side at higher value I rate
  Than a hundred moneybags bulging with pieces of eight.
  Watch how deftly I now expose his vaunted education.
  Against hot baths, first of all, he enjoins a prohibition.
  What, pray, is the rationale? What's wrong with a bath?
RIGHT LOGIC. 'Tis worst of all for a growing boy; it reduces
  him to a lath.
WRONG LOGIC. Just a minute! I've got you there; from my
  hold you'll never wrest.

Of Zeus' sons who labored most, whom do you regard
  the best?

RIGHT LOGIC. Heracles without a doubt; he's the strongest of
  the lot.

WRONG LOGIC. Were not his baths at Thermopylae always
  steaming hot?

RIGHT LOGIC. By quibbling like this are lads ruined I declare;
  The bathhouses it fills and leaves gymnasia bare.

WRONG LOGIC. Next you blame the market place; I say it's
  admirable.

If it were bad would Homer make old Nestor so voluble?
  Their tongues, says he, the young should not use; I say
  they should;

He says they must chastity keep; neither prescription is
  good.

Whoever profited from chastity, for whom did it win an
  award?

RIGHT LOGIC. For many. An instance is, it won Peleus his
  sword.

WRONG LOGIC. A prize fine for a fool! By knavery Hyperbolus
  millions made;

For our clever lampmaker no paltry blade!

RIGHT LOGIC. But Peleus for his chastity won Thetis to be his
  bride.

WRONG LOGIC. And then she levanted. An ardent woman cannot abide

Between her sheets a sluggish lover. You belong in the
  Middle Ages!

Cast up, my lad, how much it costs to earn such trifling
  wages.

Darling girls and darling boys, hors d'oeuvres, laughing,
  quaffing:

A life deprived of all these joys, who'd ever call it living?

Point one. Turn we now to consideration of nature's own
  machinery.

You yield to an illicit love, you're taken in adultery;

You're ruined for you've no defense—unless, of course,
  you've been taught by me.

Indulge your nature, gambol and frisk, you've got a ready
  plea;

With Zeus as your pattern you can strike your accuser
  dumb:

Did he not to love's lure repeatedly succumb?

And can a mortal cultivate ways too high for a god?

RIGHT LOGIC. But what if your backside's singed and rammed
    with the adulterer's rod?
  How will argument then prevail to void the stretching of
    your bum?
WRONG LOGIC. And what's the harm of a bottom stretched?
    Tell me even one.
RIGHT LOGIC. What greater harm than a bung that's sprung?
WRONG LOGIC. What will you say if I prove you wrong?
RIGHT LOGIC. I'll hold my peace. What else?
WRONG LOGIC. Answer then. Lawyers: whence do they come?
RIGHT LOGIC. I must acknowledge, from a sprung bum.
WRONG LOGIC. And whence are tragic poets fetched?
RIGHT LOGIC. From a bottom that's been stretched.
WRONG LOGIC. And politicians old or young?
RIGHT LOGIC. All from bums that have been sprung.
WRONG LOGIC. You realize your ignorance.
            And what of yonder audience?
            Look at them, do.
RIGHT LOGIC. I'm looking.
WRONG LOGIC. And the majority?
RIGHT LOGIC. The sprung bums have it, without question;
  Dozens I see in every section.
  Ah, there's my neighbor in yonder seat.
WRONG LOGIC. Will you acknowledge you've been beat?
RIGHT LOGIC. Now we've had it, ye catamite folk;
        To you I desert; take now my cloak.
  (*The* LOGICS *leave.* SOCRATES *enters from the Think-shop
  and* STREPSIADES *from his house.*)
SOCRATES. What have you decided? Will you take your son
    home,
  Or shall I teach him to speak?
STREPSIADES. Teach him, whip him, mind you hone him
    sharp;
  One jaw for little litigation, the other for bigger things.
SOCRATES. Rest easy. I'll give you an accomplished sophist.
STREPSIADES. Pale too, I hope, and a thorough rogue.
CHORUS. Get along with you then, but I'm sure you'll regret
    it.—
  To our judges now we wish to recite what profit high in
    store is
  If the prize they award, as award it they should, to our
    worthy chorus.
  When tilth in spring refreshment craves, yours first we'll
    satisfy;

On others, after yours are drenched, we will shower by
    and by.

On your crops' and vines' behalf we'll regulate our store:

No scanty sprinkle to leave them sere, to crush them no
    downpour.

The misguided mortal (your attention please!) who af-
    fronts our misty divinity,

Himself a creature of mere earth, shall not get off with
    impunity.

No wine or olive his farm will yield, all in the bud will be
    blighted;

With volleys of hail we'll strike them down in return for
    dignity slighted.

Brick or tile that he's carefully shaped we'll pepper with
    our spray.

If he or friend or relative celebrate a wedding day,

We'll pour down torrents all night long. If wrongly they
    decide,

Our judges will find it preferable in Sahara's sands to abide.

STREPSIADES. Five, four, three, two: the count down to the
    Old-and-New.

That day I fear and detest and abominate. Every creditor
Will stake his deposit and swear my utter ruin. If I request
Some settlement modest and just—*Friend, accept this,
Postpone that, cancel the other*—they reject it, abuse me
As a fraud, swear they'll sue. Let them! I don't care—
If Pheidippides has learned to speak. I'll soon know.
I'll knock at this door. Boy! Here, boy!

SOCRATES. Greetings, Strepsiades.

STREPSIADES. Same to you. Take this bag of flour. It's right
To show respect to a teacher. Tell me, that Logic
You just introduced: has my son learned it?

SOCRATES. He has so—

STREPSIADES. Cheers! Knavery omnipotent!

SOCRATES. So well that you can evade any suit you like.

STREPSIADES. Even if I borrowed before witnesses?

SOCRATES. So much the better, even if there were a thousand.

STREPSIADES. Shout and sing, my basso profundo!
Obol weighers all to the devil may go,
Principal, interest, interest's interest.
No hurt can they do me for I am blest
With a son whose tongue will crush my foes:
My champion, my savior, redeemer of my woes!

Call him out here to me, run, run!

Ah, my child, my own dear son!

SOCRATES. Here's the man himself.

STREPSIADES. Dear, dear man!

SOCRATES. Take your son and go.

STREPSIADES. Hurrah, my child hurrah! Hurrah, hurray, hurray!

What a pleasure to see your complexion! So refutatory

You now look, so disputatory, so thoroughly Athenian!

In your eye blooms the familiar *And what do you say?*

You have the rogue's trick of looking injured when you're injuring.

You've the Attic gloss on your face. Save me now,

For 'tis you who ruined me.

PHEIDIPPIDES. What is it you're afraid of?

STREPSIADES. Settlement day, the Old-and-New.

PHEIDIPPIDES. Is there such a thing as Old-and-New?

STREPSIADES. You know, the day creditors put deposits down for suits.

PHEIDIPPIDES. Then they'll lose them. One day simply cannot be two.

STREPSIADES. It can't?

PHEIDIPPIDES. How can it? Can the same woman be both old and young?

STREPSIADES. But that's the law.

PHEIDIPPIDES. I don't believe they rightly understand its meaning.

STREPSIADES. What does it mean?

PHEIDIPPIDES. Old Solon favored the people's side.

STREPSIADES. But that's nothing to do with the Old-and-New.

PHEIDIPPIDES. He fixed the summons for the two days, Old and New,

So deposits would be put down on new moon.

STREPSIADES. Then why did he add the Old?

PHEIDIPPIDES. So debtors could meet on the day before for compromise;

If they couldn't the issue would come up on new moon.

STREPSIADES. Why don't clerks accept deposits on new moon instead?

PHEIDIPPIDES. Like the official samplers, I suppose, they get a head start

On their sampling in order to grab the deposits.

STREPSIADES. You poor suckers sitting there, what chance have you got?

Shearings for the shrewd, blocks of stone, mere statistics,
A herd, stacked bottles! I'm moved to sing an encomium
For mine and my son's success.

> *Happy, happy Strepsiades,*
> *What a clever man is he!*
> *How fine a son is Pheidippides!*
> *So my neighbor will say of me,*
> *Green with envy when he sees*
> *You quashing every plea.*
> *Come in to my parlor please;*
> *We'll celebrate with a grand spree.*

(*Enter* PASIAS, *a creditor.*)

PASIAS. Must a man lose what's his? Never! Better adamant
When asked than all this bother now. For my money's sake
I must drag up witnesses, fall out with a neighbor.
But never shall I shame my country. I summon Strep-
siades—

STREPSIADES. Who's that?

PASIAS. To the Old-and-New.

STREPSIADES. Bear witness, he named two days. What for?

PASIAS. Two hundred dollars for the gray you bought.

STREPSIADES. A horse? Do you hear? All know I hate horses.

PASIAS. By Zeus, you swore by the gods you'd pay me.

STREPSIADES. By Zeus, I won't. Pheidippides hadn't learned
The irrefragable Logic.

PASIAS. You propose to default because he has?

STREPSIADES. If I didn't what good would his learning do me?

PASIAS. Would you be willing to swear your denial by the
gods?

STREPSIADES. What gods?

PASIAS. Zeus, Hermes, Poseidon.

STREPSIADES. By Zeus I would, and pay a nickel for the
privilege.

PASIAS. Curse you for a blasphemer!

STREPSIADES. The fellow could do with a salting.

PASIAS. You're making me a butt.

STREPSIADES. Capacity four gallons.

PASIAS. You'll not get off, so help me great Zeus and all the
gods.

STREPSIADES. The gods tickle me; an oath by Zeus is a joke to
those in the know.

PASIAS. You'll pay for this in good time. Do I get my money
or no?

Give me your answer and let me go.

STREPSIADES. Calm yourself. You'll have a clear answer very
　　soon.

PASIAS. What do you think he'll do?

WITNESS. Pay you, I think.

STREPSIADES. Where's that Shylock? Tell me, what is this?

PASIAS. That? A trough.

STREPSIADES. An ignoramus like you expecting money? Not
　　a penny

Would I pay a man who calls a troughette a trough.

PASIAS. Then you won't pay?

STREPSIADES. Not if I know it. Get a hump on, off with you!

PASIAS. I'm going. But sure as I'm alive I'll put my deposit
　　down.

STREPSIADES. That'll be throwing good money after bad. I
　　wouldn't want

That to happen for a silly blunder about a trough.

　　(*Exit* PASIAS; *enter* AMYNIAS, *another creditor.*)

AMYNIAS. Alas and alack!

STREPSIADES. Ha! Who's that whining? Not one of Carcinus'
　　bogies?

AMYNIAS. You want to know who I am? A victim of mis-
　　fortune.

STREPSIADES. Keep it to yourself then.

AMYNIAS. Ah, hard fate! Ah, fortune that hath shattered
　　The wheels of my horses' chariot! Ah Pallas,
　　Thou hast undone me!

STREPSIADES. Has Tlepolemus been working on you?

AMYNIAS. Scoff not, good sir, but bid your son pay me my
　　money.
　　My affairs prosper ill.

STREPSIADES. What money?

AMYNIAS. The money he borrowed.

STREPSIADES. Your affairs *are* prospering ill, it seems.

AMYNIAS. 'Twas through driving horses I fell, by Zeus.

STREPSIADES. Your gibberish sounds as if you'd been dropped
　　by an ass.

AMYNIAS. Gibberish if I want to get my money back?

STREPSIADES. Surely there's some screw loose.

AMYNIAS. What do you mean?

STREPSIADES. Your brain seems to have worked loose, I think.

AMYNIAS. And I think you'll be getting a summons if you
　　don't pay.

STREPSIADES. Tell me, do you think Zeus always rains new
water down

Or does the sun draw the old up to be reused?

AMYNIAS. I don't know and I don't care.

STREPSIADES. How do you expect to get your money if you
know nothing

About meteorology?

AMYNIAS. If you're short of cash pay me the interest.

STREPSIADES. What species of beast is interest?

AMYNIAS. A growth on money which increases daily and
monthly

As time goes by.

STREPSIADES. Good enough. Now the sea—do you think it's
bigger than it was?

AMYNIAS. No, the same; it's not right for it to grow.

STREPSIADES. So when the sea with rivers flowing into it
grows no larger,

Do you expect your money to? Chase yourself, won't you?
Where's the goad?

AMYNIAS. Witnesses!

STREPSIADES. Get on, don't dawdle. Giddyap, buster!

AMYNIAS. Assault and battery!

STREPSIADES. Jump! I'll help you along with this goad in
your rump.

You're running, are you? You and your thoroughbreds
And your sulky—I'll have them all on the run.

(*Exit* AMYNIAS.)

CHORUS. Beware of a passion deceits to weave.

The old man craves to deny his debt;
The requital he'll this day receive
Will teach him a lesson he'll never forget.
'Twas he that began the plot to deceive:
He'll be caught in the tangle of his own net.
What he long wanted now he's got—
His son is expert in gainsaying;
He can twiddle justice, he can plot,
Every decency betraying,
Saying what isn't is and what is is not.
For a son deaf-mute he'll soon be praying.

(*Enter* STREPSIADES, *beaten by* PHEIDIPPIDES.)

STREPSIADES. Ouch! Kinsmen, friends, neighbors, help! My
poor head, my poor jaws!

Scoundrel, are you beating your own father?

PHEIDIPPIDES. Yes, Daddy.

STREPSIADES. See! He confesses that he's beating me!

PHEIDIPPIDES. Of course.

STREPSIADES. Scoundrel! Parricide! Burglar!

PHEIDIPPIDES. Say it again, and more; I love being called names.

STREPSIADES. Rammed bottom!

PHEIDIPPIDES. Strew me with roses.

STREPSIADES. Beat your own father?

PHEIDIPPIDES. I'll prove I was justified.

STREPSIADES. How can it be just to beat a father, you utter villain?

PHEIDIPPIDES. I'll demonstrate and prove my point.

STREPSIADES. Prove it's right?

PHEIDIPPIDES. Very easily. Choose either Logic you will.

STREPSIADES. What Logics?

PHEIDIPPIDES. The Better or the Worse.

STREPSIADES. I did succeed in teaching you to talk all justice down

If you can persuade me it's just and proper
For son to beat father.

PHEIDIPPIDES. Oh, I think I can so convince you you'll have
not a word of objection.

STREPSIADES. I do want to hear what you can say.

CHORUS. Your task, old fellow, is to devise
How this man you may best.
Clearly there's something on which he relies,
Else he'd not throw out his chest.
The confidence of his bearing implies
A firm base on which to rest.
Tell us: How did the quarrel arise?—
Follow we now this quest.

STREPSIADES. How we first began to bicker I will tell you very soon.
You know that we'd been feasting. I asked him for a tune,
Simonides' Shearing of the Ram, with lyre accompaniment.
Lyre music, says he to me, is a stale accomplishment.
Only yokels, says he, at table sing, like grandma grinding grain.

PHEIDIPPIDES. You earned your beating on the spot. Only a cricket's brain
To singing would apply a mouth, with victuals on the table.

STREPSIADES. That's just what he said inside. Scarcely was I able

My temper to hold when Simonides the old he dubbed
poetic hack.

A snatch of Aeschylus next I begged, holding my temper
back.

That noisy mouther of trash, says he, that fashioner of
claptrap crude!

Is Aeschylus really first class?—Though my bosom heaved
I held my mood.

Then something smart of the *nouvelle vague*—so I revised
my request.

What he gave was Euripides, some tale of vile incest.

No longer could I hold it in, with abuse I'd make him
smother.

He paid me back, as you might guess; one insult provoked
another.

At last he sprang upon me full, and thwacked and choked
and beat.

PHEIDIPPIDES. And I was right, for great Euripides of his
proper praise he'd cheat.

STREPSIADES. Euripides great? What deserves the man who
calls him that?

—Don't beat me!

PHEIDIPPIDES. You deserve it.

STREPSIADES. Deserve it? I brought you up, you shameless
wretch, your lisping I understood.

If you cried *bry* I brought you drink, if *mam* I brought you
food.

Before you'd finish saying *cac* I'd rush you out to the yard.

But when I complained and cried to you that cramps were
griping me hard,

You wouldn't take me out of doors; I choked and tried to
contain me.

I couldn't forever, you heartless wretch, and now you see
I've stained me.

CHORUS. All agog are younger hearts

To hear how P. will plead,

If by virtue of speakers' arts

He evades payment for his deed,

Then old men's hides and tender parts

Are not worth a poppy seed.

Thou mover and shaker of novel words, now 'tis time to
seek

Persuasiveness, to make it seem you naught but justice speak.

PHEIDIPPIDES. How delightful is intimacy with teachings avant garde,

How sweet a thing facility established laws to disregard!

When horses were my only care not three words could I pronounce

Without a howler; but my folly now *he*'s made me to renounce.

With fine-spun words and arguments, with polemical dash,

I'll now proceed to demonstrate 'twas right my father to thrash.

STREPSIADES. Horse it up again, please Zeus. Go back to equitation;

Better far to suffer bills than utter annihilation.

PHEIDIPPIDES. To my point I now return: excuse the interruption.

Did *you* beat *me* when I was a boy? That is now the question.

STREPSIADES. Of course I did, in concern for you, a mark of my good will.

PHEIDIPPIDES. Is it then not right for me that function to fulfill?

Surely if a beating is to be counted a caress,

If I failed to beat you then I would be remiss.

I too am a Greek free-born, entitled to immunity;

Shall children then be whipped and fathers enjoy impunity?

Perhaps you'll counter by denying that children have the privilege:

Twice over childish, I reply, is the silliness of senile age.

Old men are more culpable far because of their experience;

'Tis justice then to beat them worse. There you have my evidence.

STREPSIADES. But nowhere does the law provide that fathers should so be treated.

PHEIDIPPIDES. Was he more than mortal, of different clay, who that law legislated?

Have we not the same good right by *persuasion* to innovate,

To allow sons who have beaten been on their sires to retaliate?

For old-law whippings we have got a moratorium we'll declare.—

Consider roosters and other beasts—do they their fathers
spare?

How do such creatures differ from us except that they
write no decrees?

STREPSIADES. If the cock your model you make, be consistent
please.

Off the dunghill take your meals, roost upon a bush.

PHEIDIPPIDES. Not the same at all, old man; Socrates says
as much.

STREPSIADES. Don't beat me then. If you persist one day
you'll surely rue it.

PHEIDIPPIDES. How so?

STREPSIADES. If it's right for sire to beat a son, when you
have one you'll do it.

PHEIDIPPIDES. But if I had none I'd be caught short, and you
one up when you died.

STREPSIADES. Gentlemen, as it seems to me, these arguments
are justified.

Their force is irresistible; yield to them I must;

Right it is for us elders to weep if our actions are not just.

PHEIDIPPIDES. Of the thrashing you have got what I'll say
may ease the sting.

STREPSIADES. How so? Show me the advantages my beating
can bring.

PHEIDIPPIDES. I'll go and beat my mother too.

STREPSIADES. What's that I hear? What say you?

PHEIDIPPIDES. If the Lesser Logic convinced you before,

I can beat my mother on the selfsame score.

STREPSIADES. If that's what you would do,

To the bottomless pit with you,

And take Socrates too,

And the Lesser Logic crew.

It's all your fault, Clouds; to you I trusted all my affairs.

CHORUS. You've yourself to blame, for turning to wicked ways.

STREPSIADES. Why didn't you speak out before, why egg an
old yokel on?

CHORUS. That's what we always do when we see a man's in
love with iniquity:

We pitch him into a mess and he learns fear of the gods.

STREPSIADES. Hard words, but just; I ought not have re-
pudiated my debts.—

Now come with me, dearest Pheidippides, let's destroy
accursed Chaerephon,

And Socrates too, who ruined us both.

PHEIDIPPIDES. I could not wrong my professors.

STREPSIADES. Yes, yes! Show reverence to Paternal Zeus.

PHEIDIPPIDES. Look here! Paternal Zeus? What a fogy you are!
Is there a Zeus?

STREPSIADES. There is.

PHEIDIPPIDES. There is not. Vortex turned Zeus out and is
now king.

STREPSIADES. I did think he was, but he is not. (*Pointing to a
jar called* dinos, *which is also the word translated Vortex.*)

What a fool I was! A piece of pottery, and I thought it was
a god!

PHEIDIPPIDES. Go on and rave, play the madman.

STREPSIADES. Alas for my delusion! Mad indeed I was when
for Socrates' sake

I cast out the gods. Dear Hermes, be not angry with me,
Do not crush me, pardon the glib silliness I spoke.
Advise me: shall I sue them, or what's the best course?
—Ah, that's good advice! No lingering lawsuits, but at once
I'll burn the chatterers' house down. Here, Xanthias!
Bring a ladder and a hoe, climb up the Think-shop,
Dig up the tiles, if you love me, until their house tumbles.
Bring me a lighted torch, someone, I'll pay them out
For all their grand pretensions.

DISCIPLE A. Ow, ow!

STREPSIADES. Do your job, torch, more fire!

DISCIPLE A. Man, what are you about?

STREPSIADES. A splitting argument with your rafters.

DISCIPLE B. Dear me, who's burning our house?

STREPSIADES. The fellow whose coat you stole.

DISCIPLE C. You're ruining it!

STREPSIADES. Exactly, if my hoe performs as expected.
Or I fall and break my neck.

SOCRATES. You on the roof! What are you doing up there?

STREPSIADES. I tread on air and contemplate the sun.

SOCRATES. Dear, dear! I'm choking to death, most miserably.

CHAEREPHON. And I'm burning to death, most wretchedly.

STREPSIADES. Why did you outrage the gods with your studies?
Why pry into the seats of the moon? Chase, strike, beat
them,

For many reasons, but most because they insulted the gods.

CHORUS. Lead out now. Our performance, we may state,
Has this day proven adequate.

(*Exeunt.*)

Wasps

Superficially, it is the Athenian propensity to litigiousness which is the theme of the *Wasps*; actually the play sets forth the permanent tensions between conservative and liberal politics. Bdelycleon or Cleon-hater, whom Aristophanes favors, maintains that pay for public service is a demagogue's device to purchase loyalty for himself; the opposition argues that without pay only the rich will be in position to direct policy, and that the population crowded into Athens during the war has somehow to be kept alive. Any attitude or behavior a man dislikes, Cleon charges, he castigates as subversion of democracy and invitation to tyranny. The scenes of Philocleon's attempted escapes when his son has shut him in are delightfully funny, as is the trial scene of the dog.

CHARACTERS

PHILOCLEON
BDELYCLEON, HIS SON
SOSIAS AND XANTHIAS, SLAVES
BOYS
DOGS

BAKING GIRL
GUEST
COMPLAINANT
CHORUS OF WASPS

Translated by Moses Hadas

(SOSIAS *and* XANTHIAS, *slaves, are discovered keeping watch a little before dawn, before the house of* BDELYCLEON *and his father* PHILOCLEON.)

SOSIAS. How goes it with you, poor Xanthias?

XANTHIAS. I'm teaching myself to take this all-night stint easy.

SOSIAS. A debit for your ribs. You know what manner of beast we're guarding?

XANTHIAS. I do, but I'd just like to lull myself a little.

SOSIAS. Take your chance, then. My own eyes too are sweetly suffused with drowsiness.

XANTHIAS. You're crazy or a dervish.

SOSIAS. No, but it's a yogi sleep coming over me.

XANTHIAS. You worship the same foreign Bacchus I do. A Median host,

Irresistible, just now overwhelmed my eyelids. What a dream!

SOSIAS. I dreamt too, an extraordinary dream. But tell yours first.

XANTHIAS. A big eagle, I thought, flew down into the market place,

Grabbed a bronze shield in his talons, carried it to the sky—
Then I saw it was Cleonymus who'd thrown it away.

SOSIAS. Cleonymus is a perfect riddle.

XANTHIAS. How?

SOSIAS. A man asks at table, What beast is it throws its shield away

Alike on earth, in heaven, on sea?

XANTHIAS. Something terrible will happen to me—such a dream!

SOSIAS. Don't worry, nothing terrible, I swear it.

XANTHIAS. A man throwing his shield away *is* terrible. Tell your dream.

SOSIAS. Mine's big, about the whole ship of state.

XANTHIAS. Let's have the keel of the business, right away.

SOSIAS. In my first sleep I thought I saw sheep sitting in the crowded assembly,

With cloaks and staves. Haranguing them was a rapacious shark

Who sounded like a scalded pig.

XANTHIAS. Phew.

SOSIAS. What's the matter?

XANTHIAS. Stop! Enough! Your dream stinks of putrid leather.

SOSIAS. Then the damned shark took scales and weighed out
    beef fat.

XANTHIAS. What a mess! It's the people he's going to weigh
    out.

SOSIAS. Near him I thought Theorus was sitting, with a
    crow's head.

Then Alcibiades lisped to me, *D'you thee? Theoruth
Hath got a thycobird'th head.*

XANTHIAS. Alcibiades' lisp, to the life.

SOSIAS. Strange, isn't it, for Theorus to turn crow?

XANTHIAS. Not at all; a fine thing.

SOSIAS. How so?

XANTHIAS. How? Man becomes crow—surely an omen he'll
    leave us

And go to the crows.

SOSIAS. So clever an interpreter of dreams deserves my two
    obols.

XANTHIAS. I must tell the spectators the story—after a short
    preface.

Don't expect anything grand from us, no jokes stolen from
    Megara.

We've no pair of slaves to scatter nuts from a basket to
    the audience,

No Heracles cheated of his dinner, no stale jeering at
    Euripides.

Despite Cleon's rise by sheer luck we'll not belabor the
    man again.

Ours is a little tale, with a meaning, not too subtle for you,

Yet more meaningful than ordinary farce. Up there asleep,

That big fellow on the tiles, is our master. His father he's
    shut up,

Inside; us he's ordered to keep him from getting out. The
    old man

Is sick—a strange disease none of you could know or guess

If we didn't tell you. You would guess? Amynias there,

Pronapes' son, says the old man's a dice-lover. He's wrong.

SOSIAS. A deduction from his own affliction, by Zeus.

XANTHIAS. No, but the trouble is a something-lover. It's drink-
    lover

Says Sosias to Dercylus.

SOSIAS. Not at all; that's a gentleman's failing.

XANTHIAS. Nicostratus the Scambonian says it's sacrifice-lover
    or stranger-lover.

SOSIAS. By the dog, no, Nicostratus; he's not like Stranger-lover the fairy.

XANTHIAS. All foolishness; you'll never find it. If you want to know, keep quiet.

I'll tell you master's disease. He's a lawcourt-lover, like no one else.

He loves judging, and groans if he's not in the front row. Not a wink

Of sleep does he get at night, and if he dozes ever so little his mind

Flutters round the lawyers' time clock the night through.

So used is he to holding the ballot pebble that he awakes

With three fingers pinched, as if offering incense at new moon.

If he sees scribbled on a doorway *I love Demos, Pyrilamp's son,*

He scribbles beside it, *I love ballot box.* Once the cock crowed

In the evening. *He's been bribed by officials under scrutiny,* says he,

To wake me late. He shouts for his shoes immediately supper is over,

And he goes to court to sleep, glued to a post like a limpet.

He's so strict he draws the long line to condemn everyone,

And comes home with nails full of wax like a bee. To make sure

He'll never be short of voting pebbles he keeps a beach at home.

He's psychopathic; the more he's admonished the more he judges.

That's the man we are keeping bolted in. His son takes it hard.

First he used soft words to persuade him not to wear the cloak

Or go outdoors: no use. Then ablutions and purges. Still no use.

Next he put him in the Salvation Army, but he burst into New Court,

Tambourine and all and sat there judging. When this initiation

Proved futile he took him to Asclepius' hospital at Aegina

For the dormition cure, but before dawn he was at the court railing.

After that we never let him out, but he elopes through drains
And light-holes. We calked every chink with rags; he drove pegs
Into the wall and scampered out like a magpie. Now we've circled
The yard with nets to keep him in. The old man's name is Philocleon,
And the son's Bdelycleon—a high-tempered character.

(BDELYCLEON *appears on the roof, and* PHILOCLEON *emerges from the chimney.*)

BDELYCLEON. Xanthias! Sosias! Are you asleep?

XANTHIAS. Oh my!

SOSIAS. What's the matter?

XANTHIAS. Bdelycleon is up.

BDELYCLEON. One of you run up here quick! Father's got into the oven
And is rummaging like a mouse. See he doesn't duck out
The drain. And you put your weight on the door.

SOSIAS. At once, master.

BDELYCLEON. Poseidon! What's the noise in the chimney? Who are you?

PHILOCLEON. I'm smoke escaping.

BDELYCLEON. Smoke? Of what wood?

PHILOCLEON. Fig.

BDELYCLEON. That *is* the most acrid. Down-draft, won't you? Where's the lid?
Down with you. I'll put this log on to weigh the lid down.
He's down there thinking up some new trick. Worse luck,
They'll be calling me Old Smoky's daddy.

SOSIAS. He's pushing at the door!

BDELYCLEON. Push back like a man; I'm coming. Mind the bars.
Take care he doesn't chew the peg off.

PHILOCLEON (*within*). What are you at, villains? Let me go do my judging!
Dracontides might be acquitted!

BDELYCLEON. What harm is that to you?

PHILOCLEON. I was informed by the god, when I consulted the oracle
At Delphi, that I'd shrivel if a defendant escaped me.

BDELYCLEON. Averter Apollo! What a prophecy!

PHILOCLEON. Do let me out I implore you, else I'll burst.

BDELYCLEON. Never, Philocleon, by Poseidon.

PHILOCLEON. Then I'll chew through the net.

BDELYCLEON. But you've got no teeth.

PHILOCLEON. What a fix! How can I slay you, how? Give me a sword,

Quick, or a "guilty" ticket.

BDELYCLEON. Our man may do something drastic.

PHILOCLEON. Really not. I only want to sell the draft donkey
And panniers; it's the new-moon market.

BDELYCLEON. Can't I sell them?

PHILOCLEON. Not so well as I can.

BDELYCLEON. Better, by Zeus. Bring the donkey out.

XANTHIAS. How disingenuous! What a bait for you to let
him go!

BDELYCLEON. But no haul; I'm up to the trick. But I think
I'll go

And bring the donkey out; the old man won't dodge again.
—Why are you crying, ass? At being sold? Giddyap!
Why the grunts, unless you've got an Odysseus there?

XANTHIAS. He has got one—hanging on there underneath.

BDELYCLEON. Who? Let's see!

XANTHIAS. Him.

BDELYCLEON. What's this? Who are you, mister?

PHILOCLEON. Noman, by Zeus.

BDELYCLEON. Noman? Where from?

PHILOCLEON. Ithaca, son of Levanter.

BDELYCLEON. You'll be very sorry, Mr. Noman. Quick, drag
him out!

Oh, the villain! Where he crept to! Looks to me exactly like
A summoner's foal.

PHILOCLEON. If you don't let me go quietly I'll fight.

BDELYCLEON. About what?

PHILOCLEON. The ass's shadow.

BDELYCLEON. You're rotten bad and slippery.

PHILOCLEON. Me bad? You don't realize how much the best
I am;

You will when you taste elderly judge paunch.

BDELYCLEON. Into the house, you and your donkey!

PHILOCLEON. Help, fellow judges! Help, Cleon!

BDELYCLEON. Bawl inside, behind locked doors. —Pile
stones up

To bolster the door, shoot the bolt home, roll up the big
mortar

To hold the bar in place.

SOSIAS. Ouch! Where did that brickbat fall from?

XANTHIAS. Maybe a rat loosened it up there.

SOSIAS. Rat? No, by Zeus, a judge on the rafters under the tiles.

BDELYCLEON. Worse luck, the man's turned into a sparrow and will flit off.

Where's the net? Shoo, shoo there, shoo! Scione is easier to guard

Than such a father.

SOSIAS. Come now, we've scared him inside and there's no way for him

To give us the slip; can't we take a snooze, the tiniest bit?

BDELYCLEON. You rascal, in a little while his colleagues will be calling him out.

SOSIAS. What do you mean? It's barely dawn.

BDELYCLEON. Then they must have risen late, by Zeus. After midnight usually

They come by, carrying lanterns and warbling dear old songs

Out of Phrynichus. That's how they call him.

SOSIAS. If need be we can throw stones at them.

BDELYCLEON. Provoking that species of old men, you rascal, is stirring

A wasps' nest. At the waist each carries a sharp sting.

They sting and buzz and prick like coal sparks.

SOSIAS. Don't worry. Stones in hand, I'll chase a wasp nest full of judges.

(*Enter* CHORUS—*old men dressed as wasps.*)

CHORUS. March, step smartly out! Comias; your feet are dragging:

You used to be tough as a dog-hide strap; now I find you lagging

Behind Charinades. Hi, Strymodorus of Conthyle, far the best of us!

But where's Chabes, where's Euergetes? Here we are, what's left of us,

The recruits who at Byzantium served—hep, two, three, four—

Pacing our posts, you and I. Remember how we slipped into the door

Of the bakery woman, stole her trough, and split it for kindling

To stew our greens? Forward, men! Laches' case they'll be calling.

He's a pot of money, everyone says, and to punish him for his crimes,

Cleon our patron yesterday bade us to be sure to appear betimes
With three days' rations of peppery temper. Hurry, veterans, and as you go
Beware of stumbling upon stones; all about cast your lanterns' glow.

BOY. Take care, father, watch your step, look out for the mudhole there.

CHORUS. Take a stick up off the ground and poke the wick to make it flare,

BOY. No need whatever for a stick; with my finger I'll fix it in a trice.

CHORUS. Why pull the wick so high, you fool, do you know lamp oil's price?
Of extravagant costs I have to pay you never feel the rub.

BOY. By Zeus, if to admonish us again you take your club,
We'll douse the lights and skip off home; in the dark, your worse luck,
You'll slosh around in the swampy ground like a poor benighted duck.

CHORUS. I've beaten better men than you. —But it's in mud I'm treading;
And within four days at most rain will Zeus be shedding.
The fungus on these lamps of ours betoken heavy rains;
The crops need a wetting down, and winds from northerly plains.
—Our fellow judge who here resides, what's come over him, think you?
Slack he never was before: why hasn't he joined our crew?
First of all he used to be, singing the Phrynichus song.
He's fond of music. Gentlemen, we'd better halt; it can't be very long.
We'll call him with a serenade, then he'll have no choice;
He needs must come by pleasure drawn when he hears our voice.
Why now is our elderly friend
Not at his door ready to go?
Why does he not to our call attend?
Has he lost his shoe, stubbed his toe?
Is his ankle inflamed, in his groin a tumor?
Toughest of all he used to be when any for mercy sued
His head he'd bend and remark with humor:
Go cook a stone: it'll do as much good.
Perhaps what happened yesterday gave our friend a fever:

A culprit got off by claiming in his brief
That he'd informed on Samians and was an Athens-lover.
'Twas this acquittal plunged our friend in grief.
Up, dear friend, do not eat your heart,
Do not seethe with indignation.
Today a case of treason will start—
A Thracian fat who harmed our nation.
In such a trial you must take part;
Vote with us for condemnation.
On, boy, get going!

BOY. There's something, Father, for which I pine:
    Would you grant a request of mine?

CHORUS. Certainly, child, tell me what's the pretty thing
    That you'd like for me to bring.
    Knucklebones is it, eh my laddie?

BOY. No knucklebones; figs, please, Daddy.

CHORUS. No figs; be hanged, say I.
    From my paltry pay I have to try
    Flour, wood, and groceries to buy.
    Figs indeed—up in the sky!

BOY. If the magistrate should now say
    No court will be sitting today,
    Tell me, Father, have we yet
    Other means dinner to get,
    Or must we *cross Helle's strait*?

CHORUS. Alack, alas, insoluble riddles!
    I don't know where we'd get our victuals.

BOY. Why bring me, Mother, into this mortal coil
    Where livelihood requires such toil?

CHORUS. My food bag's empty decoration.

BOY. All we've got is lamentation.

PHILOCLEON. (*appearing above*). Beloved friends, I pine for
        you—
    Your voice through crannies I hear—
    Sing I may not: what can I do?
    Yearn as I may voting urns to near
    These hold me back. Zeus lord of thunder's fire
    Turn me into smoke like Proxinides
    Son of Sellus, a most consummate liar.
    Sovereign Zeus be gracious to me,
    Take pity on sorrow and pain
    Or with thy blazing bolt speedily
    Singe me to ashes. Then again
    Inflate me and steep me in steaming brine,

Then make of me the slab of stone
On which votes are tallied line by line
Until the reckoning is done.

CHORUS. Who bars your door, who entreats you ill?
To us speak freely; we're men of good will.

PHILOCLEON. My son it is, but don't you shout. He's asleep
Out in front; your voices lower keep.

CHORUS. What's the object, silly man, of treatment so unseemly,
What excuse does he prefer for using you with contumely?

PHILOCLEON. Well enough he'll feast me, gentlemen, that I
won't deny;
But my wonted mischief I may not wreak, I may no cases
try.

CHORUS. Did that political reprobate
Venture so his sire to handle
Just because the truth you state
About the sorry naval scandal?
To bawl so loud he'd never dare
Unless himself a conspirator.
Some new dodge now must you contrive
Here below to join us, despite your guards alive.

PHILOCLEON. What'll it be? You point the way. I'll follow any
plan:
So hot I itch to go to court and defendants gloomy to scan.

CHORUS. Is there within no way for you to excavate a shaft?
Can't you dress yourself in rags, copy Odysseus' craft?

PHILOCLEON. Everything is sealed up tight, there's no exit
for a fly
You must think of another way; I can't liquefy.

CHORUS. Long ago, in the Naxos campaign, when the city was
going to fall,
You stole, remember, a bunch of spits and shinnied down
the wall.

PHILOCLEON. Yes I know, but what of that? Nothing's now
the same.
There was none to guard me, I could fly as I lusted.
Men-at-arms gimlet-eyed are at every exit now posted.
At the door, armed with spits, two of this great host
In ambush lie, as for a cat that's eloped with the roast.

CHORUS. Some contrivance for escape quick as you can conceive:
Dawn is breaking, my honey bee; it's high time to leave.

PHILOCLEON. To masticate the trammeling net is my only course I fear:

    May Dictynna forgive me now for spoiling hunting gear.

CHORUS. Spoken like a man of spirit bent upon salvation!

    Ply your jaws with right good will, on with mastication!

PHILOCLEON. Gnawed through it is, but withhold your cheer;

    We must watch our step, Bdelycleon might hear.

CHORUS. Away with all fear! If he utter a syllable

I'll make him eat his heart and fly

For his very life over hill and dale.

He'll learn not to trample the mysteries high

Of the voting pebbles' holy thurible.

Now tie a rope to the window, wind it your body round,

Work up a frenzy Diopeithean, and lower yourself to the ground.

PHILOCLEON. But if those two should see me and fish me up on my line,

    In the same old creel then stow me, how would you then incline?

CHORUS. Our hearts of oak we will summon, protect you with might and main;

    Of this let us assure you; no one will pen you again.

PHILOCLEON. Trusting in you I'll venture, but if anything befall,

    Take me up and bewail me, and bury me by the court-house wall.

CHORUS. Courage, man, you've nothing to fear. Fill your heart with hope,

    Offer prayer to your father's gods and then slide down that rope.

PHILOCLEON. O Lord Lycus, neighbor, hero, whose tastes resemble mine,

    Who takes delight in groans and tears when a culprit pays his fine;

    By the prisoners' box you fix your abode better to hear the wails,

    Alone of heroes by the mourner you sit for the pleasure grief entails:

    Pity and preserve me now, who of your fun partakes;

    Never again, I promise you, will I make your shrine my jakes.

(BDELYCLEON *awakes as* PHILOCLEON *descends.*)

BDELYCLEON. Wake up, you!

SOSIAS. What's the matter?

BDELYCLEON. There's a noise hereabouts.

SOSIAS. Has the old man found a loophole?

BDELYCLEON. He's lowering himself by a rope!

SOSIAS. Damn you, what are you about? Don't come down!

BDELYCLEON. Up the other window, and hit him with the
   door wreath:

   He'll back water when he feels the harvest-home trim-
      mings.

PHILOCLEON. Help, all who have suits this year! Smicythion,
   Chremon, Pheredeipnos, help me now if ever, before
   I'm locked up again.

CHORUS. Why wait longer your rage to vent;
   On spoiling our nest the fellow's bent.
   Out now with the lethal sting
   Sharpened fine for punishing.
   These cloaks, children, quickly take,
   Run and shout Cleon awake.
   Bid him answer the alarm;
   Here's a wretch who means to harm
   Our dear city, who in future would deny
   Our cherished privilege lawsuits to try.

BDELYCLEON. Hear my case, good friends, don't yell.

CHORUS. High as heaven our wrongs we'll tell.

BDELYCLEON. This man, I say, I'll never free.

CHORUS. What wicked, brazen tyranny!
   O my city, O Theorus,
   And any other fawning boss,
   If we perish yours the loss.

XANTHIAS. Heracles! What stings what have! Do you see them,
   Master?

BDELYCLEON. Sharp enough, well I know, to bring Philip to
   disaster.

CHORUS. You too we'll ruin. —Wheel about now, stings raised
   higher.
   Buzz in fury, draw, aim, fire!
   He'll learn to his sorrow, before we part,
   Never hostilities with a wasp swarm to start.

XANTHIAS. With stalwarts like these to fight is a most fearsome
   thing;
   When I see them buzz, by Zeus, I shudder at their sting.

CHORUS. Let go our man then. If you don't and we attack,
   You'll be envying the tortoise for the shell upon his back.

PHILOCLEON. To the charge, fellow judges, wasps of spirit
   fierce!

Their fingers, eyes, rumps, and sides now pierce.

BDELYCLEON. Midas, Phryx, Masyntias, help! Stick to him like barnacles!

You get no dinner if you let him go. I'll put you all in manacles.

Their buzzing threats are nothing more than burning fig-leaves' crackle.

CHORUS. If you don't release our man you'll feel our prickly hackle.

PHILOCLEON. Cecrops my lord, thou dragon-seed hero, will you see me mauled

By these oafs I've oft made weep when before the judges they're hauled?

CHORUS. Evils how many does old age bring! These two rogues most vilely

Their aged master manhandle, his benevolence forgetting entirely.

Coats and caps of hide he's bought them, also fleecy ponchos,

And in the freezing winter weather he even took care of their toes.

Now without shame are their eyes before the elderly jackanapes.

PHILOCLEON. Won't you let me go, you beast! Recall when you stole the grapes?

I tied you to an olive tree and manfully plied your rear.

Envied of all were you then; now you wear an ingrate leer.

Unhand me now, you and you, before my son rejoins us.

CHORUS. For this the two of you shall pay a penalty most glorious.

The righteous wrath of acrid men you'll quickly learn, you dastard;

Their spirits are bold, their flavor sharp, their very glance is mustard.

BDELYCLEON. Strike, Xanthias, strike! From the house those wasps keep shoving!

XANTHIAS. Exactly what I'm doing.

BDELYCLEON. Smoke them out, you! —Shoo, shoo! Get the devil out! —Seize

A stick to bat them down with. Ply them with Aeschines!

XANTHIAS. We were bound to extinguish them before so very long.

BDELYCLEON. You'd never escape them had they not been chewing Philocles' song.

CHORUS. Clear it is to the humble all
How stealthily does tyranny crawl!
You'd make legal safeguards nugatory,
You reactionary long-haired Tory.
Our city shields the proletariat;
But you choose to be an aristocrat.

BDELYCLEON. Can we not without melee and without unseemly billingsgate
Calmly our differences discuss and our grievances negotiate?

CHORUS. We negotiate with you, you hater of the masses,
Fringed and curled and mustachioed, friend of Brasidases?

BDELYCLEON. Better it were, so help me Zeus, to disown my
father
Than repeated shipwrecks to undergo in ever-stormy
weather.

CHORUS. Only rue and cummin yet, of our argument only a
sample.
You're unscathed now but when you hear the presentation
ample
Delivered by our advocate, you'll be galled and sore.
The very same crimes he'll lay to you; he'll call you
conspirator.

BDELYCLEON. Will you never, in heaven's name, leave me and
go away?
Is it some vote of yours to flay and be flayed all day?

CHORUS. So long as we're not laid in hearses
You can never to tyranny coerce us.

BDELYCLEON. Whatever issue is discussed, be it small or great,
Of tyranny and conspiracy incessantly you prate.
Never before have these words been heard, not for half a
century;
Like herrings in the market stalls, now they're common
currency.
If a trout is what you're after and refuse to purchase
anchovy,
Grumbles the disgrunted anchovite, *The gourmet favors
tyranny.*
If an onion you wish to buy, for your fish a savory,
The offended cabbage seller cries, *Aha, you favor tyranny.*
Must Athens then be taxed, think you, to maintain your
luxury?

XANTHIAS. Yesterday noon I called on a doxy, and asked her
to play the jockey;

Up she flounced and scolded me: *You're after Hippias'*
 tyranny!
BDELYCLEON. Such charges please the mob. Because I'd give
 my father redemption
From time-consuming, back-biting, tedious litigation,
A gentleman's life assure him, without enmity or calumny,
A conspiratorial wretch they call me, a favorer of tyranny.
PHILOCLEON. And they're right, by Zeus! I'd not exchange for
 pigeon's milk the
Agreeable life of which you seek to bilk me.
In mullet and eels and suchlike fare I take little pleasure;
The delicate aroma of lawsuit-stew is what I most treasure.
BDELYCLEON. A taste you've cultivated. Hold your tongue and
 lend an ear,
And I think that I can show that you're wrong, my daddy
 dear.
PHILOCLEON. Wrong for me to serve as judge?
BDELYCLEON. Actually you're slave and drudge.
I'll show you've been the ridiculous pawn
Of the very men on whom you fawn.
PHILOCLEON. Don't speak of slavery! I'm master, you fool.
BDELYCLEON. You think you are; in fact you're a tool.
When all are plucked, how do you profit?
PHILOCLEON. Much. Let these men judge if I should stop it.
BDELYCLEON. I too their verdict will accept. —Turn him loose,
 you!
PHILOCLEON. A sword please! —If I lose I'll stick myself
 through.
BDELYCLEON. But suppose you reject their arbitration?
PHILOCLEON. Never again may I enjoy juridical compensation.
CHORUS. The alumnus of our school
    To do credit to his teaching
    Must employ some novel tool—
BDELYCLEON. Bring me, someone, my writing slate—
I'll see what's what in this debate.
CHORUS. —The callow youth overreaching.
    He might fight through thick and thin,
    Perished else is all our preaching,
    If, heaven forbid, the young man win.
BDELYCLEON. I'll jot down here all he has to say.
PHILOCLEON. And what would you say if he wins today?
CHORUS. Old men are useless muddlers,
 Jeered at out of habit.
Men would call us olive-cane toddlers,

Brief cases for an affidavit.

Upon you it now devolves our sovereign power to vin-
    dicate.

Show us now your hardihood; your sinews flex, your tongue
    dilate.

PHILOCLEON. Directly from the starting line I shall proceed
    to demonstrate

That higher than any sovereignty is our own blessed estate.

What other happy and blessed life can with the judge's
    compare?

Powerful is he and luxurious, even with hoary hair.

Directly from bed to the court I go, where to solicit my
    grace

Great six-footers, obsequiously, show me to my place.

A hand that's picked the public purse gives me a caress;

Humbly they scrape and bow and whine with sham dis-
    tress:

Pity me, father, I beg of you; you must know what tempta-
    tions

Assail the keepers of public funds and buyers of soldiers'
    rations.

My very existence he'd never have known, except for a
    former investigation.

BDELYCLEON. Of this I must make a note: *Judges profit from*
    solicitation.

PHILOCLEON. When they've soft-soldered me and softened my
    mood

I do none of the things I promised I would.

I listen to exculpations of every imaginable sort—

The cajolery one hears in a magistrate's court!

Some cry up their poverty and credits as debits count

Until they make their total wealth equal mine in amount.

Some Aesopic fables tell; some an amusing anecdote

All calculated to make me laugh and my charity promote.

And if I'm not persuaded yet, he'll appeal to sentiment,

Dragging his children by the hand to make me hear their
    lament.

They grovel and whimper, the boys and girls, and the
    father, all aquiver,

Implores me with pleading voice from their plight to
    deliver

His bleating ramkins and his pussykins mewling,

Then a little we relent, our anger's pitch unscrewing.

Is this not power? Am I not well off?
At pelf and prestige I can freely scoff.

BDELYCLEON. Derision of wealth: for my notes point two.
—Your dominion of Hellas: What's the profit to you?

PHILOCLEON. When adolescents enter the rolls, we enjoy a
    private inspection.
If actor Aeagrus stands in the dock we demand a recitation
Of his famous Niobe role. His most elaborate aria
The piper plays in gratitude before the judge's barrier.
The dying father names his friends to care for his orphaned
    heiresses.
We flout the will with its solemn seal for men who'll
    sweetly caress us.
We give the girl, and with no accounting. Our acts enjoy
    immunity.
Judges alone, of surrogates, are from investigation free.

BDELYCLEON. For this alone, of all you said, I offer felicitation.
    But still,
Is it not high-handed to subvert the heiress' will?

PHILOCLEON. If senate and people ever are stumped in decid-
    ing some great case,
They vote that the defendants must the judges' panel face.
Evathlus and Colaconymus, the great loser of his shield,
Declare they'll never the people betray; for the people,
    their power they'll wield.
No bill can the assembly pass without this rider appended:
Judges get the whole day off after their first case is ended.
Cleon himself, the master bawler, us alone his badger-
    ing spares.
Tenderly he fondles us, brushes flies from our scanty hairs.
For *your* father you've never done as much. Theorus the
    glorious
Carried sponge and bottle—he, the peer of Euphemius—
Our shoes to clean and polish. See of what great privilege
You would deprive me and bar me: yet slavery you do
    allege!

BDELYCLEON. Talk your fill. Like a man an anus washing, at
    the end you'll see,
Scrub and scour as you will, immaculate it cannot be.

PHILOCLEON. Sweetest thing of all is this, which I forgot to
    mention.
When I come home with my judge's pay, what welcoming
    attention!

My daughter washes and salves my feet and then stoops
    for a kiss,
Calling me her daddykins; soon from my cheek I miss
The obols I'd hid there, which she, with caressing tongue
    fishes.
Affectionately my little wife brings on my special dishes.
Eat this, she insists, as she sits by my side, *Have a taste of
    that.*
I bask in the glow. I need not look to your butler, saucy
    and fat,
Wondering when to serve me he'll deign. If too long he
    dallies
I've got me now a mighty shield, impregnable to fortune's
    sallies.
If your pour me out no wine, I tilt this donkey jug of mine;
It gurgles like an army corps. I have no need of thee and
    thine.

      My own dominion, I maintain,
      Is precisely Zeus' sort.
      On hearing our din, passers-by exclaim
      How thunderous, Zeus, the court!
      When my lightning I let fly
      And my thundering bellow,
      The rich and stately I terrify;
      They stain their garments yellow.
      You fear *me*, it's very clear,
      Though you think you're clever.
      By Demeter I swear it's me you fear.
      But I fear you? Never!

CHORUS. Never before so shrewd a word,
    Never such eloquence have I heard.
PHILOCLEON. He thought my undefended vines he'd gobble
    by surprise,
But that, as now he learns, is where my own strength lies.
CHORUS. No point he omitted, but covered them all.
    As I heard him I could fancy
    That I myself was growing tall.
    The charm of his facility
    Left me quite possessed.
    A judge myself I dreamed I'd be
    In the Islands of the Blessed.
PHILOCLEON. How he fidgets, how hangdog he looks!
    Today I'll hang him on tenterhooks.

CHORUS. Every dodge must you insinuate
   Yourself from his grip to extricate.
   Hard it is for the young to assuage
   An elderly man's burning rage.
   —A heavy millstone go and seek
   Wherewith to crush my manly spirit.
   Otherwise your outlook's bleak—
   Your words alone will never do it.

BDELYCLEON. To cure the city of its disease, inveterate and
   chronic—
   That is an assignment grave, too demanding for poetry
   comic.
   And yet old Cronus, daddy mine—

PHILOCLEON. Daddy me no daddies. If you cannot prove me a
   slave in a trice,
   I will have to kill you dead—and be excluded from sacrifice.

BDELYCLEON. Then listen to me, Papa my pet, your frown for
   a little relax.
   On your fingers roughly reckon, not with abacus, just how
   much the tax
   Paid in by our subject states, plus our assorted revenues,
   Fees and imports, mining rights, interest and rents and
   harbor dues;
   Some two thousand talents, I believe, you'll find the total
   sum.
   Now count the salaries of our judges—six thousand is the
   minimum—
   One hundred and fifty talents, you see, is the total cost per
   year.

PHILOCLEON. Then hardly a tithe of the income to our salary
   goes I fear.

BDELYCLEON. By Zeus, it doesn't.

PHILOCLEON. And where does the rest of the money go? Inform me, pray.

BDELYCLEON. To the politicians whose stock in trade it is to
   say:
   Athenian masses I'll never betray! For the common people's
   sake
   Forever will I fight! Lulled by such mouthings, Father, you
   make
   Such fellows to be your kings. Then by threatening every
   city
   Fifty talents at a clip they extort, and they show no pity:

I'll aim my thunder at your city if you don't fork up.

You meanwhile are quite content on dominion's crumbs to
  sup.

When the allies perceive the populace, clinging to their
  franchise,

Thin and supine, waste and pine with starvation in their
  eyes,

You they ignore and lavish their gifts on the powerful
  politicians—

Fish and wine, sesame and honey, and soft embroidered
  cushions,

Clothing and plate and all that affords either health or
  pleasure,

And you who've toiled by land and sea and your dominion
  treasure—

For you not even a garlic clove; nothing comes to you free.

PHILOCLEON. True enough: I've had to send to Eucharides for
  money to purchase three.

But time's awasting. Tell me now: Why do you think we're
  slaves?

BDELYCLEON. Is it not the worst of slavery to have as masters
  such greedy knaves?

They and all their parasites, all feeding at the public
  trough;

Three meager obols you receive you are pleased to think
  are quite enough.

You earned those obols by your sweat, rowing, besieging,
  fighting.

Most of all I choke with spleen at an adolescent's bidding,

A fat-rumped son of Chaireas, straddling, swaying, mincing,

Ordering you to report at dawn for your daily stint of
  judging:

Whoever is tardy forfeits his pay. Himself however late he
  arrive

Pockets his drachma as advocate of the court. If a culprit
  offer a bribe,

He splits with his colleague. They manage the manner like
  two men at a saw—

One pushes, one pulls, and there goes the law.

All these tricks you never notice, only at the pay clerk stare.

PHILOCLEON. You don't say! Is that what they do? It's enough
  to raise my hair.

Your words are having an effect: I feel I'm giving ground.

BDELYCLEON. You and the others might wealthy be, and yet
  you're talked around
  By the people's patron. From Pontus unto Sardis extends
  your domination:
  What profit to you? Hardly enough to stave off starvation.
  They dribble out, drop by drop, like oil squeezed from
  wool.
  They *intend* you to be poor, as I'll explain: if life were
  bountiful
  You might not know your master's voice. Now at a whistle
  you leap
  Savagely an enemy to maul. If in opulence they wished
  to keep
  The people they could do so. A thousand cities are our
  domain;
  If each were allotted twenty Athenians to maintain,
  Twenty thousand citizens could live on sumptuous fare,
  Creams and crowns and pasties and ragout of dainty hare.
  As befits the heirs of Marathon ourselves we'd be regaling—
  Not like migrant pickers of fruit after a paymaster trailing.
PHILOCLEON. Alas for me, my hand is numb, I cannot hold
  my sword aloft.
  An enfeebling languor suffuses me; I fear me I am growing
  soft.
BDELYCLEON. But if ever *they* grow panicky, *Divide Euboea*,
  they cry!
  And promise, per man, fifty bushels of wheat. What they
  actually supply
  Is five bushels of barley stingily doled out quart by quart,
  And only on evidence of citizenship certified by a court.
                  To prevent your being bamboozled
                  We've kept you incommunicado
                  From those by whom you're dazzled.
                  I have fed and will feed you even so,
                  But not on funds embezzled.
CHORUS. Wise the saying: no judgment pass until you have
  heard either side.
  All our doubts are dissipated; with you victory will abide.
  Now our staves we'll cast away, now our passion will
  subside.
  Fraternity brother and classmate,
  Accept this prudent admonition:
  Be not stubborn and obdurate.
  I wish that I had some relation

To guide my inexperience;
Some god, 'tis plain, is your salvation:
Do not reject his benevolence.

BDELYCLEON. I'll nurture him and see he's snug
With what an old man can require,
Porridge, dressing gown, a rug,
A wench to stir his ebbing fire.—
But he stands mute with stony face,
An omen unfavorable for my case.

CHORUS. It's himself now he is chiding,
Now he sees where he transgressed.
To himself his error he's confiding
In not heeding your behest.
Now perhaps he is persuaded
To turn over a new leaf.
Now the folly old has faded;
He will lend your views belief.

PHILOCLEON. Ah me, ah!

BDELYCLEON. Why the groans?

PHILOCLEON. Promise me no promises!
There's my heart, there fain I'd sit
Where the court crier calls *Oyez*,
Vote, everyone who's not voted yet.
I'd linger till they'd voted, every one.
Hasten, my soul! where *is* my soul?
Wait, dark shadows, till our day is done;
Among the judges to sit is all my goal.
I may catch at his thieving—Cleon!

BDELYCLEON. Come, Father, in heaven's name, take my advice.

PHILOCLEON. About what? Whatever you like, except one thing.

BDELYCLEON. And what is that?

PHILOCLEON. Not to judge. Hades will do the judging before I yield.

BDELYCLEON. If that is what you like don't go *there*.
Stay here and judge your household.

PHILOCLEON. About what? This is nonsense.

BDELYCLEON. Same as there. If a maid opens a door surreptitiously
Fine her one drachma—what you used to do there. All in order.
On a fine morning you'll be sitting in the sun. If it snows
Then inside by the fire. If you sleep till noon

There's no official to shut you out.

PHILOCLEON. That's satisfactory.

BDELYCLEON. If a pleader is long-winded, moreover, you
won't go hungry
And chafe yourself—and the defendant.

PHILOCLEON. Could I draw distinctions equally fine while
masticating?

BDELYCLEON. Much finer. When testimony is false, people say
The judges have a hard problem to chew over.

PHILOCLEON. You convince me. But one thing you haven't
mentioned.
Where will I get my pay?

BDELYCLEON. From me.

PHILOCLEON. That way it'll be all mine and not shared.
Lysistratus the jester played me a dirty trick. He got a
drachma
For the two of us, went to the fishmonger to change it,
Brought back three mullet scales, which I thought obols
And put in my mouth. The taste was disgusting; I spat
them out
And brought suit.

BDELYCLEON. His defense?

PHILOCLEON. He said I had a rooster's gizzard and could
digest silver.

BDELYCLEON. Well, that's another advantage.

PHILOCLEON. And a considerable one. Do what you were
going to.

BDELYCLEON. One minute; I'll bring the things here.

PHILOCLEON. See how oracles are fulfilled! I have heard it said
The Athenians would judge suits at home. Every man
Would build a miniature court at his front door,
Like a Hecate shrine.

BDELYCLEON. What do you say now? I've brought the things
I mentioned
And more too. Here's a potty, at your need; I'll hang it on
this peg.

PHILOCLEON. Clever. Useful relief for an old man's bladder.

BDELYCLEON. And here's fire and beans to munch if you feel
the need.

PHILOCLEON. Good again. If I have a fever I can collect my
pay;
I can sit here and eat my beans. But what's the bird for?

BDELYCLEON. To wake you by crowing up there if you doze
off during a case.

PHILOCLEON. One thing I miss; the rest is satisfactory.

BDELYCLEON. What is it?

PHILOCLEON. Could you bring me the shrine of Ibycus?

BDELYCLEON. Here it is, and the hero himself.

PHILOCLEON. Master hero, how austere to see!

BDELYCLEON. To me he looks like Cleonymus.

XANTHIAS. That's why he's got no shield.

BDELYCLEON. The sooner you take your seat the sooner I can call a case.

PHILOCLEON. Call ahead. I'm on the bench.

BDELYCLEON. Let's see, what's first on the calendar? Any inmate
At fault here? Thratta has scorched the pot.

PHILOCLEON. Wait! It's murderous! Call a case with no railing?
That's the first of our sanctities.

BDELYCLEON. I have none, by Zeus.

PHILOCLEON. I'll run myself and fetch whatever's at hand.

BDELYCLEON. What a hold old habit keeps!

XANTHIAS. The devil with you! —To give such a dog house room!

BDELYCLEON. What's the matter now?

XANTHIAS. That dog Labes dashed into the kitchen, grabbed
A Sicilian cheese, and gobbled it all.

BDELYCLEON. Then this is the first offense I'll bring
Before my father. You, Xanthias, be prosecutor.

XANTHIAS Not I, by Zeus. The other dog says he'll prosecute,
If an indictment is cited.

BDELYCLEON. Go and bring them both.

XANTHIAS. The proper course.

(PHILOCLEON *enters carrying his surrogate railing.*)

BDELYCLEON. What's that?

PHILOCLEON. A pig barrier from Hestia's hearth.

BDELYCLEON. Temple robbing?

PHILOCLEON. I'll consecrate Hestia by smashing somebody.
Bring your case on. I'm all for sentencing.

BDELYCLEON. I'll bring the rolls and the briefs.

PHILOCLEON. You're wasting time, your dawdling is killing me;
I'm all set to scratch the long "guilty" mark.

BDELYCLEON. Ready!

PHILOCLEON. Make the summons.

BDELYCLEON. At your service.

PHILOCLEON. Who comes first?

BDELYCLEON. The devil! I'm sorry, I forgot to bring the voting urns.

PHILOCLEON. Where are you running off to?

BDELYCLEON. For the urns.

PHILOCLEON. Don't. I've got these sauce pans.

BDELYCLEON. Excellent; we've got all we need now, except the water clock.

PHILOCLEON. What's the potty? Isn't it a water clock?

BDELYCLEON. Well provided! The country way.
　　Quick, someone, bring out coals and incense and myrtle;
　　We must open with prayer.

CHORUS. For these prayers and these libations
　　We too offer felicitations.
　　Nobly after exacerbation
　　Have you reached reconciliation.

BDELYCLEON. The holy silence let everyone keep!

CHORUS. Phoebus Apollo in Pythia sought,
　　Bless the work this man has wrought
　　Before these doors. To an end he brought
　　Errors in which we've been caught.
　　　　Ho, Paean!

BDELYCLEON. Lord, my neighbor at my entrance gate,
　　This new rite for my father I inaugurate.
　　His oaken temper do thou moderate,
　　With honey his tartness alleviate.
　　Make him to his fellows a gentle excuser,
　　To favor accused rather than accuser,
　　To show to suppliants a kindlier temper,
　　To cease from acerbity and from rancor,
　　To amputate his nettle anger.

CHORUS. Your chants we join and heartily share
　　For your novel policy your cordial prayer.
　　For the people's cause rich fruit may it bear.
　　Among younger men such prudence is rare.

BDELYCLEON. Enter, judges, at the door. No admission after speaking's begun.

PHILOCLEON. Who's the defendant? —He'll catch it.

BDELYCLEON. Attention to the indictment! *Dog of Cydathon charges:*
　　Labes of Aexone transgressed in devouring, all by himself,
　　A Sicilian cheese. Penalty: fig-wood collar.

PHILOCLEON. No, a dog's death if he's convicted.

BDELYCLEON. Here's the defendant Labes.

PHILOCLEON. The brute! What a thievish look! Thinks he'll win me
　　With that smirk. Where's the accuser, Dog of Cydathon?

DOG. Bow-wow!

BDELYCLEON. Present!

XANTHIAS. Another Labes—good yelper and pot licker.

BDELYCLEON. Silence! Be seated! Prosecutor step forward!

PHILOCLEON. Meanwhile I'll help myself to the bean soup.

XANTHIAS (for DOG). You have heard my accusation against
him, your honors;

A heinous crime he perpetrated against me and the boys in
blue:

He sneaked into a corner and Sicilized a whole cheese in
the dark.

PHILOCLEON. A clear case. The stinker belched a cheese
stench in my face.

XANTHIAS. And wouldn't share though I begged him. Could he
Ever do kindness to you if he won't throw a bit to me, a
dog?

PHILOCLEON. Threw you nothing? Neither to me. He's hot,
like these beans.

BDELYCLEON. In heaven's name, Father, don't pass sentence
till you've heard both.

PHILOCLEON. But my good man, the case is obvious; it cries
to heaven.

XANTHIAS. Don't let him off. He's the solitariest glutton of all
hounds.

He coasted round the platter and nibbled the city's rind.

PHILOCLEON. I've not the wherewithal even to mend my jug.

XANTHIAS. Wherefore punish him. The same den cannot keep
two thieves.

Let me not bark in vain, else I shall never bark again.

PHILOCLEON. Oho, what rascality is here charged. A monster
of a thief!

Don't you agree, old cock? He nods Yes. Hi, clerk!

Hand me down the pot.

BDELYCLEON. Get it yourself. I'll call the witnesses: Plate,
Pestle, cheese-grater, griddle, and other scorched utensils.—
You, there, still on the pot? Take your place on the bench.

PHILOCLEON. I'll pot him today I think.

BDELYCLEON. Must you always be irritable and grouchy to
defendants,

Always baring your teeth? —Step up, make your defense.

Why silent? Speak up!

PHILOCLEON. Apparently he has nothing to say.

BDELYCLEON. No, I think it's the same accident that befell
Thucydides—

Sudden lockjaw. —Step aside; I'll make the defense.
It is difficult, gentlemen, to speak for a slandered dog,
But speak I shall. It's a good dog and chases wolves.

PHILOCLEON. No, a thief; moreover, a conspirator.

BDELYCLEON. The best of dogs, by Zeus, able to care for many
sheep.

PHILOCLEON. What's the use if he gobbles cheese?

BDELYCLEON. Use? He fights for you, guards your door. He's
Good all round. Forgive him an abstraction. He's no
musician.

PHILOCLEON. I wish he were as ignorant of *a-b-c*;
We'd been spared his rascally speech.

BDELYCLEON. Hear my witnesses, please. —Cheese-grater,
step up!
Speak out! You were quartermaster. Answer clearly. Did
you
Grate up all the cheese allotted our soldiers. He answers
Yes.

PHILOCLEON. He's lying, by Zeus!

BDELYCLEON. Show pity to the unfortunate, friend. Labes
here
Gets only fishbones and briers to eat, is always on the go.
The other dog is a stay-at-home, and demands his share
Of what others bring in. If denied he bites.

PHILOCLEON. I must be sick. What makes me go soft?
Something's gone wrong. I'm being won over.

BDELYCLEON. I beseech you, Father, pity him, do not destroy
him.
The puppies, where are they? Step up, poor dears;
Whimper, wail, whine!

PHILOCLEON. Step down, step down, step down, step down.

BDELYCLEON. I'll step down. That "step down" has fooled
many;
Nevertheless, step down I shall.

PHILOCLEON. Damn it, stuffing myself is no good. I was
weeping,
I thought, but it was only the beans.

BDELYCLEON. Then he's not acquitted?

PHILOCLEON. It's hard to know.

BDELYCLEON. Take the better turn, dear Papa. Dash with your
ballot
To the farther urn. Set him free!

PHILOCLEON. No, I don't understand music.

BDELYCLEON. Come, I'll lead you the shortest way.

PHILOCLEON. Is this the near urn?

BDELYCLEON. Yes.

PHILOCLEON. It's in.

BDELYCLEON. He's fooled. He's acquitted, unwittingly. I'll
dump the ballots.

PHILOCLEON. How did we make out?

BDELYCLEON. We'll see. —Labes, you're free!
What's happened to you, Father?

PHILOCLEON. Water! Where's the water?

BDELYCLEON. Pull yourself together.

PHILOCLEON. Tell me this: is he really acquitted?

BDELYCLEON. Yes.

PHILOCLEON. I'm done for.

BDELYCLEON. Don't worry sir, up with you!

PHILOCLEON. How can I face such a thing, acquitting a
defendant!
Ye gods revered, forgive me; unwittingly I did it.
It is not my character.

BDELYCLEON. Don't be distressed. I'll take good care of you,
Father,
Take you with me everywhere, to dinners, banquets, shows.
You'll spend all your life agreeably, and Hyperbolus
Shan't trick you and fool you. But let's go in.

PHILOCLEON. Very well, if you think so.

CHORUS. Go wherever you will, rejoicing.
(*The actors retire, and the* CHORUS *faces the audience for
the parabasis.*)
Spectators, myriads numberless,
Hearken now to our address.
Of intellect there is here no dearth;
Let not our remarks fall useless to earth.
Attend, people all, to what is plain-spoken if what is candid
you have loved;
To find fault with his spectators the comic poet now is
moved.
You have used him ill, he says, though he has served you
best,
In his person sometimes, entering anon another's breast
Like Eurycles the ventriloquist ghosting jests for an-
other to declaim.
Later on he shed his mask and spoke in his own name,
Working the lips of his very own and not another's Muses.
Esteem unprecedented was his, yet never did he lose his

Drive for perfection. Never was he arrogant. Never did he entertain

The lads in the gymnasium. If a disgruntled lover should complain

Of the poet's deriding his passion, calmly he ignored the slander;

The pure Muses that he served he'd never set to pander.

Mere men he disdained to attack in his plays; instead he kept his eye on

The fiercest monster, and made it his game, like Heracles charging a lion.

Straight he went for the jag-toothed beast with Cynna's fiery eyes;

Head girt with a hundred slavering sycophant tongues; raucous cries

Like a ruinous torrent's; privates unwashed like a Lamian fairy;

Stench of a rotting seal; noisome buttocks of a dromedary.

Confronting such a monster, no fear he felt, took no blackmail;

For you he fights and ever will. Last year he dared to assail

The hectic, spectral, sophist spooks who garroted your father,

Your grandfather strangled. On their beds at night they glue together

Affidavit, summons, evidence, against guiltless folk to litigate;

In terror the innocent sprang from their beds, ran for help to the magistrate.

But though a champion Heraclean you'd got to purify the state,

Last year you betrayed him. When his *Clouds* sought to disseminate

Novel notions you missed the seed he sowed. With many a libation

He swears that never a cleverer comedy was presented to our nation.

This you did not straightway see; yours the shame. In wiser eyes

My work's approved. They thought I ran in front, yet I got no prize.

> In future, friends, cosset and cherish
> The fresh and inventive poet.

Never let his fine thought perish;
In your wardrobe stow it.
All year will your garments keep the relish
Of sparkling wit, and all will know it.

High our prowess in days gone by,
High in fighting, in dancing high.
As choristers we gained great glory,
But that was back in ages hoary.
Now our cheeks are pale and wan
White our hair as plume of swan.
Yet from these embers' humble glow
Youthful vigor shall bright flame show.
Better are we to curvet and whirl
Than mincing youths who sport a curl.

If any of you spectators there sit astonished and wide-eyed
To see our middles so tightly laced, in fact waspified,
And wonder at the meaning of our sharp-pointed sting,
Though my IQ is low I'll explain the thing.
We upon whose backs you see these appendages porten-
     tous,
Athenians born we avow us, with the pride of the autoch-
     thonous,
A sturdy and a manly breed who helped this city most
When the Persian invader marched on us with his host.
With fuming smoke he blinded us, seared us with his flame,
Seeking to obliterate our wasp nest's very name.
Armed with spear and shield we rushed, all our stalwart
     swarm,
Man to man we fought amain, our glands secreting juices
     warm.
In the fury of the fray we bit our lips till they grew pale;
The very heavens were eclipsed by enemy arrows' hail.
Before the evening, with heaven's help, we smote them hip
     and thigh;
Over us the owl, Athena's bird, hovered in the sky.
We followed up harpooning them in their baggy drawers;
Routed then they fled away, stung in brows and jaws.
Now barbarians everywhere, and time out of mind,
Say no wasp is waspier than the Attic kind.

How glorious a thing it is
To have no fear of enemies,

Their poltroon armies roundly to thrash
Their country invade with galleys' dash.
The rhetoricians' eloquence
Was then no proof of excellence.
Lawyers' tricks were not the test;
The question was: Who rows the best?
Of credit, therefore, we deserve most
For laying low the Persian host.
The imperial tribute *we* earned for your weal—
Those very revenues which our juniors now steal.

Examine us from every side and surely you will find
Our habits and our characters most like the waspish kind.
First, no creature is so sharp-set, none easier to irritate;
All our business we transact in a kind of waspish state.
Into the courts we all swarm, like wasps into their haven,
Some to the Archon's, to the Odeon some, and some to the
    Court of Eleven.
Some cling to walls, with head stooped low, like grubs in a
    nesting weft.
In finding means to turn a penny we are exceedingly deft.
Any man we're ready to sting, in order our income to
    double.
Stingless drones are among us too, who without taking
    trouble
Devour what the others earn. 'Tis this that grieves us sore—
That men who evaded soldiering, who never wielded spear
    or oar,
Should with hands unblistered and soft carry off our reve-
    nue.
In future be this the rule: You carry no sting? No obols
    for you.

(*Enter* PHILOCLEON *and* BDELYCLEON.)

PHILOCLEON. Never, so long as I live, will I shed this old
    cloak.
    It saved me in the campaign of the North Wind.
BDELYCLEON. You won't let anything good happen to you.
PHILOCLEON. It's not good for me. When I gorged on fried
    fish the other day
    I had to pay the cleaner three obols to get the grease spots
    out.
BDELYCLEON. Try it anyhow. You did agree to let me treat
    you well.
PHILOCLEON. What do you want me to do?

BDELYCLEON. Take the old cloak off and drape this over you.

PHILOCLEON. We beget children and bring them up—and now he's trying to smother me.

BDELYCLEON. Take it and put it on. Don't babble.

PHILOCLEON. What *is* this nuisance, in the name of all the gods?

BDELYCLEON. Some call it Persian, some Caunaces.

PHILOCLEON. I thought it was a rug from Thymaetadae.

BDELYCLEON. No wonder, you've never been to Sardis; you'd have known it.

PHILOCLEON. Me? Never. It seems to me like a Morychus folderol.

BDELYCLEON. The material is woven in Ecbatana.

PHILOCLEON. Does tripe grow *outside* in Ecbatana?

BDELYCLEON. Those barbarians fabricate this shag at great expense;

It sucks up a talent of wool, easily.

PHILOCLEON. Why not call it, instead of Caunaces, wool consumer?

BDELYCLEON. Take it. Stand still and put it on.

PHILOCLEON. Curse the monster, what a steamy belch!

BDELYCLEON. Won't you throw it on?

PHILOCLEON. I won't, by Zeus. If you must, put a stove on me.

BDELYCLEON. Come, I'll put it on you. Now you can go.

PHILOCLEON. Put a meat hook by me too.

BDELYCLEON. What for?

PHILOCLEON. To pull me out before I'm cooked away.

BDELYCLEON. Ready, now. Take these damned brogues off and put on

These nice Laconian slippers.

PHILOCLEON. I go shod in the enemy's cursed hides?

BDELYCLEON. Put your foot in, step out firmly.

PHILOCLEON. It's no fair to put my foot in hostile territory.

BDELYCLEON. Now the other foot.

PHILOCLEON. Not that, please. One of my toes is a Spartan-hater.

BDELYCLEON. There's no way out.

PHILOCLEON. What a fix! For my old age I'll have not a—chilblain.

BDELYCLEON. Walk out in your shoes now—a stylish swagger.

PHILOCLEON. Look at my posture and tell me what nabob's my gait is most like.

BDELYCLEON. Like a boil under a garlic plaster.

PHILOCLEON. I do feel like wriggling my behind.

BDELYCLEON. Come, now. Can you converse seriously with educated and clever men?

PHILOCLEON. I can.

BDELYCLEON. What would you say?

PHILOCLEON. Many things. First, how Lamia caught broke wind,

Then how Cardopion treated his mother.

BDELYCLEON. No legends, please; domestic affairs, the kind we talk about.

PHILOCLEON. I know a very domestic affair. Once there was a cat and a mouse—

BDELYCLEON. *You ignorant oaf*, as Theagenes scolded the dung collector.

Will you talk of cats and mice among well-bred folk?

PHILOCLEON. What should I talk about?

BDELYCLEON. Important things—how you went on a mission with Androcles and Cleisthenes.

PHILOCLEON. My only mission was to Paros, for two obols a day.

BDELYCLEON. You can tell how skillfully Ephudion fought the pancratium

Against Ascondas—an old man but rugged, a chest steel-plated—

PHILOCLEON. Nonsense! How do you wrestle with steel plate?

BDELYCLEON. That's the way smart people talk sport. Tell me something else.

Suppose you're drinking with strangers. What youthful adventure

Of yours showed the most mettle?

PHILOCLEON. The most mettle? When I stole Ergasion's vine props.

BDELYCLEON. What a yokel! Tell how you hunted a boar, or a jackrabbit,

Or ran in the torch relay, some boyish stunt.

PHILOCLEON. I know. I overhauled the runner Phayllus when I was still green,

And won—by two votes in a suit for slander.

BDELYCLEON. Enough of that. Here, learn how to recline gracefully

At table, in polite society.

PHILOCLEON. Recline? How? Tell me.

BDELYCLEON. Elegantly.

PHILOCLEON. This way you mean?

BDELYCLEON. Not in the least.

PHILOCLEON. How then?

BDELYCLEON. Spread your knees, ease yourself into the cushions like a supple athlete,

Praise some *objet d'art*, inspect the ceiling, admire the hangings.—

A basin for the hands, trays in, dinner, wash, libations.

PHILOCLEON. A dream of a dinner, by the gods.

BDELYCLEON. The flute girl has tootled. Guest list: Theorus, Aeschines,

Phanos, Cleon, a visitor at Acestis's head, table verses—
Could you fling them?

PHILOCLEON. No highlander better.

BDELYCLEON. I'll find out. Say I'm Cleon and start the Harmodius catch;

You take it up. *Never have Athenians seen your equal—*

PHILOCLEON. *An unprincipled thief, a brazen rascal.*

BDELYCLEON. Would you do that? He'd shout you to destruction, annihilate you,

Drive you out of the country.

PHILOCLEON. If he threatens me I'll sing another:
Fellow by lust of power crazed, By you will our tottering city be razed.

BDELYCLEON. If Thorus sitting at Cleon's feet, should take his hand and say,

With Admetus as your model, learn to love the good; what say you?

PHILOCLEON. *Two rival parties you cannot befriend, To play the fox is no good in the end.*

BDELYCLEON. After him Aeschines son of Sellus, a clever and musical man sings:

For Cleitagoras and for me, And for the men of Thessaly—

PHILOCLEON. *How we swaggered, all we three.*

BDELYCLEON. You've got the trick well enough. Let's go to dinner to Philoctemon's.

Boy! Chrysus! Pack our dinner! There's a lot of drinking ahead.

PHILOCLEON. No, drinking is bad—leads to breaking-in, bawling, hangover, damages.

BDELYCLEON. Not if you're with gentlemen. They'll either effect reconciliation,

Or you can say something witty, Aesopic or Sybaritic,
Which you got at a party, and turn the thing into a joke:
He lets you off.

PHILOCLEON. I must learn lots of those stories if I don't have to pay

For any mischief I do. Let's go; nothing must hold us back.
(PHILOCLEON *and* BDELYCLEON *withdraw*.)

CHORUS. Often I thought I was a man of parts, stupid never;

But Amynias, Sellus' son, the Topknotter, is a man very clever.

Hungry as Antiphon, with apple and pomegranate as his contribution

He came to dine with Leogoras. At Pharsalus on a mission,

None but cockney Thessalians he met, a proper evolution

For one who'd always a cockney been at home in his own nation.

Happy Automenes we felicitate for the gifted sons he's sired.

First the virtuoso harper, by Grace herself attended, whom everyone admired

Next the actor, supple and wise. Then talented even more

Ariphrades. With none to teach him, his father swore,

Self-inspired he learned, the bawdyhouses among,

How most ingeniously to operate his tongue.

He's reconciled with Cleon, some have said. Not so. When the fellow

Persecuted and flayed me, the public laughed to hear me bellow,

Concerned not for me but only to see how I would retaliate.

Seeing this, I did for a little monkeyish antics imitate;

The very prop it leans upon will later leave the vine prostrate.

(*Enter* XANTHIAS.)

XANTHIAS. Lucky tortoises to have a shell! Thrice lucky for the casing

On your ribs, the sound roof and weather-proof tiles

Which protect your flanks. I'm tattooed to death.

CHORUS. What's the matter, boy? —Boy it must be if you're whipped;

What you are is an old man.

XANTHIAS. That old man was the worst reprobate and the drunkest

Of the company. There were Hippolytus, Antiphon, Lycon,

Lysistratus, Theophrastus, Phrynichus' gang; but of all

He was most outrageous by a mile. Stuffing done,

He cavorted around, guffawed fore and aft, like a donkey

On an emptied crib. Like a juvenile delinquent he beat me,

Yelling Boy, Boy! This was Lysistratus' figure: Old man,
   says he,
You're like a ferment working, or a brayer running to bran.
And you, the old man shouted back, are like a locust,
   bursting
Out of its shabby coat, or Sthenelus shorn of his effects.
All applauded but Theophrastus, who remarked with well-
   bred sneer;
Tell me, the old man asked him, what gives you such grand
   airs?
You're always apple-polishing the haves. One after another
The old man insulted the company, cracking country jokes
And telling boorish stories, nothing to do with anything.
Fully loaded he's off for home, beating everybody he meets.
Here he comes a-reeling. I'll get out of the way of his fists.
(*Enter* PHILOCLEON, *holding a torch in one hand and a
nude flute girl in the other. He is followed by angry
guests.*)

PHILOCLEON. Stop, get out, you silly clown
   If you keep following me through the town,
   With this torch in my hand I'll singe you brown.

GUEST. You senile delinquent, we'll never budge
   Tomorrow you can tell it to the judge.

PHILOCLEON. Judges and suits, old stuff and corny,
   Trials at law make me sick.
   Here's what I like, no canvassing a jury.
   Is that judge here? Give me a stick!
Up here, my golden little chickadee. Take hold of the rope
With your hand. Careful, it's worn out; but likes being
   rubbed.
See how cleverly I abstracted you when you were going
   to polish off
The company. In return you must be kind to the old thing.
But you won't pay up. You'll tease and trick me as you've
   done
To many another. But if you do your part now, I'll buy you
   off,
When my son's dead, sweetie, and you'll be my piggy.
Now I can't sign checks—I'm too young, and closely
   watched.
My little son's a hawk-eye, irritable, a cheese-paring skin-
   flint.
He's afraid I'll be spoiled, and I'm his only father.
There he is; it's to me he's running. Stay here and hold

the torches;

I'll catechize him, as he did me before my initiation.

BDELYCLEON. You randy old lecher—all agog for a young—coffin!

You won't get away with it, by Apollo, you won't.

PHILOCLEON. How you'd relish a marinated lawsuit!

BDELYCLEON. No cross-examination when you stole the girl from the company?

PHILOCLEON. What girl! You're raving. Stumbled in from hell?

BDELYCLEON. But there's the Dardanian creature beside you!

PHILOCLEON. That? Only a torch burning in the market place.

BDELYCLEON. She a torch?

PHILOCLEON. Yes, a torch; don't you see the color effects?

BDELYCLEON. Then what's the black in the middle?

PHILOCLEON. Pitch exuding with the heat.

BDELYCLEON. And isn't that a bottom?

PHILOCLEON. A knot in the pine.

BDELYCLEON. Knot? What are you talking about?—Come here, girl.

PHILOCLEON. Hey, what are you going to do?

BDELYCLEON. Take her away from you, because you are decayed and impotent.

PHILOCLEON. Listen to me. At the Olympics I saw old Ephudion fighting

Against Ascondas, splendidly. You'd better take care.

BDELYCLEON. You have learned sporting talk, haven't you?

(*Enter* BAKING GIRL, *with* CHAEREPHON.)

BAKING GIRL. Stand by me, in heaven's name! There's the man who ruined me.

Hit me with his torch, knocked ten obol-loaves down, then four more.

BDELYCLEON. See the trouble and lawsuits your toping brings?

PHILOCLEON. A few smart stories will straighten things; she'll be content.

BAKING GIRL. By the goddesses, you won't spoil the wares of Myrtia,

Daughter of Angkylion and Sostrate, and get away with it!

PHILOCLEON. Listen, ma'am, I'll tell you a pretty story.

BAKING GIRL. Not me, thank you.

PHILOCLEON. On his way home from dinner one evening, Aesop was barked at

By a bold, drunken bitch. Bitch, says he, you'd be smarter
To buy flour to bake, instead of that wicked tongue.

BAKING GIRL. You jeer me to boot! I summon you before the market inspectors

 For damage to merchandise. Chaerephon here is my witness.

PHILOCLEON. Dear me! Listen, this is a good one. Lasus and Simonides

 Were in competition. Said Lasus, I don't care.

BAKING GIRL. Is *that* so?

PHILOCLEON. And you, Chaerephon, will you testify for her, like pale Ino

 Hanging at Euripides' feet?

 (*Enter* COMPLAINANT.)

BDELYCLEON. Here comes another to summon you, and with a witness.

COMPLAINANT. Luckless me! Old man, I summon you for outrage.

BDELYCLEON. For outrage? Please don't. I'll make good whatever damages

 You claim, and be grateful to boot.

PHILOCLEON. I'll be glad to be reconciled. I confess assault and battery.

 Tell me, would you have me name the indemnity and be friends,

 Or would you rather name it?

COMPLAINANT. You name it; I want no troublesome lawsuits.

PHILOCLEON. A Sybarite fell out of his sulky and cracked his head:

 He was not much of a horseman. A friendly bystander said,

 Every man to his trade. You'd better see Dr. Pittalus.

BDELYCLEON. This is in keeping with the rest.

COMPLAINANT. Notice the response!

PHILOCLEON. Listen, don't go! A Sybarite woman once broke a box.

COMPLAINANT. Note this, witness!

PHILOCLEON. The box called a witness. Hang the witness. It's saner

 To buy a cord.

COMPLAINANT. Go on insulting me—till the Archon calls your case.

BDELYCLEON. You won't stay here, by Demeter. I'll hoist you and carry you—

PHILOCLEON. What are you doing?

BDELYCLEON. Out of here, inside—or the witnesses will lack complainants.

PHILOCLEON. The Delphians once charged Aesop—
BDELYCLEON. It doesn't interest me.
PHILOCLEON. With stealing the god's cup: he said the beetle—
BDELYCLEON. You and your beetles! I'll ruin you.

(BDELYCLEON *carries* PHILOCLEON *off*.)

CHORUS. Enviable is the old man's transformation
From harsh and crusty frugality;
He's profited from his education
In paths of ease and luxury.
It may be just a passing phase:
Ingrained ways are hard to change.
But many another has changed his ways
And learned an easier and wider range.
Praise unbounded to Philocleon's son
From me and all men perspicacious!
Love and admiration he has won
By filial piety and manners gracious.
A character so amiable is without peer:
My fondness for him is beyond comparing!
How skillfully did he the discussion steer
To adorn his parent with seemlier bearing.

(*Enter* XANTHIAS, *followed by* PHILOCLEON *and* BDELY-
CLEON.)

XANTHIAS. Dionysus! A desperate business has some demon
trundled
Into the house! When the old man guzzled unaccustomed
wine,
And heard the flute he was so enraptured he never stopped,
The night through, dancing the old steps Thespis first
produced.
He'll prove our tragedians are dotards, he says; presently
He's going to outdance them.
PHILOCLEON. Who by the entrance doth palely loiter?
XANTHIAS. The plague marches on.
PHILOCLEON. Barriers down! This is the first figure.
XANTHIAS. Of madness, perhaps.
PHILOCLEON. The powerful current contorts my sides, my
nostrils wheeze,
My vertebrae crack.
XANTHIAS. Take a dose of hellebore.
PHILOCLEON. Like a cock Phrynichus crouches low—
XANTHIAS. Soon you'll discharge.
PHILOCLEON. He kicks out heaven-high, his rump gapes.
XANTHIAS. Watch out!

PHILOCLEON. My joints whirl in their sockets.

BDELYCLEON. No, no, by Zeus! This is madness.

PHILOCLEON. Now I challenge all comers. Any tragedian that claims
He's a good dancer, come up and try a match with me.
Anyone? No one?

(*Enter, severally, the three stunted* SONS OF CARCINUS
["*Crab*"].)

BDELYCLEON. Here's one, alone.

PHILOCLEON. Who's the poor devil?

BDELYCLEON. Carcinus' son, the middle one.

PHILOCLEON. He'll be a casualty. I'll batter him with a tragic fling.
In rhythm he's a blank.

BDELYCLEON. Ah, but here comes his brother, another Carcinite tragedian.

PHILOCLEON. I've had crab enough for dinner.

BDELYCLEON. There's nothing but crab; here comes another Carcinite.

PHILOCLEON. What's this crawling in? A shrimp or a spider?

BDELYCLEON. He's a hermit crab, the smallest of the lot.
Writes tragedy.

PHILOCLEON. What a lucky father is Carcinus, what a brood
Of crested wrens! I must step out against them.
You get the pickle ready, in case I win.
Clear we now a space; unhindered let them pirouette.—
Proudly named offspring of the brine, by the seaside gambol and curvet.
By the strand of the unharvested main, ye brethren crustacean,
Nimbly twirl your feet in an arc, kick the high kick Phrynichean.
Let spectators enjoy a treat. Fling your legs up to the sky.
Twist, twirl, spin like a top, smack your belly and your thigh.
Carcinus himself now crabs it forward, the majestic ruler of the sea,
Rejoicing in his wriggling kinglets, proud of his proper progeny.
Dance your way out, if you please, to the door lead us prancing;
Never was a tragic chorus known to make its exit dancing.

(*Exeunt.*)

Peace

War weariness and despair of relief lead a farmer named Trygaeus to ascend to heaven on a beetle in order to procure an end to the war. The gods have washed their hands of the Greeks and left War to work his will. He has buried Peace, and the chorus eventually succeed in drawing her up, to the consternation of those who profit by war and the hearty satisfaction of all others. The text as we have it is probably a conflation of two editions, but it is full of charm and high spirits. The affectionate description of rustic festivals near the end of the play is a foreshadowing of pastoral.

CHARACTERS

Translated by B. B. Rogers

(Before TRYGAEUS' *farmhouse two slaves are seen kneading cakes of dung.)*

FIRST SERVANT. Bring, bring the beetle cake; quick there, quick! quick,

SECOND SERVANT. Here!

FIRST SERVANT.   Give it him, the abominable brute.

SECOND SERVANT. O may he never taste a daintier morsel!

FIRST SERVANT. Now bring another, shaped from asses' dung.

SECOND SERVANT. Here, here again.

FIRST SERVANT.   Where's that you brought just now?
He can't have eaten it.

SECOND SERVANT.   No; he trundled it
With his two feet, and bolted it entire.

FIRST SERVANT. Quick, quick, and beat up several, firm and tight.

SECOND SERVANT. O help me, scavengers, by all the Gods!
Or I shall choke and die before your eyes.

FIRST SERVANT. Another cake, a boy companion's bring him:
He wants one finelier molded.

SECOND SERVANT.   Here it is.
There's one advantage in this work, my masters:
No man will say I pick my dishes now.

FIRST SERVANT. Pah! more, bring more, another and another;
Keep kneading more.

SECOND SERVANT.   By Apollo, no, not I!
I can't endure this muck a moment longer;
I'll take and pitch the muck tub in and all.

FIRST SERVANT. Aye to the crows, and follow it yourself.

SECOND SERVANT. Can any one of you, I wonder, tell me
Where I can buy a nose not perforated?
There's no more loathly miserable task
Than to be mashing dung to feed a beetle.
A pig or dog will take its bit of muck
Just as it falls: but this conceited brute
Gives himself airs, and, bless you, he won't touch it,
Unless I mash it all day long, and serve it
As for a lady, in a rich round cake.
Now I'll peep in and see if he has done,
Holding the door, thus, that he mayn't observe me.
Aye, tuck away; go gobbling on, don't stop;
I hope you'll burst yourself before you know it.

Wretch! how he throws himself upon his food,
Squared like a wrestler, grappling with his jaws,
Twisting his head and hands, now here, now there,
For all the world like men who plait and weave
Those great thick ropes to tow the barges with.
'Tis a most stinking, foul, voracious brute.
Nor can I tell whose appanage he is:
I really think he can't be Aphrodite's,
Nor yet the Graces'.

FIRST SERVANT.   No? then whose?

SECOND SERVANT.   I take it
This is the sign of sulphur-bolting Zeus.
Now I suspect some pert young witling there
Is asking, *Well, but what's it all about?*
What can the beetle mean? And then I think
That some Ionian, sitting by, will answer,
Now, I've nae doubt but this is aimed at Cleon,
It eats the muck sae unco shamelessly.
But I will in, and give the beetle drink.

FIRST SERVANT. And I will tell the story to the boys,
And to the lads, and also to the men,
And to the great and mighty men among you,
And to the greatest mightiest men of all.
My master's mad; a novel kind of madness,
Not your old style, but quite a new invention.
For all day long he gazes at the sky,
His mouth wide open, thus; and rails at Zeus:
O Zeus, says he, *what seekest thou to do?*
Lay down thy besom, sweep not Hellas bare!

TRYGAEUS (*behind the scenes*). Ah me! Ah me!

SECOND SERVANT. Hush! for methinks I hear him speaking
    now.

TRYGAEUS (*behind the scenes*). O Zeus,
What wouldst thou with our people? Thou wilt drain
The lifeblood from our cities ere thou knowest!

FIRST SERVANT. Aye, there it is; that's just what I was saying:
Ye hear yourselves a sample of his ravings.
But what he did when first the frenzy seized him
I'll tell you: he kept muttering to himself,
Oh if I could but somehow get to Zeus!
With that he got thin scaling ladders made,
And tried by them to scramble up to heaven,
Till he came tumbling down, and cracked his skull.
Then yesterday he stole I know not whither,

And brought a huge Aetnaean beetle home,
And made me groom it, while he coaxed it down
Like a young favorite colt, and kept on saying,
Wee Pegasus, my flying thoroughbred,
Your wings must waft me straight away to Zeus!
Now I'll peep in and see what he's about.
Oh, mercy on us! neighbors! neighbors! help!
My master's got astride upon the beetle
And up they go ascending in the air.

TRYGAEUS. Fair and softly, my beastlet, at first.
Start not at once with a violent burst,
In the proud delight of your eager might,
Ere your joints with sweat are relaxed and wet
From the powerful swing of your stalwart wing.
And breathe not strong as we soar along;
If you can't refrain, you had best remain
Down here in the stalls of your master's halls.

SERVANT. O master of me! why how mad you must be!

TRYGAEUS. Keep silence! keep silence!

SERVANT. Why, where do you try so inanely to fly?

TRYGAEUS. My flight for the sake of all Hellas I take,
A novel and daring adventure preparing.

SERVANT. Why can't you remain at home, and be sane?

TRYGAEUS. O let not a word of ill omen be heard,
But greet me with blessings and cheers as I go,
And order mankind to be silent below;
And please to be sure with bricks to secure
All places receptive of dung and manure.

SERVANT. No, no; I won't keep still, unless you tell me
Whither you're flying off.

TRYGAEUS.   Whither, except
To visit Zeus in heaven?

SERVANT.   Whatever for?

TRYGAEUS. I'm going to ask him what he is going to do
About the Hellenic peoples, one and all.

SERVANT. And if he won't inform you?

TRYGAEUS.   I'll indict him
As giving Hellas over to the Medes.

SERVANT (*struggling with Trygaeus*). Not while I live, so help
me Dionysus!

TRYGAEUS. There is no way but this.

SERVANT.   Here! children! here!
Quick! quick! your father's stealing off to heaven,

Leaving you here deserted and forlorn.
Speak to him, plead with him, you ill-starred maidens.

GIRL. O Father, O Father, and can it be true
The tale that is come to our ears about you,
That along with the birds you are going to go,
And to leave us alone and be off to the crow?
Is it a fact, O my father? O tell me the truth if you love me.

TRYGAEUS. Yes, it appears so, my children: in truth, I am sorry to see you
Calling me dearest papa, and asking me bread for your dinner,
When I have got in the house not an atom of silver to buy it;
But if I ever return with success, ye shall soon be enjoying
Buns of enormous size, with strong fist sauce to improve them.

GIRL. And what's to be the method of your passage?
Ships will not do: they cannot go this journey.

TRYGAEUS. I ride a steed with wings: no ships for me.

GIRL. But what's the wit of harnessing a beetle
To ride on it to heaven, Papa, Papa?

TRYGAEUS. It is the only living thing with wings,
So Aesop says, that ever reached the Gods.

GIRL. O Father, Father, that's too good a story
That such a stinking brute should enter heaven!

TRYGAEUS. It went to take revenge upon the eagle,
And break her eggs, a many years ago.

GIRL. But should you not have harnessed Pegasus,
And so, in tragic style, approach the Gods?

TRYGAEUS. Nay, then I must have had supplies for two;
But now the very food I eat myself,
All this will presently be food for him.

GIRL. What if he fall in wintry watery waves,
How will his wings help extricate him then?

TRYGAEUS. Oh, I've a rudder all prepared for that:
My ship's a beetle sloop, of Naxian make.

GIRL. What bay will land you drifting drifting on?

TRYGAEUS. Why, in Peiraeus, there's the Beetle Bay.

GIRL. Yet, O be careful lest you tumble off,
And (lame for life) afford Euripides
A subject, and become a tragic hero.

TRYGAEUS. I'll see to that: good-by, good-by, my dears!
But you, for whom I toil and labor so,
Do for three days resist the calls of nature;

Since, if my beetle in the air should smell it,
He'll toss me headlong off, and turn to graze.
  Up, up, my Pegasus, merrily, cheerily,
    With ears complacent, while blithe and bold
    Your curbs shake out their clatter of gold.
(I wonder what in the world he means
By pointing his nose at those foul latrines.)
Rise, gallantly rise, from the earth to the skies,
And on with the beat of your pinion fleet
Till you come to Zeus in his heavenly seat.
From all your earthly supplies of dirt,
From ordure and muck your nostril avert.
Man! man in Peiraeus! you'll kill me I swear,
Committing a nuisance! good fellow, forbear;
Dig it down in the ground, scatter perfumes around,
  Heap, heap up the earth on the top,
Plant sweet-smelling thyme to encircle the mound,
  Bring myrrh on its summit to drop;
For if I through your folly shall tumble today,
  And my enterprise fail to succeed in,
Five talents the city of Chios shall pay
  On account of your breach—of good breeding.
(*The scene suddenly changes.*)
Zounds! how you scared me: I'm not joking now.
I say, scene-shifter, have a care of me.
You gave me quite a turn; and if you don't
Take care, I'm certain I shall feed my beetle.
But now, methinks, we must be near the Gods;
And sure enough there stand the halls of Zeus.
Oh, open! open! who's in waiting here?

HERMES. A breath of man steals o'er me: whence, whence
    comes it?
  O Heracles, what's this?

TRYGAEUS.   A beetle horse.

HERMES. O shameless miscreant, vagabond, and rogue,
  O miscreant, utter miscreant, worst of miscreants,
  How came you here, you worst of all the miscreants?
  Your name? what is it? speak!

TRYGAEUS.   The worst of miscreants.

HERMES. Your race? your country? answer!

TRYGAEUS.   Worst of miscreants.

HERMES. And who's your father?

TRYGAEUS.   Mine? the worst of miscreants.

HERMES. O by the Earth but you shall die the death
   Unless you tell me who and what you are.
TRYGAEUS. Trygaeus, an Athmonian, skilled in vines;
   No sycophant, no lover of disputes.
HERMES. Why are you come?
TRYGAEUS.   To offer you this meat.
HERMES. How did you get here, Wheedling?
TRYGAEUS.   Oho, Greedling!
   Then I'm not quite the worst of miscreants now.
   So just step in and summon Zeus.
HERMES.   O! O!
   When you're not likely to come *near* the Gods!
   They're gone: they left these quarters yesterday.
TRYGAEUS. Where on Earth are they?
HERMES.   Earth, indeed!
TRYGAEUS.   But where?
HERMES. Far, far away, close to Heaven's highest dome.
TRYGAEUS. How came they then to leave you here alone?
HERMES. I have to watch the little things they left,
   Pipkins and pannikins and trencherlets.
TRYGAEUS. And what's the reason that they went away?
HERMES. They were so vexed with Hellas: therefore here
   Where they were dwelling, they've established War,
   And given you up entirely to his will.
   But they themselves have settled up aloft,
   As high as they can go; that they no more
   May see your fightings or receive your prayers.
TRYGAEUS. Why have they treated us like that? do tell me.
HERMES. Because, though they were oftentimes for Peace,
   You always would have War. If the Laconians
   Achieved some slight advantage, they would say,
   Noo by the Twa sall master Attic catch it;
   Or if the Attics had their turn of luck,
   And the Laconians came to treat for peace,
   At once ye cried, *We're being taken in,*
   Athene! Zeus! we can't consent to this;
   They're sure to come again if we keep Pylus.
TRYGAEUS. Yes; that's exactly how we talked: exactly.
HERMES. So that I know not if ye e'er again
   Will see the face of Peace.
TRYGAEUS.   Why, where's she gone to?
HERMES. War has immured her in a deep deep pit.
TRYGAEUS. Where?

HERMES.   Here, beneath our feet. And you may see
  The heavy stones he piled about its mouth,
  That none should take her out.
TRYGAEUS.   I wish you'd tell me
  How he proposes now to deal with us.
HERMES. I only know that yester eve he brought
  Into this house a most gigantic mortar.
TRYGAEUS. What is he going to do with that, I wonder!
HERMES. He means to put the cities in and pound them.
  But I shall go. He's making such a din
  I think he's coming out.
TRYGAEUS.   Shoo! let me run
  Out of his way: methought that I myself
  Heard a great mortar's war-inspiring blast.
WAR. O mortals! mortals! wondrous-woeful mortals!
  How ye will suffer in your jaws directly!
TRYGAEUS. O King Apollo, what a great big mortar!
  Oh the mere look of War how bad it is!
  Is this the actual War from whom we flee,
  The dread tough War, the War upon the legs?
WAR (*throwing in leeks*). O Prasiae! O thrice wretched, five
    times wretched,
  And tens of times, how you'll be crushed today!
TRYGAEUS. Friends, this as yet is no concern of ours,
  This is a blow for the Laconian side.
WAR (*throwing in garlic*). O Megara! Megara! in another
    moment,
  How you'll be worn, and torn, and ground to salad!
TRYGAEUS. Good gracious! O what heavy, bitter tears
  He has thrown in to mix for Megara.
WAR (*throwing in cheese*). O Sicily! and you'll be ruined too.
TRYGAEUS. Ah, how that hapless state will soon be grated!
WAR. And now I'll pour some Attic honey in.
TRYGAEUS. Hey, there, I warn you, use some other honey:
  Be sparing of the Attic; that costs sixpence.
WAR. Ho, boy! boy! Riot!
RIOT.   What's your will?
WAR.   You'll catch it,
  You rascal, standing idle there! take that!
RIOT. Ugh, how it stings. O me! O me! why, master,
  Sure you've not primed your knuckles with the garlic?
WAR. Run in and get a pestle.
RIOT.   We've not got one;
  We only moved in yesterday, you know.

WAR. Then run at once and borrow one from Athens.

RIOT. I'll run by Zeus; or else I'm sure to catch it.

TRYGAEUS. What's to be done, my poor dear mortals, now?
Just see how terrible our danger is:
For if that varlet bring a pestle back,
War will sit down and pulverize our cities.
Heavens! may he perish, and not bring one back.

RIOT. You there!

WAR.   What! Don't you bring it?

RIOT.   Just look here, sir:
The pestle the Athenians had is lost,
The tanner fellow that disturbed all Hellas.

TRYGAEUS. O well done he, Athene, mighty mistress;
Well is he lost, and for the state's advantage,
Before they've mixed us up this bitter salad.

WAR. Then run away and fetch from Lacedaemon
Another pestle.

RIOT.   Yes, sir.

WAR.   Don't be long.

TRYGAEUS. Now is the crisis of our fate, my friends.
And if there's here a man initiate
In Samothrace, 'tis now the hour to pray
For the averting of—the varlet's feet.

RIOT. Alas! alas! and yet again, alas!

WAR. What ails you? don't you bring one now?

RIOT.   O Sir,
The Spartans too have lost their pestle now.

WAR. How so, you rascal?

RIOT.   Why, they lent it out
To friends up Thraceward, and they lost it there.

TRYGAEUS. And well done they! well done! Twin sons of Zeus!
Take courage, mortals: all may yet be well.

WAR. Pick up the things, and carry them away;
I'll go within and make myself a pestle.

TRYGAEUS. Now may I sing the ode that Datis made,
The ode he sang in ecstasy at noon,
Eh, sirs, I'm pleased, and joyed, and comforted.
Now, men of Hellas, now the hour has come
To throw away our troubles and our wars,
And, ere another pestle rise to stop us,
To pull out Peace, the joy of all mankind.
            O all ye farmers, merchants, artisans,
            O all ye craftsmen, aliens, sojourners,
            O all ye islanders, O all ye peoples,

Come with ropes, and spades, and crowbars, come in eager
    hurrying haste,

Now the cup of happy fortune, brothers, it is ours to taste.

CHORUS. Come then, heart and soul, my comrades, haste to
    win this great salvation,

Now or never, now if ever, come, the whole Hellenic na-
    tion!

Throw away your ranks and squadrons, throw your scarlet
    plagues away,

Lo, at length the day is dawning, Lamachus-detesting day!

O be thou our guide and leader, managing, presiding
    o'er us,

For I think I shan't give over in this noble task before us,

Till with levers, cranes, and pulleys once again to light we
    haul

Peace, the Goddess best and greatest, vineyard-lovingest of
    all.

TRYGAEUS. O be quiet! O be quiet! by your noisy loud delight
You will waken War, the demon, who is crouching out of
    sight.

CHORUS. O we joy, we joy, we joy, to hear your glorious procla-
    lamations,

So unlike that odious *Wanted at the camp with three days'*
    rations.

TRYGAEUS. Yet beware, beware, remember! Cerberus is down
    below:

He may come with fuss and fury (as when he was here you
    know),

Every obstacle and hindrance in the way of Peace to throw.

CHORUS. Who shall bear her, who shall tear her, from these
    loving arms away,

If I once can clasp and grasp her? O hurrah! hurrah! hurrah!

TRYGAEUS. Zounds! you'll surely be our ruin: stop your clamor,
    I entreat:

War will by and by come trampling everything beneath his
    feet.

CHORUS. Let him stamp, and tramp, and trample, let him do
    whate'er he will,

I am so immensely happy that I really can't be still.

TRYGAEUS. What the mischief! what's the matter? do not, by
    the Gods, I pray,

With your dancings and your prancings spoil our noble
    work today.

CHORUS. Really now I didn't mean to: no I didn't, I declare:

Quite without my will my ankles will perform this joyous air.

TRYGAEUS. Well, but don't go on at present; cease your dancing or you'll rue it.

CHORUS. Look, observe, I've really ceased it.

TRYGAEUS.   So you say, but still you do it.

CHORUS. Only once, I do beseech you; only just a single hop.

TRYGAEUS. Well then, one: make haste about it; only one, and then you stop.

CHORUS. Stop? of course we stop with pleasure if 'twill your designs assist.

TRYGAEUS. Well, but look: you're still proceeding.

CHORUS.   Just, by Zeus, one other twist.
Let me fling my right leg upward, and I'll really then refrain.

TRYGAEUS. This indulgence too I'll grant you, so you don't offend again.

CHORUS. Hah! but here's my left leg also: it must have its turn, 'tis plain.
(Dancing vigorously with both legs.)
I'm so happy, glad, delighted, getting rid of arms at last,
More than if, my youth renewing, I the slough of Age had cast.

TRYGAEUS. Well, but don't exult at present, for we're all uncertain still,
But, when once we come to hold her, then be merry if you will;
                    Then will be the time for laughing,
                    Shouting out in jovial glee,
                    Sailing, sleeping, feasting, quaffing,
                    All the public sights to see.
                    Then the Cottabus be playing,
                    Then be hip-hip-hip-hurrahing,
                    Pass the day and pass the night
                    Like a regular Sybarite.

CHORUS. O that it were yet my fortune those delightful days to see!
                    Woes enough I've had to bear,
                    Sorry pallets, trouble, care,
                    Such as fell to Phormio's share,
I would never more thereafter so morose and bitter be,
Nor a judge so stubborn-hearted, unrelenting, and severe;
                    You shall find me yielding then,
                    Quite a tender youth again,

When these weary times depart.
Long enough we've undergone
Toils and sorrows many a one,
Worn and spent and sick at heart,
From Lyceum, to Lyceum, trudging on with shield and
    spear.

Now then tell us what you would
Have us do, and we'll obey,
Since by fortune fair and good
You're our sovereign Lord today.

TRYGAEUS. Come let me see which way to move the stones.
HERMES. Rogue! miscreant! what are you up to now?
TRYGAEUS.   No harm;
  Everything's right, as Cillicon observed.
HEMES. Wretch! you shall die!
TRYGAEUS.   When it's my lot, of course,
  For being Hermes you'll use lots, I know.
HERMES. O you are doomed! doomed! doomed!
TRYGAEUS.   Yes? for what day?
HERMES. This very instant.
TRYGAEUS.   But I'm not prepared:
  I've bought no bread and cheese, as if to die.
HERMES. Ah, well, you're absolutely gone!
TRYGAEUS.   That's odd,
  To get such famous luck and yet not know it.
HERMES. Then don't you know that death's denounced by
    Zeus
  On all found digging here?
TRYGAEUS.   And is it so?
  And must I die indeed?
HERMES.   You must indeed.
TRYGAEUS. O then, I prithee, lend me half a crown.
  I'll buy a pig, and get initiate first.
HERMES. Ho! Zeus! Zeus! thunder crasher!
TRYGAEUS.   O pray don't.
  O by the heavenly powers don't peach upon us.
HERMES. No, no, I won't keep silence.
TRYGAEUS.   O pray do.
  O by the heavenly meat I brought you, master.
HERMES. Why, bless you, Zeus will quite demolish me
  If I don't shout and tell him all about it.
TRYGAEUS. O pray don't shout, my darling dearest Hermes.
  Don't stand gaping there, my comrades; are ye quite de-
    prived of speech?

What's the matter? speak, ye rascals! if you don't, he's safe
    to peach.

CHORUS. Do not, do not, mighty Hermes, do not, do not shout,
    I pray,

> If you e'er have tasted swine,
> Tasted sucking-pigs of mine,
> Which have soothed your throat divine,

Think upon it, think upon it, nor despise the deed today.

TRYGAEUS. King and master, won't you listen to the coaxing
    words they say?

CHORUS.   View us not with wrathful eye,
> Nor our humble prayers deny,
> From this dungeon let us hand her.
> O if you indeed detest,
> And abhor the sweeping crest
> And the eyebrows of Peisander,

Let us now, O God most gracious! let us carry Peace away.

> Then we'll glad processions bring,
> Then with sacrifices due,
> We will always, lord and king,
> We will always honor you.

TRYGAEUS. O sir, be pitiful, and heed their cry:
They never showed you such respect as now.

HERMES. Why, no; they never were such thieves as now.

TRYGAEUS. And then I'll tell you a tremendous secret,
A horrid dreadful plot against the Gods.

HERMES. Well, tell away: I'm open to conviction.

TRYGAEUS. 'Tis that the Moon and vile immoral Sun
Have long been plotting to your hurt: and now
They're giving Hellas up to the Barbarians.

HERMES. Why are they doing that?

TRYGAEUS.   Because, by Zeus!
We sacrifice to *you*, but those Barbarians
Only to *them*. So naturally they
Are very anxious that we all should perish,
And they get all the rites of all the Gods.

HERMES. Then that's the reason why they clipped the days,
And nibbled off their rounds, misguiding sinners.

TRYGAEUS. It is, it is: come, Hermes, lend a hand,
Help us to pull her out. And then for you
We'll celebrate the great Panathenaea,
And all the other rites of all the Gods,
Demeter, Zeus, Adonis, all for you;
And everywhere the cities saved from woe

Will sacrifice to you, the Savior Hermes.
Much, much besides you'll gain: and first of all
I give you this (*producing a gold cup*), a vessel for libations.

HERMES. Fie! how I soften at the sight of gold!
There, my men, the work's before you! I've got nothing more to say.
Quick, take up your spades, and enter, shoveling all the stones away.

CHORUS. Gladly, gladly will we do it, wisest of the Gods; and you,
Like a skilled superior craftsman, teach us what we ought to do.
I warrant, when the way we know, you'll find us anything but slow.

TRYGAEUS. Hold out the vessel, and we'll launch the work
With free libations and with holy prayers.

HERMES.   Pour libations.
              Silence! silence! pour libations.

TRYGAEUS. And as we pour we'll pray. O happy morn,
Be thou the source of every joy to Hellas!
And O may he who labors well today
Be never forced to bear a shield again!

CHORUS. No; may he spend his happy days in peace,
Stirring the fire, his mistress at his side.

TRYGAEUS. If there be any that delights in war,
King Dionysus, may he never cease
Picking out spearheads from his funny-bones.

CHORUS. If any, seeking to be made a Captain,
Hates to see Peace return, O may he ever
Fare in his battles like Cleonymus.

TRYGAEUS. If any merchant, selling spears or shields,
Would fain have battles, to improve his trade,
May he be seized by thieves and eat raw barley.

CHORUS. If any would-be General won't assist us,
Or any slave preparing to desert,
May he be flogged, and broken on the wheel.
But on ourselves all joy: hip, hip, hurrah!

TRYGAEUS. Don't talk of being hipped: hurrah's the word.

CHORUS. Hurrah! hurrah! hurrah's the word today.

TRYGAEUS (*pouring libations*). To Hermes, Love, Desire, the Hours, and Graces.

CHORUS. Not Ares?

TRYGAEUS (*with disgust*). No!

CHORUS.   Nor Enyalius?

TRYGAEUS.   No.

CHORUS. Now all set to, and labor at the ropes.

HERMES. Yo ho! pull away.

CHORUS. Pull away a little stronger.

HERMES. Yo ho! pull away.

CHORUS. Keep it up a little longer.

HERMES. Pull, pull, pull, pull.

TRYGAEUS. Ah they don't pull all alike.
　　Cease your craning: 'tis but feigning:
　　Pull, Boeotians! or I'll strike.

HERMES. Yo ho! pull away.

TRYGAEUS. Pull away, away, away.

CHORUS (to Trygaeus and Hermes). Verily you should be
　　helping us too.

TRYGAEUS (indignantly). Don't I strain, might and main,
　　Cling and swing, tug and haul?

CHORUS. Yet we don't advance at all.

TRYGAEUS. Now don't sit there and thwart us, Lamachus.
　　We don't require your Bugaboo, my man.

HERMES. These Argives, too, they give no help at all.
　　They only laugh at us, our toils and troubles,
　　And all the while take pay from either side.

TRYGAEUS. But the Laconians, comrade, pull like men.

HERMES. Ah, mark, 'tis only such as work in wood
　　That fain would help us: but the smith impedes.

TRYGAEUS. And the Megarians do no good: they pull, though,
　　Scrabbling away like ravenous puppy dogs.
　　Good lack! they're regularly starved and ruined.

CHORUS. We make no way, my comrades: we must try
　　A strong pull, and a long pull, all together.

HERMES. Yo ho! pull away.

TRYGAEUS. Keep it up a little longer.

HERMES. Yo ho! pull away.

TRYGAEUS. Yes, by Zeus! a little stronger.

CHORUS. Very slow, now we go.

TRYGAEUS. What a shameful dirty trick!
　　Some are working, others shirking,
　　Argives, ye shall feel the stick.

HERMES. Yo ho! pull away.

TRYGAEUS. Pull away, away, away.

CHORUS. Some of you still are designing us ill.

TRYGAEUS. Ye who fain Peace would gain,
　　Pull and strain, might and main.

CHORUS. Someone's hindering us again.

HERMES. Plague take you, men of Megara; get out!
  The Goddess hates you: she remembers well
  'Twas you that primed her up at first with garlic.
  Stop, stop, Athenians: shift your hold a little;
  It's no use pulling as you're now disposed.
  You don't do anything but go to law.
  No, if you really want to pull her out,
  Stand back a trifle farther toward the sea.

CHORUS. Come, let us farmers pull alone, and set our shoulders
  to it.

HERMES. Upon my word you're gaining ground: I think you're
  going to do it.

CHORUS. He says we're really gaining ground: cheer up, cheer
  up, my hearty.

TRYGAEUS. The farmers have it all themselves, and not another party.

CHORUS.   Pull again, pull, my men,
          Now we're gaining fast.
        Never slacken, put your back in,
          Here she comes at last.
      Pull, pull, pull, pull, every man, all he can;
          Pull, pull, pull, pull, pull,
        Pull, pull, pull, pull, all together.

(PEACE *is lifted out with her two attendants,* HARVESTHOME
and MAYFAIR.)

TRYGAEUS. Giver of grapes, O how shall I address you?
  O for a word ten thousand buckets big
  Wherewith to accost you: for I've none at hand.
  Good morning, Harvesthome: good morn, Mayfair.
  O what a lovely charming face, Mayfair!
  (*Kisses her.*)
  O what a breath! how fragrant to my heart,
  How sweet, how soft, with perfume and inaction.

HERMES. Not quite the odor of a knapsack, eh?

TRYGAEUS. Faugh! that odious pouch of odious men, I hate it.
  It has a smell of rancid-onion-whiffs;
  But *she* of harvests, banquets, festivals,
  Flutes, thrushes, plays, the odes of Sophocles,
  Euripidean wordlets.

HERMES.   O how dare you
  Slander her so: I'm sure she does not like
  That logic monger's wordy disputations.

TRYGAEUS (*continuing*). The bleating lambs, the ivy-leaf, the vat,
  Full-bosomed matrons hurrying to the farm,
  The tipsy maid, the drained and emptied flask,
  And many another blessing.

HERMES.   And look there,
  See how the reconciled cities greet and blend
  In peaceful intercourse, and laugh for joy;
  And that, too, though their eyes are swol'n and blackened,
  And all cling fast to cupping instruments.

TRYGAEUS. Yes, and survey the audience: by their looks
  You can discern their trades.

HERMES.   O dear! O dear!
  Don't you observe the man that makes the crests
  Tearing his hair? and yon's a pitchfork seller;
  Fie! how he fillips the sword cutler there.

TRYGAEUS. And see how pleased that sicklemaker looks,
  Joking and poking the spear burnisher.

HERMES. Now then give notice: let the farmers go.

TRYGAEUS. O yes! O yes! the farmers all may go
  Back to their homes, farm implements and all.
  You can leave your darts behind you: yea, for sword and
    spear shall cease.
  All things all around are teeming with the mellow gifts of
    Peace;
  Shout your Paeans, march away to labor in your fields
    today.

CHORUS. Day most welcome to the farmers and to all the just
    and true,
  Now I see you I am eager once again my vines to view,
  And the fig trees which I planted in my boyhood's early
    prime,
  I would fain salute and visit after such a weary time.

TRYGAEUS. First, then, comrades, to the Goddess be our grate-
    ful prayers addressed,
  Who has freed us from the Gorgons and the fear-inspiring
    crest.
  Next a little salt provision fit for country uses buy,
  Then with merry expedition homeward to the fields we'll
    hie.

HERMES. O Poseidon! fair their order, sweet their serried ranks
    to see:
  Right and tight, like rounded biscuits, or a thronged fes-
    tivity.

TRYGAEUS. Yes, by Zeus! the well-armed mattock seems to
   sparkle as we gaze,
And the burnished pitchforks glitter in the sun's delighted
   rays.
Very famously with those will they clear the vineyard rows.
So that I myself am eager homeward to my farm to go,
Breaking up the little furrows (long-neglected) with the
   hoe.

> Think of all the thousand pleasures,
> Comrades, which to Peace we owe,
> All the life of ease and comfort
> Which she gave us long ago:
> Figs and olives, wine and myrtles,
> Luscious fruits preserved and dried,
> Banks of fragrant violets, blowing
> By the crystal fountain's side;
> Scenes for which our hearts are yearning,
> Joys that we have missed so long—
> Comrades, here is Peace returning,
> Greet her back with dance and song!

CHORUS. Welcome, welcome, best and dearest, welcome, welcome, welcome home.

> We have looked and longed for thee,
> Looking, longing, wondrously,
> Once again our farms to see.

O the joy, the bliss, the rapture, really to behold thee come.
Thou wast aye our chief enjoyment, thou wast aye our
   greatest gain.

> We who ply the farmer's trade
> Used, through thy benignant aid,
> All the joys of life to hold.
> Ah! the unbought pleasures free
> Which we erst received of thee
> In the merry days of old,

When thou wast our one salvation and our roasted barley
   grain.

> Now will all the tiny shoots,
> Sunny vine and fig-tree sweet,
> All the happy flowers and fruits,
> Laugh for joy thy steps to greet.

Ah, but where has Peace been hiding all these long and
   weary hours?

Hermes, teach us all the story, kindest of the heavenly Powers.

HERMES. O most sapient worthy farmers, listen now and understand,

If you fain would learn the reason, why it was she left the land.

Pheidias began the mischief, having come to grief and shame,

Pericles was next in order, fearing he might share the blame,

Dreading much your hasty temper, and your savage bull-dog ways,

So before misfortune reached him, he contrived a flame to raise,

By his Megara enactment setting all the world ablaze.

Such a bitter smoke ascended while the flames of war he blew,

That from every eye in Hellas everywhere the tears it drew.

Wailed the vine, and rent its branches, when the evil news it heard;

Butt on butt was dashed and shivered, by revenge and anger stirred;

There was none to stay the tumult; Peace in silence disappeared.

TRYGAEUS. By Apollo I had never heard these simple facts narrated,

No, nor knew she was so closely to our Pheidias related.

CHORUS. No, nor I, till just this moment: that is why she looks so fair.

Goodness me! how many things escape our notice I declare.

HERMES. Then when once the subject cities, over whom ye bare the sway,

Saw you at each other snarling, growling angrier day by day,

To escape the contributions, every willing nerve they strained,

And the chief Laconian leaders by enormous bribes they gained.

These at once for filthy lucre, guest deluders as they are,

Hustling out this gracious lady, greedily embraced the War.

But from this their own advantage ruin to their farmers came;

For from hence the eager galleys sailing forth with vengeful
    aim,
Swallowed up the figs of people who were not, perchance,
    to blame.

TRYGAEUS. Very justly, very justly! richly had they earned the
    blow,
Lopping down the dusky fig tree I had loved and nur-
    tured so.

CHORUS. Very justly, very justly! since my great capacious bin,
Ugh! the rascals came across it, took a stone, and stove it in.

HERMES. Then your laboring population, flocking in from vale
    and plain,
Never dreamed that, like the others, they themselves were
    sold for gain,
But as having lost their grape stones, and desiring figs to
    get,
Every one his rapt attention on the public speakers set;
These beheld you poor and famished, lacking all your home
    supplies,
Straight they pitchforked out the Goddess, scouting her
    with yells and cries,
Whensoe'er (for much she loved you) back she turned
    with wistful eyes.
Then with suits they vexed and harassed your substantial
    rich allies,
Whispering in your ear, *The fellow leans to Brasidas*, and
    you
Like a pack of hounds in chorus on the quivering victim
    flew.
Yea, the City, sick and pallid, shivering with disease and
    fright,
Any calumny they cast her, ate with ravenous appetite.
Till at last your friends perceiving whence their heavy
    wounds arose,
Stopped with gold the mouths of speakers who were such
    disastrous foes.
Thus the scoundrels throve and prospered: whilst distracted
    Hellas came
Unobserved to wrack and ruin: but the fellow most to
    blame
Was a tanner.

TRYGAEUS.   Softly, softly, Hermes master, say not so;
Let the man remain in silence, wheresoe'er he is, below;

For the man is ours no longer: he is all your own, you
  know;
> Therefore whatsoe'er you call him,
> Knave and slave while yet amongst us,
> Wrangler, jangler, false accuser,
> Troubler, muddler, all-confuser,
> You will all these names be calling
> One who now is yours alone.

(*To* PEACE.) But tell me, lady, why you stand so mute.

HERMES. Oh, she won't speak one word before this audience:
  No, no; they've wronged her far too much for that.

TRYGAEUS. Then won't she whisper, all alone, to you?

HERMES. Will you, my dearest, speak your thoughts to me?
  Come, of all ladies most shield-handle-hating.
  (*Affects to listen.*)
  Yes, good; that's their offense: I understand.
  Listen, spectators, why she blames you so.
  She says that after that affair in Pylos
  She came, unbidden, with a chest of treaties,
  And thrice you blackballed her in full assembly.

TRYGAEUS. We erred in that; but, lady, pardon us,
  For then our wits were swaddled up in skins.

HERMES. Well then, attend to what she asks me now.
  Who in your city loves her least? and who
  Loves her the best and shrinks from fighting most?

TRYGAEUS. Cleonymus, I think, by far the most.

HERMES. What sort of man is this Cleonymus
  In military matters?

TRYGAEUS.   Excellent:
  Only he's not his so-called father's son;
  For if he goes to battle, in a trice
  He proves himself a castaway—of shields.

HERMES. Still further listen what she asks me now.
  Who is it now that sways the Assembly stone?

TRYGAEUS. Hyperbolus at present holds the place.
  But how now, Mistress? Why avert your eyes?

HERMES. She turns away in anger from the people,
  For taking to itself so vile a leader.

TRYGAEUS. He's a mere makeshift: we'll not use him now.
  'Twas that the people, bare and stripped of leaders,
  Just caught him up to gird itself withal.

HERMES. She asks how this can benefit the state.

TRYGAEUS. 'Twill make our counsels brighter.

HERMES.   Will it? how?

TRYGAEUS. Because he deals in lamps: before he came
  We all were groping in the dark, but now
  His lamps may give our council board some light.
HERMES. Oh! oh!
  What things she wants to know!
TRYGAEUS.   What sort of things?
HERMES. All the old things existing when she left.
  And first, she asks if Sophocles be well.
TRYGAEUS. He's well, but strangely metamorphosed.
HERMES.   How?
TRYGAEUS. He's now Simonides, not Sophocles.
HERMES. What do you mean?
TRYGAEUS.   He's grown so old and sordid,
  He'd put to sea upon a sieve for money.
HERMES. Lives the old wit Cratinus?
TRYGAEUS.   No; he perished
  When the Laconians made their raid.
HERMES.   How so?
TRYGAEUS. Swooned dead away: he could not bear to see
  A jolly butt of wine all smashed and wasted.
  Much, much beside we've suffered; wherefore, lady,
  We'll never never let you go again.
HERMES. Then on these terms I'll give you Harvesthome
  To be your bride and partner in your fields.
  Take her to wife, and propagate young vines.
TRYGAEUS. O Harvesthome! come here and let me kiss you.
  But, Hermes, won't it hurt me if I make
  Too free with fruits of Harvesthome at first?
HERMES. Not if you add a dose of pennyroyal.
  But, since you're going, please to take Mayfair
  Back to the Council, whose of old she was.
TRYGAEUS. O happy Council to possess Mayfair!
  O what a three days' carnival you'll have!
  What soup! what tripe! what delicate tender meat!
  But fare thee well, dear Hermes.
HERMES.   And do you
  Farewell, dear mortal, and remember me.
TRYGAEUS. Home, home, my beetle! let us now fly home.
HERMES. Your beetle's gone, my friend.
TRYGAEUS.   Why, where's he gone to?
HERMES. Yoked to the car of Zeus, he bears the thunder.
TRYGAEUS. What will he get to eat, poor creature, there?
HERMES. Why, Ganymede's ambrosia, to be sure.
TRYGAEUS. And how shall I get down?

HERMES.　　　　　　　　　　　　　O well enough.
There, by the side of Peace.

TRYGAEUS.　　　　　　　　　Now girls, now girls,
Keep close to me: our youngsters I well know
Are sore all over for the love of you.

CHORUS. Yes, go, and good fortune escort you, my friend;
　　meanwhile the machines and the wraps,
We'll give to our faithful attendants to guard, for a number
　　of dissolute chaps
Are sure to be lurking about on the stage, to pilfer and
　　plunder and steal;
Here, take them and watch them and keep them with care,
　　while we to the audience reveal
　　　The mind of our Play, and whatever we may
　　　By our native acumen be prompted to say.

'Twere proper and right for the Ushers to smite, if ever a
　　bard, we confess,
Were to fill with the praise of himself and his plays our
　　own anapaestic address.
But if ever, O daughter of Zeus, it were fit with honor
　　and praise to adorn
A Chorus Instructor, the ablest of men, the noblest that
　　ever was born,
Our Poet is free to acknowledge that he is deserving of
　　high commendation:
It was he that advancing, unaided, alone, compelled the
　　immediate cessation
Of the jokes which his rivals were cutting at rags, and the
　　battles they waged with the lice.
It was he that indignantly swept from the stage the paltry
　　ignoble device
Of a Heracles needy and seedy and greedy, a vagabond
　　sturdy and stout,
Now baking his bread, now swindling instead, now beaten
　　and battered about.
And freedom he gave to the lachrymose slave who was
　　wont with a howl to rush in,
And all for the sake of a joke which they make on the
　　wounds that disfigure his skin:
Why, how now, my poor knave? so they bawl to the slave,
　　has the whipcord invaded your back,
Spreading havoc around, hacking trees to the ground, with
　　a savage resistless attack?

Such vulgar contemptible lumber at once he bade from the
    drama depart,
And then, like an edifice stately and grand, he raised and
    ennobled the Art.
High thoughts and high language he brought on the stage,
    a humor exalted and rare,
Nor stooped with a scurrilous jest to assail some small man-
    and-woman affair.
No, he at the mightiest quarry of all with the soul of a
    Heracles flew,
And he braved the vile scent of the tan-pit, and went
    through foul-mouthed revilings for you.
And I at the outset came down in the lists with the jaggèd-
    fanged monster to fight,
Whose eyeballs were lurid and glaring with flames of
    Cynna's detestable light;
And around his forehead the thin forked tongues of a hun-
    dred sycophants quiver,
And his smell was the smell of a seal, and his voice was a
    brawling tempestuous River,
And his hinder parts like a furnace appeared, and a goblin's
    uncleansable liver.
But I recked not the least for the look of the beast; I never
    desponded or quailed,
And I fought for the safety of you and the Isles; I gallantly
    fought and prevailed.
You therefore should heed and remember the deed, and
    afford me my guerdon today,
For I never went off to make love to the boys in the schools
    of athletic display
Heretofore when I gained the theatrical prize: but I packed
    up my traps and departed,
Having caused you great joy and but little annoy, and
    mightily pleased the truehearted.

    It is right then for all, young and old, great and small,
        Henceforth of my side and my party to be,
    And each bald-headed man should do all that he can
        That the prize be awarded to me.
    For be sure if this play be triumphant today,
That whene'er you recline at the feast or the wine,
        Your neighbor will say,

Give this to the bald-head, give that to the bald-head,
    And take not away
That sweetmeat, that cake, but present and bestow it
On the man with the brow of our wonderful Poet!

Muse having driven afar this terrible business of war,
    Join with Me the chorus.
Come singing of Nuptials divine and earthly banquets,
Singing the joys of the blessed: this of old to Thee belongs.
    But and if Carcinus coming
  Ask thee to join with his sons in choral dances,
    Hearken not, come not, stand not
    As an ally beside them,
    Think of them all as merely
Little domestical quails, ballet dancers with wallet necks,
Nipped from the droppings of goats, small, stunted, ma-
   chinery hunters.
  Yea, for their father declared that the drama which
    Passed all his hopes, in the evening
    By the cat was strangled.

These are the songs of the fair sweet Graces with beautiful
   hair,
    Which it well beseemeth
This poet of wisdom to chant, while softly resting
Warbles the swallow of spring; and Morsimus no chorus
   gains,
    No, nor Melanthius either.
Well I remember his shrill discordant chatter,
    When the tragedians' chorus
    He and his brother tutored,
    Both of them being merely
Gorgons, devourers of sweets, skate worshipers, and har-
   pies,
Pests of old maids, rank fetid as goats, destroyers of fishes.
Thou having spit on them largely and heavily,
    Join in the festival dances,
    Heavenly Muse, beside me.

TRYGAEUS. O what a job it was to reach the Gods!
  I know I'm right fatigued in both my legs.
  How small ye seemed down here! why from above
  Methought ye looked as bad as bad could be,
  But here ye look considerably worse.

SERVANT. What, master, *you* returned!

TRYGAEUS.   So I'm informed.

SERVANT. What have you got?

TRYGAEUS.   Got? pains in both my legs.
Faith! it's a rare long way.

SERVANT.   Nay, tell me,

TRYGAEUS.   What?

SERVANT. Did you see any wandering in the air
Besides yourself?

TRYGAEUS.   No; nothing much to speak of,
Two or three souls of dithyrambic poets.

SERVANT. What were they after?

TRYGAEUS.   Flitting round for odes,
Those floating-on-high-in-the-airy-sky affairs.

SERVANT. Then 'tisn't true what people say about it,
That when we die, we straightway turn to stars?

TRYGAEUS. O yes it is.

SERVANT.   And who's the star there now?

TRYGAEUS. Ion of Chios, who on earth composed
Star o' the Morn, and when he came there, all
At once saluted him as *Star o' the Morn*.

SERVANT. And did you learn about those falling stars
Which sparkle as they run?

TRYGAEUS.   Yes, those are some
Of the rich stars returning home from supper,
Lanterns in hand, and in the lanterns fire.
But take this girl at once, and lead her in;
Deluge the bath, and make the water warm;
Then spread the nuptial couch for her and me:
And when you've finished, hither come again.
Meanwhile I'll give this other to the Council.

SERVANT. Whence have you brought these maidens?

TRYGAEUS.   Whence? from heaven.

SERVANT. I wouldn't give three halfpence for the Gods
If they keep brothels as we mortals do.

TRYGAEUS. No, no; yet even there some live by these.

SERVANT. Come on then, mistress: tell me, must I give her
Nothing to eat?

TRYGAEUS.   O no, she will not touch
Our wheat and barley bread: her wont has been
To lap ambrosia with the Gods in heaven.

SERVANT. Lap! we'll prepare her lap then here on earth.

CHORUS.   O what a lucky old man!

           Truly the whole of your plan
           Prospers as well as it can.

TRYGAEUS. I really wonder what you'll say when I'm a bride-
    groom spruce and gay.

CHORUS.   All men will gaze with delight.
          Old as you are you'll be quite
          Youthful and perfumed and bright.

TRYGAEUS. What, when you see her tender waist by these
    encircling arms embraced?

CHORUS. Why then we'll think you happier far than Carcinus's
    twistlings are.

TRYGAEUS.   And justly too, methinks, for I
          On beetleback essayed to fly,
          And rescued Hellas, worn with strife,
            And stored your life
          With pleasant joys of home and wife,
           With country mirth and leisure.

SERVANT. Well, sir, the girl has bathed and looks divinely:
    They mix the puddings, and they've made the cakes;
    Everything's done: we only want the husband.

TRYGAEUS. Come then and let us give Mayfair at once
    Up to the Council.

SERVANT.   What do you say? Mayfair!
    Is this May Fair? the Fair we kept at Brauron,
    When we were fresh and mellow, years ago?

TRYGAEUS. Aye, and 'twas work enough to catch her.

SERVANT.   O!
    How neat her pasterns, quite a five-year-old.

TRYGAEUS (looking round upon the audience). Now, have you
    any there that I can trust?
    One who will lead her safely to the Council?
    (To the SERVANT.)
    What are you scribbling?

SERVANT.   Marking out a place
    To pitch my tent in, at the Isthmian games.

TRYGAEUS. Well, is there none can take her? come to me then;
    I'll go myself, and set you down among them.

SERVANT. Here's someone making signs.

TRYGAEUS.   Who is it?

SERVANT.   Who!
    Ariphrades: he wants her brought his way.

TRYGAEUS. No: I can't bear his dirty, sloppy way;
    So come to me, and lay those parcels down.
    (Leads her forward toward Bouleutikon.)

Councillors! Magistrates! behold Mayfair!
And O remember what a deal of fun
That word implies: what pastimes and what feasts.
See here's a famous kitchen range she brings;
'Tis blacked a little: for in times of Peace
The jovial Council kept its saucepans there.
Take her and welcome her with joy; and then
Tomorrow morning let the sports begin:
Then we'll enjoy the Fair in every fashion,
With boxing matches and with wrestling bouts,
And tricks and games, while striplings soused in oil
Try the pancratium, fist and leg combined.
Then the third day from this, we'll hold the races;
The eager jockeys riding: the great cars
Puffing and blowing through the lists, till dashed
Full on some turning post, they reel and fall
Over and over: everywhere you see
The hapless coachmen wallowing on the plain.
You lucky Magistrate, receive Mayfair!
Just look, how pleased he seems to introduce her;
You would not though, if you got nothing by it,
No, you'd be holding a Reception day:

CHORUS.   Truly we envy your fate:
            All must allow you're a great
            Blessing and boon to the state.

TRYGAEUS. Ah, when your grapes you gather in, you'll know
    what sort of friend I've been.

CHORUS.   Nay, but already 'tis known;
            Yea, for already we own
            You have preserved us alone.

TRYGAEUS. I think you'll think so when you drain a bowl of
    new made wine again.

CHORUS. We'll always hold you first and best, except the Gods
    the ever blest.

TRYGAEUS.   In truth you owe a deal to me,
            Trygaeus, sprung from Athmone,
            For I've released the burgher crew
                And farmers too
            From toils and troubles not a few;
              Hyperbolus I've done for.

SERVANT. Now what's the next thing that we have to do?

TRYGAEUS. What but to dedicate her shrine with pipkins?

SERVANT. With pipkins! like a wretched little Hermes!

TRYGAEUS. Well then, what think you of a stall-fed bull?

SERVANT. A bull? O no! no need of bull-works now.

TRYGAEUS. Well then, a great fat pig?

SERVANT. 　　　　　　　　　No, no.

TRYGAEUS. 　　　　　　　　　　　　　　Why not?

SERVANT. Lest, like Theagenes, we grow quite piggish.

TRYGAEUS. What other victim shall we have?

SERVANT. 　　　　　　　　　　　A baa-lamb.

TRYGAEUS. A baa-lamb!

SERVANT. 　　　　　　Yes, by Zeus!

TRYGAEUS. 　　　　　　　　　But that's Ionic,
　　That word is.

SERVANT. 　　　　　All the better: then, you see,
　　If any speak for war, the whole assembly
　　Will talk Ionic and cry out Bah! Bah!

TRYGAEUS. Good, very good.

SERVANT. 　　　　　　　　And they'll be milder so,
　　And we shall live like lambs among ourselves,
　　And be much gentler toward our dear allies.

TRYGAEUS. There, get the sheep as quickly as you can,
　　I'll find an altar for the sacrifice.

CHORUS. Sure each design, when God and fortune speed it,
　　Succeeds to our mind, what is wanted we find
　　　　　　Just at the moment we need it.

TRYGAEUS. The truths you mention none can doubt, for see
　　I've brought the altar out.

CHORUS. 　　　　Then hasten the task to perform:
　　　　War, with its vehement storm,
　　　　Seems for the instant to cease;
　　　　　　Its soughings decrease,
　　　　　　Shifting and veering to Peace.

TRYGAEUS. Well, here's the basket ready stored with barley
　　grain, and wreath, and sword.
　　And here's the pan of sacred fire: the sheep alone we now
　　require.

CHORUS. 　　　Make haste, make haste: if Chaeris see,
　　　　He'll come here uninvited,
　　　　And pipe and blow to that degree,
　　　　His windy labors needs must be
　　　　　　By some small gift requited.

TRYGAEUS. Here, take the basket and the lustral water,
　　And pace the altar round from left to right.

SERVANT. See, I've been round: now tell me something else.

TRYGAEUS. Then next I'll take this torch and dip it in.

　　(*To the victim, as he sprinkles it.*) Shake your head, sirrah.

(*To the* SERVANT.) Bring the barley, you;
I'll hold the basin while you wash your hands.
Now throw the corn among the audience.

SERVANT.   There.

TRYGAEUS. What! thrown it out already?

SERVANT.   Yes, by Hermes!
There's not a single man among them all
But has at least one corn, I'll warrant you.

TRYGAEUS. Aye, but the women?

SERVANT.   If they haven't got one,
They'll get it by and by.

TRYGAEUS.   Now, then to prayers:
Who's here? where are our honest simple folk?

SERVANT. Here: these are simple folk; I'll give to them.

TRYGAEUS. What, these good simple folk?

SERVANT.   I'faith I think so;
Who, though we've poured such lots of water on them,
Yet stand stock still, and never budge a step.

TRYGAEUS. Come, let us pray, no dallying; let us pray.

    O Peace most holy, august, serene,
      O heavenborn queen
    Of the dance and song and the bridal throng,
    These offerings take which thy votaries make.

SERVANT. O mistress dear, we beseech you hear,
    And act not you as the wantons do:
    They love to spy at the passers by
      Through the half-closed door,
    And then if you heed, they are gone with speed;
    If you turn away, in an instant they
    Peep out once more as they did before.
    But deal not thus unkindly with us.

TRYGAEUS. No, by Zeus! but display in a true honest way
    Your perfect entire full form to our view,
      Who with constant desire
    These thirteen long years have been pining for you.
When our fightings are stayed, and our tumults allayed,
    We will hail thee a Lady for ever:
And O put an end to the whispers of doubt,
    These wonderful clever
Ingenious suspicions we bandy about;
And solder and glue the Hellenes anew
    With the old-fashioned true
Elixir of love, and attemper our mind
With thoughts of each other more genial and kind.

Moreover we pray that our market place may
Be furnished each day with a goodly display,
And for garlic, and cucumbers early and rare,
Pomegranates, and apples in heaps to be there,
And wee little coats for our servants to wear.
And Boeotia to send us her pigeons and widgeons,
And her geese and her plovers: and plentiful creels
Once more from Copaïs to journey with eels,
And for us to be hustling, and tussling, and bustling,
With Morychus, Teleas, Glaucetes, all
The gluttons together besieging the stall,
To purchase the fish: and then I could wish
For Melanthius to come too late for the fair,
And for *them* to be sold, and for *him* to despair,
And out of his own Medea a groan
    Of anguish to borrow,
I perish! I perish! bereaved of my sweet,
My treasure, my darling, embowered in her beet;
    And for all men to laugh at his sorrow.
These things we pray; O mistress, grant us these.

SERVANT. Here, take the cleaver: now with clever skill
    Slaughter the sheep.

TRYGAEUS.   No, no, I must not.

SERVANT.   Why?

TRYGAEUS. Peace loves not, friend, the sight of victims slain:
    Hers is a bloodless altar. Take it in,
    And when you have slain it, bring the thighs out here.
    There: now the sheep is—saved for the Choregus.

CHORUS. But you the while, outside with us remaining,
    Lay, handy and quick, these fagots of stick,
        Whatever is needful ordaining.

TRYGAEUS. Now don't you think I have laid the wood as well
    as most diviners could?

CHORUS (*admiringly*). Yes! Just what I looked for from you.
        All that is wise you can do.
        All things that daring and skill
            Suffice to fulfill
        You can perform if you will.

TRYGAEUS (*coughing*). Dear! how this lighted brand is smok-
    ing, your Stilbides is nearly choking;
    I'll bring the table out with speed; a servant's help we shall
    not need.

CHORUS. Sure all with admiration true
        Will praise a man so clever,

Who passed such toils and dangers through,
And saved the holy city too;
An envied name forever.

SERVANT. I've done the job; here, take and cook the thighs
While I go fetch the innards and the cates.

TRYGAEUS. I'll see to this: you should have come before.

SERVANT. Well, here I am: I'm sure I've not been long.

TRYGAEUS. Take these, and roast them nicely: here's a fellow
Coming this way, with laurel round his head.
Who can he be?

SERVANT.   He looks an arrant humbug.
Some seer, I think.

TRYGAEUS.   No, no; 'tis Hierocles,
The oracle-mongering chap from Oreus town.

SERVANT. What brings him here?

TRYGAEUS.   'Tis evident he comes
To raise some opposition to our truces.

SERVANT. No, 'tis the savor of the roast attracts him.

TRYGAEUS. Don't let us seem to notice him.

SERVANT.   All right.

HIEROCLES. What is this sacrifice, and made to whom?

TRYGAEUS. Roast on: don't speak: hands off the haunch, remember.

HIEROCLES. Will you not say to whom you sacrifice?
This tail looks right.

SERVANT.   Sweet Peace! it does indeed.

HIEROCLES. Now then begin and hand the firstlings here.

TRYGAEUS. It must be roasted first.

HIEROCLES.   It's roasted now.

TRYGAEUS. You're overbusy, man, whoe'er you are.
Cut on: why, where's the table? bring the wine.

HIEROCLES. The tongue requires a separate cut.

TRYGAEUS.   We know.
Now will you please?

HIEROCLES.   Yes, tell me.

TRYGAEUS.   Mind your business.
Don't talk to us: we sacrifice to Peace.

HIEROCLES. O you pitiful fools!

TRYGAEUS.   Pray speak for yourself, my good fellow.

HIEROCLES. You who, blindly perverse, with the will of the
Gods unacquainted,
Dare to traffic for Peace, true men with truculent monkeys.

SERVANT. O! O! O!

TRYGAEUS.   What's the matter?

SERVANT.   I like his truculent monkeys.

HIEROCLES. Silly and timorous gulls, you have trusted the
children of foxes

Crafty of mind and crafty of soul.

TRYGAEUS.   You utter impostor,

O that your lungs were as hot as a piece of the meat I am
roasting!

HIEROCLES. If the prophetic nymphs have not been imposing
on Bakis,

No, nor Bakis on men, nor the nymphs, I repeat, upon
Bakis,

TRYGAEUS. O perdition be yours if you don't have done with
your Bakis!

HIEROCLES. Then is the hour not come for the fetters of Peace
to be loosened.

No; for before that hour—

TRYGAEUS.   This peace is with salt to be sprinkled.

HIEROCLES. Yea, it is far from the mind of the Ever-blessed
Immortals

That we should cease from the strife, till the wolf and the
lamb be united.

TRYGAEUS. How, you scoundrel accurst, can the wolf and the
lamb be united?

HIEROCLES. Does not the beetle, alarmed, emit a most horrible odor?

Does not the wagtail yapper produce blind young in its
hurry?

So is the hour not come for Peace to be sanctioned between us.

TRYGAEUS. What then, what is to come? Are we never to cease
from the battle,

Always to chance it out, which most can enfeeble the other,

When we might both join hands, and share the dominion
of Hellas?

HIEROCLES. Can you tutor the crab to advance straight forward? you cannot.

TRYGAEUS. Will you dine any more in the Hall of Assembly?
you will not;

No, nor ever again shall your cheating knavery prosper.

HIEROCLES. You will never be able to smooth the spines of the
hedgehog.

TRYGAEUS. Will you never desist bamboozling the people of
Athens?

HIEROCLES. Say, what oracle taught you to burn the thighs
of the victim?

TRYGAEUS. This, the wisest and best, delivered by Homer
the poet:

> *When they had driven afar the detestable cloud of the*
> *battle,*
> *Then they established Peace, and welcomed her back with*
> *oblations.*
> *Duly the thighs they burned, and ate the tripe and the*
> *innards,*
> *Then poured out the libations; and I was the guide and*
> *the leader;*
> *None to the soothsayer gave the shining beautiful goblet.*

HIEROCLES. Nothing I know of these: these did not come from
the Sibyl.

TRYGAEUS. Nay, but wisely and well spake Homer the excellent poet:

> *Tribeless, lawless, and heartless is he that delights in*
> *bloodshed,*
> *Bloodshed of kith and kin, heart-sickening, horrible, hate-*
> *ful!*

HIEROCLES. Take heed, or a kite, by a trick your attention
beguiling,

> Down with a swoop may pounce.

TRYGAEUS (*to the* SERVANT). Ah! take heed really and truly.
That's an alarming hint: it bodes no good to the innards.
Pour the libation in, and hand me a piece of the innards.

HIEROCLES. Nay, but if such is the plan, I too for myself will
be caterer.

TRYGAEUS.   Pour libation; pour libation!

HIEROCLES. Pour it in also for me, and reach me a share of the
innards.

TRYGAEUS. That is far from the mind of the Ever-blessed
Immortals.

Yea, for before that hour—*you* go, *we'll* pour the libation.
Holy and reverend Peace, abide with thy servants for ever.

HIEROCLES. Now, fetch hither the tongue.

TRYGAEUS.   You, take yours off I'd advise you.

HIEROCLES. Pour the libation in.

TRYGAEUS.   Take that to assist the libation.

HIEROCLES. What! will none of you give me some meat?

TRYGAEUS.   'Tis strictly forbidden.
You no innards can have till the wolf and the lamb be
united.

HIEROCLES. Do, by your knees I beseech.

TRYGAEUS.   But fruitless are all your beseechings.
  You will never be able to smooth the spines of the hedge-
    hog.
  Come now, spectators, won't you share the mess
  Along with us?

HIEROCLES.   And I?

TRYGAEUS.   You? eat your Sibyl.

HIEROCLES. No, by the Earth, you two shan't feast alone!
  I'll snatch a piece away: 'tis all in common.

TRYGAEUS. Strike Bakis, strike!

HIEROCLES.   I call them all to witness—

TRYGAEUS. And so do I, that you're a rogue and glutton.
  Lay on him with the stick: strike, strike the rascal!

SERVANT. You manage that, while I peel off the skins
  Which he has gathered by his cozening tricks.
  Now, sacrificer, off with all your skins.
  What, won't you? here's a crow from Oreus town!
  Back to Elymnium! flutter off: shoo! shoo!

CHORUS.   What a pleasure, what a treasure,
        What a great delight to me,
        From the cheese and from the onions
        And the helmet to be free.
        For I can't enjoy a battle,
        But I love to pass my days
        With my wine and boon companions
        Round the merry, merry blaze,
        When the logs are dry and seasoned,
        And the fire is burning bright,
        And I roast the peas and chestnuts
        In the embers all alight,
        —Flirting too with Thratta
        When my wife is out of sight.

Ah, there's nothing half so sweet as when the seed is in the
  ground,
God a gracious rain is sending, and a neighbor saunters
  round.
O Comarchides! he hails me: *how shall we enjoy the hours?*
*Drinking seems to suit my fancy, what with these benig-
nant showers.*
*Therefore let three quarts, my mistress, of your kidney
beans be fried,*

*Mix them nicely up with barley, and your choicest figs
    provide;*
Syra run and shout to Manes, call him in without delay,
*'Tis no time to stand and dawdle pruning out the vines
    today,*
*Nor to break the clods about them, now the ground is soak-
    ing through.*
*Bring me out from home the field fare, bring me out the
    siskins two,*
*Then there ought to be some beestings, four good plates of
    hare beside*
(Hah! unless the cat purloined them yesterday at eventide;
*Something scuffled in the pantry, something made a noise
    and fuss);*
*If you find them, one's for father, bring the other three
    to us.*
*Ask Aeschinades to send us myrtle branches green and
    strong;*
Bid Charinades attend us, shouting as you pass along.

> *Then we'll sit and drink together,*
> *God the while refreshing, blessing*
> > *All the labor of our hands.*

> O to watch the grape of Lemnos
> Swelling out its purple skin,
> When the merry little warblings
> Of the Chirruper begin;
> For the Lemnian ripens early.
> And I watch the juicy fig
> Till at last I pick and eat it
> When it hangeth soft and big;
> And I bless the friendly seasons
> Which have made a fruit so prime,
> And I mix a pleasant mixture,
> Grating in a lot of thyme,
> —Growing fat and hearty
> In the genial summer clime.

This is better than a Captain hated of the Gods to see,
Triple-crested, scarlet-vested, scarlet bright as bright can
    be.
'Tis, he says, true Sardian tincture, which they warrant not
    to run;
But if e'er it gets to fighting, though his scarlet coat be on,

He himself becomes as pallid as the palest Cyzicene,
Running like a tawny cockhorse, he's the first to quit the
    scene;
Shake and quake his crests above him: I stood gaping
    while he flew.
Ah, but when at home they're stationed, things that can't
    be borne they do,
Making up the lists unfairly, striking out and putting down
Names at random. 'Tis tomorrow that the soldiers leave the
    town;
One poor wretch has bought no victuals, for he knew not
    he must go
Till he on Pandion's statue spied the list and found 'twas so,
Reading there his name inserted; off he scuds with aspect
    wry.
This is how they treat the farmers, but the burghers cer-
    tainly
Somewhat better: godless wretches, rogues with neither
    shame nor—shield,
Who one day, if God be willing, strict accounts to me shall
    yield.

        For they've wronged me much and sorely:
          Very lions in the city,
            Very foxes in the fight.

TRYGAEUS. Hillo! Hillo!
What lots are coming to the wedding supper!
Here, take this crest and wipe the tables down,
I've no more use for that, at all events.
And now serve up the thrushes and the cates,
And the hot rolls, and quantities of hare.

SICKLE-MAKER. Where, where's Trygaeus?
TRYGAEUS.   Stewing thrushes here.
SICKLE-MAKER. O, my best friend, Trygaeus! O what blessings
Your gift of Peace has brought us. Till today
No man would give one farthing for a sickle;
And now! I'm selling them two pounds apiece.
And my friend here sells casks for country use
Half a crown each. Trygaeus, freely take
As many casks and sickles as you please.
And take this too (*Giving money.*); out of our sales and
    gains
We bring you these, we two, as wedding presents.
TRYGAEUS. Well, lay your presents down, and hie you in
To join the marriage feast: here comes a man

Who trades in arms: he seems put out at something.

CREST-MAKER. O you've destroyed me root and branch, Trygaeus.

TRYGAEUS. How now, poor wretch! what ails you? got a crest-ache?

CREST-MAKER. You have destroyed my living and my trade, And this man's too, and yon spear-burnisher's.

TRYGAEUS. What shall I give you, then, for these two crests?

CREST-MAKER. What *will* you give?

TRYGAEUS. Faith, I'm ashamed to say: Come, there's a deal of work about this juncture; I'll give three quarts of raisins for the pair. 'Twill do to wipe my table down withal.

CREST-MAKER. Go in, then, go, and fetch the raisins out. Better have that than nothing, O my friend.

TRYGAEUS. Consume the things! here, take them, take them off. The hairs are dropping out; they're not worth having. Zounds! I'll not give one raisin for the pair.

BREASTPLATE-SELLER. O what's the use of this habergeon now? So splendidly got up: cost forty pounds.

TRYGAEUS. Well, well, you shan't lose anything by that: I'll buy it of you at its full cost price. 'Twill do superbly for my chamber pan.

BREASTPLATE-SELLER. Come, don't be mocking at my wares and me.

TRYGAEUS. Placing three stones anent it: ain't that clever?

BREASTPLATE-SELLER. And how, you blockhead, can you cleanse yourself?

TRYGAEUS. How? slip my hands in through the portholes, here, And here.

BREASTPLATE-SELLER. What, both at once!

TRYGAEUS. Yes; I'll not cheat. I'll have fair play: an arm for every hole.

BREASTPLATE-SELLER. Sure, you won't use a forty-pounder so.

TRYGAEUS. Why not, you rascal? Marry, I suppose My seat of honor's worth eight hundred shillings.

BREASTPLATE-SELLER. Well, fetch the silver out.

TRYGAEUS. Plague take the thing; It galls my stern: off with you: I won't buy it.

TRUMPETER. See, here's a trumpet, cost me two pounds ten: How in the world am I to use it now?

TRYGAEUS. I'll tell you how. Fill up this mouth with lead, Then fix a longish rod, here at the top, And there you'll have a dropping cottabus.

TRUMPETER. O me! he mocks me.

TRYGAEUS.   Here's another plan:
Pour in the lead as I advised before,
Then at the top suspend a pair of scales
With little cords, and there's a famous balance
To weigh out figs for laborers on the farm.

HELMET-SELLER. Thou hast destroyed me, dread unpitying
    Fate!
These helmets stood me in a good four pounds.
What am I now to do? who'll buy them now?

TRYGAEUS. Take them to Egypt: you can sell them there.
They're just the things they measure physic in.

TRUMPETER. O, helmet-seller, we are both undone.

TRYGAEUS. Why, *he's* received no hurt.

HELMET-SELLER.   Received no hurt!
Pray what's the use of all these helmets now?

TRYGAEUS. Just clap on each a pair of ears, like these,
They'll sell much better then than now they will.

HELMET-SELLER. O come away, spear-burnisher.

TRYGAEUS.   No, no.
I'm going to buy his spears: I really am.

SPEAR-BURNISHER. What are you going to give?

TRYGAEUS.   Saw them in two,
I'll buy them all for vine-poles, ten a penny.

SPEAR-BURNISHER. The man insults us; come away, my friend.

TRYGAEUS. Aye, go your way, for here come out the boys,
Those whom the guests have brought us; I suppose
They're going to practice what they're going to sing.
Come and stand here by me, my boy, and then
Let's hear you practice what you mean to sing.

FIRST BOY. *Sing of the younger blood, whose deeds—*

TRYGAEUS.   Plague take you, be quiet
Singing of deeds of blood: and that, you unfortunate ill-
    starred
Wretch, in the time of Peace; you're a shameful and
    ignorant blockhead.

BOY. *Slowly the hosts approached, till at length with a shock
    of encounter
Shield was dashed upon shield, and round-bossed buckler
    on buckler.*

TRYGAEUS. Buckler? you'd better be still: how dare you be
    talking of bucklers?

BOY. *Rose the rattle of war commingled with groans of the
    dying.*

TRYGAEUS. Groans of the dying? by great Dionysus, I'll make you repent it,

Singing of groans of the dying, especially such as are round-bossed.

BOY. What, then, what shall I sing? you, tell me the songs you delight in.

TRYGAEUS. *Then on the flesh of beeves they feasted;* something of *that* sort.

Then a repast they served, and whatever is best for a banquet.

BOY. *Then on the flesh of beeves they feasted, aweary of fighting;*

Then from the yoke they loosed the reeking necks of the horses.

TRYGAEUS. Good: they were tired of war, and so they feasted:

Sing on, O sing, how they were tired and feasted.

BOY. *Quickly, refreshed, they called for the casques.*

TRYGAEUS.   Casks? gladly, I warrant.

BOY. *Out from the towers they poured, and the roar of battle ascended.*

TRYGAEUS. Perdition seize you, boy, your wars and all!

You sing of nought but battles: who's your father?

BOY. Whose? mine?

TRYGAEUS.   Yes, yours, by Zeus!

BOY.   Why, Lamachus.

TRYGAEUS.   Ugh, out upon it!

Truly I marveled, and thought to myself as I heard your performance,

This is the son of some hacker, and thwacker, and sacker of cities.

Get to the spearmen, sing to *them:* begone.

Here, here, I want Cleonymus's son.

You, sing before we enter: sure I am

You won't sing wars: you've too discreet a father.

SECOND BOY. *Ah! some Saean is vaunting the targe, which I in the bushes*

Sadly, a blameless shield, left as I fled from the field.

TRYGAEUS. Tell me, you pretty baboon, are you making a mock of your father?

BOY. *Nay, but my* life *I preserved,*

TRYGAEUS.   But you shamed the parents who gave it.

Well go we in, for sure I am that you,

Being your father's son, will nevermore

Forget the song you sang about the shield.

Now then 'tis right, my jolly rogues, that you should, here remaining,

Munch, crunch, and bite with all your might, no empty vessels draining;

    With manly zeal attack the meal,

And saw and gnaw with either jaw, there's no advantage really

In having white and polished teeth unless you use them freely.

CHORUS. O aye, we know: we won't be slow; but thanks for thus reminding.

TRYPHAEUS. Set to, set to: you starving crew: you won't be always finding

    Such dishes rare of cake and hare

An easy prey in open day thus wandering unprotected.

Set to, set to: or soon you'll rue a splendid chance neglected.

CHORUS. O let not a word of ill-omen be heard, but some of you run for the bride;

Some, torches to bring while the multitudes sing and dance and rejoice by her side.

We'll carry the husbandry implements back our own little homesteads about,

When we've had our ovation, and poured our libation, and hunted Hyperbolus out.

    But first we'll pray to the Gods that they

    May with rich success the Hellenes bless,

    And that every field may its harvest yield,

    And our garners shine with the corn and wine,

    While our figs in plenty and peace we eat,

    And our wives are blest with an increase sweet;

    And we gather back in abundant store

    The many blessings we lost before;

    And the fiery steel—be it known no more.

TRYPHAEUS.   Come then, come, my bride,

        Midst the free green fields with me

           Sweetly, sweet, abide.

        Hymen, Hymenaeus O!

        Hymen, Hymenaeus O!

CHORUS.   Happy, happy, happy you,

        And you well deserve it too.

        Hymen, Hymenaeus O!

        Hymen, Hymenaeus O!

SEMICHORUS.	What shall with the bride be done,
	What be done with Harvesthome?
SEMICHORUS.	She shall yield him, one by one,
	All the joys of harvest home.
SEMICHORUS.	Ye to whom the task belongs
	Raise the happy bridegroom, raise,
	Bear him on with goodly songs,
	Bear him on with nuptial lays.
	Hymen, Hymenaeus O!
	Hymen, Hymenaeus O!
SEMICHORUS.	Go and dwell in peace:
	Not a care your lives impair,
	Watch your figs increase.
	Hymen, Hymenaeus O!
	Hymen, Hymenaeus O!
SEMICHORUS.	He is stout and big.
SEMICHORUS.	She a sweeter fig.
TRYGAEUS.	So you all will think
	When you feast and drink.
CHORUS.	Hymen, Hymenaeus O!
	Hymen, Hymenaeus O!
TRYGAEUS.	Away, away, good day, good day;
	Follow me, sirs, if ye will,
	And of bridecakes eat your fill.

(*Exeunt.*)

Birds

The *Birds* is a rich and lovely and gay fantasy. It attacks no specific abuse but is literally escapist, in that its heroes, wearied of the Athenian atmosphere, decide to build a utopia, which they call Nephelococcygia ("Cuckoonebulopolis") in the sky. There is of course an undertone of seriousness, as there must be in any thoughtful utopia; but there is no bitterness, but only playful good humor and exquisite lyricism. All of Aristophanes' qualities are here at their best, and the play is usually regarded as his masterpiece. The delegation of the gods who have come to conclude terms with the new city, which has made itself a bottleneck for sacrifices ascending from earth, is one among many delightful touches; another is the reception accorded malefactors and public nuisances who plague life on earth when they come up to exploit a virgin field. The costumes for this play must have been both gorgeous and amusing.

CHARACTERS

EUELPIDES ("HOPEFUL")
PISTHETAERUS ("TRUSTING")
HOOPOE
SERVANT OF HOOPOE
IRIS
PROMETHEUS
POSEIDON
HERACLES
TRIBALLUS

POET, PRIEST, INSPECTOR,
   LAWYER, SOOTHSAYER,
   AND THE LIKE
CHORUS OF BIRDS
CINESIAS
MESSENGERS
METON
STATUTE SALESMAN

Translated by R. H. Webb

EUELPIDES. (to his jackdaw). Straight on, you mean—beside
    that tree—or what?
PISTHETAERUS (to his crow). Damn you! —This idiot is croak-
    ing "Back!"
EUELPIDES. Oh, what's the use meandering about?
    It's deadly, shuttling to and fro for naught!
PISTHETAERUS. The fool I was, to listen to a crow,
    And travel a hundred miles to get to *this!*
EUELPIDES. Me too, to take a jackdaw for a guide,
    And knock my toenails off obeying him!
PISTHETAERUS. Where *are* we, do you know? *I* do. . . . We're
    lost!
EUELPIDES. You couldn't find the dear old Fatherland?
PISTHETAERUS. Neither could Execestides, by God!
EUELPIDES. Oh, hell!
PISTHETAERUS.   You want to go there? . . . Not with me!
EUELPIDES. That pet-shop fellow did us a nasty turn . . .
    Philocrates—the lunatic—who said,
    Well, trust a bird to find the bird you seek—
    Tereus, the Hoopoe, daddy of them all!
    This son of a midget cost us twenty cents,
    And that one yonder came to sixty more.
    But what did *they* know? Naught . . . except to bite!—
    What *now?* You want to walk us up the cliff?
    It can't be done. There isn't any path.
PISTHETAERUS. You're right. There isn't—not from where *I*
    stand.
EUELPIDES. Hasn't your crow got anything to say?
PISTHETAERUS. Not what he did before, I'm positive.
EUELPIDES. Well, what?
PISTHETAERUS.   Little enough. I *think* he says
    He'll gnaw my fingers off me, one by one!
EUELPIDES. It's just too bad that, when we merely wish
    To be allowed to go to the crows in peace,
    We cannot find the road to take us there!
    Our ailment is the opposite, my friends,
    Of that from which Acestor suffers. He,
    A foreigner, attempts to crash the polls;
    We, to the manner born as native sons,
    Whom no one could, or would, shoo off the nest,
    Have flown away with all the legs we've got.

It's not that we dislike the old home town . . .
A splendid city, Athens, rich and free,
Denying none the right to . . . pay a fine!
Indeed, while crickets chirp a month or two
Upon a bush, that stubborn folk will sit
And chirp on legal twigs till kingdom come!
That's why we started out to hit the trail;
And why, with basket, jug, and myrtle boughs,
We wander on in search of a quiet spot
Where we can settle down and live our lives.
Tereus, the hoopoe, we desire to meet,
And ask him whether, in his many flights,
He ever spied the sort of town we want.

PISTHETAERUS. Say . . .

EUELPIDES.   What?

PISTHETAERUS.   This crow of mine keeps pointing *up*.

EUELPIDES. Yes, so does this one . . . yawning at the sky
As if he wished to show me something there.
No question of it—birds are hereabouts.
We'll soon discover, if we make a noise.

PISTHETAERUS. Know what? Haul off and give the rock a kick.

EUELPIDES. You *butt* it. . . . That'll be twice as loud!

PISTHETAERUS.   Oh, well,
Then take a stone and do it.

EUELPIDES.   Good. . . . Here goes.
Hey, boy!

PISTHETAERUS. How's that? a bird is not a *boy*.
It seems to me you'd better call him *boid!*

EUELPIDES. Hey, boid! . . . No answer yet? How *boid*ensome!
Hi! Hoopoe! Yoo-hoo!

(*Enter from the thicket the bird* SERVANT *of the* HOOPOE.)

SERVANT.   Who are *you*? Such shouting!

PISTHETAERUS. Heaven preserve us! Why, he's got the gapes!

SERVANT. Dear me! Two wicked huntsmen after birds!

EUELPIDES. How impolite! And neither is it true.

SERVANT. Prepare to die!

EUELPIDES.   But we're not men.

SERVANT.   What *are* you?

EUELPIDES. I am a pale Jim Crow, from way-down-South . . .

SERVANT. Nonsense!

EUELPIDES.   And quaking in my boots. . . . You see?

SERVANT. Well, what's this other bird? . . . Or can't he talk?

PISTHETAERUS. Who? Me? . . . A yellow turtledove, from
Turkey!

EUELPIDES. What do you call *yourself*, for goodness' sake?

SERVANT. A slave bird.

EUELPIDES.   Conquered in a cock-fight, eh?

SERVANT. Oh, no . . . When Master turned into a hoopoe,
He begged that I become a bird as well,
So as to stay with him and valet him.

EUELPIDES. I shouldn't think a bird would need a valet.

SERVANT. *He* does, as having been a gentleman.
Suppose he feels a craving for sardines . . .
I take the bowl and buzz right off to market.
Or, if it's soup, I buzz around the house
For pot and ladle.

EUELPIDES.   Oh, I see. . . . A buzzard!
Listen to me, young fellow. You buzz in
And call your master.

SERVANT.   Can't. He's sleeping off
A mess of gnats and myrtle berries now.

EUELPIDES. Then wake him up.

SERVANT.   I will if you insist.
I warn you, though, it's sure to make him mad.

PISTHETAERUS (*to the crow*). Hey, damn it all, you frightened
me to death!

EUELPIDES. Oh, Lord, my jackdaw! He was scared away!

PISTHETAERUS. You were so scared yourself you let him loose.
Aren't you ashamed!

EUELPIDES.   See here, you stumped your toe
And let your crow escape. . . . Or didn't you?

PISTHETAERUS. Did not!

EUELPIDES.   Where *is* he, then?

PISTHETAERUS.   He flew away.

EUELPIDES. As if you didn't let him! . . . Lion-heart!

HOOPOE. Open my leafy gates. I go without.

EUELPIDES. Lord save us, what a freak! . . . A bird, is it?
No feathers, and a crest as big as three!

HOOPOE. *Who visits me?*

EUELPIDES.   The Mighty Twelve, at least,
To put you in *this* fix!

HOOPOE.   Ye mock my plumage?
Nay, my good friends. For I was once a man.

EUELPIDES. It isn't you we're laughing at.

HOOPOE.   Then what?

EUELPIDES. Your beak . . . so funny-looking, don't you know.

HOOPOE. That grievous wrong I owe to Sophocles.
To treat me thus—me, Tereus—on the stage!

EUELPIDES. So you are Tereus? Thought you were a peacock!

HOOPOE. Merely a bird.

EUELPIDES.   Where are your feathers, then?

HOOPOE. They've molted all away.

EUELPIDES.   Been sick . . . or what?

HOOPOE. In winter every wingèd creature molts,
    And then renews his feathered coat in spring.
    But tell me, who be ye?

EUELPIDES.   Two mortal wights.

HOOPOE. Whence come ye?

EUELPIDES.   From the land of lovely triremes!

HOOPOE. Jurymen?

EUELPIDES.   No sir, we've *ab*jured all that.
    We're down on juries.

HOOPOE.   Rare your breed must be.

EUELPIDES. A sprinkling here and there, in country parts.

HOOPOE. What enterprise has brought you hither, pray?

EUELPIDES. To seek advice from you.

HOOPOE.   Concerning what?

EUELPIDES. Time was when you were human, just like us.
    You loved to borrow money, just like us . . .
    And say you couldn't pay it, just like us!
    But then you changed into a flying thing,
    And viewed the whole wide world, both land and sea,
    Thinking the thoughts of man and bird at once.
    That's why we came—to see if you, perchance,
    Could tell us of a town where we might nest,
    As soft and fleecy as a feather bed.

HOOPOE. A nobler town than *your* fair storied heights?

EUELPIDES. Not nobler, but a trifle easier!

HOOPOE. You seek an aristocracy, I judge.

EUELPIDES. My pet aversion, Aristocrates!

HOOPOE. What kind of city, then, would be your choice?

EUELPIDES. One where the worst I had to fear would be
    A visit from a friend at breakfast time,
    Saying, *I warn you here and now, by God,*
    To be prepared to dine with us tonight;
    And don't you dare be late! . . . A wedding feast.
    I won't take no for an answer. Otherwise,
    You needn't come around when I am broke!

HOOPOE. A hard and bitter life, sir, you desire!
    (*To* PISTHETAERUS.) And your ideal . . . ?

PISTHETAERUS.   The same as his.

HOOPOE.   To wit . . . ?

PISTHETAERUS. A town in which a pretty lad's papa
    Would meet me and protest in injured tones:
    Well, you're a nice one! . . . Saw my son go by,
    All rosy from his bath and exercise,
    And didn't kiss him, hug him . . . anything!
    And yet you call yourself a friend of ours!

HOOPOE. Poor fellow! What calamities you court!—
    There *is* a city by the Eastern Sea
    To suit you both.

EUELPIDES.   Not if it's on the sea!
    At crack of dawn the *Salaminia*
    Would nose right into harbor with a writ!
    Haven't you got a place for us in Greece?

HOOPOE. Well, why not make your home in Lepreum?

EUELPIDES. I hate it, sight unseen. . . . Too *lepreous*—
    Or, if you'd rather, too *Melanthius!*

HOOPOE. Opuntian Locris, then. Go settle there.

EUELPIDES. And be a kinsman of Opuntius?
    Not for a thousand dollars on the spot!—
    But what's it like to live among the *birds?*
    You ought to know.

HOOPOE.   Not bad, for steady wear.
    First thing you do is throw away your purse.

EUELPIDES. And with it, most of man's dishonesty!

HOOPOE. We feed in gardens on white sesame
    And myrtle berries, poppy seeds and mint.

EUELPIDES. Then every day is wedding day with you!

PISTHETAERUS. Oh what a plan the race of birds could launch!
    Listen to me, and power untold is yours.

HOOPOE. By doing what?

PISTHETAERUS.   Well, to begin with, this:
    Stop fluttering about and twittering—
    A silly habit . . . so undignified!
    If anybody asks of our high-flyers,
    Now who is that bird?, Teleas will reply,
    A bird indeed . . . so flighty, so unstable . . .
    Never can put your finger on the chap!

HOOPOE. A point well taken. What is your advice?

PISTHETAERUS. Unite, and form a bird metropolis.

HOOPOE. Why, we could never organize a town!

PISTHETAERUS. *In sooth? Oh what a witless word thou sayest!*
    Look down.

HOOPOE.   So be it: down I look.

PISTHETAERUS.   Look up.

HOOPOE. I now look up.

PISTHETAERUS.   Revolve your head.

HOOPOE.   How jolly!
  Soon I shall boast, methinks, a crooked neck!

PISTHETAERUS. But what, sir, did you see?

HOOPOE.   The sky, and clouds.

PISTHETAERUS. You saw the pole of heaven and of birds.

HOOPOE. The pole? . . . *Our* pole?

PISTHETAERUS.   Quite so. One might say *perch.*
  But since the universe is *po*larized
  From there, its name at present is the *pole.*
  However, once it is settled and *po*liced,
  The pole will then become your *metropole!*
  Mankind you'll master like a midget-swarm . . .
  Blockade the gods like hungry Melians.

HOOPOE. But how?

PISTHETAERUS.   Is not the air 'twixt earth and sky?
  Well, just as we, when bound for Delphi's shrine,
  Request safe passage through Boeotia's plain,
  Just so, when men burn offerings to Heaven,
  You'll not allow the savory smoke to pass,
  Unless the gods pay tribute to your realm.

HOOPOE. Hurrah! Hurrah!
  By all the traps and tricky snares of man,
  A scheme more subtle I have never heard!
  This city I shall found with your good help,
  If all the other birds agree to join.

PISTHETAERUS. Who is to lay the plan before them?

HOOPOE.   You.
  For through the years I've taught them human speech.
  Till then, they babbled like barbarians.

PISTHETAERUS. How will you gather them?

HOOPOE.   Oh, easily.
  Stepping into the coppice here anon,
  And stirring from her sleep my nightingale,
  We'll call them, she and I, whose voices twain
  Will bring them running when they hear our chant.

PISTHETAERUS. Go, best of birds, and make no tarrying.
  Hasten within the copse this moment, pray,
  And rouse to life the feathered nightingale.

HOOPOE (*offstage*). Dear comrade, awaken. Thy slumbering
    cease,
  And the heavenly strains of that music release

Which pours from thy throat in a torrent divine
As a dirge for poor Itys, thy Itys and mine.
When thy soft russet cheek is a-quiver with song,
    Drifting out from among
Fair columbine tresses the melody beats
Up, up to the heights of the gods' holy seats,
Where golden Apollo himself, having heard
That plaint from the heart of a little brown bird,
Will attune to thy singing his ivory lyre,
And the lips of the blessed immortals inspire
To unite, as one harmonious choir,
   In a mighty Olympian chorus.

(*A flutist behind the scenes renders the answering song of
the nightingale.*)

EUELPIDES. Great goodness! What a voice the birdie has—
Like honey streaming through the foliage!

PISTHETAERUS. Hey, fellow!

EUELPIDES.   What's the matter?

PISTHETAERUS.   Quiet!

EUELPIDES.   Why?

PISTHETAERUS. The Hoopoe's tuning up again, I think.

HOOPOE. Hoop-ahoy! Hoop-hip-a-hoop-hip-ahoy!
  Oh hie ye, hie ye, hither hie to me!
  Hie hither, all ye wingèd company!
     From fields rich in seed,
     Whereon live the breed
      Of rooks and ravens,
    Come in a countless throng,
    Mustering myriad-strong.
   Fly to me, fly to me fleetly;
   Cry to me softly, sweetly.
    Come too, ye who sing
     Mid the furrows daily,
     Twittering so gaily
    Your tiny song of spring:
     Tio tio tio tio
     Tio tio tio tio.

  If in gardens, mid the bowers of the flowers,
    To ivied walls ye cling;
  Or if the mountains feed you with berries,
  Olives, arbutus, clustering cherries,
    Haste to our meeting,

Hark to the greeting
I bring you:
Trioto trio tototobrix.

Birds of marsh, birds of glen,
Bane of midges in the fen,
Ye who brighten with your mirth
Dewy meadows of the earth,
Meadows fair as Marathon,
Come, with all your kith and kin—
Thou in chief, dappled one,
Francolin, francolin.

Sons of the sea and the wild waves' daughters,
Vying with halcyons over the waters,
Hither for news, momentous decisions;
Hither we summon in tribal divisions
You long-necked birds-of-a-feather.
A visitor cometh, a shrewd old man
With a startling plan
Of venturesome doings for all our clan.

Hither, hither, hither, hither,
For a parley here together!
Toro toro toro torotix
Kikkabau kikkabau
Toro toro toro lililix.

PISTHETAERUS. See any bird?

EUELPIDES.   Not I.... No sign of one,
Although I'm searching hard enough, God knows.

PISTHETAERUS. The Hoopoe whooped it up for nothing,
then...
Deep in the rushes, like a plover's song.
(*Four birds pass across the stage.*)

HOOPOE. *Torotix torotix.*

PISTHETAERUS. Look, my friend, what's coming yonder. One,
at all events, we've got!

EUELPIDES. Right you are ... a lovely creature. Peacock, is it?
Surely not.

PISTHETAERUS. Here's the master. He can tell us. —Sir, what
kind of bird is that?

HOOPOE. Not the most familiar species. You will find his
habitat
In the marshes, by the rivers.

EUELPIDES.   Beautiful . . . as red as flame!

HOOPOE. Eminently reasonable, for Flamingo is his name!

EUELPIDES. Hey there, you there!

PISTHETAERUS.   Why the hubbub?

EUELPIDES.   Here's
a second bird. You see?

PISTHETAERUS. So there is; and, like the other, *of a* florid
augury!

EUELPIDES. *Who is this prophetic singer* climbing to a lofty
rock?

HOOPOE. He is called the Bird of Persia.

EUELPIDES.   God above! You mean a cock?
If he's Persian, he'd have flown here with his camels in a
flock!

EUELPIDES. Look! Another crested creature finds a crest to
stand upon.

PISTHETAERUS. Bless my soul! . . . A second Hoopoe! You are
not the only one?

HOOPOE. He's the offspring of that Tereus Philocles put on the
stage,
And is named for me, his Grandpa, as is nowadays the
rage:
Callias, then Hipponicus, then young Callias, the swell.

PISTHETAERUS. Say, this Callias bird is molting for a merry
fare-you-well!

EUELPIDES. Yes, a gentleman incarnate, and a multimillionaire.
So the lawyers and the ladies have between them plucked
him bare!

PISTHETAERUS. Heavens! Here's a flashy fellow!
What's he call himself, old man?

HOOPOE. He is such a gormandizer that they dubbed him
Bellican!

PISTHETAERUS. Ah . . . Cleonymus in person!

EUELPIDES.   With a crest so brave and bold?
Dear Cleonymus in battle found his own too hot to hold!

PISTHETAERUS. Why so crestified, these birdies? Will they run
an armored race?

HOOPOE. 'Tis a Carian invention. There the birdlike populace
Live on crests and roost in eyries, feeling safer, just in case!
(*Here troop in, at first singly, then pell-mell, the twenty-
four members of the* CHORUS.)

PISTHETAERUS. Great Poseidon! Now they're coming! What a
pest of birds galore!

EUELPIDES. Blessed be the Lord Apollo, clouds of birdies!
Watch them soar!
  Such a flapping and a flopping you can hardly see the door!

PISTHETAERUS. Here's a quail, the first arrival.

EUELPIDES.   There's a
freckled francolin.

PISTHETAERUS. Here, a ducky little widgeon.

EUELPIDES.   There, a halcyon sailing in.

PISTHETAERUS. What's the next one, close behind her?

EUELPIDES.   That's
a razor-bill, by gad!

PISTHETAERUS. Razor-bill! You ever see one?

EUELPIDES.   Yes, sir—Bill
the barber-lad!

HOOPOE. Next, an owl.

EUELPIDES.   What? *Owls to Athens?* Really, that
is rather bad!

HOOPOE. Magpie, turtledove, woodpecker, wheatear, osprey,
and cuckoo;
  Lark, porphyrion, reed-warbler, wren, wood-pigeon, gos-
hawk too;
  Falcon, rockdove, redshank, kestrel, grebe, and waxwing
  . . . There, I'm through!

PISTHETAERUS. Hip hooray! It's blackbird season!

EUELPIDES.   Hip
hurrah! The birds are out!

PISTHETAERUS. Hear them scream and chirp and twitter! See
them hop and skip about!

EUELPIDES. This is just a bit alarming.

PISTHETAERUS.   How they gape at you and me!
  Quite a menacing demeanor.

EUELPIDES.   Yes, I cannot but agree.

CHORUS. Wh-wh-wh-wh-wh-wh-where is our summoner?
Where does he tarry, to pay us no heed?

HOOPOE. Here am I beside you, waiting . . . loyal friend to all
your breed.

CHORUS. T-t-t-t-t-t-tell us your tidings, if haply they tune with
your brotherly words.

HOOPOE. Tidings true, and honest counsel, sure to profit all the
birds.
  Men have come, two subtle sages, on a visit to the air.

CHORUS. What? . . . Which? . . . Why? . . . Where?

HOOPOE. I repeat . . . two human beings, whom their years
have rendered wise,

Are among us, with the groundwork of a monster enter-
    prise.

CHORUS. Since my fledgling days I never knew a trick more
    scandalous!

Do you mean it?

HOOPOE.   Be not frightened.

CHORUS.   What is this you've
    done to us?

HOOPOE. Welcomed mortal men enamored of your high so-
    ciety.

CHORUS. You admit this daring action?

HOOPOE.   I admit it joyfully.

CHORUS. Are they near to us at present?

HOOPOE.   Yes, if you are near
    to me!

CHORUS.   Alas! . . . Alas!
      What a vicious and pernicious,
        What a surreptitious deed,
    That a comrade injudicious
        Who was daily wont to feed
        By our side on hill and mead,
          Should flout every or-
          Nithological law,
            And the troth
             Of his oath
           Should dishonor!
    Why, he sought to ambuscade me,
    And deceitfully betrayed me
         To a base,
         Godless race,
    That, since human life began,
    Is my foe, the race of *man!*

We shall deal with this delinquent at no very distant day;
But these mortals should be punished, I propose, without
    delay.

We must tear the rogues to pieces.

PISTHETAERUS.   Looks as if we're done
    for, eh?

EUELPIDES. *You're* to blame for this dilemma, and you needn't
    try to shirk.

Why'd you have to bring me with you?

PISTHETAERUS.   Why? To do the
    dirty work!

EUELPIDES. No . . . for tears and lamentation.

PISTHETAERUS.   *Must* you tell
    such stupid lies?
  Can you hope to do much weeping when they've peckered
    both your eyes?

CHORUS.   What ho! . . . Now go,
        To astound them, to confound them,
          To begin a bloody rout;
        To surround them, to impound them
          With your pinions all about,
          In a feathery redoubt.
      They are destined to moan
        And to wail and to groan—
          Two Greeks
          For our beaks
          To devour!
    Neither shall the misty mountains,
    Nor the ocean's foaming fountains,
          Nor the shroud
          Of a cloud
      Offer them security
      From their ancient enemy!

  Let us not defer the issue. Now's the time to scratch and
    bite.
  Hurry, Colonel! Are you ready? Wheel your troopers,
    column right.

EUELPIDES. Here it comes! There must be *some* place . . .
    Heavens!

PISTHETAERUS.   Stop, you coward! . . . Stay!

EUELPIDES. Why? To be dismembered? . . . Never!

PISTHETAERUS.   How are you to get away?

EUELPIDES. Ask me something I can answer.

PISTHETAERUS.   Listen, then
    while *I* tell *you:*
  We must stand our ground and fight them. If we take a pot
    or two . . .

EUELPIDES. Pots! And what will pots accomplish?

PISTHETAERUS.   Save us
    from the owl's attack.

EUELPIDES. But these other hook-clawed creatures . . . ?

PISTHETAERUS.   With
    a skewer from your sack
  Planted in the ground before you . . .

EUELPIDES. How can we protect our eyes?

PISTHETAERUS. Tie a bowl, or maybe saucer, to your forehead, helmetwise.

EUELPIDES. What a military genius! I must say that you surpass,

In your tactical devices, even General Nicias!

CHORUS. *Yippee yippee!* Now charge them. Steady! Couch your beaks, and tarry not.

Peck 'em, pluck 'em, scar 'em, skin 'em! First of all, go smash that pot!

HOOPOE. What is this, you wicked creatures? You intend to rob of life

Persons innocent and guileless? To engage in bitter strife

Men who are the blood relations of my dear devoted wife?

CHORUS. Why should we be told to spare them—veritable beasts of prey?

Could we ever punish others more inimical than they?

HOOPOE. What if they are foes by nature, but in fact our friends at heart,

And have come to offer counsel . . . useful knowledge to impart?

CHORUS. Useful knowledge, friendly counsel, from the lips of such as these,

Who have been for generations our ancestral enemies?

HOOPOE. Nay, but enemies can teach us many things, if we are wise.

Safety calls for due precaution, guarantees against surprise.

There's a truth that friends could never make you fully realize.

Nations learn from *hostile* nations to construct for self-defense

Mighty fleets of noble triremes, walls with lofty battlements;

And their homes, their wealth, their children, are preserved in consequence.

CHORUS. Yes, we'd better give a hearing to the rascals, I suppose.

One can get a sight of wisdom even from the worst of foes.

PISTHETAERUS. Ah! Their wrath appears to slacken. . . . To the rear! . . . Hep hep . . . Now rest.

HOOPOE (*to* CHORUS). Furthermore, it is your duty to accede to my request.

CHORUS. Never have we disregarded any previous behest.

PISTHETAERUS. Yes, sir, they are more pacific. That is plainly
    manifest.

> Helmets off! The battle's over.
> But continue under cover,
> And patrol our fortress, keeping
> Pike in hand, intently peeping
> Past the rampart of the kettle.
> No retreat, for men of mettle!

EUELPIDES.   Rightly said. But if they fell me,
> Where shall I be buried, tell me?

PISTHETAERUS. In the civic mausoleum,
> With a popular Te Deum,
> When we have informed the nation
> That we died in Aviation,
>   Fighting with a flying host!

CHORUS. Fall back to your lines. For the nonce, all clear.
Ground armor and anger, hostility, fear;
But crouch as a hoplite gripping his spear
Till we ask our visitors why they are here.

>   From what home
>   Do they come,
>   On what mission?
> Of you, sir, first would we inquire . . .

HOOPOE. Of me? And what is your desire?

CHORUS. Who *are* these travelers, and whence?

HOOPOE. *From Hellas, land of sapience.*

CHORUS. What turn of fate brings them, then—
> Brings to birds mortal men?

HOOPOE. Naught but love . . . love for you
> Your mode of life—strange, but true—
>   Hear to dwell, here to stay,
>   Near your side, day by day.

CHORUS.   Indeed!
> What reasons do they offer us?

HOOPOE. Incredible . . . nay, fabulous!

CHORUS. What profit can he now discern,
To justify a long sojourn
Among us? Does he hope to learn
Better to triumph o'er his foes,
Better to cure a comrade's woes?

HOOPOE. I scarce can credit, or describe,
The wondrous fortune of our tribe.
He'll make you think that East and West

And North and South and all the rest
Is yours, to govern from your nest.

CHORUS.   How mad! Quite inane!

HOOPOE.   Unutterably sane!

CHORUS.   But wise? I confess . . .

HOOPOE.   A fox, nothing less,
A whiz, a card, a hit,
A masterpiece of wit!

CHORUS.   Then let him speak, I beg you, sir.
Your words have set me in a stir.
In fact, I'm all a-flutter!

HOOPOE. You fellows take this panoply within,
And hang it on the hook—with God's good grace—
Next to the pot rack on the kitchen wall.
—And now, before this meeting I have called,
Explain your proposition.

PISTHETAERUS.   I refuse,
Unless they make a covenant with me—
That one the monkey made with his good wife.
There was to be, on both sides, recollect,
No biting, pinching, squeezing, poking in . . .

CHORUS. Tut, tut! You mean the . . . ?

PISTHETAERUS.   Certainly not! The eyes!

CHORUS. Well, I agree.

PISTHETAERUS.   Then promise, on your oath.

CHORUS. I swear it, as I hope to . . . win today
Unanimously!

PISTHETAERUS.   Right!

CHORUS.   And if I lie,
May I be cursed with a . . . bare majority!

HOOPOE. Hear ye! Our troopers are to shoulder arms,
And march away on furlough to their homes,
Scanning the boards for further bulletins.

CHORUS.   Mankind is imbued from his birth
With craftiness.
Yet nonetheless
Speak, speak to me, minion of earth.
For perchance, this hour,
You, sir,
Find neglected,
Nor even suspected,
Some talent or power
Surpassing the utmost that I,
In my folly, could ever descry.

Your thought declare—
        Do, sir—
To our whole delegation.
What fruit it may bear
Profits all the nation.

Your purpose in coming to visit this land, by your own
    sound logic persuaded,
Set forth unfearing. The terms of our treaty shall never
    by *me* be evaded.

PISTHETAERUS. My mind is in ferment, full of the yeast of a
    plan that is now in the making.
High time it were kneaded and worked into shape, that
    soon we may set it to baking.
A garland! And water! My hands must be washed.

EUELPIDES. Why so? Is it dinner we're taking?

PISTHETAERUS. I've long been in search of a ponderous phrase
    whereby, in a summary fashion
To break their resistance.—I feel for you all such pity, so
    deep a compassion,
Since once, in the far long-ago you were kings.

CHORUS. We? Kings? Over what, I implore you?

PISTHETAERUS. Why, everything. Yes, over me . . . over him.
    . . . Even Zeus was obliged to adore you.
More ancient than Cronus himself, you were born when
    Titans were yet to appear,
And Earth.

CHORUS.   Mother Earth?

PISTHETAERUS.   As God is my witness!

CHORUS.   I hadn't
    the slightest idea!

PISTHETAERUS. A stupid indifference, then, you displayed.
    Your Aesop you haven't been thumbing.
No claims that the lark, the original bird, preceded the
    earth in her coming.
Her father had sickened and died, and his corpse . . . she
    could find no place to inter it.
Quite desperate—five whole days had elapsed, and she
    couldn't afford to defer it—
She buried him deep in her own pretty head, by a truly
    unique operation.

EUELPIDES. The grave of the lark is in Headbury, eh? De-
    cidedly pleasant location!

PISTHETAERUS. If, then, they enjoy over gods, over earth, an authentic, recorded priority,

Their right it should be, as the eldest, to rule, to be kings of unchallenged authority.

EUELPIDES. Hear, hear!—You had better develop your beak. You'll soon have occasion to use it.

When woodpeckers call upon Zeus for his throne, he *may* be inclined to refuse it!

PISTHETAERUS. That birds, not gods, were the monarchs of men in the dark, dim ages behind you,

Is proved as a fact in a number of ways. For example, I beg to remind you,

The rooster was emperor once of the Medes, and boasted a sway continental.

Megabazus, Darius, were naught but his subjects, and many a great oriental.

Indeed he is known to us yet as "the Persian"—a sobriquet not accidental.

EUELPIDES. No wonder he struts, this cock of the walk, as a prince, with a gait magisterial;

And wears on his head, alone of the birds, that flaming tiara imperial!

PISTHETAERUS. So mighty his strength, so wide his domain, that still to this day, every morning,

As soon as he trumpets his reveille forth, intones his crepuscular warning,

Men leap from their beds to be off to their work, whether blacksmiths, potters, or bakers,

Or tanners or cobblers or armorers, grocers, or musical-instrument makers.

They fasten their shoes and are gone before light.

EUELPIDES. Ask *me*, if you've reason to doubt it.

He lost me a mantle of Phrygian wool, worse luck. I'll tell you about it.

Invited to town for a christening feast, I had drunk a bit more than I'm used to;

And waiting for dinner, I dropped off to sleep, and was roused by the crow of a rooster.

I thought it was day, poor fool; so at once for the Halimus highway I started.

But scarcely my nose had emerged from the gates, when out from the shadows there darted

A robber, who knocked me flat with a cudgel, pinched my cloak, and departed.

PISTHETAERUS. The kite, meanwhile, was ruler of Greece, and held in extreme veneration.

EUELPIDES. What? Greece?

PISTHETAERUS.   To be sure. 'Twas during his reign that he taught our entire population,

In greeting the kite, to salaam to the ground.

EUELPIDES. I know, to my mortification.

I bowed to a kite till I rolled on my back, and my money descended my gullet.

I had to go home with an empty basket ... minus the price of a mullet!

PISTHETAERUS. The cuckoo was a king of a twofold realm—Phoenicia and Egypt, her neighbor.

Whenever he sounded his *cuckoo*, they all went hurrying off to their labor,

To gather the barley and wheat from the plains at the height of the harvesting season.

EUELPIDES. "Went cuckoo," eh what? I am not surprised. With a *bird* for a boss, they had reason!

PISTHETAERUS. So great was the power of birds that a monarch who *did* have dominion in Hellas—

The Lord Agamemnon, or King Menelaus—was forced, our histories tell us,

To suffer an eagle to sit on his scepter and wangle a share of the plunder.

EUELPIDES. Now that is a point I am glad to have learned. Hitherto it awakened my wonder,

Whenever old Priam came out on the stage with an eagle who sat there inspecting

The graft he obtained. That Trojan Lysicrates surely was good at collecting!

PISTHETAERUS. More marvelous still is that Zeus, who as sovereign has won supreme recognition,

Appears with an eagle bestriding his helmet as proof of his royal position.

An owl is assigned to his daughter Athena; a hawk, to his servant Apollo.

EUELPIDES. Quite true, by Lady Demeter! But why? I fear I'm unable to follow.

PISTHETAERUS. That, when we are offering meat to a god, in accord with our national habit,

These birds, before he can reach for the present, may dart from their perches and grab it.—

And, finally, none took oaths by the gods, but swore by
   birds with conviction.

EUELPIDES. Old Lampon swears even now "by the Goose," to
   support some lying prediction!

PISTHETAERUS. Omnipotent, holy, you once were believed.
     But today, in your sad dereliction,
You're fools and nobodies—plain John Jones.
You are treated as lunatics—pelted with stones.
Around the temples they set their traps—
Those mean, detestable huntsman chaps—
Their nets and nooses, snares and decoys,
With triggers and gadgets like innocent toys.
You are carried to market cooped in a pen,
Where customers poke you . . . *A penny for ten!*
But, granting their right to subject you to this,
There's worse to be told, which I cannot dismiss.
When you come from the oven deliciously browned,
You are not to be eaten until you are drowned
In mustard and vinegar, oil and cheese,
And a hot, sweet sauce in addition to these—
         As if, *au naturel*,
           You were cursed with a hell
             Of a flavor!

CHORUS.   Ah bitter, ah bitter thy tale
         To all our race!
         My sires' disgrace,
         Their timorous hearts, I bewail.
         'Tis a woeful story—
           How, sir,
           Heirdom royal
         They squandered, disloyal,
           Untrue to my glory!
      But, thanks be to God, thou hast come,
      By the blessing of Fate, to our home!
         My chicks, my all—
           Now, sir—
         To thee I surrender,
         To live at thy call,
         Savior and Defender!

Stand forth. Instruct us in what we should do. We are
   ready for action, believe it!
We *must* have our kingship. Death be our choice, unless
   we can somehow retrieve it!

PISTHETAERUS. My counsel is, first, that the birds unite—that
    one great city be founded;
And then that the measureless regions of air 'twixt earth
    and sky be surrounded
With ramparts of brick baked hard in the kiln, like Baby-
    lon's fortification.

EUELPIDES. By Jove and mighty Porphyrion! What a stu-
    pendous circumvallation!

PISTHETAERUS. When this is completed, and battlements rise
    on top of each threatening tower,
Ask Zeus for his kingdom. Should he not listen—refuse to
    acknowledge your power—
Declare against Heaven your own Holy War, and impose
    on the gods prohibition
From using your streets as a thoroughfare, when, in a
    highly excited condition,
They're all in a swivet to get to the earth, pursuing a deli-
    cate mission
To an Alope, Semele, or an Alcmena. But, if they continue
    encroaching,
Affix your seal to them where it will put the quietus on
    amorous poaching!
A second ambassador I would suggest that you send to
    mankind, with advices
That, having succeeded to sovereign power, the birds now
    claim sacrifices
Ahead of the gods, with whom birds shall be paired in a
    suitable manner, selected
To fit the desires and habits of each, so that all may be
    duly respected.
Before Aphrodite is given a feast, to the 'pecker a pussy
    is proffered;
If one would present to Poseidon a ram, to the duck some
    grain should be offered;
Ere Heracles dines, plum cakes must be served to the cor-
    morant, also a glutton;
The kinglet, not to be slighted while Zeus is enjoying a
    banquet of mutton,
Must first be regaled with a big bull-gnat, whose throat
    has been cut with a dagger.

EUELPIDES. "Bull-gnat" is delectable. *Now let Zeus in his
    majesty thunder* and swagger!

HOOPOE. Will anyone think we are genuine gods, and not
    mere jaybirds . . . will 'e,

On seeing our feathers and watching us fly?

PISTHETAERUS.   Of course
they will. You are silly!

Is Hermes a god? Well, hasn't he wings, like many another
divinity?

Why, Victory soars on pinions of gold, and Eros flies
through infinity,

And Homer calls Iris a *tremulous dove*. . . . More still I
could easily cite you.

EUELPIDES. And Zeus, I imagine, will probably launch his own
wingèd thunder to smite you!

PISTHETAERUS. If men in their ignorance set you at naught,
if your rightful honors are scanted,

And unto the upstart gods of Olympus alone is deity
granted,

Then sparrows and rooks will descend in a cloud and
devour the seeds they have planted.

Let Lady Demeter provide, if she can, for a dole to supply
them nutrition!

EUELPIDES. She won't. She'll manage to find the excuse of a
shifty and glib politician!

PISTHETAERUS. A further experiment: order the crows to attack, at the sound of the tocsin,

Their sheep, as they pasture abroad in the meadows, and
puncture the eyes of their oxen.

And then let Doctor Apollo restore them. He's paid for
it; that's his profession!

EUELPIDES. Please wait till I market my yokeling of bullocks,
before you start this aggression!

PISTHETAERUS. But if *you* are their gods, their being, their
land, their Zeus, Poseidon, and Cronus,

All blessings will come to them.

HOOPOE.   Please name one that
would give them cause to enthrone us.

PISTHETAERUS. Well, locusts will never again nip buds from
their vines as they burst into flower;

A single squadron of kestrels and owls will destroy this
plague in an hour.

Then too, their figs will no longer be eaten by ants and
pestiferous gall-flies;

A covey of thrushes will pick them clean, bring death and
confusion to small flies.

HOOPOE. But how can we tell them the way to get rich? For
that is their darling ambition.

PISTHETAERUS. Why, when they consult you, disclose to them
where are the mines most worth acquisition.

Drop hints to the seer of lucrative bargains and commerce
in oversea quarters,

That skippers may safely embark upon voyages even in
dangerous waters.

HOOPOE. How "safely"?

PISTHETAERUS. A bird, when approached for advice, will instruct the astute navigator:

Don't sail . . . a hurricane's brewing. . . . Go now,
and your gains will be greater and greater.

EUELPIDES. Well, this is no place for a chap like me. I'm
buying a tub. . . . See you later!

PISTHETAERUS. You'll lead them to treasures of silver and gold
interred years past by a miser,

And long forgotten by all but you, who are now their sole
supervisor.

None knows of my hoard, save maybe a bird, men boast—
and think they are funny!

EUELPIDES. I'm selling my tub for to buy me a mattock and
dig me some pots of old money!

HOOPOE. But *we* cannot offer them health, which the gods
have retained in their keeping securely.

PISTHETAERUS. Why not? Good health is a state of well-being,
and that is prosperity, surely?

Whereas, if in business a man's "bad off," he is certain to
feel rather poorly!

HOOPOE. And how can we bring them to ripeness of age? The
Olympians only can give it.

Must many a lad be deprived of his life before he can
properly live it?

PISTHETAERUS. Three centuries more you could add to their
span.

HOOPOE. But where in the world would we get them?

PISTHETAERUS. From *yours. Five cycles of sons of the earth
lives the crow.* You'd never regret them.

EUELPIDES. Hooray! These birdies are able to govern us better
than Zeus, if we let them!

PISTHETAERUS. Far better, indeed!
To begin with, none of us mortals would need
To erect stone temples with glittering floors,
Adorned with porches and golden doors.
But in forest and covert, in shadowy dell,
Our gods will forever contentedly dwell;

And the shrine of the highest and noblest shall be
That glory of glories, a fair olive tree.
No journeys to Ammon or Delphi for us;
No sacrifice, no ceremonial fuss!
But amid the arbutus at dawn we shall stand,
With kernels of barley and wheat in our hand,
And, arms uplifted to heaven, shall pray
That a bit of good fortune may wander our way . . .
    Which it does, in a twinkling . . .
    For naught but a sprinkling
      Of birdseed!

CHORUS. Once hatefulest foeman I ever shall know, now comrade the like of no other,
I'll never be brought to consider the thought of rejecting
  your counsel, dear brother!
      Assured, nay,
    Bold of heart, I make this oath,
      This threat, yea,
    Here and now I pledge my troth:
      If with me you join alliance
      As a friend and staunch crusader,
      In harmonious defiance
      Of this Heavenly invader,
      Soon, I swear,
      Will Zeus forbear
      Still to wear
      My scepter!

No strenuous work are we going to shirk; in the field we
  shall fight without slacking.
But plans of campaign must be yours; for, in brain, I confess we are grievously lacking!

HOOPOE. No idle daydreams, then. The time has come.
Procrastinicianitis is ruled out!
So let's be up and doing.—First of all,
Please enter, will you not, my humble home,
Whose sticks and twigs are proud to welcome you.
And may I know your names?

PISTHETAERUS.   With pleasure, sir.
I'm Pisthetaerus; and this gentleman,
Euelpides.

HOOPOE.   Happy to meet you both.

PISTHETAERUS. We thank you.

HOOPOE.   Will you kindly step inside?

PISTHETAERUS. Delighted. Lead the way.

HOOPOE.   Then follow me.

PISTHETAERUS. I say . . . er . . . you! . . . Back water, will you
    please?
  See here, we cannot fly. We haven't wings.
  So how are we to live with you at all?

HOOPOE. No trouble there.

PISTHETAERUS.   But look. That fox, you know,
  The one in Aesop, had a sorry time
  As friend and partner of the eagle, eh?

HOOPOE. Fear not. There is a certain magic root . . .
  One bite apiece, and you will both grow wings.

PISTHETAERUS. Enough, sir! In we go.—Come, Xanthias,
  Come, Manodorus, take our baggage up.

CHORUS. One moment, mister!

HOOPOE   What now?

CHORUS.   Just this. Enter-
  tain our friends at your leisure;
  But Procne, peer of the Muses, nor fearing to join them in
    rhythmical measure,
  Call hither, to stay with us, sing, and be gay. 'Twould be
    a superlative pleasure.

PISTHETAERUS. Oh do by all means grant them what they ask!
  Do call the birdie. Make her leave the copse,
  And bring her here at once, I beg of you.
  We too desire to see the nightingale.

HOOPOE. Why certainly, if such is your request.—
  Procne, come out and greet our visitors.
  (*Enter an attractive young* FLUTIST.)

PISTHETAERUS. Great Zeus in Heaven! What a pretty bird!
  How white and soft she is!

EUELPIDES.   Nice chick! . . . Know what?
  I'd love to be a *rooster*-nightingale!

PISTHETAERUS. She's all dressed up in jewels, like a girl.

EUELPIDES. Believe I'll kiss her, if you don't object.

PISTHETAERUS. You'd kiss a pair of skewers, idiot?

EUELPIDES. No . . . peel them off . . . just shell her like an egg,
  And smack her on the lips.

HOOPOE.   Now let us go.

PISTHETAERUS. And may good luck go with us! . . . After you.
                              (*Exeunt.*)

CHORUS.   Golden one, belovèd!
      O fairest of birds to me,

Playmate, mistress of melody,
Late, so late, thou appearest.
Come, my own, my dearest,
Sound thy silvery flute to sing
Songs in tune with the voice of spring,
Music poured from thy heart to bring
Charm to verse anapaestic.

Dim creatures of earth, who attain unto birth like leaves,
in blind fecundation,
Ye men of a day, frail figures of clay, mere phantoms in
wild agitation,
Ungifted with wings, poor suffering things whose life is
a vision diurnal,
I beg you, attend unto us, the unending, the truly and only
eternal,
Who airily fly, and the years defy, whose thoughts are the
thoughts of the ages.
From us you may learn high wisdom, discern the trans-
cendent lore of the sages—
How Erebus, Space, the Olympian race, the birds and the
streams were created.
Thereafter, when Prodicus bores you, by God you can tell
him *his* Science is *dated!*—
First, Void, and the Night. No glimmer of light pierced
Tartarus' boundless dominions;
Nor Earth nor Air nor Firmament there. Then Night of the
ebony pinions
Brought forth in her nest within Erebus' breast an Egg, by
the Whirlwind sired;
From whence was born, as the months rolled on, great
Eros, the ever desired,
With wings on his shoulders of scintillant gold, as swift as
the storm in his flying,
Who mated with Space in a darkling embrace, in the
bosom of Tartarus lying.
'Twas thus that our breed was engendered, the seed
hatched out by this epochal union.
No gods were above us till turbulent Love had effected a
cosmic communion.
From mystic espousals, atomic carousals—a vast, cataclys-
mic commotion—
Arose the Divinities, Heaven's infinities, Earth, and the
billows of Ocean.

So, nothing can be as primeval as we. Our sonship to
    Eros, moreover,
Is proved by our flight and our constant delight in be-
    friending a passionate lover.
Fair lads of allure who have sworn to be pure, when they
    ought to be ripe for romances,
Admirers persuade, enlisting our aid, to be open to all
    their advances—
Presenting a rooster, a quail, or a goose . . . some pet their
    favorite fancies.—
We merit your praise in numberless ways, and your thanks,
    for the soundest of reasons.
We herald the coming of winter and summer, the annual
    round of the seasons.
You scatter your grain at the croak of the crane, south-
    bound for Libyan waters,
When mariners willingly hang up the tiller and snooze in
    their snug winter quarters,
And prudent Orestes knits him a waistcoat, for warmth
    while he strips other fellows!
The kites appear at the turn of the year, when the cold
    wind softens and mellows,
To say that your flocks should be sheared of their locks.
    You're finally warned by the swallow
To peddle your woolies and buy something cool for the
    sweltering days that will follow.
Then, too, we alone are your Ammon, Dodona, and Pythian
    shrine hieratic:
To us you apply, 'tis from us that you try to secure some
    augury vatic,
Ere risking a trade, espousing a maid, or essaying a quest
    problematic.
Remember that *bird* is a popular word for whatever you
    count as a presage;
A sneeze is a *bird*, or a rumor you've heard, or anything
    fraught with a message;
A *bird* is a meeting, a *bird* is a greeting, the voices of serv-
    ants or asses.
So can you not see very plainly that we are Apollo himself
    for the masses?

    If, then, you will only believe us divine,
    We shall serve you as prophets and musical Nine.
    The winds and the weather, in spring, in fall,

In winter and summer, will be at your call.
Nor ever, like Zeus, will we sit on a cloud,
Indulging in lofty disdain of the crowd;
But, near you, we'll see that the life of each one—
Both you and your wife and your son and *his* son—
> Is a round of good fun.
With health, with wealth, with peace and with play,
Youth, laughter, and dances, and banquetings—yea,
Bird's milk for your breakfast—I venture to say
That, embarrassed with riches, fatigued, blasé,
> You will pray
> For a stay
> Of good fortune!

> Muse of the woodland
> (*Tio tio tio tiotinx*),
Changeful ever is thy singing,
Through the valleys and hilltops ringing
> (*Tio tio tio tiotinx*),
Where, amid greenery tresses beside thee I raise
> (*Tio tio tio tiotinx*)
From my fawn-yellow throat, in melodious praise,
Hymns unto Pan of the forests and fountains,
Dances to Rhea, the Queen of the mountains
> (*Tototo tototo totototinx*),
Whence, like honey-bee from flower,
Phrynichus drank, in my lyrical bower,
> Nectar so sweet that its savor
> All his song doth flavor
> (*Tio tio tio tiotinx*).

Gentlemen, if any of you wish to weave your web of life
With the birds, forever happy and forever free from strife,
Come. For deeds on earth disgraceful, under human law taboo,
Here with us are recommended as the proper thing to do.
Father-beating, for example, you believe a wicked shame;
We, however, laud a bantam who with sure and sudden aim
Smacks his pompous parent, saying, *Lift your spur, if you are game!*
Any truant slave among you, branded with a mark of sin,
Will be domiciled in birdland as a freckled francolin.
Spintharus the Turk, who maybe feels in Athens out of place,

Will consort with turkey buzzards, members of Philemon's
  race
Execestides, despairing of an Attic pedigree,
We'll adopt, as baby bunting of a feathered family.
Any Meles who's enfranchise all expatriated Micks,
Could become a polly parrot and perform his daddy's tricks.
No discredit here whatever to indulge in poli . . . tics!

> Such was the music
> (*Tio tio tio tiotinx*)
> Made by swans for Phoebus' greeting,
> Quire of voices and pinions beating
> (*Tio tio tio tiotinx*).
> Wafted afar from the moors above Maritza's bed
> (*Tio tio tio tiotinx*),
> To the clouds of high heaven the melody sped.
> Beasts of the wilds were crouching in wonder;
> Breathless, the billows were quenching their thunder
> (*Tototo tototo tototinx*).
> Gods were awed. Olympus' portal
> Rang, when the Muses and Graces immortal
> Sang, to the birds replying,
> *Hail! Hosanna!* crying
> (*Tio tio tio tiotinx*).

Naught is better, naught more pleasant, than to grow a
  pair of wings.
At the theater, for instance, they'd be quite convenient
  things.
Bored with tragedies, and hungry . . . never mind, you
  needn't stay;
You could wing it home, eat luncheon in a comfortable
  way,
Then, replete, fly back among us for a comic matinee.
If a Patrocleides present got the gripes, would he in pain
Sit here sweating? Not a moment! Up he'd soar with might
  and main,
Blow off steam with sighs of rapture, and cavort back here
  again.
Or an ardent lover, haply, is on tenterhooks because
Down in front he spies her husband, seated with the
  Senators.
Well, he'd ruffle up his feathers and away from you he'd
  go;

Then, when he had loved his lady, back he'd fly to see the
show.
Are not wings a priceless blessing? 'Tis as plain as plain
can be.
Take Dieitrephes whose pinions sprouted on his pottery;
Yet, a nobody, he's risen till he's anybody's peer—
First a Captain, then a Colonel, now a *light-horse Chan-*
ticleer!
(*Re-enter* EUELPIDES *and* PISTHETAERUS, *awkward in their*
new plumage.)

PISTHETAERUS. Well, here we are!

EUELPIDES (*laughing*). Good Lord! I've never seen
A funnier spectacle since I was born!

PISTHETAERUS. Than what?

EUELPIDES. Than you, in feathers. . . . Oh,
those wings!
Want me to tell you what you look most like?
A jackleg painter's portrait of a goose!

PISTHETAERUS. A jayhawk with a crew cut goes for *you!*

EUELPIDES. Well, each of us might say, with Aeschylus:
This wrong my own fair plumage wrought, none else!

CHORUS. What is our plan of action?

PISTHETAERUS. First of all,
Christen our city with a big fine name,
Then sacrifice to the bird gods.

EUELPIDES. So say I.

CHORUS. Now let me see, what *shall* we call the city?

PISTHETAERUS. How do you like that noble Spartan word,
High-sounding *Lacedaemon?*

EUELPIDES. God above!
Saddle the town with such a name as that?
I love no *lassie* who's a *demon* too!

PISTHETAERUS. What shall it be, then?

CHORUS. Something fanciful . . .
A touch of clouds and airy spaciousness
And lightness.

PISTHETAERUS. Cuckoo . . . nebulopolis?

CHORUS. Hurrah! Hurrah!
Splendid! An absolutely gorgeous name!

EUELPIDES. Is that the Cuckooonebulopolis
Where Aeschines has millions in the bank,
And poor Theogenes hides most of his?

PISTHETAERUS. Best bet for them, perhaps, is Phlegra's plain,
In which the gods outbragged the Giant host!

CHORUS. A glorious city, ours, indeed. What god
    Shall be her Patron . . . wear Athena's robe?

EUELPIDES. The Warrior Maid herself. What better choice?

PISTHETAERUS. How can you have a decent government
    Where women pose in panoply of bronze,
    And leave the distaff side to Cleisthenes?

CHORUS. Who *will* be master of our ramparts, then?

PISTHETAERUS. A bird.

CHORUS.   Like *us?* What breed?

PISTHETAERUS.   Persian—the cock,
    Doughtiest fighter in the world today,
    True chick of Ares.

EUELPIDES.   Cheers for Captain Chick!

PISTHETAERUS. No rock too high for *him* to roost upon!
    (*To* EUELPIDES.) Come now, you hurry out into the air
    And serve the builders of our city wall.
    Roll up your sleeves, tote gravel, mix the mortar,
    Carry the hod . . . and tumble off the ladder,
    Set guards, and bank the fires, and go the rounds
    With torch and bell, and sleep there on the job;
    Dispatch a herald to the gods above,
    Another to humanity below,
    And then report to me.

EUELPIDES.   *You* can report,
    For all *I* care, to hell!

PISTHETAERUS.   Now run along,
    Nobody else can do the things I said.—
    We'll sacrifice to the new divinities.
    I'll go and find a priest to lead our march.—
    Bring out the basket, boys, and holy water.

CHORUS.   *In full accord, I with thee*
          Ply the oar in harmony,
    To hymn the gods in a holy procession,
    To slaughter a victim—with proper discretion
    (A bit of a goat might make an impression).
           So hear us:
       Let one, let all, now raise
       A Pythian strain of praise,
       Intoned while Chaeris plays
          To cheer us.

PISTHETAERUS. Hey, stop that noise! . . . Lord save us, what
    is this?
    Strange sights a-plenty in my time I've seen,

But never yet a clarinetist crow!—

Well, Priest, begin the service. You're in charge.

PRIEST. I will, sir. (*To* SLAVE.) First, the basket, if you please.
Pray ye to the birdland Vestal, to the Kite, Guardian
of the Home, and to all the Olympian Birds and Bird-
esses: Osprey of Sunium . . .

PISTHETAERUS. All hail, Kingfisher, Monarch of the Spray!

PRIEST. Swan of Delphi and of Delos; Leto, Maternal Stork;
Phoebe-Artemis . . .

PISTHETAERUS. So Phoebus calls his sister "Phoebe" now?

PRIEST. Lenaean Linnet; Ostrich, Mountain-Mother of Gods
and men . . .

PISTHETAERUS. The image of her son Cleocritus!

PRIEST. That they grant health and happiness to all the folk
of Cuckoonebulopolis *and her allies of Chios* . . .

PISTHETAERUS. Ha! Good old Chios gets there every time!

PRIEST. And to all Bird-Heroes and their sons: Porphyrion,
Woodpecker, Pelican, Spotted Eagle, Grouse, Peacock,
Reed-Warbler, Teal, Gull, Heron, Gannet, Black-Cap,
Titmouse . . .

PISTHETAERUS. Stop it, you fool . . . stop calling them! My
God,

What sort of victim do you think we have,

For all that vulture flock to feed upon?

One single kite would soon make off with it!

Get out . . . you and your precious garlands! . . . Go!

I shall perform this sacrifice myself.

CHORUS.   Another song, once again,
                 Must we sing, a pure refrain

Befitting this moment of pious lustration,

And summon the Blessed—no large delegation . . .

Just one, if *we* are to share the collation.

                 For, clearly,
                 This victim you have brought
                 Is, frankly speaking, naught
                 But horns *plus* beard. Now *ought*
                 You, *really?*

PISTHETAERUS. Let us invoke the wingèd gods with prayer.
(*Enter* POET.)

POET.   City of Birds, Paradise,
                         Blest in story!
                         Give forth, my Muse,
                         Strains of exalted price.
                         Hymn her glory!

PISTHETAERUS. Now where did *this* come from? . . . Who *are*
　　you, eh?

POET. 　　　　　　　A prelude drips
　　　　　　　　From my honeyed lips,
　　　　　　　　Pure, sweet, esoteric.
　　　　Trusty squire of the Muses call me—
　　　　　　In language Homeric!

PISTHETAERUS. A *servant*, is it? Then your hair's too long!

POET. Why, don't you know, sir, all we learnèd bards
　　　　Trusty squires of the Muses are labeled,
　　　　　　In language Homeric?

PISTHETAERUS. As *trusty* as that rusty cloak of yours!—
　　Well, Bard, my friend, what ill wind blows *you* here?

POET. Full many a noble song have I composed
　　To praise your Cuckoonebulopolis—
　　Chorales and rounds, Simonidean odes . . .

PISTHETAERUS. Composed already, did you say? . . . Since
　　when?

POET. Long, long have I extolled this city's name.

PISTHETAERUS. She hasn't any, yet. She's just been born!
　　We're setting out to christen her right now.

POET. Sped by the Nine, Rumor spreadeth fast perforce,
　　　　Fleet as the flashing feet of a courser.
　　　　　Thou great Sire of Aetna,
　　　　Who in name unto Piety art wed,
　　　　　　Wilt grant me a boon,
　　　　　Whate'er is thy joy eftsoon
　　　　To give, bending thy royal head?

PISTHETAERUS. This chap is likely to become a pest.
　　Let's give him *something* and get shut of him.
　　　(*To* SLAVE.) That leather vest—you have a shirt beneath—
　　Off with it. . . . Give it to our brilliant bard.
　　　(*To* POET.) Here, take it, son. You need it, goodness knows!

POET. 　　　　Never ungracious, the Muse I revere
　　　　Welcomes the gift proffered me here.
　　　　　　Yet 'tis her due
　　　　To ponder the word of Pindar anew:

PISTHETAERUS. We thought we'd shake the fellow? . . . Not a
　　chance!

POET. 　　　　*From a Scythian caravan*
　　　　　Is outcast, a man
　　　　　　Who hath for his ain
　　　　　　No woven skein
　　　　　　　To house him.

>   *Inglorious, one*
>   *With vest, if none*
>   *Will blouse him!*
>   *Hearken. My speech is plain.*

PISTHETAERUS. Aye, plain enough to show you want that shirt!
   (*To* SLAVE.) Well, take it off. The poet must be served.—
   It's yours. And, now you've got it, go!

POET.   I go;
   And, once away, will laud your city thus:

>   Sing, *thou gold-enthronèd,*
>   This quivering, shivering home!
>   Through snowy moors bemoanèd,
>   Through draughty downs I roam,
>   *Tra-la-la-la!*

PISTHETAERUS. Forget it! Proud possessor of a shirt,
   Shiver no more . . . not here, at any rate!—
   Well, *this* calamity I looked for least—
   That he should learn about our town so soon.—
   (*To* SLAVE.) Now take the holy water round again.
   Let all be silent!
   (*Enter* SOOTHSAYER.)

SOOTHSAYER. Stop this sacrifice!

PISTHETAERUS. And who are you?

SOOTHSAYER.   A seer.

PISTHETAERUS.   Then go to grass!

SOOTHSAYER. Misguided man, be not irreverent.
   This oracle of Bakis prophesies
   Concerning Cuckoonebulopolis.

PISTHETAERUS. Why tell me *now?* The city has been founded!
   You should have come . . .

SOOTHSAYER.   God's will impeded me.

PISTHETAERUS. Oh well, no harm in hearing it, I guess.

SOOTHSAYER. *Hearken to me. When the silvery crows and the*
       wolves are united,
   Building a joint habitation "where Sicyon marches with
       Corinth". . .

PISTHETAERUS. And what has Corinth, pray, to do with *us?*

SOOTHSAYER. A riddle, that. Good Bakis means the Air.
   Offer the Bounteous One a ram snow-white in its tresses.
   Then, if a prophet shall come to expound my words to the
       people,
   Give unto him an immaculate cloak and a brace of new
       sandals . . .

PISTHETAERUS. Are *sandals* in it?

SOOTHSAYER.   Read it for yourself!

   Aye, and a goblet; and laden his hands with meats from the
     altar . . .

PISTHETAERUS. Meats! Does it say so?

SOOTHSAYER.   Read it for yourself!

   If, divine youth, thou obeyest the bidding of these my
     injunctions,
   "High in the clouds shalt thou soar as the eagle." But if
     thou refusest,
   Devil an eagle thou'lt be, nor a dove, nor a woodpecker
     even!

PISTHETAERUS. Is all that in it?

SOOTHSAYER.   Read it for yourself!

PISTHETAERUS. Your oracle is nothing like the one

   Apollo gave to *me*. I wrote it down:
   When to thy sacrifice cometh unbidden a mountebank
     prophet,
   Troubling thy people at prayer, to demand a taste of the
     victim,
   Then shalt ·thou flog him behind, where his backside
     marches with . . .

SOOTHSAYER.   Nonsense!

   I don't believe it!

PISTHETAERUS.   Read it for yourself!

   Spare him not, though perchance he may soar in the clouds
     as the eagle . . .
   Lampon himself though he happen to be, or the great
     Diopeithes!

SOOTHSAYER. Is all that in it?

PISTHETAERUS.   Read it for yourself!

   So move on, now. . . . Get out!

SOOTHSAYER.   Ah, woe is me!

PISTHETAERUS. Just run along and soothsay somewhere else!

   (*Enter* METON, *a surveyor.*)

METON. I come to you . . .

PISTHETAERUS.   Damn it, another bore!—

   For what, milord . . . what mission, what design,
   What deep intent? And why the buskined tread?

METON. I would survey for you the Realm of Air . . .

   Partition it in lots.

PISTHETAERUS.   For heaven's sake,

   Who are you, anyway?

METON.   Meton, by name.

   All Hellas knows me . . . and Colonus!

PISTHETAERUS.   Say,
  What have you there?

METON.   Measures, to plot the sky.
  To illustrate, the air, in total form,
  Is very like an oven top. So, then,
  Applying from above this metric arc,
  With compasses thereon. . . . You follow?

PISTHETAERUS.   No!

METON. I use a ruler, thus, until at length
  The circle has been squared, and in the midst
  A market place is set, from which the streets
  Are drawn, to radiate as from a star,
  The beams of which, itself a circle, shine
  Straight forth to every point.

PISTHETAERUS.   The man's a Thales!
  Meton . . .

METON.   What is it?

PISTHETAERUS.   Well . . . you know I love you . . .
  Do me a favor—go away from here!

METON. Am I in danger?

PISTHETAERUS.   As in Spartan law,
  Today is moving day for foreigners.
  The town is in a tumult.

METON.   Civil war?

PISTHETAERUS. Oh, no.

METON.   Then what?

PISTHETAERUS.   Unanimous consent
  To wallop every humbug in the land!

METON. I'll just slip off.

PISTHETAERUS.   You'd better. . . . No, too late!
  They're after you. . . . They're coming closer. . . . There!

METON. Oh mercy me!

PISTHETAERUS.   I warned you, didn't I?
  Now go survey yourself some other place!
  (*Enter* INSPECTOR.)

INSPECTOR. Where are the Consuls?

PISTHETAERUS.   Sardanapalus, what?

INSPECTOR. I come to Cuckoonebulopolis
  Commissioned as Inspector.

PISTHETAERUS.   Yes? By whom?

INSPECTOR. Teleas made the motion, curse the luck!

PISTHETAERUS. Oh. . . . Would it suit you, then, to go right
    home . . .
  No work, full pay?

INSPECTOR. It would. I begged postponement
   Till the Assembly met and passed upon
   A certain deal I've made with Pharnaces.

PISTHETAERUS. Well, here's your salary. . . . Now move!

INSPECTOR. What's this?

PISTHETAERUS. Assembly meeting. . . . Good old Pharnaces!

INSPECTOR. Stop! I protest! Beating an officer?

PISTHETAERUS. Now shoo! . . . And take your ballot urns along!

   (*Exit* INSPECTOR; *enter* STATUTE SALESMAN.)

   Think of it . . . sending their Inspectors here
   Before our sacrifice is even made!

STATUTE SALESMAN. *If any citizen of Cuckoonebulopolis commits a tort against an Athenian . . .*

PISTHETAERUS. Another pesky document! . . . What now?

STATUTE SALESMAN. I am a statute salesman, coming here
   With brand-new laws to sell you.

PISTHETAERUS. Such as what?

STATUTE SALESMAN. *The Cuckoonebulopolitans shall employ
      the same weights and measures and the same decrees,
      as the Olophyxians.*

PISTHETAERUS. And you, the same as the Hell-of-a-fixians!

STATUTE SALESMAN. What are you doing?

PISTHETAERUS. Take your laws and go!

   (*Exit* STATUTE SALESMAN; *re-enter* INSPECTOR.)

INSPECTOR. I summon Pisthetaerus to appear in court next
      month. I charge him with assault and battery!

PISTHETAERUS. Is that so? . . . Oh, it's you still hanging round!

STATUTE SALESMAN. *Whoever shall expel the magistrates, and
      refuse to admit them in accordance with the Charter . . .*

PISTHETAERUS. The Lord preserve us all! . . . *You* here again?

INSPECTOR. I'll bring a twenty-thousand-dollar suit . . .

PISTHETAERUS. Only to have me rip it up the back?

STATUTE SALESMAN. Who took the Charter to the johnny? . . .
   Yah!

PISTHETAERUS. Oh shucks! Somebody catch him! . . . Hey
      there, stop!—
   This is no place for us. Let's go within,
   And make our sacrifice without chagrin.

   (*Exeunt.*)

CHORUS. Unto me, the all-mighty, all-seeing,
         Now come burnt offerings from man,

The prayers of his inmost being.
The length and breadth of the world I scan.
To safeguard fruit and flower
From tribes of savage power
Whose ravening jaws devour
Every little bud that bloweth,
At the moment of its birth,
Blighting every tree that groweth,
Feeding on the crops of earth.
I slaughter, I slay them; the sweet-scented bloom
Of the garden I rescue from hideous doom.
Death to creepy-crawly creatures, worm or fly!
Death to such as dare my puissant wing defy!
Death, say I!

On this day by proclamation you outlaw your enemies:
For the head of one Diagoras, who profaned the Mysteries,
You will get a thousand dollars; and to win a thousand
  more,
Kill a dead-and-buried Tyrant deader than he was before!
So upon this same occasion, *we* would make announce-
  ment, too:
Kill Philocrates the Sniper, and a thousand comes to you;
If you want to earn four thousand, you can bring him back
  alive—
Traitor to the breed of finches . . . strings and sells them six
  for five!
Thrushes too he treats with outrage . . . blows them up to
  make them plump;
Sticks into the blackbirds' noses feathers in a gaudy clump.
Doves with equal spite he catches, to be shamefully con-
  fined
In a hunting net, and ordered basely to decoy their kind!
Thus do *we* proclaim. Moreover, if perchance you keep for
  fun
Birds imprisoned in your houses, go release them, every
  one.
Else, if you neglect my warning, you will see your precious
  boys
Caught by us and put in cages and compelled to play
  decoys!

O race of the wingèd, what blessing
Is banned for the birds? Come ice, come snow,

What cloak need they for their dressing?
When stifling summer with light is aglow,
No hurt from its rays can betide me;
For flowery meadows provide me
With bosoms of leafage to hide me,
When the troubadour cicada
Chants his lay so piercing sweet,
An immortal serenader,
Frenzied by the noontide heat.
I winter in caverns of rock, where I play
With nymphs of the mountain the livelong day;
While, in spring, I feast on food of pure delight,
Berries from the Graces' garden, soft and white,
Maiden-white.

Now we wish to tell the judges, ere for balloting they rise,
What rewards we guarantee them if they offer us the
prize—
Gifts surpassing all that Paris ever found in women's eyes.
First—a boon at which our critics of the drama seldom
mock—
Owls, the nestlings of Laureion, in a never-failing flock.
They will build within your houses, in your purses they will
breed.
And will hatch sufficient pennies to supply your every
need.
Homes you'll have as grand as temples—flying buttresses
and things;
And our architects will fit them with a noble pair of *wings!*
If you'd be a petty grafter, yet remain within the law,
You shall have a hawk attendant, with a sharp and crooked
claw.
For digestion we shall give you, when you're dining out, a
craw!
But, if we are not the victors, you had better forge full soon
Disks the like of those on statues—each a tiny crescent
moon.
Otherwise, when at a party, spick and span in evening
dress,
You will pay. For birds are naughty, and they make an
awful mess!

PISTHETAERUS. Well, birds, the rites are done, the omens good.
Too bad we've had no runner from the walls

To tell us what is going on out there.—
Ah, here he comes, in true Olympic form!
(*Enter* MESSENGER.)

MESSENGER. Wh-where . . . where is . . . where . . . where's the
Chief?
I want . . . Pisthetaerus . . .

PISTHETAERUS.   Here I am.

MESSENGER. Your wall is ready . . . finished!

PISTHETAERUS.   Good for you!

MESSENGER. A splendid structure, most magnificent . . .
So wide that on the top Proxenides
The Braggadocian and Theogenes
Could pass each other in two chariots
With racers bigger than the Wooden Horse!

PISTHETAERUS. My God!

MESSENGER.   Its height—*I measured it myself*—
A hundred fathoms.

PISTHETAERUS.   Heavens! What a wall!
Who can have *built* the thing as high as that?

MESSENGER. Why birds, none else. No hardy sons of Egypt,
Masons or engineers or porters. No,
Just birds, barehanded. Marvelous it was!
A fleet of thirty thousand Libyan cranes
Sailed in, ballasted with foundation stones,
Which longbills neatly chiseled into shape.
Still others carried brick—ten thousand storks.
Water was taken up into the air
By curlews and related river fowl.

PISTHETAERUS. Who fetched the mortar for them?

MESSENGER.   Herons did.

PISTHETAERUS. How did they ever get it in the hods?

MESSENGER. That was the very smartest trick of all.
The geese dug in with those flat feet of theirs . . .
As good as any shovel you could find.

PISTHETAERUS. *What task too great for willing feet to do?*

MESSENGER. Then ducks, with apron strings around their
necks,
Passed brick along, swallow apprentices
Flitting about with mortar in their mouths,
And wearing their own trowels right behind them!

PISTHETAERUS. Why should a man hire labor after this?
What of the carpentry? Did birds do that?

MESSENGER. Woodpeckers—craftsmen better than the best.
Those long sharp beaks can make the shavings fly!

Such hammering and sawing as went on,
You'd think it was a shipyard you were in!—
Well, there's your wall, with gates and everything,
Bolted and barred, completely garrisoned.
Patrols are out, the watchman rings his bell,
The guards are at their posts, and beacon fires
Are blazing on the towers. —Now I'll go
And take a bath. The rest is up to you.

CHORUS. What ails you? Aren't you very much surprised
Our city has been fortified so soon?

PISTHETAERUS. Oh, yes indeed. It's just too wonderful!
Truthfully, don't you think it's all a lie?—
But look . . . a guard is coming! See him run . . .
Grim as a war dance! News from the front, no doubt.
(*Enter* SECOND MESSENGER.)

SECOND MESSENGER. Halloa halloo, halloo halloa! What ho!

PISTHETAERUS. What is it? Something wrong?

SECOND MESSENGER.   An outrage, sir!
A god . . . from Heaven . . . one of Zeus's gods . . .
Flew straight into our city through the gates,
Eluding every jackdaw sentinel!

PISTHETAERUS. Oh monstrous deed! Oh shameless miscreant!
What god?

SECOND MESSENGER. We know not, save that he is wingèd.

PISTHETAERUS. Didn't you, then, detail a band of scouts
To bring him down?

SECOND MESSENGER.   We did . . . the race of hawks . . .
A flying squadron, thirty thousand strong
Of mounted archers, talons curved to kill—
Buzzard and kestrel, vulture, eagle, owl.
The whiz and whir of pinion shakes the air,
And ether pulses as they seek the god.
By now the hunt should be not far from here.
Then should we not have slings and bows in hand?
Ho! Hither, everyone! We need your help!
Come, shoot and smite! A sling, a sling I want!

CHORUS.   'Tis war! War doth rise,
                    Like none seen nor heard,
             A battle in the skies
                    Betwixt god and bird!

             The murky realm of Air,
                    Begotten child of Night,

Defend, yea, beware
Lest they evade our sight!

Scan every quarter keenly, one and all!
A sound of eddying wing doth greet my ear,
As though a god sublime were hov'ring near.
(*Enter* IRIS.)

PISTHETAERUS. Hi! . . . You there! Whither away, young
woman? Stop!

Who are you? . . . Wait! . . . Hey, calm yourself! Slow
down!

Where are you from? You might at least say that!

IRIS. From Heaven . . . from Olympus, and the gods.

PISTHETAERUS. And what's your name? What *are* you—boat, or
bonnet?

IRIS. *Iris the fleet.*

PISTHETAERUS.   You can't be *all* of it!

IRIS. I do not understand . . .

PISTHETAERUS.   Will not some bull-bat
Mount and subdue this heifer?

IRIS.   Me? . . . But why?
You'll treat me . . . ?

PISTHETAERUS.   To a good long crying spell!

IRIS. But how absurd, how strange!

PISTHETAERUS.   Now look here, wench . . .
What gate did you come in by, when you came?

IRIS. I'm sure I do not know, sir. Gates, indeed!

PISTHETAERUS. Won't answer me, you see? All innocence!
—Did you apply to the jackdaw captains? No?
You got a visa from the storks?

IRIS.   Why, what . . . ?

PISTHETAERUS. You didn't!

IRIS.   Are you sane?

PISTHETAERUS.   You mean to say
No bird official left his mark upon you?

IRIS. Certainly *not!* For shame, sir! I should hope . . .

PISTHETAERUS. And yet you dare come sneaking on your wings
Through other people's towns and private air?

IRIS. Where are the gods to fly, if not in air?

PISTHETAERUS. *I'm sure I do not know,* but somewhere else!
If any Iris ever was, you're guilty.
Listen. If you should get what you deserve,
You'd be arrested and condemned to death!

IRIS. I am immortal!

PISTHETAERUS.   I don't care; you'd die!
  In my opinion, it is scandalous
  That, when the whole wide world accepts our rule,
  You still are rebels . . . cannot realize
  That now it's *your* turn to obey the boss!—
  Where are you sailing to with all those wings?
IRIS. To earth. My father sent me down to say
  The Olympian gods desire a sacrifice.
  Mankind must slaughter sheep on holy hearths,
  And fill their streets with smoke.
PISTHETAERUS.   Did you say "gods"?
  What gods?
IRIS.   Why, us, of course . . . the gods of Heaven.
PISTHETAERUS. So *you* are gods?
IRIS.   What others can there be?
PISTHETAERUS. The birds, my lass! Men are to worship *them,*
  And not the gods any more at all . . . by God!
IRIS. You fool, you fool! Rouse not dread wrath divine,
  For fear your breed may perish, root and branch,
  Felled by the ax of Justice and of Jove;
  And lest your frame, your home's encircling walls,
  Be burned to ashes by Licymnian fires!
PISTHETAERUS. Now wait a minute! Blustering's no good.
  Am I a Lydian or a Phrygian slave,
  That you should try to frighten me with spooks?
  If Zeus, I tell you, bothers me too much,
  His palace, *yea, Amphion's mighty halls,*
  My flaming eagles shall incinerate!
  Porphyrions, clad in skins of pards, forsooth,
  Shall take the air against him at my call,
  Six hundred strong. And yet there was a time
  When *one* Porphyrion gave him fits, you know!
  As for his envoy, if *you* worry me,
  I'll tip you up and part those pretty legs.
  Then Mistress Iris will be much surprised
  To find in this old goat so tough a ram!
IRIS. Confusion seize you, sir, for talking so!
PISTHETAERUS. Be off, now! Hurry! Scoot! . . . And also, scat!
IRIS. Father will end your horrid insolence!
PISTHETAERUS. Good heavens! Won't you kindly fly away,
  And seek some younger victim for your "fires"?

                                         (*Exit* IRIS.)

CHORUS.   The way now is barred,
                And never more again

> May bold Sons of God
>> Traverse my domain.
>
> No sacrificial flame
>> From Earth's prostrate floor
> In pious mortal's name
>> Shall to Olympus soar.

PISTHETAERUS. That messenger we sent to men below . . .
I wonder if he's ever coming back.
(*Enter* HERALD.)

HERALD. O blessed one, thrice blessed! O most wise!
O brilliant, glorious, wise—I said that once—
O . . . Help me, will you? . . .

PISTHETAERUS.   What's it all about?

HERALD. Your wisdom earns for you this golden crown.
The nations honor you with one accord.

PISTHETAERUS. Thank you . . . But *why* should nations
honor me?

HERALD. Founder of this celestial commonwealth,
You do not know what widespread fame is yours,
What lovers for your country you have won.
Before you built this city in the clouds,
Sparta was all the fashion everywhere;
The world was full of little Socrateses . . .
Hungry and dirty, shaggy, toting canes.
But now birds are the craze, and men delight
To act as much like us as possible.
No sooner are they out of bed at dawn
Than off they fly to Commons in a flock,
Where, perching each upon his special twig,
They scratch and claw and fight each others' *bills!*
So manifest, indeed, the mania is,
That some are even nicknamed after birds.
A certain pegleg huckster is "the Partridge";
"Swallow" Menippus is a foreign chap;
Opuntius they call "the One-Eyed Crow";
"The Lark" is Philocles; Theogenes
Is dubbed a silly "Goose"; Lycurgus, "Crane";
"The Bat" is Chaerephon, who never sleeps;
"The Jay" is Syracosius; "the Quail"
Is Meidias, who wears the vacant look
Of one that totters groggy from the ring.
Oh yes indeed, they love the birds so much
That in their songs they sing of nothing else

But doves and eagles, wrens and nightingales.
A poem without *wings* is not a poem!—
Well, that is how it stands. And one word more:
Thousands will soon be coming here to us—
A flock of birds of prey in search of plumage!

PISTHETAERUS. This is no time to dilly-dally, then.
You go at once and heap the hampers high ...
Baskets and baskets full of fluffy feathers.
Manes can bring them out of doors to me.
I shall remain and greet our visitors.

CHORUS. "Well manned" will our city be called, 'tis clear,
On her debut ... bless her!

PISTHETAERUS. May Fortune, too, caress her!

CHORUS. The name of her suitors is legion, I hear.
Come now, step lively! Hurry!
What need will endanger
The joy of a stranger?
For Wisdom and Love, the Graces and Peace
And smiling Tranquillity offer release
From every doubt and worry.

PISTHETAERUS. You lazy thing ...
Malingering!
Why can't you bring
Them faster?

CHORUS. More feathers! Another big hamper at once!
—Arouse him. Do! Back, sir!

PISTHETAERUS. By giving *you* a smack, sir!

CHORUS. An obstinate donkey, a loafer, a dunce!

PISTHETAERUS. A wretched disposition!

CHORUS. First gather together
Each order of feather—
Prophetical, nautical, musical. Then
You may fittingly fledge and accouter your men
To match the man's ambition.

PISTHETAERUS. By all the ... Goslings, what a good-for-
naught!
It makes my fingers itch to look at you!
(*Enter* YOUTH.)

YOUTH. *A bird! Aye, grant me an eagle to be,*
To soar aloft, high over the waste of the Sea,
Above her silvery waters!

PISTHETAERUS. Apparently that herald told the truth ...
Here's *one* who sings of eagles, anyhow!

YOUTH. Hurrah!

No boon is sweeter than the boon of flight!
My heart's a-flutter with a mad desire
To live with you . . . be governed by your laws!

PISTHETAERUS. Which laws, my lad? The birds have many
laws.

YOUTH. All of them! But especially the one
That bids a bantam bite and choke his sire.

PISTHETAERUS. Oh yes, a very manly trait, we think,
For a chick to give his pa a peck or two.

YOUTH. Well, that is why I've come up here to stay—
I want to choke my Dad and be his heir!

PISTHETAERUS. Oh, but we have another law, you see,
Kept in the ancient archives of the storks:
If any father cherishes his brood,
Cares for his storklings till they leave the nest,
The young, in turn, must duly care for him.

YOUTH. A lot of good it did me, then, to come!
You mean I have to *work* for my old man?

PISTHETAERUS. Never you mind. You came here in good faith.
I shall equip you as an orphan bird,
And give to you, my son, the counsel sage
That I received when I was at your age.
You mustn't beat your daddy any more.
Here is a wing for you . . . and here's a spur . . .
And here's a crest as fine as any cock's.
Take them, and guard your land, and earn your keep,
And let your father live. If fight you must,
Fly off to Thrace and fight the enemy!

YOUTH. By George, sir, I believe you're right. . . . I will!

PISTHETAERUS. Now you are talking like a man of sense.

(*Exit* YOUTH; *enter* CINESIAS, *a poet.*)

CINESIAS. *Olympus I seek, skyward I fly, wafted on airy*
pinions,
Blazing a song-way, flitting afar, hither and yon.

PISTHETAERUS. This creature needs a whole cargo of feathers!

CINESIAS. *Fearless of body, spirit undaunted, seeking a new . . .*

PISTHETAERUS. Welcome to Thistledown, Cinesias!
Why wheel your whirling course to us, my friend?

CINESIAS. *A bird, a bird, a nightingale I'd be, songster melo-*
dious!

PISTHETAERUS. Stop warbling, now, and tell me what you
want.

CINESIAS. Great wings, great wings, whereon to soar aloft,

And find me in the regions of the clouds
New themes, full of the storm wind and the snows!

PISTHETAERUS. What! Get a theme from clouds? Why, no one
    could.

CINESIAS. We are dependent on them utterly.
    The brightest jewels of the lyric art
    Are dark with swirling shadows ... misty ... dim.
    But let me quote. Then you will understand.

PISTHETAERUS. Oh no I won't!

CINESIAS.   Oh yes indeed, you must!
    I shall conduct you through that dusky realm.
        Weird ghosts of the cloud world,
            Airily awing,
      The bird phantoms of a great flock ...

PISTHETAERUS.   Heave ho!

CINESIAS.   *May I go, bounding on seaward courses,*
        With the gales of gusty breezes!

PISTHETAERUS. *I'll give you breeze enough to last your life!*

CINESIAS.   *Now to a southern track I veer,*
        Now to almighty Boreas' arms
    Yielding my frame, plowing the portless
    Furrows of air, voyaging on!
    A pleasant game, old fellow ... happy thought!

PISTHETAERUS. Don't like to be a *swirling shadow,* eh?

CINESIAS. Such treatment for a famous choralist
    Whose services are in acute demand!

PISTHETAERUS. How would you like to stay right here with us,
    And train a dancing choir of featherweights
    For Leotrophides to sponsor?

CINESIAS.   Mock,
    If so you wish: but on and up I fare
    Until I wing my way through all the air!
    (*Exit* CINESIAS; *enter* LAWYER.)

LAWYER.   *Yon birds, whence do they come,*
      Dappled of wing, knowing nor wealth nor care?
      Wilt thou pause in thy flight and tell,
        Bright swallow?

PISTHETAERUS. A veritable plague has broken out ...
    Another warbler comes to visit us!

LAWYER. I repeat ... *Wilt thou pause and tell,*
          Bright swallow?

PISTHETAERUS. With rags like those, he'll need a swallow *flock,*
    To make a summer warm enough for *him!*

LAWYER. Where is the man who feathers colonists?

PISTHETAERUS. Present. But first inform me what you want.

LAWYER. *'Tis wings, 'tis wings I crave!* Ask me no more.

PISTHETAERUS. To fly to Pellene for an overcoat?

LAWYER. Oh no; to drum up trade. I work the islands,
Snooping for cases, shystering.

PISTHETAERUS.   Indeed?
A fine profession!

LAWYER.   Think how fine 'twould be
If I could *fly* around with summonses!

PISTHETAERUS. A summons is a summons, wings or no.

LAWYER. Yes, but when pirates bothered me, you see,
I'd join a caravan of homing cranes,
Ballasted with a bellyful of briefs!

PISTHETAERUS. Is *this* your business—strong young chap like
you—
Practicing blackmail on colonials?

LAYER. What can I do? Dig ditches? Not for me!

PISTHETAERUS. But heaven knows there must be decent ways
For able-bodied youths to make a living,
Better than framing honest citizens.

LAWYER. Now, my dear sir, it's wings I want, not words!

PISTHETAERUS. The very words I speak can lend you wings.

LAWYER. What! Give me wings by *talking* to me? . . . How?

PISTHETAERUS. By *winged words* that make the spirit soar.

LAWYER. You mean . . . ?

PISTHETAERUS.   Haven't you heard some father say
Chatting with cronies in the barbershop,
It's simply dreadful how Dieitrephes
Carries away my son with horsy talk?
Another says his boy is stage-struck . . . *Yes,*
The lad's transported . . . swept right off his feet!

LAWYER. Can words transport a person?

PISTHETAERUS.   Certainly.
By words the mind is raised to higher things . . .
Uplifted. So my good advice, I hope,
Will elevate and guide your thoughts to seek
A lawful occupation.

LAWYER.   I refuse!

PISTHETAERUS. What will you do?

LAWYER.   I won't disgrace my folks!
My father was a shyster. So was his!—
Come now, the lightest, fastest wings you've got—
A hawk's, we'll say—to take me first abroad
To serve a writ, then home to enter suit,

Then back to foreign parts.

PISTHETAERUS.   Ah yes, I see;
   The case will go against him by default.
   You beat him to it, eh?

LAWYER.   Exactly so.

PISTHETAERUS. And then, while he is still en route to Athens,
   Flying back east, *you* snatch his property!

LAWYER. Precisely; spinning like a top . . . that's me!

PISTHETAERUS. Then I've the very thing to make you hum—
   The plumage worn by Corcyrean cops!

LAWYER. Mercy! A whip!

PISTHETAERUS.   Oh no, a pair of wings . . .
   To spin you as you've never spun before!

LAWYER. God help me!

PISTHETAERUS.   Fly! Come on now, damn you, fly!
   Take off, you scoundrel! And I hope you'll say
   Your kind of legal racket doesn't pay!
   Let's pick our feathers up and get away.

                                          (*Exeunt.*)

CHORUS.   Marvels yet unknown to Science
                  Have I seen in bird's-eye view,
                  Miracles and wonders new.

               Growing in the land of giants,
               Miles removed from Fort Reliance,
                  Stands the great Cleonymus tree,
                  Tall and spreading, but, ah me,
                  Naught is here but vanity.

               In the spring this vegetation
               Blossoms into legislation,
               But in winter trepidation
                  Makes it shed its panoply!

               In the darkness of perdition,
                  Set amid a lampless waste,
                  Is a certain spot debased,
               Where, without undue suspicion,
               Man may dine with apparition.
                  Through the day 'tis patronized:
                  But from nightfall, be apprised,
                  Safety isn't advertised!
               If a mortal, there benighted,
               By Orestes' ghost be sighted,
               He will make for home affrighted—
                  Stripped, and all but paralyzed!

(*Enter* PROMETHEUS, *shielding his face.*)

PROMETHEUS. Dear me, I hope that Zeus won't see me here!
  Where's Pisthetaerus?

PISTHETAERUS.   Heavens! What is this?
  Why all the rigging?

PROMETHEUS.   Look behind me, will you?
  Is there a god in sight?

PISTHETAERUS.   No, thank the Lord!
  But who are *you?*

PROMETHEUS.   How late is it, about?

PISTHETAERUS. Oh, somewhere in the afternoon, I guess.
  Who *are* you, anyway?

PROMETHEUS.   Teatime, perhaps?

PISTHETAERUS. You make me sick!

PROMETHEUS.   What is the weather like?
  Cloudy, I mean to say, or clearing off?

PISTHETAERUS. Oh, go to hell!

PROMETHEUS.   In that case, I'll unwrap.

PISTHETAERUS. My dear Prometheus! You?

PROMETHEUS.   *Sh!* Not so loud!

PISTHETAERUS. But why?

PROMETHEUS.   Quiet! And please don't call my name!
  You'll ruin me if Zeus finds out I'm here.
  Before I tell you how things are up there,
  Just hold this parasol above my head,
  To keep the gods from catching sight of me.

PISTHETAERUS. Ha ha! That's good!
  A clever notion . . . quite Promethean!
  Duck under. There you are, all safe. Proceed.

PROMETHEUS. Well, listen, then.

PISTHETAERUS.   I'm listening. Go on.

PROMETHEUS. The hour of Zeus has struck!

PISTHETAERUS.   What time was it?

PROMETHEUS. The moment when you occupied the air.
  Since then, no mortal sacrifice from earth,
  No smoke nor savor of burnt offering,
  Has risen to the gods. And so we fast,
  As if it were the Thesmophoria.
  Besides, those barbarous hordes of gods above us,
  Howling with hunger like Illyrians,
  Are threatening to levy war on Zeus,
  Unless the ports are opened up again,
  So they can get their chops and tenderloins.

PISTHETAERUS. Barbarian gods there are, on top of *you?*

PROMETHEUS. Of course. Remember Execestides!
   Where, do you think, are *his* ancestral shrines?
PISTHETAERUS. What do you call the dirty foreigners?
PROMETHEUS. Triballi.
PISTHETAERUS.   Oh! Those savages in Thrace.
   To ballyhack with all the likes of *them!*
PROMETHEUS. I quite agree. But here's the point, my friend:
   Envoys are on their way, to treat for peace,
   From *our* Triballi and from Zeus as well.
   But don't you grant it, save upon these terms—
   That Zeus restore the scepter to the birds,
   And also marry Royalty to you.
PISTHETAERUS. Who is this Royalty?
PROMETHEUS.   A comely maid
   Who keeps his thunderbolts et cetera—
   His famous statesmanship, his navy yards,
   His Law-and-Order, sheriffs, jury fees,
   His Golden Mean . . . and mean vocabulary!
PISTHETAERUS. She runs his whole establishment?
PROMETHEUS.   She does.
   Take her away from him, and all is yours.
   That's why I came—to give you this advice.
   For since Time was, I've been the friend of man.
PISTHETAERUS. Yes, but for you we couldn't fry our fish!
PROMETHEUS. And how I loathe the race of gods, you know.
PISTHETAERUS. Surely . . . and they return the compliment!
PROMETHEUS. A veritable Timon.—I must run. . . .
   My parasol! If Zeus should see me now,
   He'll take me for a girl in a parade.
PISTHETAERUS. Then add this campstool to your cavalcade!

CHORUS.   Near the Shadefoot reservation
           Is a lake where Socrates . . .
           Washes? No! . . . but, if you please,
      Raises spooks! There in vexation
      Came Peisander, for oblation
           To his spirit, long since dead.
           Half in hope and half in dread,
      Like Odysseus, then, he waited,
           After slaughtering a camel,
      For his ghost. But, ah, he baited
           By that gore of massive mammal,
           Chaerephon the Bat, instead!

(*Enter* POSEIDON, HERACLES, *and* TRIBALLUS)

POSEIDON. Well, here is Cuckoonebulopolis,
   The destination of our embassy.—
   (*To* TRIBALLUS.) What ails you, sir? Your cloak is all awry!
   A gentleman should wear it thus . . . with grace.
   Who do you think you are—Laespodias?
   Democracy! What *will* it bring us to?
   Electing *this* to represent the gods!
   Keep still, and let me try. . . . Be damned to you!
   A god less civilized I never saw!—
   Well, Hercales, what now?
HERACLES.   I told you once . . .
   I'd like to choke him and be done with it—
   Whoever built these walls across the sky!
POSEIDON. But we were sent here to negotiate.
HERACLES. Well, anyway, I'd choke him . . . all the more!
   (*Enter* PISTHETAERUS, *followed by slaves carrying cooking
   utensils and poultry.*)
PISTHETAERUS. Hand me the grater. . . . Now the mustard
   pot. . . .
   A bit of cheese. . . . You'd better poke the fire.
POSEIDON. Our hearty greetings to a son of earth.
   Three gods are we.
PISTHETAERUS.   Sprinkle the mustard on.
HERACLES. Whose stuff is this you're cooking?
PISTHETAERUS.   Just some birds
   Found guilty of an oligarchic plot
   Against the State.
HERACLES.   And so you season them
   Before cremation, eh?
PISTHETAERUS.   What's that? Well, well!
   Hi, Heracles! How are you?
POSEIDON.   We have come,
   As envoys from the gods, to offer peace.
PISTHETAERUS. Look at this bottle, will you? . . . Not a drop!
HERACLES. Too bad! Why, birds are ruined without oil!
POSEIDON. Nothing to gain have *we* from waging war;
   And think of what our friendship means to *you*:
   Water in every cistern, rain or shine;
   A life of halcyon days throughout the year!
   On all these matters we have power to act.
PISTHETAERUS. We didn't start the war—remember that—
   But if you wish it, we shall not oppose—
   Provided you are willing to play fair—
   A covenant. And playing fair means this:

Zeus must restore the scepter to the birds.
If we can get together on these terms,
Your excellencies will be asked to lunch.

HERACLES. Suits me! I vote right now that we accept!

POSEIDON. What! You're a glutton, and a fool besides!
You'd rob your father of his very throne?

PISTHETAERUS. Indeed! Will not you gods be stronger still,
If birds hold sway between mankind and you?
For now the world is hidden by the clouds,
And men can get away with perjury.
But if you make alliance with the birds,
The crow, when one has sworn by him and Zeus,
Will sneak up on the rascal furtively
And peck his eyes out, if he told a lie.

POSEIDON. Now, by Poseidon, that's a point well made!

HERACLES. Hear, hear!

PISTHETAERUS (*to* TRIBALLUS). And what say you?

TRIBALLUS.   Na! I . . . I . . . teenk . . .

PISTHETAERUS. He says "aye aye"! You heard him?—Then
    again,
Another favor will we do for you:
If any mortal vows a sacrifice,
But won't pay up—the stingy things—and says,
Laughing it off, *The gods are patient fellows!*
We can collect it for you.

POSEIDON.   Oh? And how?

PISTHETAERUS. When he is counting up his precious hoard,
Or sitting in his bath, with sudden swoop
A kite will snatch and carry to the god
The market price of those two sheep he lost!

HERACLES. Question! . . . Restore the scepter, that's my vote!

POSEIDON. Well, get Triballus's.

HERACLES.   See here, Triballus . . .
Looking for trouble, eh?

TRIBALLUS.   Da beega steeck! . . .
No do!

HERACLES. He says I'm absolutely right.

POSEIDON. If you two are agreed, I vote the same.

HERACLES. Your proposition is accepted, sir.

PISTHETAERUS. By Jove, there's something else. . . . Almost
    forgot!
Hera I willingly concede to Zeus,
But I must have that maiden Royalty
To be my wife.

POSEIDON. *You've* no desire for peace!—
  Come, let's be going home!
PISTHETAERUS.   A lot *I* care!—
  Here, chef, this dressing must be sweetened up.
HERACLES. Whither away, Poseidon, my good man?
  Are we to fight a war for one lone girl?
POSEIDON. But what are we to do, then?
HERACLES.   Do? . . . Make peace!
POSEIDON. Idiot, don't you know that you've been duped?
  You stand in your own light. If Zeus should die
  After surrendering his throne to them,
  You'll be a pauper—you, his rightful heir,
  Who should inherit his entire estate!
PISTHETAERUS. Oh, how distressing—fooling you like that!
  Come over here and let me talk to you.
  Your uncle is deceiving you, my boy.
  Of all that money not one cent is yours.
  By legal right. Remember you're a bastard!
HERACLES. Bastard, you say? . . . Good heavens! . . . Me?
PISTHETAERUS.   Of course.
  Your mother was an álien. Furthermore,
  Athena is "the Heiress." *Could* she be,
  If Zeus has *sons* who were legitimate?
HERACLES. Suppose the old man names me in his will?
PISTHETAERUS. The law won't let him. You're a foreigner.
  And this Poseidon here, who eggs you on,
  Will be the first to claim your father's wealth
  As the legitimate *brother* of the dead!
  But let me quote you Solon's very words:
  A bastard shall have no part or share in his deceased
    father's estate, if there be surviving sons of legitimate
    birth. If no legitimate sons survive, said estate shall be
    divided between those nearest of kin to the deceased.
HERACLES. Then I'll get nothing when my father dies?
PISTHETAERUS. No, not a penny—that is . . . tell me this:
  You weren't adopted, were you, legally?
HERACLES. No, and I often wondered why it was!
PISTHETAERUS. Don't stand there looking daggers at the sky.
  You side with us and I'll make you a king,
  And feed you bird's milk by the bucketful!
HERACLES. I've always thought you right about that girl.
  You ought to have her. That's the way *I* vote.
PISTHETAERUS (*to* POSEIDON). What's *your* opinion?
POSEIDON.   I am still opposed!

PISTHETAERUS. It rests with you, Triballus. What's the word?

TRIBALLUS. Me gif da plitty leddy, granda gal,
  For birdie queen?

HERACLES.   He says to give her up!

POSEIDON. Why, damn it, he did *not* say give her up . . .
  Unless it's pidgin Greek the fellow talks!

HERACLES. That's *it!* He *gives* her to the pigeons, see?

POSEIDON. Well, you two go ahead and settle it.
  I'm voted down. There's nothing more to say.

HERACLES. Sir, we agree to grant your terms in full.
  So come on back to Heaven with us now,
  And get your Royalty and all the rest.

PISTHETAERUS. These rebels, then, were slaughtered just in time
  To make my marriage feast.

HERACLES.   Suppose I stay
  And do the cooking, while you fellows go?

POSEIDON. The cooking *and* the eating! . . . Come along!

HERACLES. I could have been so happy! Dear, oh dear!

PISTHETAERUS (*to servant*). Get me a wedding garment.
  Bring it here.

                               (*Exeunt.*)

CHORUS.   On the shores of Inquisition
        Is a Bar whose arid soil
        Horny-throated sons of toil
     Cultivate in competition,
     Sowing with the tongue suspicion,
        Harvesting impeachment fruit.
        Foreigners of low repute,
     They're of Gorgias's communion;
        And we so despise the vices
     Of this Rhetoricians' Union,
        That in all our sacrifices
        Tongues are severed at the root!

(*Enter* MESSENGER.)

MESSENGER. O happy creatures, O ineffable,
  O blessed, O thrice blessed, race of birds,
  Receive your Prince into his royal home!
  He cometh as no gleaming star above
  Doth sparkle in its realm with flash of gold.
  No piercing ray of sun hath ever shone
  As shineth he, companioned by a bride
  So beautiful that she doth beggar speech,
  Wielding the wingèd thunderbolt of Zeus.

A nameless perfume unto heaven's arch
Doth mount, and curling wreaths of incense smoke
The breezes waft—a wondrous spectacle.
But lo, the Master! Let the Muse benign
Open her lips—your lips—in song divine!
(*Enter* PISTHETAERUS, *crowned and escorting Royalty.*)
CHORUS. Way for the King! Into columns deploy ye;
     Flying, convoy ye
   To blessedness joyous so blest a pair!
    All hail! Hail to the fair,
     Hail to the youthful!
   Hail unto thee, mate of a bride
     Who is the pride
      Of Heaven!

  A wonderful, wonderful fortune indeed,
  For the birds and their breed,
This mortal hath wrought. So come, let us sing
Glad strains hymeneal to welcome our king,
   And to give Miss Royalty greeting!

   Yea, thus did the Fates intoné
    Hymns telling of wedded love,
    When, great among gods above,
   Zeus placed on his lofty throne
    Hera, Queen of Olympus.
    Hymen, O Hymenaeus!
    Hymen, O Hymenaeus!
   Who guided the nuptial train?
    One wingèd with golden wealth,
    One bright with the bloom of health.
   Lo, sitting beside the Twain,
    Eros, lover of lovers.
    Hymen, O Hymenaeus!
    Hymen, O Hymenaeus!
PISTHETAERUS. I rejoice in your songs, I delight in your lays;
 Your words are enchantment. Sing me the praise
Of his thunders, the tremor of earth at their crash,
His lightnings—*my* lightnings—their terrible flash,
   The *baneful blaze of the levin!*
CHORUS. Fire of the storm, thou glittering wonder,
   Sword of the heavenly powers;
  Voice of the storm, reverberant thunder,
   Herald of imminent showers,

Here is your Lord, who hath shaken
Earth in his anger, and taken
Royalty, mistress of Zeus, for his consort.
Hymen, O Hymenaeus!

PISTHETAERUS. Ho for the wedding feast. Come all,
Flying friends wherever bred,
Follow me on to the palace hall,
Where the bridal couch is spread.

Now hand to hand and wing to wing,
Let us dance, dear Lady—*so*—
Faster and faster, till we swing
Round and round, and *up* you go!

CHORUS. *Bravo! Huzza! Hosanna!* cry!
Tarantara, the victor! aye,
Noblest of the gods on high!

(*Exeunt.*)

Lysistrata

In *Acharnians* an individual escapes the hardships of war by negotiating a private peace; in *Peace* an ambassador ascends to heaven to put a stop to war; in *Lysistrata*, presented after the Sicilian disaster of 413 B.C., the scheme for ending war is a sex strike on the part of the women. The operation of the strike is exceedingly funny, especially where the young wife teases her panting husband so unmercifully, but the play as a whole is sad. Now, the poet implies, no rational solution of the political problem seems possible. His sympathetic understanding of the plight of women, whose lives war leaves sunless and empty, is touching and timeless in its relevance. Talk of state policy in the interstices of the sexual theme is quite grave, and the political message of the whole is on a high level; what Aristophanes advocates, in effect, is Panhellenic harmony to save Greece from destruction.

CHARACTERS

LYSISTRATA

CALONICE

MYRRHINE

LAMPITO

STRATYLLIS

CINESIAS

HERALD OF THE
  LACEDAEMONIANS

CHORUS OF OLD MEN

CHORUS OF WOMEN

ATHENIANS

SPARTANS

MAGISTRATE

LOUNGER

Translated by Jack Lindsay

(LYSISTRATA *stands alone with the Propylaea at her back.*)

LYSISTRATA. If they were trysting for a Bacchanal,
A feast of Pan or Colias or Genetyllis,
The tambourines would block the rowdy streets.
But now there's not a woman to be seen
Except—ah, yes—this neighbor of mine yonder.
(*Enter* CALONICE.)
Good day, Calonice.

CALONICE.   Good day, Lysistrata.
But what has vexed you so? Tell me, child.
What are these black looks for? It doesn't suit you
To knit your eyebrows up glumly like that.

LYSISTRATA. Calonice, it's more than I can bear,
I am hot all over with blushes for our sex.
Men say we're slippery rogues—

CALONICE.   And aren't they right?

LYSISTRATA. Yet summoned on the most tremendous business
For deliberation, still they snuggle in bed.

CALONICE. My dear, they'll come. It's hard for women, you
know,
To get away. There's so much to do.
Husbands to be patted and put in good tempers:
Servants to be poked out: children washed
Or soothed with lullays or fed with mouthfuls of pap.

LYSISTRATA. But I tell you, here's a far more weighty object.

CALONICE. What is it all about, dear Lysistrata,
That you've called the women hither in a troop?
What kind of an object is it?

LYSISTRATA.   A very large one!

CALONICE. Is it long too?

LYSISTRATA.   Both large and long to handle—

CALONICE. And yet they're not all here!

LYSISTRATA.   O I didn't mean that.
If that was the prize, they'd soon come fluttering along.
No, no, it concerns an object I've felt over
And turned this way and that for sleepless nights.

CALONICE. It must be fine to stand such long attention.

LYSISTRATA. So fine it comes to this—Greece saved by Woman!

CALONICE. By Woman! Wretched thing, I'm sorry for it.

LYSISTRATA. Our country's fate is henceforth in our hands:
To destroy the Peloponnesians root and branch—

CALONICE. What could be nobler!

LYSISTRATA. Wipe out the Boeotians—

CALONICE. Not utterly. Have mercy on the eels!

LYSISTRATA. But with regard to Athens, note I'm careful
    Not to say any of these nasty things;
    Still, thought is free. . . . But if the women join us
    From Peloponnesus and Boeotia, then
    Hand in hand we'll rescue Greece.

CALONICE. How could we do
    Such a big wise deed? We women who dwell
    Quietly adorning ourselves in a back room
    With gowns of lucid gold and gawdy toilets
    Of stately silk and dainty little slippers. . . .

LYSISTRATA. These are the very armaments of the rescue.
    These crocus gowns, this outlay of the best myrrh,
    Slippers, cosmetics dusting beauty, and robes
    With rippling creases of light.

CALONICE. Yes, but how?

LYSISTRATA. No man will lift a lance against another—

CALONICE. I'll run to have my tunic dyed crocus.

LYSISTRATA. Or take a shield—

CALONICE. I'll get a stately gown.

LYSISTRATA. Or unscabbard a sword—

CALONICE. Let me buy a pair of slippers.

LYSISTRATA. Now, tell me, are the women right to lag?

CALONICE. They should have turned birds, they should have
    grown wings and flown.

LYSISTRATA. My friend, you'll see that they are true Athenians:
    Always too late. Why, there's not a woman
    From the shoreward demes arrived, not one from Salamis.

CALONICE. I know for certain they were up at dawn,
    Rocking aboard their husbands if not the skiffs.

LYSISTRATA. And I'd have staked my life the Acharnian dames
    Would be here first, yet they haven't come either!

CALONICE. Well anyhow there is Theagenes' wife
    We can expect—she consulted Hecate.
    But look, here are some at last, and more behind them.
    See . . . where are they from?

LYSISTRATA. From Anagyra they come.

CALONICE. Yes, they generally manage to come first.
    (*Enter* MYRRHINE.)

MYRRHINE. Are we late, Lysistrata? . . . What is that?
    Nothing to say?

LYSISTRATA. I've not much to say for you,
Myrrhine, dawdling on so vast an affair.

MYRRHINE. I couldn't find my girdle in the dark.
But if the affair's so wonderful, tell us, what is it?

LYSISTRATA. No, let us stay a little longer till
The Peloponnesian girls and the girls of Boeotia
Are here to listen.

MYRRHINE. That's the best advice.
Ah, there comes Lampito.
(*Enter* LAMPITO.)

LYSISTRATA. Welcome Lampito!
Dear Spartan girl with a delightful face,
Washed with the rosy spring, how fresh you look
In the easy stride of your sleek slenderness,
Why you could strangle a bull!

LAMPITO. I think I could.
It's frae exercise and kicking at my arse.

LYSISTRATA. What lovely breasts to own!

LAMPITO. Oo . . . your fingers
Assess them, ye tickler, wi' such tender chucks
I feel as if I were an altar victim.

LYSISTRATA. Who is this youngster?

LAMPITO. A Boeotian lady.

LYSISTRATA. There never was much undergrowth in Boeotia,
Such a smooth place, and this girl takes after it.

CALONICE. Yes, I never saw a lawn so primly kept.

LYSISTRATA. This girl?

LAMPITO. A sonsie open-looking jinker!
She's a Corinthian.

LYSISTRATA. Yes, isn't she?
Very open, in some parts particularly.

LAMPITO. But who's garred this Council o' Women to meet
here?

LYSISTRATA. I have.

LAMPITO. Propound then what you want o' us.

MYRRHINE. What is the amazing news you have to tell?

LYSISTRATA. I'll tell you, but first answer one small question.

MYRRHINE. As you like.

LYSISTRATA. Are you not sad your children's fathers
Go endlessly off soldiering afar
In this plodding war? I am willing to wager
There's not one here whose husband is at home.

CALONICE. Mine's been in Thrace, keeping an eye on Eucrates
For five months past.

MYRRHINE.   And mine left me for Pylos
  Seven months ago at least.

LAMPITO.   And as for mine
  No sooner has he slipped out frae the line
  He straps his shield and he's snickt off again.

LYSISTRATA. And not the slightest glitter of a lover!
  And since the Milesians betrayed us, I've not seen
  An eight-inch toy to give a proper grip
  And be a leathern consolation to us.
  Now will you help me, if I find a means
  To stamp the war out.

MYRRHINE.   By the two Goddesses, Yes!
  I will though I've to pawn this very dress
  And drink the barter money the same day.

CALONICE. And I too though I'm split up like a turbot
  And half is hackt off as the price of peace.

LAMPITO. And I too! Why, to get a peep at the shy thing
  I'd clamber up to the tip-top o' Taygetus.

LYSISTRATA. Then I'll expose my mighty mystery.
  O women, if we would compel the men
  To bow to Peace, we must refrain—

MYRRHINE.   From what?
  O tell us!

LYSISTRATA.   Will you truly do it then?

MYRRHINE. We will, we will, if we must die for it.

LYSISTRATA. We must refrain from all touch of baubled
    love. . . .
  Why do you turn your backs? Where are you going?
  Why do you bite your lips and shake your heads?
  Why are your faces blanched? Why do you weep?
  Will you or won't you, or what do you mean?

MYRRHINE. No, I won't do it. Let the war proceed.

CALONICE. No, I won't do it. Let the war proceed.

LYSISTRATA. You too, dear turbot, you that said just now
  You didn't mind being split right up in the least?

CALONICE. Anything else! O bid me walk in fire
  But do not rob us of that darling pet.
  What else is like it, dearest Lysistrata?

LYSISTRATA. And you?

MYRRHINE.   O please give me the fire instead.

LYSISTRATA. Lewd to the least drop in the tiniest vein,
  Our sex is fitly food for Tragic Poets,
  Our whole life's but a pile of kisses and babies.

But, hardy Spartan, if you join with me
All may be righted yet. O help me, help me.

LAMPITO. It's a sair, sair thing to ask of us, by the Twa,
A lass to sleep her lane and never fill
Love's gap except wi' makeshifts. . . . But let it be.
Peace maun be thought of first.

LYSISTRATA.   My friend, my friend!
The only one amid this herd of weaklings.

CALONICE. But if—which heaven forbid—we should refrain
As you would have us, how is Peace induced?

LYSISTRATA. By the two Goddesses, now can't you see
All we have to do is idly sit indoors
With smooth roses powdered on our cheeks,
Our bodies burning naked through the folds
Of shining Amorgos' silk, and meet the men
With our dear Venus plats plucked trim and neat.
Their stirring love will rise up furiously,
They'll beg our knees to open. That's our time!
We'll disregard their knocking, beat them off—
And they will soon be rabid for a Peace.
I'm sure of it.

LAMPITO.   Just as Menelaus, they say,
Seeing the breasties of his naked Helen
Flang down the sword.

CALONICE.   But we'll be tearful fools
If our husbands take us at our word and leave us.

LYSISTRATA. There's only left then, in Pherecrates' phrase,
To flay a skinned dog—flay further our flayed toys.

CALONICE. Bah, proverbs are no satisfaction in bed.
But what avail will your scheme be if the men
Drag us for all our kicking on to the couch?

LYSISTRATA. Cling to the doorposts.

CALONICE.   But if they should rape us?

LYSISTRATA. Yield then, but with a sluggish, cold indifference.
There's no pleasure for them if they rasp it in.
Besides we have other ways to madden them;
They cannot stand up long, and they've no delight
Unless we fit their aim with merry succor.

CALONICE. Well if you must have it so, we'll all agree.

LAMPITO. For us I ha' no doubt. We can persuade
Our men to strike a fair an' decent Peace,
But how will ye pitch out the battle frenzy
O' the Athenian populace?

LYSISTRATA.   I promise you
  We'll wither up that curse.

LAMPITO.   I don't believe it.
  Not while they own ane trireme oared an' rigged,
  Or a' those stacks an' stacks an' stacks o' siller.

LYSISTRATA. I've thought the whole thing out till there's no
    flaw.
  We shall surprise the Acropolis today:
  That is the duty set the older dames.
  While we sit here talking, they are to go
  And under pretense of sacrificing, seize it.

LAMPITO. Certie, that's fine; all's warking for the best.

LYSISTRATA. Now quickly, Lampito, let us tie ourselves
  To this high purpose as tightly as the hemp of words
  Can knot together.

LAMPITO.   Set out the terms in detail
  And we'll a' swear to them.

LYSISTRATA.   Of course. . . . Well then
  Where is our Scythianess? Why are you staring?
  First lay the shield, boss downward, on the floor
  And bring the victim's innards.

CALONICE.   But, Lysistrata,
  What is this oath that we're to swear?

LYSISTRATA.   What oath!
  In Aeschylus they take a slaughtered sheep
  And swear upon a buckler. Why not we?

CALONICE. O Lysistrata, Peace sworn on a buckler!

LYSISTRATA. What oath would suit us then?

CALONICE.   Something we could ride
  Would be our best insignia. . . . A white horse!
  Let's swear upon its entrails.

LYSISTRATA.   A horse indeed!

CALONICE. Then what will symbolize us?

LYSISTRATA.   This, as I tell you—
  First set a great dark bowl upon the ground
  And disembowel a skin of Thasian wine,
  Then swear that we'll not add a drop of water.

LAMPITO. Ah, what aith could clink pleasanter than that!

LYSISTRATA. Bring me a bowl then and a skin of wine.

CALONICE. My dears, see what a splendid bowl it is;
  I'd not say No if asked to sip it off.

LYSISTRATA. Put down the bowl. Lay hands, all, on the victim.
  Skiey Queen who givest the last word in arguments,

And thee, O Bowl, dear comrade, we beseech:
Accept our oblation and be propitious to us.

CALONICE. What healthy blood, la, how it gushes out!

LAMPITO. An' what a leesome fragrance through the air.

LYSISTRATA. Now, dears, if you will let me, I'll speak first.

CALONICE. Only if you draw the lot, by Aphrodite!

LYSISTRATA. So, grasp the brim, you, Lampito, and all.
You, Calonice, repeat for the rest
Each word I say. Then you must all take oath
And pledge your legs to the same stern conditions—
To husband or lover I'll not open thighs

CALONICE. *To husband or lover I'll not open thighs*

LYSISTRATA. Though he bring proof-of-love of monstrous size

CALONICE. *Though he bring proof-of-love of monstrous size*
O, O, my knees are failing me, Lysistrata.

LYSISTRATA. But still at home, ignoring him, I'll stay

CALONICE. *But still at home, ignoring him, I'll stay*

LYSISTRATA. Beautiful, clad in saffron silks all day

CALONICE. *Beautiful, clad in saffron silks all day*

LYSISTRATA. That so his passion I may swell and pinch

CALONICE. *That so his passion I may swell and pinch*

LYSISTRATA. I'll fight him to the very latest inch

CALONICE. *I'll fight him to the very latest inch*

LYSISTRATA. If, spite of hostile knees, he rapes me there

CALONICE. *If, spite of hostile knees, he rapes me there*

LYSISTRATA. I'll put him out, so frigid and aloof

CALONICE. *I'll put him out, so frigid and aloof*

LYSISTRATA. Nor wriggle with my toes stretched at the roof

CALONICE. *Nor wriggle with my toes stretched at the roof*

LYSISTRATA. Nor crouch like carven lions with arse in air

CALONICE. *Nor crouch like carven lions with arse in air*

LYSISTRATA. If I keep faith, then bounteous cups be mine

CALONICE. *If I keep faith, then bounteous cups be mine*

LYSISTRATA. If not, to nauseous water change this wine.

CALONICE. *If not, to nauseous water change this wine.*

LYSISTRATA. Do you all swear to this?

MYRRHINE. We do, we do.

LYSISTRATA. Then I shall immolate the victim thus.
(*She drinks.*)

CALONICE. Here now, share fair, haven't we made a pact?
Let's all quaff down that friendship in our turn.

LAMPITO. Hark, what caterwauling hubbub's that?

LYSISTRATA. As I told you,
The women have appropriated the citadel.

So, Lampito, dash off to your own land
And raise the rebels there. These will serve as hostages,
While we ourselves take our places in the ranks
And drive the bolts right home.

CALONICE. But won't the men
March straight against us?

LYSISTRATA. And what if they do?
No threat shall creak our hinges wide, no torch
Shall light a fear in us; we will come out
To Peace alone.

CALONICE. That's it, by Aphrodite!
As of old let us seem hard and obdurate.

(LAMPITO *and some go off, the others go up into the Acropolis.*)

(CHORUS OF OLD MEN *enter to attack the captured Acropolis.*)

CHORUS OF OLD MEN. Make room, Draces, move ahead;
  why your shoulder's chafed, I see,
With lugging uphill these lopped branches of the olive tree.
How upside-down and wrong-way-round a long life sees
  things grow.
Ah, Strymodorus, who'd have thought affairs could tangle so?
    The women whom at home we fed,
    Like witless fools, with fostering bread,
    Have impiously come to this—
    They've stolen the Acropolis,
    With bolts and bars our orders flout
        And shut us out.

Come Philurgus, bustle thither; lay our faggots on the
  ground,
In neat stacks beleaguering the insurgents all around;
And the vile conspiratresses, plotters of such mischief dire,
Pile and burn them all together in one vast and righteous
  pyre:
Fling with our own hands Lycon's wife to fry in the thick-
  est fire.

By Demeter, they'll get no brag while I've a vein to beat!
Cleomenes himself was hurtled out in sore defeat.
    His stiff-backed Spartan pride was bent.
    Out, stripped of all his arms, he went:

A pygmy cloak that would not stretch
To hide his rump (the draggled wretch),
Six sprouting years of beard, the spilth
        Of six years' filth.

That was a siege! Our men were ranged in lines of seven-
    teen deep
Before the gates, and never left their posts there, even to
    sleep.
Shall I not smite the rash presumption then of foes like
    these,
Detested both of all the gods and of Euripides—
Else, may the Marathon plain not boast my trophied vic-
    tories!

        Ah, now, there's but a little space
        To reach the place!
        A deadly climb it is, a tricky road
        With all this bumping load:
        A pack-ass soon would tire. . . .
        How these logs bruise my shoulders; farther still
        Jog up the hill,
        And puff the fire inside,
        Or just as we reach the top we'll find it's died.
                Ough, phew!
                I choke with the smoke.

        Lord Heracles, how acrid-hot
        Out of the pot
        This mad-dog smoke leaps, worrying me
        And biting angrily. . . .
        'Tis Lemnian fire that smokes,
        Or else it would not sting my eyelids thus. . . .
        Haste, all of us;
        Athene invokes our aid.
        Laches, now or never the assault must be made!
                Ough, phew!
                I choke with the smoke.

Thanked be the gods! The fire peeps up and crackles as it
    should.
Now why not first slide off our backs these weary loads of
    wood
And dip a vine branch in the brazier till it glows, then
    straight

Hurl it at the battering-ram against the stubborn gate?
If they refuse to draw the bolts in immediate compliance,
We'll set fire to the wood, and smoke will strangle their
defiance.

Phew, what a spluttering drench of smoke! Come, now from
off my back. . . .
Is there no Samos general to help me to unpack?
Ah there, that's over! For the last time now it's galled my
shoulder.
Flare up thine embers, brazier, and dutifully smolder,
To kindle a brand, that I the first may strike the citadel.
Aid me, Lady Victory, that a triumph trophy may tell
How we did anciently this insane audacity quell!

CHORUS OF WOMEN. What's that rising yonder? That ruddy
glare, that smoky skurry?
O is it something in a blaze? Quick, quick, my comrades,
hurry!

Nicodice, helter-skelter!
Or poor Calyce's in flames
And Cratylla's stifled in the welter.
O these dreadful old men
And their dark laws of hate!
There, I'm all of a tremble lest I turn out to be too late.
I could scarcely get near to the spring though I rose before
dawn,
What with tattling of tongues and rattling of pitchers in
one jostling din
With slaves pushing in! . . .

Still here at last the water's drawn
And with it eagerly I run
To help those of my friends who stand
In danger of being burned alive.
For I am told a dribbling band
Of graybeards hobble to the field,
Great fagots in each palsied hand,
As if a hot bath to prepare,
And threatening that out they'll drive
These wicked women or soon leave them charring into
ashes there.
O Goddess, suffer not, I pray, this harsh deed to be done,
But show us Greece and Athens with their warlike acts
repealed!

> For this alone, in this thy hold,
> Thou Goddess with the helm of gold,
> We laid hands on thy sanctuary,
> Athene.... Then our ally be
> And where they cast their fires of slaughter
> Direct our water!

STRATYLLIS (*caught*). Let me go!

WOMEN. You villainous old men, what's this you do?
No honest man, no pious man, could do such things as you.

MEN. Ah ha, here's something most original, I have no doubt:
A swarm of women-sentinels to man the walls without.

WOMEN. So then we scare you, do we? Do we seem a fearful host?
You only see the smallest fraction mustered at this post.

MEN. Ho, Phaedrias, shall we put a stop to all these chattering tricks?
Suppose that now upon their backs we splintered these our sticks.

WOMEN. Let us lay down the pitchers, so our bodies will be free,
In case these lumping fellows try to cause some injury.

MEN. O hit them hard and hit again and hit until they run away,
And perhaps they'll learn, like Bupalus, not to have too much to say.

WOMEN. Come on then, do it! I won't budge, but like a bitch I'll snap
Till you can show no more than I myself beneath the lap.

MEN. Be quiet, or I'll pash you out of any years to come.

WOMEN. Now you just touch Stratyllis with the top joint of your thumb.

MEN. What vengeance can you take if with my fists your face I beat?

WOMEN. I'll rip you with my teeth and strew your entrails at your feet.

MEN. Now I appreciate Euripides' strange subtlety:
Woman is the most shameless beast of all the beasts that be.

WOMEN. Rhodippe, come and let's pick up our water-jars once more.

MEN. Ah cursed drab, what have you brought this water hither for?

WOMEN. What is your fire for then, you smelly corpse? Yourself to burn?

MEN. To build a pyre and make your comrades ready for the
urn.

WOMEN. And I've the water to put out your fire immediately.

MEN. What, you put out my fire?

WOMEN.   Yes, sirrah, as you soon will see.

MEN. I don't know why I hesitate to roast you with this flame.

WOMEN. If you have any soap you'll go off cleaner than you
came.

MEN. Cleaner, you dirty slut?

WOMEN.   A nuptial bath in which to lie!

MEN. Did you hear that insolence?

WOMEN.   I'm a free woman, I.

MEN. I'll make you hold your tongue.

WOMEN.   Henceforth you'll serve in no more juries.

MEN. Burn off her hair for her.

WOMEN.   Now forward, water, quench their furies!

MEN. O dear, O dear!

WOMEN.   So . . . was it hot?

MEN. Hot! . . . Enough, O hold.

WOMEN. Watered, perhaps you'll bloom again—why not?

MEN. Brrr, I'm wrinkled up from shivering with cold.

WOMEN. Next time you've fire you'll warm yourself and leave
us to our lot.

(MAGISTRATE *enters with attendant Scythians.*)

MAGISTRATE. Have the luxurious rites of the women glittered
Their libertine show, their drumming tapped out crowds,
The Sabazian Mysteries summoned their mob,
Adonis been wept to death on the terraces,
As I could hear the last day in the Assembly?
For Demostratus—let bad luck befoul him—
Was roaring, *We must sail for Sicily,*
While a woman, throwing herself about in a dance
Lopsided with drink, was shrilling out *Adonis,*
Woe for Adonis. Then Demostratus shouted,
We must levy hoplites at Zacynthus,
And there the woman, up to the ears in wine,
Was screaming *Weep for Adonis* on the house top,
The scoundrelly politician, that lunatic ox,
Bellowing bad advice through tipsy shrieks:
Such are the follies wantoning in them.

MEN. O if you knew their full effrontery!
All of the insults they've done, besides sousing us
With water from their pots to our public disgrace

For we stand here wringing our clothes as though we'd
    pissed 'em.
MAGISTRATE. By Poseidon, justly done! For in part with us
The blame must lie for dissolute behavior
And for the pampered appetites they learn.
Thus grows the seedling lust to blossoming:
We go into a shop and say, *Here, goldsmith,*
You remember the necklace that you wrought my wife;
Well, the other night in fervor of a dance
Her clasp broke open. Now I'm off for Salamis;
If you've the leisure, would you go tonight
And stick a bolt pin into her opened clasp.
Another goes to a cobbler, a soldierly fellow,
Always standing up erect, and says to him,
Cobbler, a sandal strap of my wife's pinches her,
Hurts her little toe in a place where she's sensitive.
Come at noon and see if you can stretch out wider
This thing that troubles her, loosen its tightness.
And so you view the result. Observe my case—
I, a magistrate, come here to draw
Money to buy oar blades, and what happens?
The women slam the door full in my face.
But standing still's no use. Bring me a crowbar,
    And I'll chastise this their impertinence.
What do you gape at, wretch, with dazzled eyes?
Peering for a tavern, I suppose.
Come, force the gates with crowbars, prise them apart!
I'll prise away myself too. . . .

(LYSISTRATA *appears.*)

LYSISTRATA.   Stop this banging.
I'm coming of my own accord. . . . Why bars?
It is not bars we need but common sense.
MAGISTRATE. Indeed, you slut! Where is the archer now?
Arrest this woman, tie her hands behind.
LYSISTRATA. If he brushes me with a finger, by Artemis,
The public menial, he'll be sorry for it.
MAGISTRATE. Are you afraid? Grab her about the middle.
Two of you then, lay hands on her and end it.
CALONICE. By Pandrosos! if your hand touches her
I'll spread you out and trample on your guts.
MAGISTRATE. My guts! Where is the other archer gone?
Bind that minx there who talks so prettily.
MYRRHINE. By Phosphor, if your hand moves out her way
You'd better have a surgeon somewhere handy.

MAGISTRATE. You too! Where is that archer? Take that
    woman.

I'll put a stop to these surprise parties.

STRATYLLIS. By the Tauric Artemis, one inch nearer
    My fingers, and it's a bald man that'll be yelling.

MAGISTRATE. Tut tut, what's here? Deserted by my arch-
    ers. . . .

But surely women never can defeat us;
Close up your ranks, my Scythians. Forward at them.

LYSISTRATA. By the Goddesses, you'll find that here await you
    Four companies of most pugnacious women
    Armed cap-a-pie from the topmost louring curl
    To the lowest angry dimple.

MAGISTRATE.   On, Scythians, bind them.

LYSISTRATA. On, gallant allies of our high design,
    Vendors of grain-eggs-pulse-and-vegetables,
    Ye garlic-tavern-keepers of bakeries,
    Strike, batter, knock, hit, slap, and scratch our foes,
    Be finely imprudent, say what you think of them. . . .
    Enough! retire and do not rob the dead.

MAGISTRATE. How basely did my archer force come off.

LYSISTRATA. Ah, ha, you thought it was a herd of slaves
    You had to tackle, and you didn't guess
    The thirst for glory ardent in our blood.

MAGISTRATE. By Apollo, I know well the thirst that heats you—
    Especially when a wineskin's close.

MEN. You waste your breath, dear magistrate, I fear, in an-
    swering back.

What's the good of argument with such a rampageous
    pack?

Remember how they washed us down (these very clothes
    I wore)

With water that looked nasty and that smelt so even more.

WOMEN. What else to do, since you advanced too danger-
    ously nigh.

If you should do the same again, I'll punch you in the eye.

Though I'm a stay-at-home and most a quiet life enjoy,

Polite to all and every (for I'm naturally coy),

Still if you wake a wasps' nest then of wasps you must
    beware.

MEN. How may this ferocity be tamed? It grows too great to
    bear.

Let us question them and find if they'll perchance declare
    The reason why they strangely dare

To seize on Cranaos' citadel,
This eyrie inaccessible,
This shrine above the precipice,
The Acropolis.
Probe them and find what they mean with this idle talk;
    listen, but watch they don't try to deceive.
You'd be neglecting your duty most certainly if now this
    mystery unplumbed you leave.

MAGISTRATE. Women there! Tell what I ask you, directly....
    Come, without rambling, I wish you to state
What's your rebellious intention in barring up thus on our
    noses our own temple gate.

LYSISTRATA. To take first the treasury out of your manage-
    ment, and so stop the war through the absence of gold.

MAGISTRATE. Is gold then the cause of the war?

LYSISTRATA.   Yes, gold
    caused it and miseries more, too many to be told.
'Twas for money, and money alone, that Pisander with all
    of the army of mob agitators
Raised up revolutions. But, as for the future, it won't be
    worth while to set up to be traitors.
Not an obol they'll get as their loot, not an obol! while we
    have the treasure chest in our command.

MAGISTRATE. What then is that you propose?

LYSISTRATA.   Just this—
    merely to take the exchequer henceforth in hand.

MAGISTRATE. The exchequer!

LYSISTRATA.   Yes, why not? Of our
    capabilities you have had various clear evidences.
Firstly remember we have always administered soundly the
    budget of all home expenses.

MAGISTRATE. But this matter's different.

LYSISTRATA.   How is it different?

MAGISTRATE. Why, it deals chiefly with wartime supplies.

LYSISTRATA. But we abolish war straight by our policy.

MAGISTRATE.   What will you do if emergencies arise?

LYSISTRATA. Face them our own way.

MAGISTRATE.   What, *you* will?

LYSISTRATA.   Yes, *we* will!

MAGISTRATE. Then there's no help for it: we're all destroyed.

LYSISTRATA. No, willy-nilly you must be safeguarded.

MAGISTRATE. What madness is this?

LYSISTRATA.   Why, it seems you're annoyed.
It must be done, that's all.

MAGISTRATE.   Such awful oppression
    never, O never in the past yet I bore.
LYSISTRATA. You must be saved, sirrah—that's all there is to it.
MAGISTRATE.   If we don't want to be saved?
LYSISTRATA.   All the more.
MAGISTRATE. Why do women come prying and meddling in
    matters of state touching wartime and peace?
LYSISTRATA. That I will tell you.
MAGISTRATE.   O tell me or quickly I'll—
LYSISTRATA. Hearken awhile and from threatening cease.
MAGISTRATE. I cannot, I cannot; it's growing too insolent.
WOMEN. Come on; you've far more than we have to dread.
MAGISTRATE. Stop from your croaking, old carrion crow
    there. . . .
    Continue.
LYSISTRATA.   Be calm then and I'll go ahead.
  All the long years when the hopeless war dragged along,
    we, unassuming, forgotten in quiet,
  Endured without question, endured in our loneliness all
    your incessant child's antics and riot.
  Our lips we kept tied, though aching with silence, though
    well all the while in our silence we knew
  How wretchedly everything still was progressing by listen-
    ing dumbly the day long to you.
  For always at home you continued discussing the war and
    its politics loudly, and we
  Sometimes would ask you, our hearts deep with sorrowing,
    though we spoke lightly, though happy to see,
  What's to be inscribed on the side of the Treaty-stone?
    What, dear, was said in the Assembly today?
  Mind your own business, he'd answer me growlingly, *hold*
    your tongue, woman, or else go away.
  And so I would hold it.
WOMEN.   I'd not be silent for any man
    living on earth, no, not I!
MAGISTRATE. Not for a staff?
LYSISTRATA.   Well, so I did nothing but
    sit in the house, feeling dreary, and sigh,
  While ever arrived some fresh tale of decisions more fool-
    ish by far and presaging disaster.
  Then I would say to him, *O my dear husband, why still do*
    they rush on destruction the faster?
  At which he would look at me sideways, exclaiming,
    Keep for your web and your shuttle your care,

Or for some hours hence your cheeks will be sore and hot;
*   leave this alone, war is Man's sole affair!*

MAGISTRATE. By Zeus, but a man of fine sense, he.

LYSISTRATA.   How sensible?
    You dotard, because he at no time had lent
His intractable ears to absorb from our counsel one
    temperate word of advice, kindly meant?
But when at the last in the streets we heard shouted
    (everywhere ringing the ominous cry)
Is there no one to help us, no savior in Athens?
    and, *No, there is no one,* come back in reply.
At once a convention of all wives through Hellas
    here for a serious purpose was held,
To determine how husbands might yet back to wisdom
    despite their reluctance in time be compelled.
Why then delay any longer? It's settled.
    For the future you'll take up our old occupation.
Now in turn you're to hold tongue, as we did, and listen
    while we show the way to recover the nation.

MAGISTRATE. *You* talk to *us!* Why, you're mad. I'll not stand it.

LYSISTRATA. Cease babbling, you fool; till I end, hold your
    tongue.

MAGISTRATE. If I should take orders from one who wears veils,
    may my neck straightaway be deservedly wrung.

LYSISTRATA. O if that keeps pestering you,
    I've a veil here for your hair,
    I'll fit you out in everything
    As is only fair.

CALONICE. Here's a spindle that will do.

MYRRHINE. I'll add a wool basket too.

LYSISTRATA. Girdled now sit humbly at home,
    Munching beans, while you card wool and comb.
        For war from now on is the Women's affair.

WOMEN.   Come then, down pitchers, all,
                 And on, courageous of heart,
                 In our comradely venture
                 Each taking her due part.

I could dance, dance, dance, and be fresher after,
I could dance away numberless suns,
To no weariness let my knees bend.
Earth I could brave with laughter,
Having such wonderful girls here to friend.
O the daring, the gracious, the beautiful ones!

Their courage unswerving and witty
  Will rescue our city.

O sprung from the seed of most valiant-wombed grand-
  mothers, scions of savage and dangerous nettles!
Prepare for the battle, all. Gird up your angers.
  Our way the wind of sweet victory settles.

LYSISTRATA. O tender Eros and Lady of Cyprus,
  some flush of beauty I pray you devise
To smooth twixt our nipples and O Aphrodite
  prettily slip twixt our valorous thighs!
Joy will raise up its head through the legions warring
  and all of the far-serried ranks of mad love
Bristle the earth to the pillared horizon,
  pointing in vain to the heavens above.
I think that perhaps then they'll give us our title—
  Peacemakers.
MAGISTRATE.   What do you mean? Please explain.
LYSISTRATA. First, we'll not see you now flourishing arms
  about into the Marketing-place clang again.
WOMEN. No, by the Paphian.
LYSISTRATA.   Still I can conjure them
  as past where the herbs stand or crockery's sold
Like Corybants jingling (poor sots) fully armored, they
  noisily round on their promenade strolled.
MAGISTRATE. And rightly; that's discipline, they—
LYSISTRATA.   But what's sillier
  than to go on an errand of buying a fish
Carrying along an immense Gorgon buckler
  instead of the usual platter or dish?
A phylarch I lately saw, mounted on horseback,
  dressed for the part with long ringlets and all,
Stow in his helmet the omelet bought steaming
  from an old woman who kept a food stall.
Nearby a soldier, a Thracian, was shaking
  wildly his spear, like Tereus in the play,
To frighten a fig girl while unseen the ruffian
  filched from her fruit trays the ripest away.
MAGISTRATE. How, may I ask, will your rule re-establish
  order and justice in lands so tormented?
LYSISTRATA. Nothing is easier.
MAGISTRATE.   Out with it speedily—
  what is this plan that you boast you've invented?

LYSISTRATA. If, when yarn we are winding, it chances to tangle,
  then, as perchance you may know, through the skein
This way and that still the spool we keep passing
  till it is finally clear all again:
So to untangle the War and its errors,
  ambassadors out on all sides we will send
This way and that, here, there and round about—
  soon you will find that the War has an end.
MAGISTRATE. So with these trivial tricks of the household,
  domestic analogies of threads, skeins, and spools,
You think that you'll solve such a bitter complexity,
  unwind such political problems, you fools!
LYSISTRATA. Well, first as we wash dirty wool so's to cleanse it,
  so with a pitiless zeal we will scrub
Through the whole city for all greasy fellows;
  burrs too, the parasites, off we will rub.
That verminous plague of insensate place seekers
  soon between thumb and forefinger we'll crack.
All who inside Athens' walls have their dwelling
  into one great common basket we'll pack.
Disenfranchised or citizens, allies or aliens,
  pell-mell the lot of them in we will squeeze
Till they discover humanity's meaning. . . .
  As for disjointed and far colonies,
Them you must never from this time imagine as
  scattered about just like lost hanks of wool.
Each portion we'll take and wind in to this center,
  inward to Athens each loyalty pull,
Till from the vast heap where all's piled together
  at last can be woven a strong Cloak of State.
MAGISTRATE. How terrible is it to stand here and watch them
  carding and winding at will with our fate,
Witless in war as they are.
LYSISTRATA.   What of us then,
  who ever in vain for our children must weep
Borne but to perish afar and in vain?
MAGISTRATE. Not that, O let that one memory sleep!
LYSISTRATA. Then while we should be companioned still mer-
  rily, happy as brides may, the livelong night,
Kissing youth by, we are forced to lie single. . . .
  But leave for a moment our pitiful plight,
It hurts even more to behold the poor maidens
  helplessly wrinkling in staler virginity.
MAGISTRATE. Does not a man age?

LYSISTRATA.   Not in the same way.
    Not as a woman grows withered, grows he.
  He, when returned from the war, though gray-headed,
      yet if he wishes can choose out a wife.
  But she has no solace save peering for omens,
      wretched and lonely the rest of her life.

MAGISTRATE. But the old man who still can erect—

LYSISTRATA. O why not finish and die?
  A bier is easy to buy,
  A honey cake I'll knead you with joy,
  This garland will see you are decked.

CALONICE. I've a wreath for you too.

MYRRHINE. I also will fillet you.

LYSISTRATA. What more is lacking? Step aboard the boat.
  See, Charon shouts ahoy.
  You're keeping him, he wants to shove afloat.

MAGISTRATE. Outrageous insults! Thus my place to flout!
  Now to my fellow magistrates I'll go
  And what you've perpetrated on me show.

LYSISTRATA. Why are you blaming us for laying you out?
  Assure yourself we'll not forget to make
  The third day offering early for your sake.

        (MAGISTRATE *retires*, LYSISTRATA *returns within*.)

MEN. All men who call your loins your own, awake at last, arise
  And strip to stand in readiness. For as it seems to me
  Some more perilous offensive in their heads they now devise.

        I'm sure a Tyranny
        Like that of Hippias
        In this I detect. . . .
        They mean to put us under
        Themselves I suspect,
        And that Laconians assembling
        At Cleisthenes' house have played
        A trick-of-war and provoked them
        Madly to raid
        The Treasury, in which term I include
        The pay for my food.

        For is it not preposterous
        They should talk this way to us
        On a subject such as battle!

And, women as they are, about bronze bucklers dare to
    prattle—
Make alliance with the Spartans—people I for one
Like very hungry wolves would always most sincerely
    shun. . . .
        Some dirty game is up their sleeve,
        I believe.
A Tyranny, no doubt . . . but they won't catch me, that I
    know.
        Henceforth on my guard I'll go,
A sword with myrtle branches wreathed forever in my
    hand,
And under arms in the Public Place I'll take my watchful
    stand,
Shoulder to shoulder with Aristogeiton. Now my staff I'll
    draw
        And start at once by knocking
          that shocking
        Hag upon the jaw.

WOMEN. Your own mother will not know you when you get
    back to the town.
But first, my friends and allies, let us lay these garments
    down,
And all ye fellow-citizens, hark to me while I tell
        What will aid Athens well.
        Just as is right, for I
        Have been a sharer
        In all the lavish splendor
        Of the proud city.
        I bore the holy vessels
        At seven, then
        I pounded barley
        At the age of ten,
        And clad in yellow robes,
        Soon after this,
        I was Little Bear to
        Brauronian Artemis;
        Then neckleted with figs,
        Grown tall and pretty,
        I was a Basket bearer.
        And so it's obvious I should
        Give you advice that I think good,
        The very best I can.
It should not prejudice my voice that I'm not born a man,

If I say something advantageous to the present situation.
For I'm taxed too, and as a toll provide men for the nation.
> While, miserable graybeards, you,
> > It is true,

Contribute nothing of any importance whatever to our
needs;
> But the treasure raised against the Medes

You've squandered, and no nothing in return, save that you
make
Our lives and persons hazardous by some imbecile mistake.
What can you answer? Now be careful, don't arouse my
spite,
Or with my slipper I'll take you napping,
> > faces slapping
> > > Left and right.

MEN. What villainies they contrive!
Come, let vengeance fall,
You that below the waist are still alive,
Off with your tunics at my call—
> Naked, all.

For a man must surely savor of a man.
No quaking, brave steps taking, careless what protrudes,
white-shooed,
> in the nude, onward bold,
> > All ye who garrisoned Leipsidrion of old....
> > > Let each one wag
> > > As youthfully as he can,
> > > And if he has the cause at heart
> > > Rise at least a span.

We must take a stand and keep to it,
For if we yield the smallest bit
> To their importunity,

Then nowhere from their inroads will be left to us immunity.
But they'll be building ships and soon their navies will
attack us,
As Artemisia did, and seek to fight us and to sack us.
> And if they mount, the Knights they'll rob
> > Of a job.

For everyone knows how talented they all are in the saddle,
> Having long practiced how to straddle;
No matter how they're jogged there up and down, they're
never thrown.

Then think of Myron's painting, and each horsebacked
  Amazon

In combat hand-to-hand with men. . . . Come, on these
  women fall,

> And in pierced wood-collars let's stick
>   quick
> The necks of one and all.

WOMEN. Don't cross me or I'll loose
> The Beast that's kenneled here. . . .
> And soon you will be howling for a truce,
> Howling out with fear.
> But my dear,
>   Strip also, that women may savor of woman's pas-
>   sion. . . .

But you, you'll be too sore to eat garlic more, or one black
  bean, I really mean, so great's my spleen, to kick you
  black and blue

> With these my dangerous legs.
> I'll hatch the lot of you,
> If my rage you dash on,
> The way the relentless Beetle
> Hatched the Eagle's eggs.

> Scornfully aside I set
> Every silly old-man threat
> While Lampito's with me.

Or dear Ismenia, the noble Theban girl. Then let decree
Be hotly piled upon decree; in vain will be your labors,
You futile rogue abominated by your suffering neighbors.

> To Hecate's feast I yesterday went—
> Off I sent

To our neighbors in Boeotia, asking as a gift to me
> For them to pack immediately

That darling dainty thing . . . a good fat eel I meant of
  course;

But they refused because some idiotic old decree's in force.

O this strange passion for decrees nothing on earth can
  check,

Till someone puts a foot out tripping you,
>   and slipping you
> Break your neck.

(LYSISTRATA *enters in dismay*.)

WOMEN. Dear Mistress of our martial enterprise,
  Why do you come with sorrow in your eyes?

LYSISTRATA. O 'tis our naughty femininity,
  So weak in one spot, that hath saddened me.
WOMEN. What's this? Please speak.
LYSISTRATA. Poor women, O so weak!
WOMEN. What can it be? Surely your friends may know.
LYSISTRATA. Yea, I must speak it though it hurt me so.
WOMEN. Speak; can we help? Don't stand there mute in need.
LYSISTRATA. I'll blurt it out then—our wombs, our wombs have
    mutinied.
WOMEN. O Zeus!
LYSISTRATA. What use is Zeus to our anatomy?
  Here is the gaping calamity I meant:
  I cannot shut their ravenous appetites
  A moment more now. They are all deserting.
  The first I caught was sidling through the postern
  Close by the Cave of Pan: the next hoisting herself
  With rope and pulley down: a third on the point
  Of slipping past: while a fourth malcontent seated
  For instant flight to Orsilochus' brothel
  On bird-back I dragged off by the hair in time. . . .
  They are all snatching excuses to sneak home.
  Look, there goes one. . . . Hey, what's the hurry?
FIRST WOMAN. I must get home. I've some Milesian wool
  Packed wasting away, and moths are pushing through it.
LYSISTRATA. Fine moths indeed, I know. Get back within.
FIRST WOMAN. By the Goddesses, I'll return instantly.
  I only want to stretch it on my bed.
LYSISTRATA. You shall stretch nothing and go nowhere either.
FIRST WOMAN. Must I never use my wool then?
LYSISTRATA.   If needs be.
SECOND WOMAN. How unfortunate I am. O my poor flax!
  It's left at home unstript.
LYSISTRATA.   So here's another
  That wishes to go home and strip her flax.
  Inside again!
SECOND WOMAN. No, by the Goddess of Light,
  I'll be back as soon as I have flayed it properly.
LYSISTRATA. You'll not flay anything. For if you begin
  There'll not be one here but has a patch to be flayed.
THIRD WOMAN. O holy Eilithyia, stay this birth
  Till I have left the precincts of the place!
LYSISTRATA. What nonsense is this?
THIRD WOMAN.   I'll drop it any minute.
LYSISTRATA. Yesterday you weren't with child.

THIRD WOMAN.   But I am today.
  O let me find a midwife, Lysistrata.
  O quickly!

LYSISTRATA.   Now what story is this you tell?
  What is this hard lump here?

THIRD WOMAN.   It's a male child.

LYSISTRATA. By Aphrodite, it isn't. Your belly's hollow,
  And it has the feel of metal. . . . Well, I soon can see.
  You hussy, it's Athene's sacred helm,
  And you said you were with child.

THIRD WOMAN.   And so I am.

LYSISTRATA. Then why the helm?

THIRD WOMAN.   So if the throes should take me
  Still in these grounds I could use it like a dove
  As a laying nest in which to drop the child.

LYSISTRATA. More pretexts! You can't hide your clear intent,
  And anyway why not wait till the tenth day
  Meditating a brazen name for your brass brat?

FOURTH WOMAN. And I can't sleep a wink. My nerve is gone
  Since I saw that snake sentinel of the shrine.

FIFTH WOMAN. And all those dreadful owls with their weird
        hooting!
  Though I'm wearied out, I can't close an eye.

LYSISTRATA. You wicked women, cease from juggling lies.
  You want your men. But what of them as well?
  They toss as sleepless in the lustful night.
  I'm sure of it. Hold out awhile, hold out,
  But persevere a teeny-weeny longer.
  An oracle has promised Victory
  If we don't wrangle. Would you hear the words?

WOMEN. Yes, yes, what is it?

LYSISTRATA.   Silence then, your chatterboxes.
  Here—
  *Whenas the swallows flocking in one place from the
      hoopoes*
  Deny their legs love's gambols any more,
  *All woes shall then have ending and great Zeus the
      Thunderer*
  Shall put above what was below before.

WOMEN. Are the men then always to be underneath?

LYSISTRATA. *But if the swallows squabble among themselves
      and fly away*
  Out of the temple, refusing to agree,
  Then The Most Lascivious Birds in all the World

They shall be named forever. That's his decree.

WOMEN. It's obvious what it means.

LYSISTRATA. Now by all the gods

We must let no agony deter from duty.

Back to your quarters. For we are base indeed,

My friends, if we betray the oracle. (*She goes out.*)

OLD MEN. I'd like to remind you of a fable they used to employ,

When I was a little boy:

How once through fear of the marriage bed a young man,

Melanion by name, to the wilderness ran,

And there on the hills he dwelt.

For hares he wove a net

Which with his dog he set—

Most likely he's there yet.

For he never came back home, so great was the fear he felt.

I loathe the sex as much as he,

And therefore I no less shall be

As chaste as was Melanion.

MAN. Grann'am, do you much mind rape?

WOMAN. Onions you won't need, to cry.

MAN. From my foot you shan't escape.

WOMAN. What thick forests I espy.

MEN. So Myronides' fierce beard

And ponderous black arse were feared,

That the foe fled when they were shown—

Brave he 'as Phormion.

WOMEN. Well, I'll relate a rival fable just to show to you

A different point of view:

There was a rough-hewn fellow, Timon, with a face

That glowered as through a thorn-bush in a wild, bleak place.

He too decided on flight,

This very Furies' son,

All the world's ways to shun

And hide from everyone,

Spitting out curses on all knavish men to left and right.

But though for men he reared this hate,

With women still he loved to mate

And never thought them enemies.

WOMAN. O your jaw I'd like to break.

MAN. That I fear do you suppose?

WOMAN. Learn what kicks my legs can make.

MAN. Hair and more than hair expose.

WOMAN. Nay, you'll see there, I engage,
   All is well kept despite my age,
   And tended smoothly so's to please,
   Scorched for emergencies.

 (LYSISTRATA *appears.*)

LYSISTRATA.   Hollo, there, hasten hither to me.
 Skip fast along.

WOMAN.   What is this? Why the noise?

LYSISTRATA. A man, a man! I spy a frenzied man!
 He carries Love before him like a staff.
 O Lady of Cyprus, and Cythera, and Paphos,
 I beseech you, keep our minds and hands to the oath.

WOMAN. Where is he, whoever he is?

LYSISTRATA.   By the Temple of Chloe.

WOMAN. Yes, now I see him, but who can he be?

LYSISTRATA. Look at him. Does anyone recognise his face?

MYRRHINE. I do. He is my husband, Cinesias.

LYSISTRATA. You know how to work. Play with him, lead
 him on,
 Seduce him to the cozening point—kiss him, kiss him,
 Then slip your mouth aside just as he's sure of it,
 Ungirdle every caress his mouth feels at
 Save that the oath upon the bowl has locked.

MYRRHINE. You can rely on me.

LYSISTRATA.   I'll stay here to help
 In stroking up his passion to its height
 Of vain magnificence. . . . The rest to their quarters.

 (*Enter* CINESIAS.)

 Who is this that stands within our lines?

CINESIAS.   I.

LYSISTRATA. A man?

CINESIAS.   Too much a man!

LYSISTRATA.   Then be off at once.

CINESIAS. Who are you that thus eject me?

LYSISTRATA.   Guard for the day.

CINESIAS. By all the gods, then call Myrrhine hither.

LYSISTRATA. So, call Myrrhine hither! Who are you?

CINESIAS. I am her husband, Cinesias, son of Penis.

LYSISTRATA. Welcome dear friend. That glorious name of
 yours
 Is quite familiar in our ranks. Your wife
 Continually has it in her mouth.
 She cannot touch an apple or an egg
 But she must say, *This to Cinesias!*

CINESIAS. O is that true?

LYSISTRATA. By Aphrodite, it is.
If the conversation strikes on men, your wife
Cuts in with, *All are boobies by Cinesias.*

CINESIAS. Then call her here.

LYSISTRATA. And what am I to get?

CINESIAS. This, if you want it. . . . See, what I have here.
I'll give it you to dandle.

LYSISTRATA. Then I'll call her.

CINESIAS. Be quick, be quick. All grace is wiped from life
Since she went away. O sad, sad am I
When there I enter on that loneliness,
And wine is unvintaged of the sun's flavor,
And food tasteless, since I've grown this extra limb.

MYRRHINE (*above*). I love him O so much! but he won't
have it.
Don't call me down to him.

CINESIAS. Sweet little Myrrhine!
What do you mean? Come here.

MYRRHINE. O no I won't.
Why are you calling me? You don't want me.

CINESIAS. Not want you! with this week's old length of love.

MYRRHINE. Farewell.

CINESIAS. Don't go, please don't go, Myrrhine.
At least you'll hear our child. Call your mother, lad.

CHILD. Mummy . . . mummy . . . mummy!

CINESIAS. There now, don't you feel pity for the child
He's not been fed or washed now for six days.

MYRRHINE. I certainly pity him with so heartless a father.

CINESIAS. Come down, my sweetest, come for the child's sake.

MYRRHINE. A trying life it is to be a mother!
I suppose I'd better go.
(*She comes down.*)

CINESIAS. How much younger she looks,
How fresher and how prettier! Myrrhine,
Lift up your lovely face, your disdainful face;
And your ankle . . . let your scorn step out its worst;
It only rubs me to more passion here.

MYRRHINE (*playing with the child*). You're as innocent as he's
iniquitous.
Let me kiss you, honey petling, mother's darling.

CINESIAS. How wrong to follow other women's counsel
And let loose all these throbbing voids in yourself
As well as in me. Don't you go throb-throb?

MYRRHINE. Take away your hands.

CINESIAS. Everything in the house
Is being ruined.

MYRRHINE. I don't care at all.

CINESIAS. The roosters are picking all your web to rags.
Do you mind that?

MYRRHINE. Not I.

CINESIAS. What time we've wasted
We might have drenched with Paphian laughter, flung
On Aphrodite's Mysteries. O come here.

MYRRHINE. Not till a treaty finishes the war.

CINESIAS. If you must have it, then we'll get it done.

MYRRHINE. Do it and I'll come home. Till then I am bound.

CINESIAS. Well, let us have a quick one on the ground.

MYRRHINE. No . . . no . . . still I'll not say that I don't love you.

CINESIAS. You love me! Then, dear girl, let me get above you.

MYRRHINE. You must be joking. The boy's looking on.

CINESIAS. Here, Manes, take the child home. . . . There, he's
      gone.
There's nothing in the way now. Come, lie down.

MYRRHINE. But, villain, where shall we do it?

CINESIAS. In Pan's cave.
A splendid place!

MYRRHINE. Where shall I make my ablutions
Before returning to the citadel?

CINESIAS. You can easily wash yourself in the Clepsydra.

MYRRHINE. But how can I break my oath?

CINESIAS. Leave that to me,
I'll take all risk.

MYRRHINE. Well, I'll get you a small couch.

CINESIAS. Don't worry. I'd as soon lie on the ground.

MYRRHINE. No, by Apollo, in spite of all your faults
I won't have you lying on the nasty earth.

(*From here* MYRRHINE *keeps on going off to fetch things.*)

CINESIAS. Ah, how she loves me.

MYRRHINE. Get into the bed,
While I take off my clothes. O what a nuisance,
I must find a mattress first.

CINESIAS. Why a mattress?
Please don't get one!

MYRRHINE. Lie on crude sacking!
Never, by Artemis! That would be too vulgar.

CINESIAS. Open your legs.

MYRRHINE. No. Wait a second.

CINESIAS.   O . . .
  Then hurry back again.
MYRRHINE.   Here's a mattress, now
  ,Lie down while I undress. But what a shame,
  You have no pillow.
CINESIAS.   I don't want one, dear.
MYRRHINE. But I do.
CINESIAS.   Miserable Comrade mine,
  They treat you just like Heracles at a feast
  With cheats of dainties, O disappointing legs!
MYRRHINE. Raise up your head.
CINESIAS.   There, that's everything at last.
MYRRHINE. Yes, all.
CINESIAS.   Then run to my arms, you golden girl.
MYRRHINE. I'm undoing my girdle now. But you've not for-
    gotten?
  You're not deceiving me about the Treaty?
CINESIAS. No, by my life, I'm not.
MYRRHINE.   Why, you've no blanket.
CINESIAS. It's not the blanket but you I want to ravish.
MYRRHINE. Never mind. You'll do that soon. I'll come straight
    back.
CINESIAS. The woman will choke me with her coverlets.
MYRRHINE. Get up a moment.
CINESIAS.   Something else is up.
MYRRHINE. Would you like me to perfume you?
CINESIAS.   By Apollo, no!
MYRRHINE. By Aphrodite, I'll do it anyway.
CINESIAS. Lord Zeus, may she soon use up all the myrrh.
MYRRHINE. Stretch out your hand. Take it and rub it in.
CINESIAS. Hmm, it's not as fragrant as might be; that is,
  Not before it's smeared. It doesn't smell of kisses.
MYRRHINE. How silly I am: I've brought you Rhodian scents.
CINESIAS. It's good enough, leave it, love.
MYRRHINE.   You must be jesting.
CINESIAS. Plague rack the man who first compounded scent!
MYRRHINE. Here, take this flask.
CINESIAS.   I've a far better one.
  Don't tease me, lie down, and get nothing more.
MYRRHINE. I'm coming . . . I'm just drawing off my shoes. . . .
  You're sure you will vote for Peace?
CINESIAS.   I'll think about it.
                                        (She runs off.)
  I'm dead: the woman's worn me all away.

She's gone and left me with an anguished pulse.
What shall I put thee in (O woe!)
Since into something thou must go,
Poor little lad . . . he pines and peeks.
Our lovely girl has proved a curse.
(Where's Cynalopex?)
A nurse to cherish him, a nurse!

MEN. Balked in your amorous delight
How melancholy is your plight.
With sympathy your case I view!
What loins, I ask, what liver too,
What cods, what buttocks, could sustain
This awful stretch and stiffening strain,
    And not a single trace
Of lewd-thighed wenches in the place!

CINESIAS. O Zeus, what sinewy suffering!

MEN. She did it all, the harlot, she
With her atrocious harlotry.

WOMEN. Nay, rather call her darling sweet.

MEN. What, sweet? She's a rude, wicked thing.

CINESIAS. A wicked thing, as I repeat.
    O Zeus, O Zeus,
Canst thou not suddenly let loose
Some twirling hurricane to tear
Her flapping up along the air
And drop her, when she's whirled around,
    Here to the ground
Neatly impaled upon this stake
That rises only for her sake.

                                    (He goes out.)

(Enter Spartan HERALD. The MAGISTRATE comes forward.)

HERALD. Where gabs the Senate an' the Prytanes?
I've fetched dispatches for them.

MAGISTRATE.   Are you a man
Or a Priapus, pray?

HERALD.   My scrimp-brained lad,
I'm a herald, as ye see, who hae come frae Sparta
Anent a Peace.

MAGISTRATE.   Then why do you hide that lance
That sticks out under your arms?

HERALD.   I've brought no lance.

MAGISTRATE. Then why do you turn aside and hold your cloak
So far out from your body? Is your groin swollen
With stress of traveling?

HERALD. By Castor, I'll swear
The man is wud.

MAGISTRATE. Why, look, it stands right out,
My rascal fellow.

HERALD. But I tell ye No!
Enow o' fleering!

MAGISTRATE. Well, what is it then?

HERALD. It's my dispatch cane.

MAGISTRATE. Of course—a Spartan cane!
But speak right out. I know all this too well.
Are new privations springing up in Sparta?

HERALD. Och, hard as could be: in lofty lusty columns
Our allies stand united. We maun get Pellene.

MAGISTRATE. Whence has this evil come? Is it from Pan?

HERALD. No. Lampito first ran asklent, then the ithers
Sprinted after her example, and blocked, the hizzies,
Their wames unskaithed against our every fleech.

MAGISTRATE. What did you do?

HERALD. We are broken, and bent double
Limp like men carrying lanthorns in great winds
About the city. They winna let us even
Wi' lightest neif skim their primsie howes
Till we've concluded Peace-terms wi' a' Hellas.

MAGISTRATE. So the conspiracy is universal;
This proves it. Then return to Sparta, bid them
Send envoys with full powers to treat of Peace;
And I will urge the Senate here to choose
Plenipotentiary ambassadors,
As argument adducing this erection.

HERALD. I'm off. Your wisdom nane could contravert.

(*They retire.*)

MEN. There is no beast, no rush of fire, like woman so un-
tamed.
She calmly goes her way where even panthers would be
shamed.

WOMEN. And yet you are fool enough, it seems, to dare to war
with me,
When for your faithful ally you might win me easily.

MEN. Never could the hate I feel for womankind grow less.

WOMEN. Then have your will. But I'll take pity on your naked-
ness.
For I can see just how ridiculous you look, and so
Will help you with your tunic if close up I now may go.

MEN. Well, that, by Zeus, is no scoundrel deed, I frankly will
admit.

I only took them off myself in a scoundrel raging fit.

WOMEN. Now you look sensible, and that you're men no one
could doubt.

If you were but good friends again, I'd take the insect out
That hurts your eye.

MEN. Is that what's wrong? That nasty bitie thing.

Please squeeze it out, and show me what it is that makes
this sting.

It's been paining me a long while now.

WOMEN. Well I'll agree to that,

Although you're most unmannerly. O what a giant gnat.

Here, look! It comes from marshy Tricorysus, I can tell.

MEN. O thank you. It was digging out a veritable well.

Now that it's gone, I can't hold back my tears. See how
they fall.

WOMEN. I'll wipe them off, bad as you are, and kiss you after
all.

MEN. I won't be kissed.

WOMEN. O yes, you will. Your wishes do not matter.

MEN. O botheration take you all! How you cajole and flatter.

A hell it is to live with you; to live without, a hell:

How truly was that said. But come, these enmities let's
quell.

You stop from giving orders and I'll stop from doing wrong.

So let's join ranks and seal our bargain with a choric song.

CHORUS. Athenians, it's not our intention

    To sow political dissension

    By giving any scandal mention;

But on the contrary to promote good feeling in the state

By word and deed. We've had enough calamities of late.

    So let a man or woman but divulge

    They need a trifle, say,

    Two minas, three or four,

    I've purses here that bulge.

    There's only one condition made

    (Indulge my whim in this I pray)—

    When Peace is signed once more,

    On no account am I to be repaid.

    And I'm making preparation

    For a gay select collation

    With some youths of reputation.

I've managed to produce some soup and they're slaughter-
    ing for me
A sucking pig: its flesh should taste as tender as could be.
        I shall expect you at my house today.
        To the baths make an early visit,
        And bring your children along;
        Don't dawdle on the way.
        Ask no one; enter as if the place
        Was all your own—yours henceforth is it.
        If nothing chances wrong,
        The door will then be shut bang in your face.

(*The* SPARTAN AMBASSADORS *approach.*)

CHORUS. Here come the Spartan envoys with long, worried
    beards.
        What's there?
That contraption like a wattled pig-sty jumbled twixt their
    thighs?
        Hail, Spartans how do you fare?
        Did anything new arise?
SPARTAN. No need for a clutter o' words. Do ye see our
    condition?
CHORUS. The situation swells to greater tension.
    Something will explode soon.
SPARTAN.   It's awfu' truly.
But come, let us wi' the best speed we may
Scribble a Peace.
CHORUS.   I notice that our men
Like wrestlers poised for contest, hold their clothes
Out from their bellies. An athlete's malady!
Since exercise alone can bring relief.
ATHENIAN. Can anyone tell us where Lysistrata is?
There is no need to describe our men's condition,
It shows up plainly enough.
CHORUS.   It's the same disease.
Do you feel a jerking throb there in the morning?
ATHENIAN. By Zeus, yes! In these straits I'm racked all
    through.
Unless Peace is soon declared, we shall be driven
In the void of women to try Cleisthenes.
CHORUS. Be wise and put your tunics on; who knows,
One of the Hermes castrators may perceive you.
ATHENIAN. By Zeus, you're right.
SPARTAN.   By the Twa Goddesses,
Indeed ye are. Let's put our tunics on.

ATHENIAN. Hail O my fellow sufferers, hail Spartans.

SPARTAN. O hinnie darling, what a waefu' thing
  If they had seen us wi' our lunging waddies!

ATHENIAN. Tell us then, Spartans, what has brought you here?

SPARTAN. We come to treat o' Peace.

ATHENIAN.   Well spoken there!
  And we the same. Let us call out Lysistrata
  Since she alone can settle the Peace terms.

SPARTAN. Call out Lysistrata too if ye don't mind.

CHORUS. No indeed. She hears your voices and she comes.
  (Enter LYSISTRATA.)
  Hail, Wonder of all women! Now you must be in turn
  Hard, shifting, clear, deceitful, noble, crafty, sweet, and
    stern.
  The foremost men of Hellas, smitten by your fascination,
  Have brought their tangled quarrels here for your sole
    arbitration.

LYSISTRATA. An easy task if their love's raging homesickness
  Doesn't start trying out how well each other
  Will serve instead of us. But I'll know at once
  If they do. O where's that girl, Reconciliation?
  Bring first before me the Spartan delegates,
  And see you lift no rude or violent hands—
  None of the churlish ways our husbands used.
  But lead them courteously, as women should.
  And if they grudge fingers, catch what's a better handle.
  And introduce them with ready tact. The Athenians
  Draw by whatever offers you a grip.
  Now, Spartans, stay here facing me. Here you,
  Athenians. Both hearken to my words.
  I am a woman, but I'm not a fool.
  And what of natural intelligence I own
  Has been filled out with the remembered precepts
  My father and the city elders taught me.
  First I reproach you both sides equally
  That when at Pylae and Olympia,
  At Pytho and the many other shrines
  That I could name, you sprinkle from one cup
  The altars common to all Hellenes, yet
  You wrack Hellenic cities, bloody Hellas
  With deaths of her own sons, while yonder clangs
  The gathering menace of barbarians.

ATHENIAN. I cannot hold it in much longer now.

LYSISTRATA. Now unto you, O Spartans, do I speak.

Do you forget how your own countryman,
Pericleidas, once came hither suppliant
Before our altars, pale in his purple robes,
Praying for an army when in Messenia
Danger growled, and the Sea god made earth quaver.
Then with four thousand hoplites Cimon marched
And saved all Sparta. Yet base ingrates now,
You are ravaging the soil of your preservers.

ATHENIAN. By Zeus, they do great wrong, Lysistrata.

SPARTAN. Great wrang, indeed. O what a pretty arse.

LYSISTRATA. And now I turn to the Athenians.
Have you forgotten too how once the Spartans
In days when you wore slavish tunics, came
And with their spears broke a Thessalian host
And all the partisans of Hippias?
They alone stood by your shoulder on that day.
They freed you, so that for the slave's short skirt
You should wear the trailing cloak of liberty.

SPARTAN. I've never seen a nobler woman anywhere.

ATHENIAN. Nor I one with such prettily jointing hips.

LYSISTRATA. Now, brethren twined with mutual benefactions,
Can you still war, can you suffer such disgrace?
Why not be friends? What is there to prevent you?

SPARTAN. We're agreed, gin that we get this tempting Mole,

LYSISTRATA. Which one?

SPARTAN.   That ane we've wanted to get into,
O for sae lang. . . . Pylos, of course.

ATHENIAN.   By Poseidon,
Never!

LYSISTRATA. Give it up.

ATHENIAN.   Then what will we do?
We need some ticklish place united to us—

LYSISTRATA. Ask for some other lurking-hole in return.

ATHENIAN. Then, ah, we'll choose this snug thing here,
    Echinus,
Shall we call the nestling spot? And this backside haven,
These desirable twin promontories, the Maliac,
And then of course these Megarean Legs.

SPARTAN. Not that, O surely not that, never that.

LYSISTRATA. Agree! Now what are two legs more or less?

ATHENIAN. I want to strip at once and plow my land.

SPARTAN. And I too—but I want to dung it first.

LYSISTRATA. And so you can, when Peace is once declared.

If you mean it, get your allies' heads together
  And come to some decision.
ATHENIAN.   What allies?
  There's no distinction in our politics:
  We've risen as one man to this conclusion;
  Every ally is jumping-mad to drive it home.
SPARTAN. And ours the same, for sure.
ATHENIAN.   The Carystians first!
  I'll bet on that.
LYSISTRATA.   I agree with all of you.
  Now off and cleanse yourselves for the Acropolis,
  For we invite you all in to a supper
  From our commissariat-baskets. There at table
  You will pledge your good behavior to our loins;
  Then each man's wife is his to hustle home.
ATHENIAN. Come, as quickly as possible.
SPARTAN.   As quick as ye like.
  Lead on.
ATHENIAN. O Zeus, quick, quick, lead quickly on.

                                    (*They hurry off.*)

CHORUS.   Broidered stuffs on high I'm heaping,
              Fashionable cloaks and sweeping
              Trains, not even gold gawds keeping.
  Take them all, I pray you, take them all (I do not care)
  And deck your children—your daughter, if the Basket she's
    to bear.
              Come, everyone of you, come in and take
              Of this rich hoard a share.
              Nought's tied so skillfully
              But you its seal can break
              And plunder all you spy inside.
              I've laid out all that I can spare,
              And therefore you will see
              Nothing unless than I you're sharper-eyed.
              If lacking corn a man should be
              While his slaves clamor hungrily
              And his excessive progeny,
  Then I've a handful of grain at home which is always to
    be had,
  And to which in fact a more-than-life-size loaf I'd gladly
    add.
              Then let the poor bring with them bag or sack
              And take this store of food.
              Manes, my man, I'll tell

To help them all to pack
Their wallets full. But O take care.
I had forgotten; don't intrude,
Or terrified you'll yell.
My dog is hungry too, and bites—beware!

(*Some* LOUNGERS *from the Market with torches approach the Banqueting hall. The* PORTER *bars their entrance.*)

FIRST LOUNGER. Open the door.

PORTER. Here, move along.

FIRST LOUNGER. What's this?
You're sitting down. Shall I singe you with my torch?
That's vulgar! O I couldn't do it . . . yet
If it would gratify the audience,
I'll mortify myself.

SECOND LOUNGER. And I will too.
We'll both be crude and vulgar, yes we will.

PORTER. Be off at once now or you'll be wailing
Dirges for your hair. Get off at once,
And see you don't disturb the Spartan envoys
Just coming out from the splendid feast they've had.

(*The banqueters begin to come out.*)

FIRST ATHENIAN. I've never known such a pleasant banquet
before,
And what delightful fellows the Spartans are.
When we are warm with wine, how wise we grow.

SECOND ATHENIAN. That's only fair, since sober we're such
fools.
This is the advice I'd give the Athenians—
See our ambassadors are always drunk.
For when we visit Sparta sober, then
We're on the alert for trickery all the while
So that we miss half of the things they say,
And misinterpret things that were never said,
And then report the muddle back to Athens.
But now we're charmed with each other. They might cap
With the Telamon-catch instead of the Cleitagora,
And we'd applaud and praise them just the same;
We're not too scrupulous in weighing words.

PORTER. Why, here the rascals come again to plague me.
Won't you move on, you sorry loafers there!

LOUNGER. Yes, by Zeus, they're already coming out.

SPARTAN. Now hinnie dearest, please tak' up your pipe
That I may try a spring an' sing my best
In honor o' the Athenians an' oursels.

ATHENIAN. Aye, take your pipe. By all the gods, there's noth-
    ing
  Could glad my heart more than to watch you dance.
SPARTANS. Mnemosyne,
    Let thy fire storm these younkers,
    O tongue wi' stormy ecstasy
       My Muse that knows
    Our deeds and theirs, how when at sea
    Their navies swooped upon
    The Medes at Artemision—
    Gods for their courage, did they strike
    Wrenching a triumph frae their foes;
       While at Thermopylae
  Leonidas' army stood: wild boars they were like,
    Wild boars that wi' fierce threat
    Their terrible tusks whet;
  The sweat ran streaming down each twisted face,
    Faem blossoming i' strange petals o' death
      Panted frae mortal breath,
  The sweat drenched a' their bodies i' that place,
  For the hurlyburly o' Persians glittered more
      Than the sands on the shore.

    Come, Hunting Girl, an' hear my prayer—
  You whose arrows whizz in woodlands, come an' bless
      This Peace we swear.
    Let us be fenced wi' agelong amity,
  O let this bond stick ever firm through thee
      In friendly happiness.
  Henceforth no guilefu' perjury be seen!
      O hither, hither O
      Thou wildwood queen.
LYSISTRATA. Earth is delighted now, peace is the voice of
    earth.
  Spartans, sort out your wives: Athenians, yours.
  Let each catch hands with his wife and dance his joy,
  Dance out his thanks, be grateful in music,
  And promise reformation with his heels.
ATHENIANS. O Dancers, forward. Lead out the Graces,
      Call Artemis out;
  Then her brother, the Dancer of Skies,
      That gracious Apollo.
      Invoke with a shout
      Dionysus out of whose eyes

Breaks fire on the maenads that follow;
And Zeus with his flares of quick lightning, and call
      Happy Hera, Queen of all,
And all the Daimons summon hither to be
      Witnesses of our revelry
And of the noble Peace we have made,
      Aphrodite our aid.
      Io Paieon, Io, cry—
      For victory, leap!
      Attained by me, leap!
      Euoi Euoi Euai Euai.

SPARTAN. Piper, gie us the music for a new sang.

SPARTANS. Leaving again lovely lofty Taygetus
Hither O Spartan Muse, hither to greet us,
And wi' our choric voice to raise
To Amyclean Apollo praise,
And Tyndareus' gallant sons whose days
Alang Eurotas' banks merrily pass,
An' Athene o' the House o' Brass.

     Now the dance begin;
Dance, making swirl your fringe o' woolly skin,
     While we join voices
To hymn dear Sparta that rejoices
     I' a beautifu' sang,
      An' loves to see
Dancers tangled beautifully,
For the girls i' tumbled ranks
     Alang Eurotas' banks
     Like wanton fillies thrang,
     Frolicking there
An' like Bacchantes shaking the wild air
     To comb a giddy laughter through the hair,
Bacchantes that clench thyrsi as they sweep
     To the ecstatic leap.

     An' Helen, Child o' Leda, come
Thou holy, nimble, gracefu' Queen,
Lead thou the dance, gather thy joyous tresses up i' bands
An' play like a fawn. To madden them, clap thy hands,
And sing praise to the warrior goddess templed i' our lands,
     Her o' the House o' Brass.

                    (*Exeunt.*)

Thesmophoriazusae

The Thesmophoria was a festival to Demeter and Persephone, sacred to women: the title of the present play means *"Women Celebrating the Thesmophoria."* At this private festival the women are to try Euripides for traducing their sex, and after applying in vain to Agathon, Euripides persuades his kinsman Mnesilochus to attend disguised as a woman and to protect his interests. The scene where Mnesilochus is singed and scraped and dressed for his role is riotous. One speaker for the prosecution charges that Euripides' plays have opened all husbands' eyes to feminine failings so that they now keep closer watch. Another, who sells appurtenances of sacrifice, charges that Euripides' plays have spoiled her livelihood by casting doubts on religion. When Mnesilochus suggests that Euripides has not revealed a fraction of women's iniquities he is suspected and put under guard. Euripides in disguise tries to save him by brilliant parodies of rescue scenes from his own *Telephus, Palamedes, Helen,* and *Andromeda. Thesmophoriazusae* is irresistible for its energetic and highly literate fooling, and is rather flattering to Euripides than otherwise. There is no ridicule in the parodies, the charges of the women are proven unjust, and Euripides is spared the broad insinuations made about Agathon. The play was presented in 411 B.C., only a few months after the *Lysistrata.*

CHARACTERS

Translated by B. B. Rogers

(EURIPIDES *and* MNESILOCHUS *are discovered pacing along an Athenian street.*)

MNESILOCHUS. Zeus! is the swallow *never* going to come?
Tramped up and down since daybreak! I can't stand it.
Might I, before my wind's *entirely* gone,
Ask where you're taking me, Euripides?

EURIPIDES. You're not to hear the things which face to face
You're going to see.

MNESILOCHUS.   What! Please say that again.
I'm not to hear?

EURIPIDES.   The things which you shall see.

MNESILOCHUS. And not to see?

EURIPIDES.   The things which you shall hear.

MNESILOCHUS. A pleasant jest! a mighty pleasant jest!
I'm not to hear or see at all, I see.

EURIPIDES (*in high philosophic rhapsody*). To hear! to see!
full different things, I ween;
Yea verily, generically diverse.

MNESILOCHUS. What's "diverse"?

EURIPIDES.   I will explicate my meaning.
When Ether first was mapped and parceled out,
And living creatures breathed and moved in her,
She, to give sight, implanted in their heads
The Eye, a mimic circlet of the Sun,
And bored the funnel of the Ear, to hear with.

MNESILOCHUS. *Did she!* That's why I'm not to hear or see!
I'm very glad to get that information!
O, what a thing it is to talk with Poets!

EURIPIDES. Much of such knowledge I shall give you.

MNESILOCHUS.   O!
Then p'raps (excuse me) you will tell me how
Not to be lame tomorrow, after this.

EURIPIDES (*loftily disregarding the innuendo*). Come here and
listen.

MNESILOCHUS (*courteously*).   Certainly I will.

EURIPIDES. See you that wicket?

MNESILOCHUS.   Why, by Heracles,
Of course I do.

EURIPIDES.   Be still.

MNESILOCHUS.   Be still the wicket?

EURIPIDES. And most attentive.

MNESILOCHUS.   Still attentive wicket?

EURIPIDES. There dwells, observe, the famous Agathon,
   The Tragic Poet.

MNESILOCHUS (*considering*). Agathon. Don't know him.

EURIPIDES. He is that Agathon—

MNESILOCHUS (*interrupting*).   Dark, brawny fellow?

EURIPIDES. O no, quite different; don't you know him really?

MNESILOCHUS. Big-whiskered fellow?

EURIPIDES.   Don't you know him really?

MNESILOCHUS. No. (*Thinks again.*) No, I don't; at least I
   don't remember.

EURIPIDES (*severely*). I fear there's much you don't remem-
   ber, sir.
   But step aside: I see his servant coming.
   See, he has myrtles and a pan of coals
   To pray, methinks, for favorable rhymes.

SERVANT. All people be still!
   Allow not a word from your lips to be heard,
   For the Muses are here, and are making their odes
      In my Master's abodes.
   Let Ether be lulled, and forgetful to blow,
   And the blue sea waves, let them cease to flow,
      And be noiseless.

MNESILOCHUS.   Fudge!

EURIPIDES.   Hush, hush, if you please.

SERVANT. Sleep, birds of the air, with your pinions at ease;
   Sleep, beasts of the field, with entranquilized feet;
      Sleep, sleep, and be still.

MNESILOCHUS.   Fudge, fudge, I repeat.

SERVANT. For the soft and terse professor of verse,
   Our Agathon now is about to—

MNESILOCHUS (*scandalized*).   No, no!

SERVANT. What's that?

MNESILOCHUS.   'Twas the *ether, forgetting to blow!*

SERVANT (*beginning pettishly, but soon falling back into his
   former tone*). I was going to say he is going to lay
   The stocks and the scaffolds for building a play.
   And neatly he hews them, and sweetly he glues them,
   And a proverb he takes, and an epithet makes,
   And he molds a most waxen and delicate song,
   And he tunnels, and funnels, and—

MNESILOCHUS.   Does what is wrong.

SERVANT. What clown have we here, so close to our eaves?

MNESILOCHUS. Why, one who will take you and him, by your leaves,

Both you and your terse professor of verse,

And with blows and with knocks set you both on the stocks,

And tunnel and funnel, and pummel, and worse.

SERVANT. Old man, you must have been a rare pert youngster.

EURIPIDES. O, heed not *him;* but quickly call me out

Your master Agathon; do pray make haste.

SERVANT. No need of prayer: he's coming forth directly.

He's molding odes; and in the cold hard winter

He cannot turn, and twist, and shape his strophes

Until they are warmed and softened in the sun.

MNESILOCHUS. And what am I to do?

EURIPIDES. You're to keep quiet.

O Zeus! the Hour is come, and so's the Man!

MNESILOCHUS. O, what's the matter? what disturbs you so?

O, tell me what: I really want to know.

Come, I'm your cousin; won't you tell your cousin?

EURIPIDES. There's a great danger brewing for my life.

MNESILOCHUS. O, tell your cousin what.

EURIPIDES. This hour decides

Whether Euripides shall live or die.

MNESILOCHUS. Why, how is that? There's no tribunal sitting,

No Court, no Council, will be held today.

'Tis the Mid-Fast, the third Home Festival.

EURIPIDES. It is! it is! I wish enough it wasn't.

For on this day the womankind have sworn

To hold a great assembly, to discuss

How best to serve me out.

MNESILOCHUS. Good gracious! Why?

EURIPIDES (*with the mild surprise of injured innocence*). Because, they say, I write lampoons upon them.

MNESILOCHUS. Zeus and Poseidon! they may well say that.

But tell your cousin what you mean to do.

EURIPIDES. I want to get the poet Agathon

To go among them.

MNESILOCHUS. Tell your cousin why.

EURIPIDES. To mingle in their Assembly and speak

On my behalf.

MNESILOCHUS. What, openly, do you mean?

EURIPIDES. O no, disguised: dressed up in women's clothes.

MNESILOCHUS. A bright idea that, and worthy you:

For in all craftiness we take the cake.

EURIPIDES. O, hush!

MNESILOCHUS. What now?

EURIPIDES. Here's Agathon himself.

MNESILOCHUS. Where? Which?

EURIPIDES. Why there: the man in the machine.

MNESILOCHUS. O dear, what ails me? Am I growing blind?
  I see Cyrene; but I see no man.

EURIPIDES. Do, pray, be silent; he's just going to sing.

MNESILOCHUS. Is it *The Pathway of the Ants*, or what?

AGATHON (*as actor*). *Move ye slowly, with the holy*
  Torchlight dear to Awful Shades,
  Singing sweetly, dancing featly,
  Yes, and neatly, freeborn maids.

(*As Chorus.*) *Whose the song of festal praise?*
  Only tell us, we are zealous
  Evermore our hymns to raise.

(*As actor.*) *Sing of Leto, sing of thee too*
  Archer of the golden bow,
  Bright Apollo, in the hollow
  Glades where Ilian rivers flow,
  Building buildings, long ago.

(*As Chorus.*) *Raise the music, softly swelling*
  To the fame of Leto's name,
  To the god in song excelling,
  Brightest he, of all there be,
  Giving gifts of minstrelsy.

(*As actor.*) *Sing the maiden, quiver-laden,*
  From the woodland oaks emerging,
  Haunted shades of mountain glades,
  Artemis, the ever virgin.

(*As Chorus.*) *We rejoice, heart and voice,*
  Hymning, praising, gently phrasing,
  Her, the maiden quiver-laden.

(*As actor.*) *Soft pulsation of the Asian*
  Lyre, to which the dancers go,
  When the high and holy Graces
  Weave their swiftly whirling paces,
  Phrygian measure, to and fro.

(*As Chorus.*) *Lyre Elysian, heavenly vision,*
  When thy witching tones arise,
  Comes the light of joy and gladness
  Flashing from immortal eyes.
  Eyes will glisten, ears will listen,
  When our manful numbers ring.
  Mighty master, son of Leto,

Thine the glory, thou the King.
(MNESILOCHUS *utters a cry of delight.*)

MNESILOCHUS. Wonderful! Wonderful!
How sweet, how soft, how ravishing the strain!
What melting words! and as I heard them sung,
You amorous Powers, there crept upon my soul
A pleasant, dreamy, rapturous titillation.
And now, dear youth, for I would question you
And sift you with the words of Aeschylus,
Whence are you, what your country, what your garb?
Why all this wondrous medley? Lyre and silks,
A minstrel's lute, a maiden's netted hair,
Girdle and wrestler's oil! a strange conjunction.
How comes a sword beside a looking glass?
What are you, man or woman? If a man,
Where are his clothes? his red Laconian shoes?
If woman, 'tis not like a woman's shape.
What are you, speak; or if you tell me not,
Myself must guess your gender from your song.

AGATHON. Old man, old man, my ears receive the words
Of your tongue's utterance, yet I heed them not.
I choose my dress to suit my poesy.
A poet, sir, must needs adapt his ways
To the high thoughts which animate his soul.
And when he sings of women, he assumes
A woman's garb, and dons a woman's habits.

MNESILOCHUS (*aside to* EURIPIDES). When you wrote *Phaedra,*
did you take her habits?

AGATHON. But when he sings of men, his whole appearance
Conforms to man. What nature gives us not,
The human soul aspires to imitate.

MNESILOCHUS (*as before*). Zounds, if I'd seen you when you
wrote the *Satyrs!*

AGATHON. Besides, a poet never should be rough,
Or harsh, or rugged. Witness to my words
Anacreon, Alcaeus, Ibycus,
Who when they filtered and diluted song,
Wore soft Ionian manners and attire.
And Phrynichus, perhaps you have seen him, sir,
How fair he was, and beautifully dressed;
Therefore his plays were beautifully fair.
For as the Worker, so the Work will be.

MNESILOCHUS. Then that is why harsh Philocles writes harshly,
And that is why vile Xenocles writes vilely,

And cold Theognis writes such frigid plays.

AGATHON. Yes, that is why. And I perceiving this
    Made myself womanlike.

MNESILOCHUS.   My goodness, how?

EURIPIDES. O, stop that yapping: in my youthful days
    I too was such another one as he.

MNESILOCHUS. Good gracious! I don't envy you your schooling.

EURIPIDES (*sharply*). Pray, let us come to business, sir.

MNESILOCHUS.   Say on.

EURIPIDES. A wise man, Agathon, compacts his words,
    And many thoughts compresses into few.
    So, I in my extremity am come
    To ask a favor of you.

AGATHON.   Tell me what.

EURIPIDES. The womankind at their Home feast today
    Are going to pay me out for my lampoons.

AGATHON. That's bad indeed, but how can I assist you?

EURIPIDES. Why, every way. If you'll disguise yourself,
    And sit among them like a woman born,
    And plead my cause, you'll surely get me off.
    There's none but you to whom I dare entrust it.

AGATHON. Why don't you go yourself, and plead your cause?

EURIPIDES. I'll tell you why. They know me well by sight;
    And I am gray, you see, and bearded too,
    But you've a baby face, a treble voice,
    A fair complexion, pretty, smooth, and soft.

AGATHON. Euripides!

EURIPIDES.   Yes.

AGATHON.   Wasn't it you who wrote
    You value life; do you think your father doesn't?

EURIPIDES. It was: what then?

AGATHON.   Expect me not to bear
    Your burdens; that were foolishness indeed.
    Each man must bear his sorrows for himself.
    And troubles, when they come, must needs be met
    By manful acts, and not by shifty tricks.

MNESILOCHUS. Aye, true for you, your wicked ways are shown
    By sinful acts, and not by words alone.

EURIPIDES. But tell me really why you fear to go.

AGATHON. They'd serve me worse than you.

EURIPIDES.   How so?

AGATHON.   How so?
    I'm too much like a woman, and they'd think
    That I was come to poach on their preserves.

MNESILOCHUS. Well, I must say that's not a bad excuse.

EURIPIDES. Then won't you really help?

AGATHON. I really won't.

EURIPIDES. Thrice luckless I! Euripides is done for!

MNESILOCHUS. O friend! O cousin! don't lose heart like this.

EURIPIDES. Whatever can I do?

MNESILOCHUS. Bid *him* go hang!
See, here am I; deal with me as you please.

EURIPIDES (*striking while the iron is hot*).
Well, if you'll really give yourself to me,
First throw aside this overcloak.

MNESILOCHUS. 'Tis done.
But how are you going to treat me?

EURIPIDES. Shave you here,
And singe you down below.

MNESILOCHUS (*magnanimously*). Well, do your worst;
I've said you may, and I'll go through with it.

EURIPIDES. You've always, Agathon, got a razor handy;
Lend us one, will you?

AGATHON. Take one for yourself
Out of the razor case.

EURIPIDES. Obliging youth!
(*To* MNESILOCHUS.) Now sit you down, and puff your right
cheek out.

MNESILOCHUS. Oh!

EURIPIDES. What's the matter? Shut your mouth, or else
I'll clap a gag in.

MNESILOCHUS. Lackalackaday!

EURIPIDES. Where are you fleeing?

MNESILOCHUS. To sanctuary I.
Shall I sit quiet to be hacked like that?
Demeter, no!

EURIPIDES. Think how absurd you'll look,
With one cheek shaven, and the other not.

MNESILOCHUS (*doggedly*). Well, I don't care.

EURIPIDES. O, by the Gods, come back.
Pray don't forsake me.

MNESILOCHUS. Miserable me!

EURIPIDES. Sit steady; raise your chin; don't wriggle so.

MNESILOCHUS (*wincing*). O tchi, tchi, tchi!

EURIPIDES. There, there, it's over now.

MNESILOCHUS. And I'm, worse luck, a Rifled Volunteer.

EURIPIDES. Well, never mind; you're looking beautiful.
Glance in this mirror.

MNESILOCHUS.   Well then, hand it here.

EURIPIDES. What see you there?

MNESILOCHUS (*in disgust*).   Not me, but Cleisthenes.

EURIPIDES. Get up: bend forward. I've to singe you now.

MNESILOCHUS. O me, you'll scald me like a sucking pig.

EURIPIDES. Someone within there, bring me out a torch.
  Now then, stoop forward: gently; mind yourself.

MNESILOCHUS. I'll see to that. Hey! I've caught fire there. Hey!
  O, water! water! neighbors, bring your buckets.
  Fire! Fire! I tell you; I'm on fire, I am!

EURIPIDES. There, it's all right.

MNESILOCHUS.   All right, when I'm a cinder?

EURIPIDES. Well, well, the worst is over; 'tis indeed.
  It won't pain now.

MNESILOCHUS.   Faugh, here's a smell of burning!
  Drat it, I'm roasted all about the stern.

EURIPIDES. Nay, heed it not. I'll have it sponged directly.

MNESILOCHUS. I'd like to catch a fellow sponging *me*.

EURIPIDES. Though you begrudge your active personal aid,
  Yet, Agathon, you won't refuse to lend us
  A dress and sash: you can't deny you've got them.

AGATHON. Take them, and welcome. I begrudge them not.

MNESILOCHUS. What's first to do?

EURIPIDES.   Put on this yellow silk.

MNESILOCHUS. By Aphrodite, but 'tis wondrous nice.

EURIPIDES. Gird it up tighter.

MNESILOCHUS.   Where's the girdle?

EURIPIDES.   Here.

MNESILOCHUS. Make it sit neatly there about the legs.

EURIPIDES. Now for a snood and hair net.

AGATHON.   Will this do?
  It's quite a natty hairdress; it's my nightcap.

EURIPIDES. The very thing: i'faith, the very thing.

MNESILOCHUS. Does it look well?

EURIPIDES.   Zeus! I should think it did!
  Now for a mantle.

AGATHON.   Take one from the couch.

EURIPIDES. A pair of woman's shoes.

AGATHON.   Well, here are mine.

MNESILOCHUS. Do they look well?

EURIPIDES.   They are loose enough, I trow.

AGATHON. You see to that; I've lent you all you need.
  Will someone kindly wheel me in again?

EURIPIDES. There then, the man's a regular woman now,

At least to look at; and if you've to speak,
Put on a feminine mincing voice.

MNESILOCHUS (*in a shrill treble*).   I'll try.

EURIPIDES. And now begone, and prosper.

MNESILOCHUS.   Wait a bit.

Not till you've sworn—

EURIPIDES.   Sworn what?

MNESILOCHUS.   That if I get

In any scrape, you'll surely see me through.

EURIPIDES. I swear by Ether, Zeus's dwelling place.

MNESILOCHUS. As well by vile Hippocrates's cabin.

EURIPIDES. Well, then, I swear by every blessèd God.

MNESILOCHUS. And please remember 'twas your *mind* that
  swore,
Not your tongue only; please remember that.

EURIPIDES. O, get you gone: for there's the signal hoisted
Over the Temple; they are assembling now.
I think I'll leave you.

MNESILOCHUS.   Thratta, come along.
O Thratta, Thratta, here's a lot of women
Coming up here! O, what a flare of torches!
O sweet Twain-goddesses, vouchsafe me now
A pleasant day, and eke a safe return.
Set down the basket, Thratta; give me out
The sacred cake to offer to the Twain.
O dread Demeter, high unearthly one,
O Persephassa, grant your votaress grace
To join in many festivals like this,
Or if not so, at least escape this once.
And may my daughter, by your leaves, pick up
A wealthy husband, and a fool to boot;
And little Bull-calf have his share of brains.
Now, then, I wonder which is the best place
To hear the speeches? Thratta, you may go.
These are not things for servant girls to hear.

CRIERESS.   Worldly clamor
                     Pass away!
                  Silence, silence,
                     While we pray;
To the Twain, the Home-bestowers,
Holy Parent, holy Daughter,
And to Wealth, and Heavenly Beauty,
And to Earth the foster mother,
And to Hermes and the Graces,

That they to this important high debate
    Grant favor and success,
Making it useful to the Athenian State,
    And to ourselves no less.
And O, that she who counsels best today
    About the Athenian nation,
And our own commonwealth of women, may
    Succeed by acclamation.
These things we pray, and blessings on our cause.
Sing Paean, Paean, ho! with merry loud applause.

CHORUS. We in thy prayers combine,
    And we trust the Powers Divine
    Will on these their suppliants' smile,
    Both Zeus the high and awful,
    And the golden-lyred Apollo
    From the holy Delian isle.
    And thou, our mighty maiden,
    Lance of gold, and eye of blue,
    Of the God-contested city,
        Help us too:
    And the many-named, the Huntress,
    Gold-fronted Leto's daughter;
    And the dread Poseidon ruling
    Over Ocean's stormy water;
    Come from the deep where fishes
    Swarm, and the whirlwinds rave;
    And the Oreads of the mountain,
    And the Nereids of the wave.
    Let the Golden Harp sound o'er us
    And the gods with favor crown
    This Parliament of Women,
    The free and noble matrons
    Of the old Athenian town.

CRIERESS. Oyez! Oyez!
Pray ye the Olympian gods—and goddesses,
And all the Pythian gods—and goddesses,
And all the Delian gods—and goddesses,
And all the other gods—and goddesses,
Whoso is disaffected, ill-disposed
Toward this commonwealth of womankind,
Or with Euripides, or with the Medes
Deals to the common hurt of womankind,
Or aims at tyranny, or fain would bring
The Tyrant back; or dares betray a wife

For palming off a baby as her own;
Or tells her master tales against her mistress;
Or does not bear a message faithfully;
Or, being a suitor, makes a vow, and then
Fails to perform; or, being a rich old woman,
Hires for herself a lover with her wealth;
Or, being a girl, takes gifts and cheats the giver;
Or, being a trading man or trading woman,
Gives us short measure in our drinking cups—
Perish that man, himself and all his house;
But pray the gods—and goddesses—to order
To all the women always all things well.

CHORUS.　　　　　We also pray,
　　　　　　　　And trust it may
　　　　　Be done as you premise,
　　　　　　　　And hope that they
　　　　　　　　Will win the day
　　　　　Whose words are best and wisest.
　　　　　　　　But they who fain
　　　　　　　　Would cheat for gain,
　　　　　Their solemn oaths forgetting,
　　　　　　　　Our ancient laws
　　　　　　　　And noble cause
　　　　　And mystic rites upsetting;
　　　　　　　　Who plot for greed,
　　　　　　　　Who call the Mede
　　　　　With secret invitation,
　　　　　　　　I say that these
　　　　　　　　The gods displease,
　　　　　And wrong the Athenian nation.
　　　　　　　　O Zeus most high
　　　　　　　　In earth and sky,
　　　　　All-powerful, all-commanding,
　　　　　　　　We pray to thee,
　　　　　　　　Weak women we,
　　　　　But help us notwithstanding.

CRIERESS. Oyez! Oyez! The Women's Council-Board
Hath thus enacted (moved by Sostrata,
President Timocleia, clerk Lysilla),
To hold a morning Parliament today
When women most have leisure; to discuss
What shall be done about Euripides,
How best to serve him out; for that he's guilty
We all admit. Who will address the meeting?

FIRST WOMAN. I wish to, I.

CRIERESS.   Put on this chaplet first.
   Order! order! Silence, ladies, if you please.
   She's learnt the trick; she hems and haws; she coughs in
      preparation;
   I know the signs; my soul divines a mighty long oration.

FIRST WOMAN. 'Tis not from any feeling of ambition
I rise to address you, ladies, but because
I long have seen, and inly burned to see
The way Euripides insults us all,
The really quite interminable scoffs
This market gardener's son pours out against us.
I don't believe that there's a single fault
He's not accused us of; I don't believe
That there's a single theater or stage,
But there is he, calling us double-dealers,
False, faithless, tippling, mischief-making gossips,
A rotten set, a misery to men.
Well, what's the consequence?

                      The men come home
Looking so sour—O, *we* can see them peeping
In every closet, thinking friends are there.
Upon my word we can't do *anything*
We used to do; he has made the men so silly.
Suppose I'm hard at work upon a chaplet,
Hey, she's in love with somebody; suppose
I chance to drop a pitcher on the floor,
And straightway 'tis, *For whom was that intended?*
I warrant now, for our Corinthian friend.
Is a girl ill? Her brother shakes his head;
The girl's complexion is not to my taste.
Why, if you merely want to hire a baby,
And palm it off as yours, you've got no chance,
They sit beside our very beds, they do.
Then there's another thing; the rich old men
Who used to marry us, are grown so shy
We never catch them now; and all because
Euripides declares, the scandalmonger,
An old man weds a tyrant, not a wife.
You know, my sisters, how they mew us up,
Guarding our women's rooms with bolts and seals
And fierce Molossian dogs. That's all his doing.
We might put up with that; but, O my friends,
Our little special perquisites, the corn,

The wine, the oil, gone, gone, all gone forever.
They've got such keys, our husbands have, such brutes,
Laconian-made, with triple rows of teeth.
Then in old times we only had to buy
A farthing ring, and pantry doors flew open.
But now this wretch Euripides has made them
Wear such worm-eaten perforated seals,
'Tis hopeless now to try it. Therefore, ladies,
What I propose is that we slay the man,
Either by poison or some other way;
Somehow or other he must die the death.
That's all I'll say in public: I'll write out
A formal motion with the clerkess there.

CHORUS. Good heavens! what force and tact combined!
          O, what a many-woven mind!
          A better speech, upon my word,
          I don't believe I ever heard.
          Her thoughts so clean dissected,
          Her words so well selected,
          Such keen discrimination,
          Such power and elevation,
'Twas really quite a grand, superb, magnificent oration.
So that if, in opposition, Xenocles came forth to speak,
               Compared with her
               You'd all aver
All his grandest, happiest efforts are immeasurably weak!

SECOND WOMAN. Ladies, I've only a few words to add.
I quite agree with the honorable lady
Who has just sat down: she has spoken well and ably.
But I can tell you what I've borne myself.
My husband died in Cyprus, leaving me
Five little chicks to work and labor for.
I've done my best, and bad's the best, but still
I've fed them, weaving chaplets for the gods.
But now this fellow writes his plays, and says
There are no gods; and so, you may depend,
My trade is fallen to half; men won't buy chaplets.
So then for many reasons he must die;
The man is bitterer than his mother's potherbs.
I leave my cause with you, my sisters: I
Am called away on urgent private business,
An order, just received, for twenty chaplets.

CHORUS.   Better and better still.
          A subtler intellect, a daintier skill.

Wise are her words, and few;
Well timed and spoken too.
A many-woven mind she too has got, I find.
And he must clearly,
This rascal man, be punished most severely.

MNESILOCHUS. Mrs. Speaker and ladies,
I'm not surprised, of course I'm not surprised,
To find you all so angry and aggrieved
At what Euripides has said against us.
For I myself—or slay my babies else—
Hate him like poison, to be sure I do,
He's most provoking, I admit he is.
But now we're all alone, there's no reporter,
All among friends, why not be fair and candid?
Grant that the man has really found us out,
And told a thing or two, sure they're all *true*,
And there's a many thousand still behind.
For I myself, to mention no one else,
Could tell a thousand plaguy tricks I've played
On my poor husband; I'll just mention one.
We'd been but three days married; I'm abed,
Husband asleep beside me; when my lover
(I'd been familiar with him from a child)
Came softly scratching at the outer door.
I hear; I know *the little clinking sound*,
And rise up stealthily, to creep downstairs.
Where go you, pray? says husband. *Where!* say I,
*I've such a dreadful pain in my inside
I must go down this instant. Go,* says he.
He pounds his anise, juniper, and sage,
To still my pains: *I* seize the water jug,
And wet the hinge, to still its creaking noise,
Then open, and go out: and I and lover
Meet by Aguieus and his laurel shade,
Billing and cooing to our hearts' content.
(*With vivacity.*) Euripides has never found out that.
Nor how a wife contrived to smuggle out
Her frightened lover, holding up her shawl
To the sun's rays for husband to admire.
Nor how we grant our favors to bargees
And muleteers, if no one else we've got.
Nor how, arising from a night's debauch,
We chew our garlic, that our husbands, coming
Back from the walls at daybreak, may suspect

Nothing amiss at home. Then what's the odds
If he does rail at Phaedra? Let him rail.
What's that to us? Let him rail on, say I.
Phaedra indeed! He might come nearer home.
I knew a woman, I won't mention names,
Remained ten days in childbirth. Why, do you think?
Because she couldn't buy a baby sooner.
Her husband runs to every medicine man
In dreadful agitation; while he's out,
They bring a little baby in a basket,
Bunging its mouth up that it mayn't cry out,
And stow it safe away till he comes home.
Then at a given sigh she feebly says,
My time is come: please, husband, go away.
He goes; they open basket; baby cries.
O, what delight, surprise, congratulations!
The man runs in; the nurse comes running out,
(The same that brought the baby in the basket),
A prodigy! a lion! such a boy!
Your form, your features: just the same expression:
Your very image: lucky, lucky man!
Don't we do this? By Artemis, we do.
Then wherefore rail we at Euripides?
We're not one bit more sinned against than sinning.

CHORUS. What a monstrous, strange proceeding!
　　　　Whence, I wonder, comes her breeding?
　　　　From what country shall we seek her,
　　　　Such a bold, audacious speaker?
　　　　That a woman so should wrong us,
　　　　Here among us, here among us,
I could never have believed it; such a thing was never
　　known.
　　　　But what *may* be, no man knoweth,
　　　　And the wise old proverb showeth,
That perchance a poisonous sophist lurketh under every
　　stone.
O, nothing, nothing in the world so hateful you will find
As shameless women, save of course the rest of womankind.

FIRST WOMAN. What can possess us, sisters mine? I vow by
　　old Agraulus,
We're all bewitched, or else have had some strange mis-
　　chance befall us,
To let this shameless hussy tell her shameful, bold, im-
　　proper,

Unpleasant tales, and we not make the least attempt to stop her.

If anyone assist me, good; if not, alone we'll try,

We'll strip and whip her well, we will, my serving maids and I.

MNESILOCHUS. Not strip me, gentle ladies; sure I heard the proclamation,

That every freeborn woman now might make a free oration;

And if I spoke unpleasant truths on this your invitation,

Is that a reason why I now should suffer castigation?

FIRST WOMAN. It is, indeed: how dare you plead for him who always chooses

Such odious subjects for his plays, on purpose to abuse us?

Phaedras and Melanippes too: but ne'er a drama made he

About the good Penelope, or such-like virtuous lady.

MNESILOCHUS. The cause I know; the cause I'll show: you won't discover any

Penelope alive today, but Phaedras very many.

FIRST WOMAN. You will? you dare? how *can* we bear to hear such things repeated,

Such horrid, dreadful, odious things?

MNESILOCHUS.　　　　　　O, I've not near completed

The things I know; I'll give the whole: I'm not disposed to grudge it.

FIRST WOMAN. You can't, I vow; you've emptied now your whole disgusting budget.

MNESILOCHUS. No, not one thousandth part I've told: not even how we take

The scraper from the bathing room, and down the corn we rake,

And push it in, and tap the bin.

FIRST WOMAN.　　　　　Confound you and your slanders!

MNESILOCHUS. Nor how the Apaturian meat we steal to give our panders,

And then declare the cat was there.

FIRST WOMAN.　　　　　You nasty telltale you!

MNESILOCHUS. Nor how with deadly ax a wife her lord and master slew,

Another drove her husband mad with poisonous drugs fallacious,

Nor how beneath the reservoir the Acharnian girl—

FIRST WOMAN.　　　　　　　Good gracious!

MNESILOCHUS. Buried her father out of sight.

FIRST WOMAN.　　　　　Now really this won't do.

MNESILOCHUS. Nor how when late your servant bare a child
    as well as you,
  You took her boy, and in his stead your puling girl you
    gave her.

FIRST WOMAN. O, by the Two, this jade shall rue her insolent
    behavior.
  I'll comb your fleece, you saucy minx.

MNESILOCHUS. By Zeus, you had best begin it.

FIRST WOMAN. Come on!

MNESILOCHUS.   Come on!

FIRST WOMAN.   You will? you will?
  (*Flinging her upper mantle to* PHILISTA.) Hold this, my
    dear, a minute.

MNESILOCHUS. Stand off, or else, by Artemis, I'll give you such
    a strumming—

CHORUS. For pity's sake, be silent there: I see a woman
    coming,
  Who looks as if she'd news to tell. Now prithee both be
    quiet
  And let us hear the tale she brings, without this awful riot.

CLEISTHENES. Dear ladies, I am one with you in heart;
  My cheeks, unfledged, bear witness to my love,
  I am your patron, aye, and devotee.
  And now, for lately in the market place
  I heard a rumor touching you and yours,
  I come to warn and put you on your guard,
  Lest this great danger take you unawares.

CHORUS. What now, my child? for we may call thee child,
  So soft, and smooth, and downy are thy cheeks.

CLEISTHENES. Euripides, they say, has sent a cousin,
  A bad old man, among you here today.

CHORUS. O, why and wherefore, and with what design?

CLEISTHENES. To be a spy, a horrid, treacherous spy,
  A spy on all your purposes and plans.

CHORUS. O, how should he be here, and we not know it?

CLEISTHENES. Euripides has tweezered him, and singed him,
  And dressed him up, disguised in women's clothes.

MNESILOCHUS (*stamping about with a lively recollection of his
    recent sufferings*). I don't believe it; not one word of it;
  No man would let himself be tweezered so.
  Ye goddesses, I don't believe there's one.

CLEISTHENES. Nonsense: I never should have come here else,
  I had it on the best authority.

CHORUS. This is a most important piece of news.
    We'll take immediate steps to clear this up.
    We'll search him out: we'll find his lurking-place.
    Zounds, if we catch him! r-r-r! the rascal man.
    Will you, kind gentleman, asisst the search?
    Give us fresh cause to thank you, patron mine.

CLEISTHENES (*to* FIRST WOMAN). Well, who are you?

MNESILOCHUS (*aside*).   Wherever can I flee?

CLEISTHENES. I'll find him, trust me.

MNESILOCHUS (*aside*).   Here's a precious scrape!

FIRST WOMAN. Who? I?

CLEISTHENES.   Yes, you.

FIRST WOMAN.   Cleonymus's wife.

CLEISTHENES. Do you know her, ladies? Is she speaking truth?

CHORUS. O yes, we know her: pass to someone else.

CLEISTHENES. Who's this young person with the baby here?

FIRST WOMAN. O, she's my nursemaid.

MNESILOCHUS (*aside*).   Here he comes; I'm done for.

CLEISTHENES. Hey! where's she off to? Stop? Why, what the
    mischief!

CHORUS (*aside to* CLEISTHENES). Yes, sift her well; discover
    who she is.
    We know the others, but we don't know her.

CLEISTHENES. Come, come, no shuffling, madam, turn this way.

MNESILOCHUS (*fretfully*). Don't pull me, sir, I'm poorly.

CLEISTHENES.   Please to tell me
    Your husband's name.

MNESILOCHUS.   My husband's name? my husband's?
    Why What-d'ye-call-him from Cothocidae.

CLEISTHENES. Eh, what? (*Considers.*) There was a What-d'ye-
    call-him once—

MNESILOCHUS. He's Who-d'ye-call-it's son.

CLEISTHENES.   You're trifling with me.
    Have you been here before?

MNESILOCHUS.   O, bless you, yes.
    Why, every year.

CLEISTHENES.   And with what tent companion?

MNESILOCHUS. With What's-her-name.

CLEISTHENES.   This is sheer idling, woman.

FIRST WOMAN (*to* CLEISTHENES). Step back, sir, please, and let
    me question her
    On last year's rites; a little further, please;
    No *man* must listen now. (*To* MNESILOCHUS.) Now,
    stranger, tell me

What first we practiced on that holy day.

MNESILOCHUS. Bless me, what was it? first? why, first we—
drank.

FIRST WOMAN. Right; what was second?

MNESILOCHUS.   Second? Drank again.

FIRST WOMAN. Somebody's told you this. But what was third?

MNESILOCHUS. Well, third, Xenylla had a drop too much.

FIRST WOMAN. Ah, that won't do. Here, Cleisthenes, approach.

   This is the *man* for certain.

CLEISTHENES.   Bring him up.

FIRST WOMAN. Strip off his clothes! for there's no truth in him.

MNESILOCHUS. What! strip the mother of nine little ones?

CLEISTHENES. Loosen that belt, look sharp, you shameless
thing.

FIRST WOMAN. She does appear a stout and sturdy one:
   Upon my word, she has no breasts like ours.

MNESILOCHUS. Because I'm barren, never had a child.

FIRST WOMAN. Yes, *now;* but *then* you had nine little ones!

CLEISTHENES. Stand up and show yourself. See! he's a man!

FIRST WOMAN. O, this is why you mocked and jeered us so!
   And dared defend Euripides like that!
   O, villain, villain.

MNESILOCHUS.   Miserable me!
   I've put my foot in it, and no mistake.

FIRST WOMAN. What shall we do with him?

CLEISTHENES.   Surround him here.
   And watch him shrewdly that he 'scape you not.
   I'll go at once and summon the police.

                      (CLEISTHENES *goes out.*)

CHORUS. Light we our torches, my sisters, and manfully gird-
ing our robes,

Gather them sternly about us, and casting our mantles
aside

On through the tents and the gangways, and up by the tiers
and the rows,

Eyeing, and probing, and trying, where men would be
likely to hide.

Now 'tis time, 'tis time, my sisters, round and round and
round to go,

Soft, with light and airy footfall, creeping, peeping, high
and low.

Look about in each direction, make a rigid, close inspection,
Lest in any hole or corner, other rogues escape detection.
      Hunt with care, here and there,
Searching, spying, poking, prying, up and down, and every-
    where.

      For if once the evildoer we can see,
He shall soon be a prey to our vengeance today,
    And to all men a warning he shall be
Of the terrible fate that is sure to await
The guilty sin schemer and lawless blasphemer.
And then he shall find that the gods are not blind
      To what passes below;
      Yea, and all men shall know
It is best to live purely, uprightly, securely,
      It is best to do well,
And to practice day and night what is orderly and right,
    And in virtue and in honesty to dwell.
But if anyone there be who a wicked deed shall do
In his raving, and his raging, and his madness, and his
    pride,
Every mortal soon shall see, aye, and every woman too,
      What a doom shall the guilty one betide.
For the wicked evil deed shall be recompensed with speed,
    The Avenger doth not tarry to begin,
Nor delayeth for a time, but he searcheth out the crime,
    And he punisheth the sinner in his sin.

Now we've gone through every corner, every nook surveyed
    with care,
And there's not another culprit skulking, lurking any-
    where.

FIRST WOMAN. Hoy! Hoy there! Hoy!
He's got my child, he's got my darling, O!
He's snatched my little baby from my breast.
O, stop him, stop him! O, he's gone. O! O!

MNESILOCHUS. Aye, weep! you ne'er shall dandle him again,
Unless you loose me. Soon shall these small limbs,
Smit with cold edge of sacrificial knife,
Incarnadine this altar.

FIRST WOMAN.   O! O! O!
Help, women, help me. Sisters, help, I pray.
Charge to the rescue, shout, and rout, and scout him.
Don't see me lose my baby, my one pet.

CHORUS. Alas! Alas!
    Mercy o' me! what do I see?
        What can it be?
  What, will deeds of shameless violence never, never, never,
    end?
  What's the matter, what's he up to, what's he doing now,
    my friend?

MNESILOCHUS. Doing what I hope will crush you out of all
    your bold assurance.

CHORUS. Zounds, his words are very dreadful; more than
    dreadful, past endurance.

FIRST WOMAN. Yes, indeed, they're very dreadful, and he's
    got my baby too.

CHORUS. Impudence rare! Look at him there,
    Doing such deeds, and I vow and declare
    Never minding or caring—

MNESILOCHUS.   Or likely to care.

FIRST WOMAN. Here you are come: here you shall stay,
    Never again shall you wander away;
    Wander away, glad to display
    All the misdeeds you have done us today,
    But dear you shall pay.

MNESILOCHUS. There at least I'm hoping, ladies, I shall find
    your words untrue.

CHORUS. What God do you think his assistance will lend,
    You wicked old man, to escort you away?

MNESILOCHUS. Aha, but I've captured your baby, my friend,
  And I shan't let her go, for the best you can say.

CHORUS. But no, by the goddesses twain,
    Not long shall our threats be in vain,
    Not long shall you flout at our pain.
    Unholy your deeds, and you'll find
    That we shall repay you in kind,
    And perchance you will alter your mind
    When Fate, veering round like the blast,
    In its clutches has seized you at last,
        Very fast.
  Comrades, haste, collect the brushwood: pile it up without
    delay:
  Pile it, heap it, stow it, throw it, burn and fire and roast
    and slay.

FIRST WOMAN. Come, Mania, come; let's run and fetch the
    fagots.

(*To* MNESILOCHUS.) Ah, wretch, you'll be a cinder before
    night.

MNESILOCHUS (*busily engaged in unpacking the baby*). With
    all my heart. Now I'll undo these wrappers,
These Cretan long clothes; and remember, darling,
It's all your mother that has served you thus.
What have we here? a flask, and not a baby!
A flask of wine, for all its Persian slippers.
O ever thirsty, ever tippling women,
O ever ready with fresh schemes for drink,
To vintners what a blessing: but to us
And all our goods and chattels what a curse!

FIRST WOMAN. Draw in the fagots, Mania; pile them up.

MNESILOCHUS. Aye, pile away; but tell me, is this baby
    Really your own?

FIRST WOMAN.   My very flesh and blood.

MNESILOCHUS. Your flesh and blood?

FIRST WOMAN.   By Artemis it is.

MNESILOCHUS. Is it a pint?

FIRST WOMAN.   O, what have you been doing?
O, you have stripped my baby of its clothes.
Poor tiny morsel!

MNESILOCHUS (*holding up a large bottle*). Tiny?

FIRST WOMAN.   Yes, indeed.

MNESILOCHUS. What is its age? Three Pitcher feasts or four?

FIRST WOMAN. Well, thereabouts, a little over now.
    Please give it back.

MNESILOCHUS.   No, thank you, not exactly.

FIRST WOMAN. We'll burn you then.

MNESILOCHUS.   O, burn me by all means;
But anyhow I'll sacrifice this victim.

FIRST WOMAN. O! O! O!
Make *me* your victim, anything you like;
But spare the child.

MNESILOCHUS.   A loving mother truly.
But this dear child must needs be sacrificed.

FIRST WOMAN. My child! my child! give me the basin, Mania,
    I'll catch my darling's blood at any rate.

MNESILOCHUS. And so you shall; I'll not deny you that.

FIRST WOMAN. You spiteful man! you most ungenerous man!

MNESILOCHUS. This skin, fair priestess, is your perquisite.

FIRST WOMAN. What is my perquisite?

MNESILOCHUS.   This skin, fair priestess.

CRITYLLA. O Mica, who has robbed thee of thy flower,
  And snatched thy babe, thine only one, away?
FIRST WOMAN. This villain here: but I'm so glad you're come.
  You see he doesn't run away, while I
  Call the police, with Cleisthenes, to help us.
MNESILOCHUS (*soliloquizes*). O me, what hope of safety still
    remains?
  What plan? what stratagem? My worthy cousin,
  Who first involved me in this dreadful scrape,
  He cometh not. Suppose I send him word.
  But how to send it? Hah, I know a trick
  Out of his *Palamede.* I'll send a message
  Written on oar blades. Tush! I've got no oar blades.
  What shall I do for oar blades? Why not send
  These votive slabs instead? The very thing.
  Oar blades are wood, and slabs are wood. I'll try.
      Now for the trick; fingers be quick;
      Do what you can for my notable plan.
      Slab, have the grace to permit me to trace
      Grooves with my knife on your beautiful face.
      The tale of my woe it is yours for to show.
      O, o, what a furrow! I never did see
      Such a horrible "*r*" as I've made it to be.
      Well, that must do; so fly away you,
      Hither and thither, off, off, and away.
      Do not delay for a moment, I pray.
CHORUS. Now let us turn to the people, our own panegyric to
    render.
  Men never speak a good word, never one, for the feminine
    gender,
  Every one says we're a Plague, the source of all evils to
    man,
  War, dissension, and strife. Come, answer me this, if you
    can;
  Why, if we're *really* a Plague, you're so anxious to have us
    for wives;
  And charge us not to be peeping, nor to stir out of doors for
    our lives.
  Isn't it silly to guard a Plague with such scrupulous care?
  Zounds! how you rave, coming home, if your poor little wife
    isn't there.
  Should you not rather be glad, and rejoice all the days of
    your life,

Rid of a *Plague*, you know, the source of dissension and
strife?

If on a visit we sport, and sleep when the sporting is over,
O, how you rummage about; what a fuss, your lost Plague
to discover.

Everyone stares at your Plague if she happens to look on
the street:

Stares all the more if your Plague thinks proper to blush
and retreat.

Is it not plain then, I ask, that Women are really the best?

What, can you doubt that we are? I will bring it at once to
the test.

We say Women are best; you men (just like you) deny it,

Nothing on earth is so easy as to come to the test, and to
try it.

I'll take the name of a Man, and the name of a Woman, and
show it.

Did not Charminus give way to Miss-Fortune? Do you not
know it?

Is not Cleophon viler than vile Salabaccho by far?

Is there a Man who can equal, in matters of glory and war,

Lady Victoria, Mistress of Marathon, queen of the Sea?

Is not Prudence a Woman, and who is so clever as she?

Certainly none of your statesmen, who only a twelvemonth
ago

Gave up their place and their duty. Would women demean
themselves so?

Women don't ride in their coaches, as Men have been doing
of late,

Pockets and purses distended with cash they have filched
from the State.

We, at the very outside, steal a wee little measure of corn,

Putting it back in the even, whatever we took in the morn.

But this is a true description of you.
Are you not gluttonous, vulgar, perverse,
Kidnapers, housebreakers, footpads, and worse?
And we in domestic economy too
Are thriftier, shiftier, wiser than you.
For the loom which our mothers employed with such
skill,
With its Shafts and its Thongs—we are working it still.
And the ancient umbrella by no means is done,
We are wielding it yet, as our Shield from the Sun.

But O for the Shafts, and the Thong of the Shield,
Which your Fathers in fight were accustomed to wield.
Where are they today? Ye have cast them away
As ye raced, in hot haste, and disgraced, from the fray!

Many things we have against you, many rules we justly blame;
But the one we now will mention is the most enormous shame.
What, my masters! ought a lady, who has borne a noble son,
One who in your fleets and armies great heroic deeds has done,
Ought she to remain unhonored? ought she not, I ask you, I,
In our Stenia and our Scira still to take precedence high?
Whoso breeds a cowardly soldier, or a seaman cold and tame,
Crop her hair, and seat her lowly; brand her with the marks of shame;
Set the nobler dame above her. Can it, all ye Powers, be right
That Hyperbolus's mother, flowing-haired, and robed in white,
Should in public places sit by Lamachus's mother's side,
Hoarding wealth, and lending monies, gathering profits far and wide?
Sure 'twere better every debtor, calm, resolving not to pay,
When she comes exacting money, with a mild surprise should say,
Keeping principal and income, *You to claim percentage due!*
Sure a son so capital is capital *enough for you.*

MNESILOCHUS. I've strained my eyes with watching; but my poet,
He cometh not. Why not? Belike he feels
Ashamed of his old frigid *Palamede.*
Which is the play to fetch him? O, I know;
Which but his brand-new *Helen?* I'll be Helen.
I've got the woman's clothes, at all events.
CRIERESS. What are you plotting? What is that you're muttering?
I'll Helen you, my master, if you don't
Keep quiet there till the policeman comes.

MNESILOCHUS (*as Helen*). These are the fair-nymphed waters of the Nile,

> Whose floods bedew, in place of heavenly showers,
> Egypt's white plains and black-dosed citizens.

CRIERESS. Sweet-shining Hecate, what a rogue it is.

MNESILOCHUS. Ah, not unknown my Spartan fatherland,

> Nor yet my father Tyndareus.

CRIERESS.   My gracious!

> Was *he* your father? Sure, Phrynondas was.

MNESILOCHUS. And I was Helen.

CRIERESS.   What, again a woman?

> You've not been punished for your first freak yet.

MNESILOCHUS. Full many a soul, by bright Scamander's stream,

> Died for my sake.

CRIERESS.   Would yours had died among them!

MNESILOCHUS. And now I linger here; but Menelaus,

> My dear, dear lord, ah wherefore comes he not?
> O sluggish crows, to spare my hapless life!
> But soft! some hope is busy at my heart,
> A laughing hope—O Zeus, deceive me not.

EURIPIDES. Who is the lord of this stupendous pile?

> Will he extend his hospitable care
> To some poor storm-tossed, shipwrecked mariners?

MNESILOCHUS. These are the halls of Proteus.

EURIPIDES.   Proteus, are they?

CRIERESS. O, by the Twain, he lies like anything.

> I knew old Protteas; he's been dead these ten years.

EURIPIDES. Then whither, whither have we steered our bark?

MNESILOCHUS. To Egypt.

EURIPIDES.   O, the weary, weary way!

CRIERESS. Pray don't believe one single word he says.

> This is the holy temple of the Twain.

EURIPIDES. Know you if Proteus be at home or not?

CRIERESS. Why, don't I tell you, he's been dead these ten years!

> You can't have quite got over your seasickness,
> Asking if Proteas be at home or not.

EURIPIDES. Woe's me! is Proteus dead? and where's he buried?

MNESILOCHUS. This is his tomb whereon I'm sitting now.

CRIERESS. O, hang the rascal; and he *shall* be hanged!

> How dare he say this altar is a tomb?

EURIPIDES. And wherefore sitt'st thou on this monument,

> Veiled in thy mantle, lady?

MNESILOCHUS.   They compel me,
  A weeping bride, to marry Proteus' son.
CRIERESS. Why do you tell the gentleman such fibs?
  Good gentleman, he's a bad man; he came
  Among the women here, to steal their trinkets.
MNESILOCHUS. Aye, aye, rail on: revile me as you list.
EURIPIDES. Who is the old woman who reviles you, lady?
MNESILOCHUS. Theonoë, Proteus' daughter.
CRIERESS.   What a story!
  Why, I'm Critylla, of Gargettus, sir,
  A very honest woman.
MNESILOCHUS.   Aye, speak on.
  But never will I wed thy brother, no,
  I won't be false to absent Menelaus.
EURIPIDES. What, lady, what? O, raise those orbs to mine.
MNESILOCHUS. O sir, I blush to raise them, with these cheeks.
EURIPIDES. O dear, O dear, I cannot speak for trembling.
  Ye Gods, is't possible? Who art thou, lady?
MNESILOCHUS. O, who art thou? I feel the same myself.
EURIPIDES. Art thou Hellenic, or a born Egyptian?
MNESILOCHUS. Hellenic I: O, tell me what art thou.
EURIPIDES. O surely, surely, thou art Helen's self.
MNESILOCHUS. O, from the greens thou must be Menelaus.
EURIPIDES. Yes, yes, you see that miserable man.
MNESILOCHUS. O, long in coming to these longing arms,
    O, carry me, carry me, from this place,
    O, wrap me in thy close embrace,
  O, carry me, carry me, carry me home, by this fond and
    loving kiss,
  O, take me, take me, take me hence.
CRIERESS.   I say now, none of this.
  Let go there, or I'll strike you with this link!
EURIPIDES. Let go my wife, the child of Tyndareus,
  Not take her home to Sparta? O, what mean you?
CRIERESS. O, that's it, is it? You're a bad one too!
  Both of one gang. That's what your gypsying meant!
  But he at any rate shall meet his due.
  Here's the policeman, and the Scythian coming.
EURIPIDES. Ah, this won't do: I must slip off awhile.
MNESILOCHUS. And what am I to do?
EURIPIDES.   Keep quiet here,
  Be sure I'll never fail you while I live;
  I have ten thousand tricks to save you yet.
MNESILOCHUS. Well, you caught nothing by *that* haul, I think.

POLICEMAN. O archer, here's the vagabond, of whom Cleisthenes told us. (*To* MNESILOCHUS.) Why do you hang
your head?

(*To* SCYTHIAN.) Take him within; there tie him on the
plank;

Then bring him here and watch him. Let not any
Approach too near him: should they try to, take
The whip, and smite them.

CRIERESS. Aye, one came but now
Spinning his yarns, and all but got him off.

MNESILOCHUS. O sir! policeman! grant me one request,
O, by that hand I pray you, which you love
To hold out empty, and to draw back full.

POLICEMAN. What should I grant you?

MNESILOCHUS. Don't expose me thus;
Do tell the Scythian he may strip me first;
Don't let a poor old man, in silks and snoods,
Provoke the laughter of the crows that eat him.

POLICEMAN. Thus hath the Council ordered it, that so
The passers-by may see the rogue you are.

MNESILOCHUS. Alas! alas! O yellow silk, I hate ye!
O, I've no hope, no hope of getting free.

CHORUS. Now for the revels, my sisters, which we to the great
Twain Powers
Prayerfully, carefully raise, in the holy festival hours.
And Pauson will join in our worship today,
And Pauson will join in the fasting,
And, keen for the fast, to the Twain he will pray
For the rite to be made everlasting, I ween,
For the rite to be made everlasting.

Now advance
In the whirling, twirling dance,
With hand linked in hand, as we deftly trip along,
Keeping time to the cadence of the swiftly flowing song;
And be sure as we go
That we dart careful glances, up and down, and to and fro.

Now 'tis ours
To entwine our choicest flowers,
Flowers of song and adoration to the great Olympian
Powers.
Nor expect
That the garland will be flecked

With abuse of mortal men; such a thought is incorrect.
>> For with prayer
>> And with sacred loving care,
A new and holy measure we will heedfully prepare.

>> To the high and holy Minstrel
>> Let the dancers onward go,
>> And to Artemis, the maiden
>> Of the quiver and the bow;
O, hear us, Far-controller, and the victory bestow.
>> And we trust our merry music
>> Will the matron Hera please,
>> For she loves the pleasant Chorus
>> And the dances such as these,
>> —Wearing at her girdle
>> The holy nuptial keys.

>> To Pan and pastoral Hermes
>> And the friendly Nymphs we pray,
>> That they smile with gracious favor
>> On our festival today,
With their laughter-loving glances beaming brightly on our
>> Play,
>> As we dance the Double chorus
>> To the old familiar strain,
>> As we weave our ancient pastime
>> On our holy day again,
>> —Keeping fast and vigil
>> In the Temple of the Twain.

Turn the step, and change the measure,
Raise a loftier music now;
Come, the Lord of wine and pleasure,
Evoi, Bacchus, lead us thou!
>> Yea, for Thee we adore!
>> Child of Semele, thee
>> With thy glittering ivy wreaths,
>> Thee with music and song
>> Ever and ever we praise.
Thee with thy wood nymphs delightedly singing,
>> Evoi! Evoi! Evoi!
Over the joyous hills the sweet strange melody ringing.
>> Hark! Cithaeron resounds,
>> Pleased the notes to prolong;

> Hark! the bosky ravines
> And the wild slopes thunder and roar,
> Volleying back the song.
> Round thee the ivy fair
> With delicate tendril twines.

SCYTHIAN. Dere now bemoany to de ouder air.

MNESILOCHUS. O, I entreat you.

SCYTHIAN. Nod endread me zu.

MNESILOCHUS. Slack it a little.

SCYTHIAN. Dat is vat I does.

MNESILOCHUS. O mercy! mercy! O, you drive it tighter.

SCYTHIAN. Dighder zu wiss him?

MNESILOCHUS. Miserable me!
Out on you, villain.

SCYTHIAN. Zilence, bad ole man.
I'se fetch de mad, an' vatch zu comfibly.

MNESILOCHUS. These are the joys Euripides has brought me!
O gods! O Savior Zeus! there's yet a hope.
Then he won't fail me! Out he flashed as Perseus.
I understand the signals, I'm to act
The fair Andromeda in chains. Ah, well,
Here are the chains, worse luck, wherewith to act her.
He'll come and succor me; he's in the wings.

EURIPIDES. Now to peep, now to creep
> Soft and slyly through.
> Maidens, pretty maidens,
> Tell me what I am to do.
> Tell me how to glide
> By the Scythian Argus-eyed,
> And to steal away my bride.
Tell me, tell me, tell me, tell me, tell me, tell me, tell,
Echo, always lurking in the cavern and the dell.

MNESILOCHUS. A cold unpitying heart had he
> Who bound me here in misery.
> Hardly escaped from moldy dame,
> I'm caught and done for, just the same.
> Lo, the Scythian guard beside me,
> Friendless, helpless, here he tied me;
> Soon upon these limbs of mine
> Shall the greedy ravens dine.
> See you? not to me belong
> Youthful pleasures, dance and song,
> Never, never more shall I
> With my friends sweet lawsuits try,

But woven chains with many a link surround me,
Till Glaucetes, that ravening whale, has found me.

> Home I nevermore shall see;
> Bridal songs are none for me,
> Nought but potent incantations;
> Sisters, raise your lamentations,
> Woe, woe, woeful me,
> Sorrow, and trouble, and misery.
> Weeping, weeping, endless weeping,
> Far from home and all I know,
> Praying him who wronged me so.
>> O! O! Woe! woe!
> First with razor keen he hacks me,
> Next in yellow silk he packs me,
> Sends me then to dangerous dome,
> Where the women prowl and roam.
> O heavy Fate! O fatal blow!
> O woeful lot! and lots of woe!

O, how they will chide me, and gibe, and deride me!
And O that the flashing, and roaring, and dashing
Red bolt of the thunder might smite me in sunder—
> The Scythian who lingers beside me!
For where is the joy of the sunshine and glow
To one who is lying, distracted and dying,
With throat-cutting agonies riving him, driving him
Down, down to the darkness below.

ECHO. O welcome, daughter; but the gods destroy
Thy father Cepheus, who exposed thee thus.

MNESILOCHUS. O, who are you who mourn for my woes?

ECHO. Echo, the vocal mockingbird of song,
I who, last year, in these same lists contended,
A faithful friend, beside Euripides.
And now, my child, for you must play your part,
Make dolorous wails.

MNESILOCHUS. And you wail afterward?

ECHO. I'll see to that; only begin at once.

MNESILOCHUS. O Night most holy,
> O'er dread Olympus, vast and far,
>> In thy dark car
>> Thou journeyest slowly
> Through Ether ridged with many a star.

ECHO. With many a star.

MNESILOCHUS. Why on Andromeda ever must flow
Sorrow and woe?

ECHO.   Sorrow and woe?

MNESILOCHUS. Heavy of fate.

ECHO.   Heavy of fate.

MNESILOCHUS. Old woman, you'll kill me, I know, with your prate.

ECHO.   Know with your prate.

MNESILOCHUS. Why, how tiresome you are: you are going too far.

ECHO.   You are going too far.

MNESILOCHUS. Good friend, if you kindly will leave me in peace,

    You'll do me a favor, O prithee, cease.

ECHO.   Cease.

MNESILOCHUS. O, go to the crows!

ECHO.   O, go to the crows!

MNESILOCHUS. Why can't you be still?

ECHO.   Why can't you be still?

MNESILOCHUS (*spitefully*). Old gossip!

ECHO (*spitefully*).   Old gossip!

MNESILOCHUS. Lackaday!

ECHO.   Lackaday!

MNESILOCHUS.   And alas!

ECHO.   And alas!

SCYTHIAN. O, vat does zu say?

ECHO.   O, vat does zu say?

SCYTHIAN. I'se calls de police.

ECHO.   I'se calls de police.

SCYTHIAN. Vat nosense is dis?

ECHO.   Vat nosense is dis?

SCYTHIAN. Vy, vere is de voice?

ECHO.   Vy, vere is de voice?

SCYTHIAN (*to* MNESILOCHUS). Vos id zu?

ECHO.   Vos id zu?

SCYTHIAN. Zu'll catch id.

ECHO.   Zu'll catch id.

SCYTHIAN. Does zu mocksh?

ECHO.   Does zu mocksh?

MNESILOCHUS. 'Tisn't I, I declare: it is that woman there.

ECHO.   It is that woman there.

SCYTHIAN. Vy, vere is de wretch?

                   Me mush catch, me mush catch.

    Her's a gone, her's a fled.

ECHO.   Her's a gone, her's a fled.

SCYTHIAN. Zu'll a suffer for dis.

ECHO.   Zu'll a suffer for dis.

SCYTHIAN. Vat again?

ECHO.   Vat again?

SCYTHIAN. Zeege ole o' de mix.

ECHO.   Zeege ole o' de mix.

SCYTHIAN. Vat a babbled an' talketing ooman.

EURIPIDES. Ah me, what wild and terrible coast is this?
  Plying the pathless air with wingèd feet,
  Steering for Argos, bearing in my hand
  The Gorgon's head—

SCYTHIAN.   Vat dat zu say o' Gorgo?
  Dat zu has gots de writer Gorgo's head?

EURIPIDES. *Gorgon,* I say.

SCYTHIAN.   An' me says *Gorgo* too.

EURIPIDES. Alas, what crag is this, and lashed upon it
  What maiden, beautiful as shapes divine,
  A lovely craft too rudely moored?

MNESILOCHUS.   O stranger,
  Pity the sorrows of a poor young woman,
  And loose my bonds.

SCYTHIAN.   Vat, vill zu no be quiet?
  Vat, talkee, talkee, ven zu're goin' to die?

EURIPIDES. Fair girl, I weep to see thee hanging there.

SCYTHIAN. Disn't von gal: dis von ole vilain man,
  Von vare bad rascal fellow.

EURIPIDES.   Scythian, peace!
  This is Andromeda, King Cepheus' daughter.

SCYTHIAN. Von dawder! Dis? Vare obvious man, metinks.

EURIPIDES. O, reach thy hand, and let me clasp my love;
  O Scythian, reach. Ah me, what passionate storms
  Toss in men's souls; and as for mine, O lady,
  Thou art my love!

SCYTHIAN.   Me nod admire zure dasde.
  Sdill zu may tiss her, if zu wiss id, dere.

EURIPIDES. Hardhearted Scythian, give me up my love,
  And I will take her—take her aye to wife.

SCYTHIAN. Tiss her, me says; me nod objex to dat.

EURIPIDES. Ah me, I'll loose her bonds.

SCYTHIAN.   Zu bedder nod.

EURIPIDES. Ah me, I will.

SCYTHIAN.   Den, me'se cut off zure head.
  Me draw de cudless, and zu die, zu dead.

EURIPIDES. Ah, what avails me? Shall I make a speech?
  His savage nature could not take it in.

> True wit and wisdom were but labor lost
> On such a rude barbarian. I must try
> Some more appropriate, fitter stratagem.

(He goes out.)

SCYTHIAN. O, de vile vox! He jocket me vare near.

MNESILOCHUS. O, Perseus, Perseus, wilt thou leave me so?

SCYTHIAN. Vat, does zu askin' for de vip again?

CHORUS. Pallas we call upon,
>   Chastest and purest one,
>   Maiden and Virgin, our
>   Revels to see:
>   Guarding our portals
>   Alone of Immortals,
>   Mightily, potently,
>   Keeping the key.
>   Hater of Tyranny,
>   Come, for we call thee, we
>   Women in Chorus.
>   Bring Peace again with thee,
>   Jocundly, merrily,
>   Long to reign o'er us.
>
>   Sacred, unearthly ones,
>   Awfullest Shades,
>   Graciously, peacefully,
>   Come to your glades.
>   Man must not gaze on the
>   Rites at your shrine,
>   Torch-glimmer flashing o'er
>   Features divine.
>   Come, for we're pouring
>   Imploring, adoring,
>   Intense veneration;
>   Dawn on your worshipers,
>   Givers of Home and our
>   Civilization.

EURIPIDES. Ladies, I offer terms. If well and truly
> Your honorable sex befriend me now,
> I won't abuse your honorable sex
> From this time forth forever. This I offer.

CHORUS (suspiciously). But what's your object in proposing
> this?

EURIPIDES. That poor old man there, he's my poor old cousin.
> Let him go free, and nevermore will I

Traduce your worthy sex; but if you won't,
I'll meet your husbands coming from the Wars,
And put them up to all your goings-on.

CHORUS. We take your terms, so far as we're concerned,
But you yourself must manage with the Scythian.

EURIPIDES. I'll manage *him*. Now, Hop-o'-my-thumb, come
  forward,

(A DANCING GIRL *enters*.)

And mind the things I taught you on the way.
Hold up your frock: skip lightly through the dance.
The Persian air, Teredon, if you please.

SCYTHIAN. Vy, vat dis buzbuz? revels come dis vay?

EURIPIDES. She's going to practice, Scythian, that is all.
She's got to dance in public by-and-by.

SCYTHIAN. Yesh, practish, yesh. Hoick! how se bobs about!
Now here, now dere: von vlea upon de planket.

EURIPIDES. Just stop a moment; throw your mantle off;
Come, sit you down beside the Scythian here,
And I'll unloose your slippers. That will do.
We must be moving homeward.

SCYTHIAN.   May I tiss her?

EURIPIDES. Once, only once.

SCYTHIAN (*kissing her*).   O, O, vat vare sweet tiss!
Dat's vare moche sweeter dan zure Attish honies.
Dooze let me tiss her tecon time, ole lady.

EURIPIDES. No, Scythian, no; we really can't allow it.

SCYTHIAN. O doozy, doozy, dear ole lady, doozy.

EURIPIDES. Will you give silver for one kiss?

SCYTHIAN.   Yesh! yesh!

EURIPIDES. Well, p'raps on that consideration, Scythian,
We won't object; but give the silver first.

SCYTHIAN. Silver? Vy, vere? I'se got none. Take dis bow-cus.
Zu, vat I call zu?

EURIPIDES.   Artemisia.

SCYTHIAN. Yesh. Hartomixer.

EURIPIDES.   Hillo, what's that? She's off.

SCYTHIAN. I'se fetch her pack; zu, look to bad ole man.

EURIPIDES. O tricky Hermes, you befriend me still.
Good-by, old Scythian; catch her if you can.
Meanwhile I'll free your prisoner: and do you
(*To* MNESILOCHUS.) Run like a hero, when I've loosed your
  bonds,
Straight to the bosom of your family.

MNESILOCHUS. Trust me for that, so soon as these are off.

EURIPIDES. There then, they are off: now run away, before
    The Scythian come and catch you.

MNESILOCHUS.   Won't I just!

SCYTHIAN. Ole lady, here's—vy, vere's ole lady fannish?
    Vere's dat ole man? O bah, I smells de trick.
    Ole lady, dis vare bad o' zu, ole lady!
    Me nod expex dis of zu. Bad ole lady.
        Hartomixer!
    Bow-cusses? Yesh, zu von big howcus-bowcus.
    Vat sall I does? vere can ole lady was?
        Hartomixer!

CHORUS. Mean you the ancient dame who bore the lute?

SCYTHIAN. Yesh, does zu saw her?

CHORUS.   Yes, indeed I did.
    She went *that* way: there was an old man with her.

SCYTHIAN. Von yellow-shilk ole man?

CHORUS.   Exactly so.
    I think you'll catch them if you take *that* road.

SCYTHIAN. Vare bad ole lady, did se vich vay run?
        Hartomixer!

CHORUS. Straight up the hill; no, no, not that direction.
    You're going wrong: see, that's the way she went.

SCYTHIAN. O dear, O dear, but Hartomixer runnish.
                (He runs out the wrong way.)

CHORUS. Merrily, merrily, merrily on to your own confusion go.
    But we've ended our say, and we're going away,
    Like good honest women, straight home from the Play.
    And we trust that the twain-Home-givers will deign
    To bless with success our performance today.

                      (Exeunt.)

Frogs

The *Frogs*, presented in 405 B.C., is not only a rollicking
farce but our earliest example of literary criticism of a high
technical order. Dionysus goes to Hades to fetch Euripides
(who died in 406) because Athens has no good tragic poets
left. The adventures of Dionysus and his slave Xanthias on
their way to Pluto's court are delightfully amusing; the songs
of the chorus of initiates in Hades are enchanting. What
emerges from the elaborate competition is that Euripides is
prosaic in diction, deals with vulgar themes, corrupts manners, and debases music. The criticism of Aeschylus' turgidity
and obscurity, it must be noted, is almost as severe. When
artistic tests prove inconclusive, the decision favors Aeschylus
on the basis of his superior solution of a *political* problem:
what to do about Alcibiades. The play documents not only the
high literacy of an audience capable of following technical
criticism, but also the view of the poet as a responsible public
teacher.

CHARACTERS

XANTHIAS, SERVANT OF
  DIONYSUS
DIONYSUS
HERACLES
A CORPSE
CHARON
AEACUS
A HOUSEMAID OF PERSEPHONE

LANDLADY, KEEPER OF
  COOKSHOP
PLATHANE, HER PARTNER
EURIPIDES
AESCHYLUS
PLUTO
CHORUS OF FROGS
CHORUS OF BLESSED MYSTICS

Translated by R. H. Webb

(DIONYSUS *with the lion skin of* HERACLES *over his saffron robe, and his slave* XANTHIAS *on a donkey, carrying the luggage on a pole, appear as travelers. The house of* HERACLES *is in the background.*)

XANTHIAS. Boss, would you mind it if I started off
With a good old gag that always gets a laugh?
DIONYSUS. Any you like—except *I got the pip!*
My stomach just can't take it any more.
XANTHIAS. Some other pearl?
DIONYSUS.   Except *I'm fit to pop!*
XANTHIAS. What about one that really is a *scream?*
DIONYSUS. Go right ahead—but don't you dare . . .
XANTHIAS.   Dare what?
DIONYSUS. To shift your load and say that you are *pooped!*
XANTHIAS. Or, that if nobody will relieve the strain,
I'm going to "relieve *myself*"?
DIONYSUS.   No, please—
Unless you see that I am sick already!
XANTHIAS. Why do I have to pack this stuff around
And not have fun like all the other boys—
Phrynichus, Lycis, and Ameipsias?
DIONYSUS. Because you can't! . . . I never miss a play;
And every time I hear that sort of wit
I go home twelve months older than I was!
XANTHIAS. Pity a poor old neck that's *fit to pop,*
And isn't allowed to crack a single joke!
DIONYSUS. Dear me, what airs! What pampered insolence—
When Dionysus, Earl of Brandywine,
Struggles along on foot, and gives his slave
An ass to bear his burden and himself.
XANTHIAS. Do *I* not bear it?
DIONYSUS.   How, when you are *borne?*
XANTHIAS. By carrying *this.*
DIONYSUS.   But how . . . ?
XANTHIAS.   With pain, *that's how!*
DIONYSUS. Doesn't the donkey bear the weight *you* bear?
XANTHIAS. This load I'm toting on my back? No *sir!*
DIONYSUS. How *can* you tote it when *he's* toting *you?*
XANTHIAS. All I know is, my shoulder's *got the pip!*
DIONYSUS. Well, since the donkey isn't helping you,
Suppose you take *your* turn and carry *him?*

XANTHIAS. I wish to God I'd signed up with the fleet.
　Then I could say to *you*, Oh go to hell!

DIONYSUS. Get down, you rascal. Here is where we stop—
　First stop upon the way to journey's end.
　My legs have made it! —Hi there! Open up!

HERACLES. Who's hammering my door? Might be a centaur,
　Throwing his weight around! —Say, what on earth . . . ?

DIONYSUS (*aside to* XANTHIAS). Psst!

XANTHIAS. 　　　　　　　　　　　　　Well?

DIONYSUS. 　　　　　　　　　　　　Didn't you notice?

XANTHIAS. 　　　　　　　　　　　　　Notice what?

DIONYSUS. How scared he was of me.

XANTHIAS. 　　　　　　　　　Scared you were *crazy!*

HERACLES. Honest to God, I can't control myself—
　Biting my lips in two, but all the same . . .

DIONYSUS. Hey, listen, can't you? I've a request to make.

HERACLES. Ha ha! Shiver me timbers, what a sight—
　A lion skin on top of yellow silk!
　What's the idea? Club and buskins *both*? . . .
　Where go you?

DIONYSUS. 　　　　Shipping aboard the *Cleisthenes* . . .

HERACLES. Get in the fight?

DIONYSUS. 　　　　　　　*And,* incidentally,
　We sank some twelve or thirteen Spartan ships . . .

HERACLES. The *two* of you?

DIONYSUS. 　　　　　　Quite so.

XANTHIAS (*aside*). 　　　　　　Then *I* woke *up!*

DIONYSUS. And, bless you, sitting on the deck one day,
　Reading once more that dear *Andromeda,*
　My heart was smitten by desire so strong . . .

HERACLES. *How* strong?

DIONYSUS. 　　　　A "Tiny" Molon of desire!

HERACLES. For whom? A woman?

DIONYSUS. 　　　　　　　　No!

HERACLES. 　　　　　　　　　A boy?

DIONYSUS. 　　　　　　　　　　　No, no!

HERACLES. A man?

DIONYSUS. Oh gee!

HERACLES. 　　　Have you and Cleisthenes . . . ?

DIONYSUS. Don't tease me, Brother. Truly, I am ill.
　This love is making havoc of my life!

HERACLES. Tell me about it, son.

DIONYSUS. 　　　　　　Impossible!
　I can't describe it . . . only illustrate.

You've felt a sudden passion for pea soup?

HERACLES. Thousands of times!

DIONYSUS. Do I reveal my thought, then?
Or shall I tell thee in another way?

HERACLES. About pea soup? No, *that* I understand!

DIONYSUS. Such is the longing that devours my soul
For sweet ... Euripides.

HERACLES. A *dead* man?

DIONYSUS. Yes!
And no one can dissuade me on this earth
From going for him!

HERACLES. Down to *Hades*?

DIONYSUS. Yes,
And lower still, if such a place there be.

HERACLES. But why?

DIONYSUS. I want a poet who can *write!*
Some are no more, and they that live are base.

HERACLES. Iophon's living, isn't he?

DIONYSUS. That's true—
The only blessing that remains to us ...
If it's a blessing. I am not quite sure.

HERACLES. Why resurrect, if resurrect you must,
Euripides, instead of Sophocles?

DIONYSUS. Because I want to test young Iophon,
And see what he can do all by himself.
Besides, Euripides, the clever rogue,
Would aid my kidnap scheme; while Sophocles,
Gentleman always, is a gentleman still.

HERACLES. And what of Agathon?

DIONYSUS. Too bad, he's gone.
Good poet, sadly missed.

HERACLES. Poor chap! Gone where?

DIONYSUS. To the Elysian Feasts of Macedon.

HERACLES. How about Xenocles?

DIONYSUS. Bad cess to *him!*

HERACLES. Pythangelus?

XANTHIAS. Nobody thinks of *me*—
My shoulder rubbed until it's raw!

HERACLES. But surely myriads of little men
Still scribble for the Tragic Boards up there,
Outprattling your Euripides a mile.

DIONYSUS. Mere nubbins, with a silly gift of gab;
Shrill swallow choirs, murderers of Art!
One single play produced, and they are spent—

Small piss-ants, fouling the bed of Tragedy!
What potent poet can you find today,
To father one full-bodied, ringing phrase?

HERACLES. Potent? You mean . . . ?

DIONYSUS.   A poet who will risk
A bold, a reckless utterance, such as
Aether, the Inglenook of Zeus; Time's tread;
The mind refused its solemn oath to plight,
The tongue was perjured, in the mind's despite!

HERACLES. You like that stuff?

DIONYSUS.   I'm mad about it!

HERACLES.   Pshaw!
Cheap hocus-pocus, and you know it is!

DIONYSUS. *My mind, sir, is my castle.* Mind your own!

HERACLES. Well anyway, it's pure humbuggery.

DIONYSUS. I'll *listen*, when you lecture me on *food!*

XANTHIAS. Nobody thinks of *me!*

DIONYSUS.   Now look, here's why
I came here in this toggery of yours—
To learn what hospitality you found,
That time you went down after Cerberus:
Who put you up, the highways, harbors, springs,
Bakeries, bawdyhouses, restrooms, towns,
Madams and lodgings, inns with fewest bugs . . .
I want them all.

XANTHIAS.   Nobody thinks of *me!*

HERACLES. Poor kid! You dare attempt this journey? *You?*

DIONYSUS. No more of that, now! Tell me first the roads—
The quickest way to get from here to Hell—
Neither too hot, however, nor too cold.

HERACLES. Well, let me see, what shall I recommend?
The Lynch-Gate Road is one of the easiest—
You hang yourself!

DIONYSUS.   Too hot—a *stifling* way!

HERACLES. A slippery cutoff, known as Evergreen Lane,
Mid the murmuring pine and the . . .

DIONYSUS.   Hemlock?

HERACLES.   Right you are!

DIONYSUS. Br-r-r! Makes me shiver just to think of it!
You're frozen stiff—numb from the ankles up!

HERACLES. A shorter route, then, but precipitate . . .

DIONYSUS. Shorter the better. Walking's not my forte!

HERACLES. Stroll to the Ceramicus . . .

DIONYSUS.   Well, what next?

HERACLES. And climb the tower—that high one—

DIONYSUS. And do what?

HERACLES. Watch till the torch race is about to start;
And when the crowd is shouting *Let 'em go!*
You let *yourself* go.

Where?

Headforemost . . . *down!*

DIONYSUS. I'd ruin two potential brain croquettes!
That road I'll *never* take!

HERACLES. Which *will* you take?

DIONYSUS. The one *you* took.

HERACLES. But that's a lengthy *cruise*.
First you will come to an enormous lake,
Bottomless, huge.

DIONYSUS. How will I get across?

HERACLES. In a tiny boat—so big—an aged salt
Rows people over for two bits a head.

DIONYSUS. Aha! Good old two bits will get you anywhere!
How did they get down *there?*

HERACLES. Theseus, of course.
Next, you will see big snakes and dreadful beasts
Past counting.

DIONYSUS. Don't you try to frighten me.
You cannot scare me out of it.

HERACLES. Then, mud,
Masses of mud, and streams of muck, in which
Is every man who ever wronged a guest,
Or beat his ma or slapped his father's face,
Or took a girl to bed and wouldn't pay,
Or swore an oath he knew he couldn't keep,
Or copied out some lines by Morsimus.

DIONYSUS. And likewise everyone, I hope, who danced
That Pyrrhic number by Cinesias!

HERACLES. Then flutes will breathe sweet music through the
air,
A light as brilliant as the sun will shine,
And myrtle groves and blissful throngs appear
Of men and women clapping their hands for joy.

DIONYSUS. Who *are* they?

HERACLES. Those who have entered into Bliss.

XANTHIAS. And I'm the ass they tie outside the gate!
Damned if I tote this stuff another yard!

HERACLES. And they will tell you all you need to know.
Their happy homes are yonder by the road,

Close to the very doors of Pluto's house.
And now good-by, dear brother.

DIONYSUS. Same to you.
Keep well. (*To* XANTHIAS, *as* HERACLES *retires.*) And you
pick up your pack again.

XANTHIAS. Before I've set it down?

DIONYSUS. Get going, there!

XANTHIAS. Oh please. . . . Why don't you hire another boy—
Some dead man coming from his funeral?

DIONYSUS. Suppose I cannot find one.

XANTHIAS. Then take me.

DIONYSUS. All right. . . . Yonder's a bier approaching now.
(*Enter a* CORPSE *with* BEARERS.)
Hey, you! —Not *you*. . . . I'm talking to the corpse.
Look, will you carry a small pack for me?

CORPSE. *How* small?

DIONYSUS. This here.

CORPSE. A dollar, shall we say?

DIONYSUS. Too much!

CORPSE (*to* BEARERS). We might as well be getting on.

DIONYSUS. Wait, my good man. I'm sure we can agree.

CORPSE. One dollar, cash, or not another word!

DIONYSUS. Six bits!

CORPSE. I'd sooner come to life again!

XANTHIAS. Stuck up, now, ain't he? Shucks! Be damned to
him!
I'll go, sir.

DIONYSUS. Spoken like a gentleman!
Let's find the boat.
(CHARON *is heard offstage.*)

CHARON. Avast! Bring her ashore.

XANTHIAS. What's that I see?

DIONYSUS. What's what? . . . Oh, that? . . . A lake—
The one he told us of. And look—a boat!

XANTHIAS. Yes, by Poseidon, yes . . . and Charon too!

DIONYSUS. *Ahoy there, Charon!*

XANTHIAS. *Hi there, Cap!*

DIONYSUS. }
XANTHIAS. } *Ahoy!*

CHARON. All passengers for the Land of Sweet Repose,
Bound for Oblivion, or Ass's Locks,
The Doghouse, Hell, or Taenarum—*Aboard!*

DIONYSUS. Here's *one.*

CHARON. Then get aboard. Step lively, please!

DIONYSUS. You really go to Hell?

CHARON.   For *you* we will!
  Get *in!*

DIONYSUS.   Come, boy.

CHARON.   Sorry, no slaves allowed,
  Unless they fought to free their carcasses.

XANTHIAS. I couldn't—had the pink-eye . . . just my luck!

CHARON. Then you will have to run around the lake.

XANTHIAS. Where shall I meet you?

CHARON.   Rest-in-Peace Hotel,
  At Tombstone Point.

DIONYSUS.   You understand?

XANTHIAS.   Too well!
  What evil omen crossed my path this day?

CHARON (*to* DIONYSUS). You take an oar. —Time's up, now.
    All aboard!
  What do you think you're doing?

DIONYSUS.   What you said—
  Told me to take an oar . . . I *took* an oar!

CHARON. Sit *down* there, Fatty, on that bench!

DIONYSUS.   All right.

CHARON. Stretch out your arms . . . full length.

DIONYSUS.   Well, there you are.

CHARON. Now stop this silly clowning. Brace your legs
  And row . . . row like a good one.

DIONYSUS.   Never learned—
  Complete landlubber . . . *most* unnautical.
  How *can* I row?

CHARON.   Easily. You will hear,
  Once you have started, lovely songs . . .

DIONYSUS.   By whom?

CHARON. Our minstrel frogs . . . wonderful!

DIONYSUS.   Give me the count.

CHARON. Stroke. . . . Stroke. . . .
  (*The* CHORUS OF FROGS *is heard offstage, croaking in rhythm
  with the oarsmen.*)

CHORUS.   *Brekekekex ko-ax ko-ax*
               Brekekekex ko-ax ko-ax
              From marsh and mere
                Sound again
                Your fair refrain
               Deep and clear,
               O humid race,
              Booming the bass

Cadenza
Ko-ax ko-ax.
In sweet accord
Thus we laud
Divine Dionysus, when,
Beside his temple in the Fen,
Townsmen and villagers journey,
Tankards replete for the Tourney,
So tipsily reeling around
My hallowed ground.
Brekekekex ko-ax ko-ax.

DIONYSUS.   My poor behind begins to ache.
Ko-ax yourself, for heaven's sake!
But *you* don't care, you maniacs.

CHORUS.   *Brekekekex ko-ax ko-ax.*

DIONYSUS.   Be damned to you, *ko-ax* and all!
Ko-ax and nothing else you bawl!

CHORUS.   'Tis our right and proper chorus,
Meddlesome wight.
For the lyric Nine adore us,
As doth goat-footed Pan, who merrily
Plays his pipes on hillock, in hollow,
And the Harpist, Lord Apollo,
Rendering thanks for the reed that I verily
Nurse for the lyre in swampy lands.
Brekekekex ko-ax ko-ax.

DIONYSUS.   I'm raising blisters on my hands;
My rump is in a fearful stew,
And soon he'll up and say to you . . .

CHORUS.   *Brekekekex ko-ax ko-ax.*

DIONYSUS.   O tuneful breed,
Pray give o'er!

CHORUS.   Nay, nay! Indeed
All the more
Shall we chant,
If e'er before
On a sunlit morn we capered
Where the flags and rushes tapered,
Trilling arias ecstatic
Suited to our sports aquatic,
Or, in flight from rainy weather,
Danced in wat'ry regions nether,
Brightly caroling together
Many a bubble-and-spray gavotte . . .

DIONYSUS. *Brekekekex ko-ax ko-ax—*
I beat you that time, did I not?

CHORUS. Fearsome fate for me to suffer!

DIONYSUS. Mine will certainly be tougher
If I row until I split!

CHORUS. *Brekekekex ko-ax ko-ax.*

DIONYSUS. Do *I* care, damn you? Not a bit!

CHORUS. 'Tis our song. We'll not forsake it—
Never, as long as throat can take it—
Crying loudly through the day . . .

DIONYSUS. *Brekekekex ko-ax-ko-ax.*
You cannot win in this affray!

CHORUS. Nor can *you* put *us* to rout, sir!

DIONYSUS. Nor can *you*! With conqu'ring might
Will I lift my voice and shout, sir,
Be there need, into the night,
Brekekekex ko-ax ko-ax.
And press the fight
Until I out-*ko-ax* you, son.

(*Belligerently.*)
Brekekekex ko-ax ko-ax.

(*Silence from the* FROGS.)
Well, was I right?
Not one *ko-ax* I hear. . . . You're done!

CHARON. Slow up, there! . . . Easy! . . . Bring her in! . . . Now,
then,
Ashore! . . . All tickets, please!

DIONYSUS. Here's mine—two bits.
Hey, Xanthias! . . . Where are you, Xanthy? . . . Hi!

XANTHIAS. Yoo-hoo!

DIONYSUS. Come over here! . . .

XANTHIAS. How are you, boss?

DIONYSUS. What is it like out yonder?

XANTHIAS. Darkness . . . Mud . . .

DIONYSUS. You saw the parricides and perjurers
He told us of?

XANTHIAS. Certainly. Didn't you?

DIONYSUS. Oh yes, I saw them . . .
And I see them *now*! . . .
All right, what next?

XANTHIAS. We'd better move along.—
This is the place in which he said we'd find
Those awful animals.

DIONYSUS.   To hell with him—
  A show-off, telling tales to frighten me.
  He's jealous of my well-known fortitude.
  Nothing is haughtier than . . . Heracles!
  I only wish I *could* meet one of them,
  And win a trophy worthy of my tour.

XANTHIAS. What's that? . . . I hear a funny kind of noise.

DIONYSUS. Which way?

XANTHIAS.   Back yonder.

DIONYSUS.   Walk behind me, then.

XANTHIAS. No, it's in front.

DIONYSUS.   Then go ahead of me.

XANTHIAS. I see it now. I see a great beast!

DIONYSUS. Wh-what sort?

XANTHIAS.   Ghastly. . . . Never stays the same—
  A bull, first . . . then a mule . . . and now a *girl* . . .
  Good looker, too.

DIONYSUS.   Where? Lemme get to her!

XANTHIAS. She isn't there. She's turned into a bitch.

DIONYSUS. Empusa!

XANTHIAS.   Maybe. Her face is all ablaze
  With fire.

DIONYSUS.   And has she got one leg of brass?

XANTHIAS. By George, she has! and the other one's pure *gall!*

DIONYSUS. I want to go away from here.

XANTHIAS.   Me too.

DIONYSUS (*appealing to his priest in the audience*). Save me
    Your Eminence—till supper-time!

XANTHIAS. May Heracles preserve us!

DIONYSUS.   Stop it, man!
  For heaven's sake, don't speak my name out loud!

XANTHIAS. Well, Dionysus, then.

DIONYSUS.   That's even worse! . . .
  Now get along with you.

XANTHIAS.   Here, Master, here!

DIONYSUS. What is it?

XANTHIAS.   Calm yourself. Fair Fortune smiles.
  We now may say, *à la* Hegelochus,
  The storm is spent. The ocean is a tease.
  Empusa's gone.

DIONYSUS.   You swear?

XANTHIAS.   Honest to God!

DIONYSUS. You cross your heart?

XANTHIAS.   Yes.

DIONYSUS.   Hope you may die?

XANTHIAS.   I do.—

I must admit she turned me green with fright . . .
And you turned yellow. . . . Look, you're yellow still!

DIONYSUS. What brought these miseries upon my head?
Who up in heaven wants to ruin me?

XANTHIAS. *Aether, God's Tenement? . . . The tread of Time?*
(*Sound of music offstage.*)

DIONYSUS. Hey!

XANTHIAS.   What's the matter?

DIONYSUS.   Didn't you hear it?

XANTHIAS.   What?

DIONYSUS. That *breath of flutes.*

XANTHIAS.   Yes, and another breath,
The mystic scent of torches, comes to me.

DIONYSUS. Let's squat down here and listen silently.

CHORUS.   All hail, hail, Iacchus!
                    All hail, hail, Iacchus!

XANTHIAS. That's who it is—the Saved, the Blessed Ones
He told us of, in joyful song nearby . . .
The very same they sing in the Agora.

DIONYSUS. You're right, I do believe. In any case
We'd best keep quiet till we know for sure.
(*Enter the* CHORUS OF MYSTICS.)

CHORUS.   Divine Babe, here residing
                In a fane built for thy biding,
              All hail, hail, Iacchus!
                    Join our throng,
                    Ever by us
                  In the dance song
                    Of the pious
                  Through the moorland;
          On thy fair forehead, the gleaming
          Of a wreath with berries teeming,
              Set aquiver by the measure
            That with bold foot thou dost beat
              In a bold rite, and replete
            With a pure, a holy pleasure
          And the sweet charm of the graces
                    That are meet
              For the Mystics' hallowed paces.

XANTHIAS. O great and glorious Persephone,
How redolent, that song, of barbecue!

DIONYSUS. Be still, then, if you want some sausage too!

CHORUS.
        The firebrand must awaken;
      For our Day-Star is uptaken—
        All hail, hail, Iacchus!—
           Doth arise,
          And a splendor
           In the dark skies
          Doth engender
      Through the meadow
    Where the aged limb is leaping,
    And our woes away are creeping,
    And the sore burden is lightened
      Of the years' wearisome pain
    By the dance thou dost ordain
    In a vale with blossoms brightened.
    Mid the torch glow that is o'er us
        Lead amain,
    Blessed Youth, a youthful chorus!

Be silent. Attend. Let no one offend by his presence our ritual dances,

Whose taste is impure, nor knows the lure of the Word, the art that entrances;

Nor shared the delights of the elegant rites of the Muse, the Mistress of Glamour;

Nor deeply the wine has imbibed of Cratinus, the dauntless Bull of the Drama;

Nor feels malaise at a scene that displays a malapropos vulgarity;

Nor seeks to quiet political riot by preaching and practicing charity,

But quite unashamedly fans the flame to further his private ambitions;

Or, mid the unrest of a country distressed, takes gold from corrupt politicians

A ship or a fort to betray, to export from Aegina a contraband cargo—

Thus aping Thoricion, that blackguard official of *five per cent, or embargo!*—

The contents of which—sails, oarlocks, pitch—Epidaurus will have in an hour;

Or cash would entreat for the enemy's fleet from a certain imperial power;

Or, while he's rehearsing his chorus, perversely gives Hecate's precinct a shower;

Or nibbles away at the dramatists' pay—some demagogue
    fain to attack us

Because we had twitted the fellow a bit in accord with the
    rubrics of Bacchus:

All these do I warn, *Begone, begone! Avaunt!* is my stern
    exhortation.

Make way for the mystic, the pure, the artistic, who, roused
    by a holy elation,

Will dance till the dawn and will rest in the morn, as is
    meet for this fair celebration.

> March onward, all ye blessèd,
> By pasture bloom caressèd,
> Your step firm and lithesome,
> 'Mid quip and jest
> And mocking banter blithesome—
> Though lunch was none too good, at best!
> Stride on. The Maid applaud ye,
> Our Virgin Savior laud ye;
> Her praise hymn forever,
> Who guards this spot,
> And vows to fail us never—
> Although Thoricion likes it not!

Now raise ye another refrain for the Mother, the Queen of
    the Harvest to honor,

Adorning with beauty of voice and of flute Demeter, our
    Holy Madonna.

> O Mistress of this solemn rite,
> Stand thou beside me in the fight,
> And lead thy graceful choir aright,
> To utter naught that in thy sight
>   Is stupid or immoral!
> O grant me witty things to say,
> And earnest things in a witty way,
> All worthy of thy festal day,
> That I may win the merry fray
>   And wear the victor's laurel!

> Now hear ye!

Call forth the Holy Child with song; summon the Babe
    Iacchus,

That he may join our pilgrim throng, votaries of Bacchus.

Thou who the fairest of festal music inspirèd,
Come seek with us, O Infant ever desirèd,
Thy Mother's fane,
And prove thee able to sustain
The toilsome course untirèd.
Iacchus, lover of song and dance, lead thou me on.

This tattered tunic here, let none misjudge it;
This battered shoe I wear, let none begrudge it;
'Tis thy decree,
As aiding in our jollity—
And balancing the budget!
Iacchus, lover of song and dance, lead thou me on.

A comely maid beside us, thanks to you, sir,
Afforded me a stimulating view, sir,
When from her shirt
One little bosom like a flirt
Peeped out and said *How-do, sir!*
Iacchus, lover of song and dance, lead thou me on.

DIONYSUS.   Processions I could never eschew.
A whirl with yonder girlie
I'd simply love—I mean that peekaboo!
XANTHIAS.   Me too!
CHORUS.   Methinks it would beseem us
To jeer at Archidemus,
The snaggle-tooth Bicuspidorian,
Who nowadays, God love us,
Commands the dead above us,
Top villain of the hyphenated clan.

Young Cleisthenes, the queerie,
Intones a *miserere*
For sweet Sebinus, prostrate in despair.
His manly features mauling,
Incontinently bawling,
He beats his breast and plucks his bottom bare.

And Callias, the fearless,
In navel battles peerless,
Engaged the foe bedight in pussy skin.
DIONYSUS.   Could any of you tell us
Where Pluto lives? From Hellas'
Shores we only recently got in.

CHORUS.   It is not far away, sir;
               Nor ask again, I pray, sir.
               Behind yon very portal he doth dwell.
DIONYSUS.   Then bring the baggage, fellow.
XANTHIAS.   The old refrain—how mellow!
               But toting baggage is no bagatelle!

CHORUS.   Now onward,
To enter the Deity's holy ground, tread its carpet of
    flowers,
Glad partners in a solemn round dear to Potent Powers.
And I will bear the torch to light blessed maids and matrons
Who through the night in darkling rite laud our Heavenly
    Patrons.
           Aye, onward to the meadows bright
               With asphodel and roses,
            To dance in our native way
            That beauteous dance and gay.
            For thus on this happy day
               Fair Fortune disposes.

           On us alone the sun doth smile
               With face benign—stout yeomen,
            True Saints of the Mystic Band,
            Who greet with a guileless hand
            All friends from an alien land,
              All . . . parvenu showmen!

(DIONYSUS *and* XANTHIAS *approach the palace of Pluto.*)

DIONYSUS. Well, I suppose I ought to knock. But how?
    I wonder how they do it hereabouts.
XANTHIAS. Quit dawdling. Go and have a try at it.
    The *mood* of Heracles should match his *model!*
DIONYSUS (*knocking*). Hello!

(AEACUS *appears.*)

AEACUS.   Who's there?
DIONYSUS (*striking a pose*). The valiant Heracles!
AEACUS. You reckless rogue, you barefaced good-for-naught,
    You scamp, you utter scamp, you . . . scalawag!
    Our watchdog Cerberus, my special care,
    First luring from his post, you seized and choked,
    And off you ran with him. But now you're caught,
    Hemmed in by yon blackhearted Stygian peak,
    Acheron's canyon that with gore doth reek,
    Cocytus' wanton bitches, swift and sleek!

Echidna's fivescore mouths thy veins will tear;
Bloodsuckers of Tartessus will not spare
Thy severed lungs, Teithrasian Gorgon hags
Thy very vitals ripping into rags,
Thy entrails mangling to a scarlet shred!
To summon them I presently am sped.

> (*Exit* AEACUS; DIONYSUS *collapses.*)

XANTHIAS. I say, what *have* you done? . . . Ridiculous!

DIONYSUS. *Propississiation for my shins. Amen.*

XANTHIAS. Get up! Somebody'll *see* you!

DIONYSUS.   I am faint.
Water! A sponge, to press upon my heart!

XANTHIAS. Well, here's one. . . . Take it.

DIONYSUS.   Where?

XANTHIAS.   Ye golden gods!
That's where you keep your heart?

DIONYSUS.   It got so scared
It went into a tailspin, so to speak!

XANTHIAS. Of all the cowards, human or divine . . . !

DIONYSUS. A coward, eh? I asked you for a sponge,
When anybody else would have . . .

XANTHIAS.   Done what?

DIONYSUS. Just lain there, stinko—any *coward* would.
But I got up, and wiped myself besides!

XANTHIAS. God, what a *man!*

DIONYSUS.   Exactly what *I* think.
Weren't *you* afraid, when all that hell broke loose?

XANTHIAS. Why no, I never even thought of it.

DIONYSUS. All right, then, since you are a dauntless soul,
With such a hero complex, *you* be *me.*
Put on the lion skin and take the club,
And I will tote the baggage for a change.

XANTHIAS. No sooner said than done. Your word is law.—
Well, look me over—Xanthias—Heracles!
You'll see a better brand of spunk than yours.

DIONYSUS. What *I* see is the Meletean *punk!*
But first, to get this luggage on my back.

> (*A* HOUSEMAID *appears.*)

HOUSEMAID. Heracles! Darling! Here at last! . . . Come in.
My mistress, learning you'd arrived, at once
Put loaves into the oven, made pea soup—
Oh, pots and pots of it—and cakes and rolls,
And barbecued an ox. . . . But do come in!

XANTHIAS. No, thank you very much, but . . .

HOUSEMAID.   I insist!
   I simply cannot let you go like this.
   Roast chicken, and delectable desserts,
   And wines the sweetest ever. Come with me.

XANTHIAS. I'm much obliged, but . . .

HOUSEMAID.   Don't be silly, now.
   You've *got* to! Think of all those lovely girls
   We have, to play the flute and dance for you—
   A half a dozen of them!

XANTHIAS.   How's that? *Girls?*

HOUSEMAID. The cutest things—so young and soft and smooth.
   Now hurry. Cook was taking off the fish
   When I came out, ready to send it in.

XANTHIAS. Oh very well, then. You may run ahead
   And tell the girls that I am on the way.—
   Up with the baggage, boy, and follow me.

DIONYSUS. Hey, *wait* a minute! You aren't *serious?*
   Dressing you up like that was just a joke!
   Now stop this foolishness at once, my lad.
   Pick up these bundles here and be yourself.

XANTHIAS. You don't intend to rob me of this rig
   You *gave* me?

DIONYSUS.   Not at all. . . . I'm *doing* it!
   Remove that lion skin, sir.

XANTHIAS.   I protest!
   I call upon the gods to . . .

DIONYSUS.   *What* gods? . . . *Me?*
   How vain, how stupid, to suppose that you,
   A common slave, could be Alcmena's son!

XANTHIAS. Here, take it, by all means. But some fine day
   Perhaps you'll need me yet—God grant you may!

CHORUS.   'Tis the mark of one sagacious,
       Practical and perspicacious,
         Who hath sailed the seven seas,
       That he roll across to larboard
       If it's stormy on the starboard—
         Not immobile, if you please,
       As a graven image, never
       Shifting in a smart endeavor
         To secure a softer breeze.
       Such a man is jolly clever—
         Aye, a born Theramenes!

DIONYSUS.   Would it not have been diverting
       If old Xanthias, while flirting

With a maiden minus clothes,
Had declared an intermission
For a privy expedition;
    Whereupon I, on my toes,
Seeing what was up, had darted
In to finish what he started;
    But he peppered me with blows,
Knocking out—the lionhearted—
    From my kisser both front rows!

(*Enter* LANDLADY *and* PLATHANE.)

LANDLADY. Here, Plathane, look yonder. . . . That's the scamp
  Who came—remember?—to my boardinghouse
  And ate up sixteen loaves of bread . . .

PLATHANE.   It is—
  The very same!

XANTHIAS. Bad news for *somebody!*

LANDLADY. And twenty portions of roast beef besides,
  At four bits *per* . . .

XANTHIAS.   Somebody's in for it!

LANDLADY. And nearly all my garlic . . .

DIONYSUS.   Nonsense, madam.
  Surely you cannot mean that . . .

LANDLADY.   So? You thought
  I wouldn't know you in those fancy shoes?
  And *fish*—I haven't even mentioned that!

PLATHANE. Nor yet, dear me, the elegant fresh cheese
  That he devoured, drying cloth and all!

LANDLADY. And then, when I informed him what he owed,
  He glared at me and bellowed like a bull . . .

XANTHIAS. Quite typical. That's how he always acts.

LANDLADY. And drew his dagger, like a crazy man.

PLATHANE. Oh heavens, yes!

LANDLADY.   We, horrified, of course,
  Went scrambling up the ladder to the loft.
  But out he rushed—and took my pallet, too!

XANTHIAS. He would. Just like him.

PLATHANE.   Something must be *done.*

LANDLADY. Go get my lawyer, Cleon. Bring him here.

DIONYSUS (*to* XANTHIAS). You go and find, for *me*, Hyperbolus!

LANDLADY. I'll have revenge!—You greedy gullet, you!
  Oh how I'd love to take a stone and crack
  Those grinders that cleaned up my pantry shelves!

XANTHIAS. *I'd* love to fling him on the city dump!

PLATHANE. Or take a scythe and slice right off his neck
   The throat that gobbled my delicious tripe!
   I'm going after Cleon, who this day
   Will serve a writ and wind the business up.
                    (*Exeunt* LANDLADY *and* PLATHANE.)

DIONYSUS. Damme if I don't love my Xanthias!

XANTHIAS. I know what *that* means! . . . Not another word!
   I *won't* be Heracles . . . I *won't!*

DIONYSUS.   Now, Xanthy,
   Please do not talk like that!

XANTHIAS.   But how could I,
   A common slave, become Alcmena's son?

DIONYSUS. *I* know, *I* know. . . . You're mad. . . . You've a right
    to be.
   I wouldn't blame you if you slapped my face.
   If ever I rob you of the role again,
   A curse on me, my spouse, my little brood . . .
   And Archidemus of the bleary eye!

XANTHIAS. That does it! I accept. It's worth a try!

CHORUS.   Now that you once more are wearing
         An investiture so daring,
           'Tis your task with might and main
         To renew your youth, acquiring
         An expression awe-inspiring,
           Mindful of the brawn and brain
         Of your great heroic model.
         For if, prone to silly twaddle,
           You emit one word inane,
         'Tis your destiny to toddle
           'Round beneath that load again.

XANTHIAS. Good advice, my friends; but, queerly,
         It just happens that I really
           Thought of it myself, by chance.
         True, when things are looking better,
         He will rob me, and forget a
           Promise made me in advance.
         Nonetheless you shall behold a
         Man of spirit even bolder,
           And with mustard in his glance.—
         Hark! . . . I'll need, before I'm older,
           'Twould appear, all vigilance.

  (*Enter* AEACUS *with* POLICEMEN.)

AEACUS. Arrest this dog thief here without delay.
   We'll show him! Quick!

DIONYSUS. Bad news for *somebody!*

XANTHIAS. To hell with you! Stand back!

AEACUS. Resisting, eh?
What ho! Ditylas, Pardocus, Sceblyas,
Come out and help us overcome this rogue!

DIONYSUS. Isn't it terrible—a thief like him
Assaulting an officer?

AEACUS. Monstrous, indeed!

DIONYSUS. Outrageous . . . oh dear me!

XANTHIAS. I hope to die,
If ever I came near this place before,
Or stole a cent's worth of your property!
Now here's a sporting offer, freely made:
You give this slave of mine the third degree,
And if you prove me guilty, kill me dead!

AEACUS. What may we do to him?

XANTHIAS. Why, anything!
The rack, the wheel, the whip. . . . Skin him alive . . .
Vinegar up his nose . . . bricks on his chest . . .
Or hang him by his thumbs . . . what have you. . . . *But*
No lashing with a leek or onion top!

AEACUS. That's fair enough. And if I lame the boy
In any way, you shall be reimbursed.

XANTHIAS. Not I! Just take him off and torture him.

AEACUS. Here, rather. Let him say it to your face.—
Put down your pack. . . . No lies, now! Understand?

DIONYSUS. To whom it may concern I give due warning:
I'm an Immortal. If you torture *me,*
You'll have yourself to blame.

AEACUS. What did you say?

DIONYSUS. That I am Dionysus, son of Zeus.
This person is my slave.

AEACUS (*to* XANTHIAS). Hear that?

XANTHIAS. I do.
All the more reason, then, to torture him . . .
Won't even feel it, if he is a god!

DIONYSUS. *You* claim to be a god too—Heracles.
So shouldn't *you* be beaten, just as much?

XANTHIAS. Sounds logical.—Whichever one of us
Shows that he minds it, or lets fall a tear,
You may be certain he is not a god.

AEACUS. I must admit that you're a gentleman—
Completely fair and square. —Take off your coats.

XANTHIAS. But how can *you* be fair?

AEACUS.   Oh easily—
A blow for you, a blow for him.

XANTHIAS.   All right.

(AEACUS *strikes him.*)
Well, go ahead. And watch whether I flinch.

AEACUS. But I've already *hit* you!

XANTHIAS.   No-o-o! You swear?

AEACUS. I'll go and hit the other fellow.

(*He strikes* DIONYSUS.)

DIONYSUS.   When?

AEACUS. Just *did* it!

DIONYSUS.   Wouldn't you think I'd *sneeze* or something?

AEACUS. Funny . . . I'll try this other chap again.

XANTHIAS. What are you waiting for, then?

(AEACUS *strikes him.*)

Oh!

AEACUS.   Why "Oh"?
It didn't *hurt* you?

XANTHIAS.   No. . . . Suddenly thought
'Twas time my Diomean rites were held!

AEACUS. The man's a marvel! . . . Now back over here.

(*Strikes* DIONYSUS.)

DIONYSUS. Hey!

AEACUS.   *What?*

DIONYSUS.   Hey look! Yonder's the cavalry!

AEACUS. Why *weep* about it?

DIONYSUS.   Onions. . . . Can't you smell?

AEACUS. No *pain*, by any chance?

DIONYSUS.   Not in the least!

AEACUS. I'll step across and take a crack at *him.*

XANTHIAS. Golly!

AEACUS.   You mean . . . ?

XANTHIAS.   My foot. . . . A blasted thorn!

AEACUS. Now what the deuce . . . ? Well, back again we go.

DIONYSUS. O Lord! . . . *of Delphi and of Delos fair!*

XANTHIAS. Aha! *That* stung him! Did you hear?

DIONYSUS.   Not me!
Just trying to recall Hipponax' words.

XANTHIAS. You're getting nowhere. Crack him in the ribs.

AEACUS. Ribs nothing! Stand up. . . . Stick your belly out.

DIONYSUS. Great God! . . .

XANTHIAS.   He felt it *that* time!

DIONYSUS. . . . *whose realm, far beneath Aegean's silver sea,*
                    Monarch of headland heights . . .

AEACUS. I give it up! I simply cannot tell
Which of you is a god. —But let's go in.
My Master and his Queen, Persephone,
Will surely know, for they are gods themselves.

DIONYSUS. Right, but I wish it had occurred to you
Before you tried to beat me black and blue!

(Exeunt.)

CHORUS.   Lead us, O Muse, in the maze
                         Of a dance, of a song
                         To enrapture thy heart.
                         Lift thy gaze
                         Over this throng
                         Of the gallant—
                         Numberless lovers of art,
                         Famed for wit and talent,
                         More avid of hon-
                         Or than great Cleophon,
                         Whose babbling, bilingualist lips
                         Sudden anxiety grips.
                         Lo, a Thracian swallow
                         Hath perched on his tongue—
                         That barbarous bloom—
                         And hath plaintively sung
                         A cadenza of gloom:
                         Though the jury be hung,
                         My hanging soon will follow!

'Tis indeed the bounden duty of this consecrated band
That they offer worthy counsel to the people of this land.
First, let all our folk be equal, and be free from civic fear.
If, with Phrynichus entangled, one was thrown upon his
   ear,
Slipping into grievous error, barking painfully his shins,
True confession and repentance should absolve his former
   sins.
Furthermore, no son of Athens ever ought to lose his vote.
Why, a slave who manned a trireme in a certain scrap of
   note,
Straightway was a good . . . Plataean—his own master over-
   night.
Not that I would want to argue that this action wasn't right;
'Twas the only deed of wisdom you have done, it seems to
   me.

But the men who've fought your battles o'er and o'er upon
  the sea,
As their fathers did before them, men of pure Athenian
  stock,
Surely ought to be forgiven if just once they ran amok.
Let us put away resentment, let us use our native wit,
Welcoming into our household for the common benefit
Every loyal friend and neighbor who has battled at our
  side.
For if we persist in showing such a vain and snobbish pride
When our Ship of State is struggling *in the billows' wild*
  caress,
History will not be likely to applaud our cleverness!

> *If into life I have looked,*
> *Into man and the heart*
> *Of a man . . .* 'ittlekin's doom,
> *One* is booked
> Soon to depart,
> And doth fidget,
> Pestilent ape, in his gloom—
> Cleigenes the Midget—
> That niggardly Knight
> Of the Baths, downright
> Dictator, who forced us to buy
> Soap that was nothing but lye
> Mixed with gritty gravell
> No pacifist, he.
> For he's sorely afraid
> That when off on a spree
> He'll be bashed on the head,
> And will impotent be
> Without his trusty *gavel!*

It appears to us that Athens shows the selfsame attitude
To the fairest and the purest and the noblest of her brood,
As toward our silver coinage and the later wartime gold,
Both of which are out of fashion, though their worth has
  been extolled
As the finest ever minted. All men everywhere agree
That their weight and sterling soundness are unique in
  currency,
Whether here at home in Hellas or abroad. But recently
We ourselves no longer like them, and prefer to use for cash

A debased, barbaric tender—this new-fangled copper trash!
So, too, *men* of weight and substance, Hellenes to the
manner born,
Men of rounded education and of sterling worth, we scorn.
Aye, a gentleman, a sportsman, and the cream of Athens'
crop
We reject for something trashy, for a half-breed carrot top!
In the old days we were chary of preferment for a scamp,
Nor would rashly put in office persons of a shabby stamp;
And not even as a scapegoat did we use a common tramp!
Pick *deserving* public servants, as of old, my foolish friends,
And once more you'll seem to merit any luck that Fortune
sends;
While, despite your reformation if you meet adversity,
You'll escape the shame of hanging from a *sour* apple tree!
(*Enter* AEACUS *and* XANTHIAS.)

AEACUS. By Jove, your master is a splendid chap—
A perfect gentleman!

XANTHIAS.   Of course he is—
Knows how to drink and wench . . . and nothing else!

AEACUS. Proved you had been impersonating him,
And didn't even whip you. Think of it!

XANTHIAS. He'd better *not* have!

AEACUS.   *That's* the talk, my boy!
Below-stairs lingo. . . . How I love the sound!

XANTHIAS. Really? You do?

AEACUS.   Why, I'm in paradise
When I can damn the boss behind his back.

XANTHIAS. And grumble at him when you're safe outside,
After a licking?

AEACUS.   It delights my soul!

XANTHIAS. And meddling in his business?

AEACUS.   Can't be beat!

XANTHIAS. My twin! My long-lost twin! . . . Eavesdropping,
now,
On private conversation?

AEACUS.   Ravishing!

XANTHIAS. And blabbing to the parlor maids?

AEACUS.   Oh God!
At that point, brother, I ejaculate!

XANTHIAS. Then put it there! . . . The old fraternal grip!
Blest be the tie that binds the servants' hall!
Let me enfold you in a fond embrace.—

I say, what's all the rumpus? What goes on—
A row?

AEACUS.   Aeschylus and Euripides—
At it again. We've had a great to-do
Down here—amounts to civil war, in fact.

XANTHIAS. What caused it?

AEACUS.   There's a statute on our books
That the most skillful craftsman in each art—
I mean the fine arts, poetry and such—
Be asked to dinner in the City Hall,
And have a chair by Pluto's side . . .

XANTHIAS.   I see.

AEACUS. Until a better artist in that line
Appears among us. Then he has to move.

XANTHIAS. But why should this have worried Aeschylus?

AEACUS. The Tragic Throne was naturally his,
As being master of his trade.

XANTHIAS.   Who else?

AEACUS. Well, when Euripides appeared, of course
He started showing off to the underworld.
Pickpockets, gangsters, burglars, parricides—
And we've a lot of them around—went wild
Over his fancy footwork in debate,
And cheered him as the champ. That turned his head,
And thereupon he claimed the right to sit
Where Aeschylus had sat.

XANTHIAS.   Wasn't he lynched?

AEACUS. Oh no, the mob kept yelling for a trial,
To prove which poet really was the best.

XANTHIAS. That convict crowd?

AEACUS.   Aye, screaming to the skies.

XANTHIAS. But weren't there others backing Aeschylus?

AEACUS. Few *decent* people anywhere—Just look!

XANTHIAS. Well, what are Pluto's plans? What will he do?

AEACUS. He'll hold a competition, here and now—
A contest in poetic skill.

XANTHIAS.   But, say,
Why hasn't Sophocles put in a claim?

AEACUS. Not he! Look what he did the day he came—
Gave Aeschylus a hug and shook his hand,
And tacitly conceded him the throne.
Now he intends, Clidemides reports,
To watch from the side lines, and if Aeschylus wins,
He'll stay there. But if Aeschylus should lose,

He's ready to take on Euripides.

XANTHIAS. It's really coming off?

AEACUS. Oh yes, quite soon.
And when it does, you'll see strange goings-on:
Poetry will be measured by the pound . . .

XANTHIAS. What? Weighed in scales like so much butcher's meat?

AEACUS. Yardsticks and rulers will be put to work,
Rectangular forms . . .

XANTHIAS. Who's making any brick?

AEACUS. Wedges and miter squares. Euripides
Will overhaul each drama verse by verse.

XANTHIAS. I dare say Aeschylus resents all this?

AEACUS. *'Neath pendent brows he glowered like a bull.*

XANTHIAS. Who'll judge the case?

AEACUS. Difficult question, that.
They found a dearth of qualified referees.
Aeschylus balked at an Athenian . . .

XANTHIAS. Too many crooks, no doubt!

AEACUS. Yet all the rest,
As judges of poetic genius, were,
To him, a joke. So finally they chose
An expert in dramatic art—your boss.—
But come. *When masters are on business bent,*
Tears are the wages of the indolent.

(*Exeunt.*)

CHORUS. Wrath, dread wrath will be his whose voice is as thunder,
While his antagonist whets his tusk—that voluble wonder!
    Ah, what a terrible frenzy will torture his soul—
        Yea,
      How his angry orbs will roll!

Strife, dire strife will ensue, as verse that is helmeted, plumèd,
Battles with splinters and shavings that fall from a style that is groomèd,
    Fending itself from the prancing phrases designed—
        Yea,
      Fathered by a matchless mind.

Lo, yon mane that does stream from the neck of the champion bristles.

Fury does furrow his brow. With a roar he hurls his mis-
    siles—
        Riveted timbers of verbiage ripped from the stage—
            Aye,
        Heavèd with a giant's rage.

Then will the tongue *précieuse*, suave master of arts belle-
    tristic,
Smoothly uncoiling its length, give rein to a rancor
    phlogistic,
        Mincing the mightiest words into fragments of naught—
            Aye,
        Words by toil of Titan wrought.

(*Enter* DIONYSUS, EURIPIDES, *and* AESCHYLUS.)

EURIPIDES. I'll *not* renounce my claim. Don't ask me to.
    For I'm a better dramatist than he.

DIONYSUS. You hear his statement, Aeschylus? . . . Speak up!

EURIPIDES. Too proud to speak. The same old *silence* gambit,
    Used to create an awesome atmosphere.

DIONYSUS. Now, now, sir! Easy does it. Draw it mild!

EURIPIDES. I know the fellow—know him through and
    through—
    Arrogant, wanton savage that he is,
    Of speech unbridled, passionate, unfenced,
    A ranting, pompous portmantologist!

AESCHYLUS. *What, scion of the Mistress of the Peas?*
    You scoff at *me*, cliché anthologist,
    Maker of ragamuffin manikins?
    You'll rue the day that . . .

DIONYSUS.   Come come, Aeschylus,
    Heat not thy heart with vengeful bitterness.

AESCHYLUS. Nay, I must show this cripple puppeteer
    Just who he *is*, to be so impudent!

DIONYSUS. A lamb, a *black* lamb, bring me here forthwith!
    A monstrous storm is threatening to burst.

AESCHYLUS. Importing lovesick monodies from Crete,
    Vile, godless passions that degrade our Art!

DIONYSUS. One moment, pray, most noble Aeschylus.—
    My poor Euripides, be sensible,
    Take cover from this blizzard for the nonce.
    Some headlong hailstone, sir, may smite your brow
    And smash to smithereens your . . . Telephus!—
    Now calm down, Aeschylus, and let us have
    A quiet give-and-take, without abuse.

Poets should not be fishwives, gentlemen.

(*To* AESCHYLUS.) You come out roaring like a forest fire!

EURIPIDES. I'll face him in the cockpit any time,
  To peck and claw—and let him claw *me* first—
  Dialogue, lyrics—tear them limb from limb
  And rip them up the back—*Meleager, Peleus,*
  Aeolus, even *Telephus,* by God!

DIONYSUS. Well, what do *you* think, Aeschylus? Speak up.

AESCHYLUS. To hold a contest here was not my wish,
  For I should be at a disadvantage.

DIONYSUS.   How?

AESCHYLUS. Because my dramas did not die with me ...
  His did, and are available for use.
  If you approve, however, I concur.

DIONYSUS. Some incense, and an altar! I would make,
  Before this war of wits begins, a plea
  That I may judge their art with artistry.—
  You sing to the Muses while I pray to them.

CHORUS.   Heavenly Nine, pure Maids everlasting,
  Rapt spectators of bouts between critical minds magistratic,
  Wrestlers in bitter dispute, sagacious, trenchant, Socratic,
  Crafty contortionists, fain to exhibit a skill acrobatic,
      Hark to a duel 'twixt power and guile.
      Here is a genius at blinding and blasting;
      There, an adept at the saw and the file.
      Haste ye! This trial of talents contrasting
          Neareth heights dramatic.

DIONYSUS (*to* AESCHYLUS *and* EURIPIDES). You too should pray,
  before you speak your lines.

AESCHYLUS. Demeter, nurse and mother of my art,
  Let me be worthy of thy Mysteries.

DIONYSUS. And now it's your turn.

EURIPIDES.   No, I thank you. No.
  The gods I worship are of another stamp.

DIONYSUS. Your own? You have a private mint?

EURIPIDES.   Quite so.

DIONYSUS. Rank amateurs, at best! ... Well, pray to them.

EURIPIDES. Aether, my Bread of Life, O vibrant Tongue,
  O Mother Wit, O Nose fastidious,
  Grant that I neatly pin him to the mat!

CHORUS. Right eager are we to behold these twain
      Militant rounds of Logic dancing,
          Tripping amain—
          How entrancing!—

Λ

> *Treading the way of war.* 'Tis plain,
> Frenzied is the tongue, advancing
> To attack, the spirit prancing
> In its pride, alert the brain.
> This one doubtless will endeavor
> To be eminently clever—
> Polished, pointed, and urbane.
> On will rush his foe, refuting
> And disputing,
> Massive verbiage uprooting,
> Till he wrecks the whole terrain.

DIONYSUS. Begin. . . . And plead your case with wit—no cheap forensic shoddy—

The sort of thing that we may hear from almost anybody!

EURIPIDES. Postponing to the end discussion—which indeed I owe you—

Of *my* achievements as a playwright, first I wish to show you

The kind of mountebank *he* was, and how he fascinated

The simple folk whom Phrynichus had newly graduated.

To start with, up there on the stage some creature he would set out—

Achilles, say, or Niobe—who, muffled as all-get-out,

Was Tragedy incarnate, but no word, no sound, would let out.

DIONYSUS. No, not a peep!

EURIPIDES. The Chorus, meanwhile, duty never shunning,

Assailed that silent figure with a string of odes hand-running,

But got no answer.

DIONYSUS. Good! I liked it . . . found it far more pleasant

Than all this modern talky-talk.

EURIPIDES. The viewpoint of a peasant!

DIONYSUS. No doubt. . . . But why did what's-his-name *do* that, whereas at present . . . ?

EURIPIDES. A faker's trick, to keep the house on tenterhooks, uncertain

If Niobe would *ever* speak. . . . And then, down came the curtain!

DIONYSUS. The old rapscallion! How he fooled me! Unashamed hijackery!—

Why squirm and twist, my man?

EURIPIDES. Because I'm showing up his quackery.—

And when the play was halfway done, with all this fiddle-
  faddle,
He'd spout a stream of beefy words, gigantic forms astrad-
  dle
Great steeds with beetling brows and crests—a literary diet
That Athens never ate before!

AESCHYLUS. Oh oh! I cannot ...

DIONYSUS. Quiet!

EURIPIDES. *Nothing* a chap could *understand!*

DIONYSUS (*to* AESCHYLUS). No use to grit your grinders!

EURIPIDES. *Scamander* this, *Scamander* that. . . . Such moun-
  tainous spellbinders
As *griffin-eagles built of bronze*—a *shield,* in *his* cryptology.
But how was anyone to *know?*

DIONYSUS. As to his ornithology,
  Through weary watches of the night I've thought on what
    in thunder
  That *gilded centaur-chanticleer* could be . . . and *still* I
    wonder!

AESCHYLUS. A figurehead upon a ship, you dullard!

DIONYSUS. Always foxin' us!
  I fancied 'twas the gilded jockey fathered by Philoxenus!

EURIPIDES. And after all, in tragedy, why introduce a *rooster?*

AESCHYLUS. Think of the monsters in *your* works that we are
  introduced to!

EURIPIDES. No horse-cocks, anyway, or goat-stags—heathen
  hyphenations
  Less fitting in Greek dramas than in Persian decorations!
  When you bequeathed to me this Art, she was a curiosity—
  Swollen with bombast, corpulent with verbal ponderosity.
  Well, first of all, a slenderizing regimen I gave 'er
  Of beet juice, exercises, verse of light and pleasant flavor,
  A broth of bookish hand-me-downs from my immense col-
    lection;
  Then built her up on monodies.

DIONYSUS. Cephisophon's confection?

EURIPIDES. My prologues never were confused, abrupt, and
  desultory,
  But gave at once the pedigree, the outline of the story.

DIONYSUS. Good thing they went no further. . . . *Yours* is not
  so hunky-dory!

EURIPIDES. My characters were kept at work right through to
  the finale;

The prince, the pauper, young or old—no one could dilly-
dally;

Servants and masters, women, men, were equally loquacious.

AESCHYLUS. And shouldn't you have hung for it?

EURIPIDES. For what?

Why, goodness gracious,

It is the democratic way!

DIONYSUS. I'd stop, if I were you, sir.

Discourse upon *that* topic you had better not pursue, sir!

EURIPIDES. I taught these people how to use their tongues . . .

AESCHYLUS. A frightful blunder!

And, ere you made it, I could wish that you had burst
asunder!

EURIPIDES. And eyes and heads—to comprehend, to dodge and
weave, to wrangle,

To gauge a style with nicety and test its every angle,

Prove all things and suspect the worst.

AESCHYLUS. You did, and I
could strangle . . . !

EURIPIDES. By choosing themes that were concerned with
everyday reality,

I taught them how to criticize a play with rationality,

Their sober reason undisturbed by mere theatricality,

Like tinkling-brass-accoutered-colts cavorting to amaze
them,

A Cycnus or a Memnon flashing foreign arms to daze them.

My true alumni you can tell from those of this word heaver:

His are Megaenetus the Wop, Phormisius the Beaver—

Mustachioed swashbucklers both, and frolicsome Pine
Benders;

Theramenes and Cleitophon, *my* graduate defenders.

DIONYSUS. Theramenes? Now there's a chap that's clever in
the clinches.

When trouble gets him in its grip, the fellow never
flinches—

He throws a lucky flip-flop and escapes defeat by inches!

EURIPIDES. These wholesome habits, then, of thought

To this democracy I taught;

I showed them logic on the stage

Till logic now is all the rage.

They reason, they discriminate,

And everything investigate.

Their homes they manage better, too:

What goes on here? they ask. *Hey, you!*
Where's so-and-so? Who took my new . . . ?
DIONYSUS. I grant you that, by God! They do!
  As soon as they are past the door,
  They have the servants in, and roar
  What's happened to the soup tureen?
  Who bit the head off this sardine?
  That handsome bowl I bought last year
  Has gone to glory—'tisn't here!
  And where is Sunday's garlic, pray?
  Who nibbled at this olive, eh?
  Time was when they were stupid clods,
  Mere Simple Simon noddynods
        And lazy mollycoddles!
CHORUS (*to* AESCHYLUS).
      Thou seest the hazard, illustrious thane.
    How wilt thou answer a charge so black, sir?
                    Prithee maintain
            Care lest passion seize the rein,
        Sweeping thee beyond the track, sir.
        Calmly meet this dread attack, sir;
            Wrath, my noble prince, restrain,
            Nor indulge in bitter censure.
        Reef thy sails before thou venture
            Out upon the stormy main.
        Watch the angry winds, awaiting
                    Their abating;
        Then, with caution navigating,
        Launch with vigor thy campaign.
DIONYSUS (*to* AESCHYLUS). Thou first to impart to theatrical
  art a style as sublime as the mountains,
  With lofty disdain for the flat and the plain, release thy
  rhetorical fountains.
AESCHYLUS. That I should be forced to reply to this person
  arouses my deep indignation;
  Yet, lest he assert that I haven't the means of disproving
  his bold accusation,
  (*To* EURIPIDES.) What gifts do you hold that a poet should
  have, to be worthy of men's admiration?
EURIPIDES. Superlative artistry, craftsmanship, and the skill of
  a talented teacher
  To make men better by counsel sage.
AESCHYLUS.   And if, as a teacher—
  or preacher—

You've failed, and have turned into villainous rogues sound
youngsters, the pride of our city,

What punishment ought you to suffer?

DIONYSUS.   Ask *me*: to be hung,
sans mercy or pity!

AESCHYLUS. Consider the audience I had bequeathed him:
cowardly loafers and laggards?

Degenerate scamps like the youth of today, who are naught
but promising blackguards?

No! Fine six-footers with courage so sturdy that nothing
could ever o'erwhelm it,

Each breathing the spirit of spear, of lance, of the pure
white plume of the helmet,

Hearts booted and spurred for the rout of the foe, that
highest and noblest of missions.

DIONYSUS. Hey, stop it! Enough of your helmets and spears.
I am sick unto death of *munitions!*

EURIPIDES. Just what did you do that another did not, to develop this spirit, I pray you?

DIONYSUS. Speak out! Why stand there preening yourself and
nursing your dudgeon? . . . What say you?

AESCHYLUS. By writing a drama *instinct with Mars.*

DIONYSUS.   What drama?

AESCHYLUS.   The
Seven, which fired

In every spectator a passion for war and for deeds of daring
inspired.

DIONYSUS. 'Twas the *Thebans* you taught to be daring, and
they have in this very war been pursuing

The principles given by you to their sires—and you ought
to be flogged for so doing!

AESCHYLUS. Those lessons you too might have learned, but you
wanted your ease, all hardship eschewing.—

And again, by producing my *Persians*, this aim was
achieved once more—to enamor

Our youth of a yearning for victory won by a feat of illustrious glamour.

DIONYSUS. I was charmed when Darius emerged from his
coffin and published the doom of his nation,

The Chorus wringing their hands, meanwhile, indulging in
loud lamentation!

AESCHYLUS. For such are the paths that a poet should tread.
Our earliest civilization

We owe to the poets, who helped us escape from the laws
   of barbaric society.

'Twas Orpheus who taught us to reverence life, a religion
   of mystical piety;

Musaeus who brought us oracular wisdom, and magical
   methods of healing;

And Hesiod told of the tillage of earth, her opulent beauty
   revealing;

The fame of the godlike Homer was won by the lessons he
   gave to our heroes:

Good discipline, courage, the wearing of arms . . .

DIONYSUS.   Well,
   Pantacles' marks were all zeros!

While puffing along in a recent parade, poor chap—he's a
   bit on the stout side—

His helmet agleam on his head, he was trying to fasten the
   plume from the *outside!*

AESCHYLUS. But many another, like masterful Lamachus,
   learned what Homer imparted;

And his was the matrix from which I have molded the
   forms of my own *lionhearted*

Patroclus and Teucer, whose valor, I trusted, would arouse
   Athenian yeomen

To rival their deeds at the sound of the trumpet and vanquish the finest of foemen.

This further: loose women I never created—no Phaedras, no
   Stheneboeas.

And who can assert that in dramas of mine any lovelorn
   lady appears?

EURIPIDES. Ah no! Aphrodite had left you untouched, with
   none of her graces endowered.

AESCHYLUS. Thank heaven! On you and on yours, I am told,
   her charms in such volume were showered

That wreckage and ruin were brought to your home.

DIONYSUS (*to* EURIPIDES).   *Touché!* By
   Jove, it is true, sir:

The things you had written of other men's wives, your own
   inflicted on you, sir!

EURIPIDES. My poor Stheneboeas! What harm has been done
   to the world by their tragic romances?

AESCHYLUS. Why, virtuous spouses of virtuous husbands, ap-
   palled by their brazen advances,

Drink hemlock, feeling vicarious shame at their lurid Bellerophon fancies.

EURIPIDES. And Phaedra . . . you think that her story is false,
  imagined by *me*, a mere fiction?
AESCHYLUS. Unhappily, no. She is real. But a poet should seek
  to avoid the depiction
Of evil—should hide it, not drag into view its ugly and
  odious features.
For children have tutors to guide them aright; young man-
  hood has poets for teachers.
And so we must write of the fair and the good.
EURIPIDES.   In language
  to dwarf Lycabettus?
In words to outweigh the Parnassian cliffs? Quite frankly,
  where does it get us,
As teachers, to talk in a tongue superhuman?
AESCHYLUS. .   Pedestrian
  spirit, in *my* style
Great words are begotten to match great thoughts. Sub-
  limity speaks in the high style.
Then too it is right that a hero of drama should use words
  larger than ours,
When even the costume he wears is designed to reflect his
  superior powers.
These noble devices of mine you spoiled.
EURIPIDES.   Just how? By
  what indiscretion?
AESCHYLUS. By wrapping your princes in beggarly rags, to
  produce a pathetic impression
Of woe that would soften the hearts of their hearers.
EURIPIDES.   Was
  that so dire a transgression?
AESCHYLUS. A plutocrat, chosen to captain a trireme, swears
  that he hasn't a dollar,
Tricked out as a tatterdemalion Telephus living in absolute
  squalor.
DIONYSUS. And sporting a *tunic* of elegant wool! If he wins a
  reprieve by his fakery,
He's sure to pop up next morning in market, ready to buy
  out a bakery!
AESCHYLUS. Besides, you are guilty of training our youth in the
  art of sophistical gabble.
The playgrounds are empty; our athletes sit on their well-
  worn haunches and babble.
Our prize bluejackets today, I am told, are bandying words
  with the skipper.

In *my* time, none of them *knew* any, even aboard our fan-
ciest clipper.

Ahoy! he could bellow, *Avast! Aye aye, sir,* and shout for
his "grub" from the steward . . .

DIONYSUS. And, firing a jet from his ample exhaust, asphyxiate
all to the leeward!

The menacing mucker would then go ashore for thieving
and raising a rumpus.

> Now they argue and never row
> And let the ship a-bobbing go.

AESCHYLUS. Of what ills is Euripides *not* the cause?
Pimps he brings on in defiance of laws,
A woman in a temple becoming a mother,
A woman lying with her own brother,
No-life equals life asserting,
Our whole city thus subverting,
Filling it with clowns of diverse shapes,
Half-educted demagogue apes,
Whose study it is the people to debauch.
None can now carry the relay-race torch
For none works out in the gymnasium.

DIONYSUS. I near died laughing at the Panathenaeum!
A stooped-over fellow, short, fat, and pale
Was puffing along at the race's tail;
At the Ceramicus gate folk thwacked his flanks,
His belly, his rump, his sides, his shanks.
The beating caused his wind to fan:
Out blew the torch and away he ran.

CHORUS. Sharp the strife, violent the collision,
Difficult 'twill be to reach a decision.
The one will press with energy immense, the
Other dodge with footwork fancy.
Keep not always the same stance:
Attack however there's a chance.
Bring all your resources into play;
Wrangle, tangle, be flayed and flay.
Draw arguments old from out your store,
Venture subtleties never used before.
If you fear your audience uninitiate,
Unable profundities to penetrate,
Rest easy; out of fashion is naïveté.
Veteran campaigners of many a fray,
The spectators come well-girt:
Each has book in hand, each has wits alert.

You've a sage and clever audience;
There's naught to fear, take heart, advance!

EURIPIDES. To your prologues I'll address myself first. I'll test
The opening lines of this able playwright's work.
His statement of subject is opaque.

DIONYSUS. Which will you choose for examination?

EURIPIDES. Many, but first give me the opening of the
Oresteia.

DIONYSUS. Silence, everyone! Speak, Aeschylus!

AESCHYLUS. Hermes of the nether world who surveys paternal
power,
Be savior and ally at my supplication:
I come to this land, here I return.

DIONYSUS. Do you find any fault in these lines?

EURIPIDES. More than a dozen.

DIONYSUS. But there are only three lines in all.

EURIPIDES. And twenty slips in each.

DIONYSUS. Aeschylus, I beg you, do be quiet. If you don't
You'll be more than three lines short.

AESCHYLUS. Me be quiet for him?

DIONYSUS. If you take my advice.

EURIPIDES. Right away he blundered sky-high.

AESCHYLUS. You see, Dionysus, how foolish your advice?

DIONYSUS. I don't much care.

AESCHYLUS. What blunder are you referring to?

EURIPIDES. The opening again, please.

AESCHYLUS. Hermes of the nether world who surveys paternal
power—

EURIPIDES. Is it Orestes speaking at the grave of his murdered father?

AESCHYLUS. Precisely.

EURIPIDES. Would a man whose father had been treacherously
murdered
By a woman's intrigue speak of Hermes as surveying?

AESCHYLUS. Not that Hermes, but Hermes the Helper, as he
demonstrated
By assigning paternal surveillance.

EURIPIDES. A worse fault than I thought. If he held nether
paternal surveillance—

DIONYSUS. He would be a grave robber at his father's bidding.

AESCHYLUS. Dionysus, the wine you drink is flat.

DIONYSUS. Recite another line, and you, Euripides, keep an
eye out for mistakes.

AESCHYLUS. *Be savior and ally at my supplication:*
  I come to this land, here I return.

EURIPIDES. Our sage Aeschylus gives us the same thing twice.

DIONYSUS. How twice?

EURIPIDES. Look at the text and I'll explain. *I come to this land,*
  Says he, *and I return,* the meaning's the same.

DIONYSUS. By Zeus, it is—as if a man said to his neighbor
  Lend me your skillet, your frying pan lend me.

AESCHYLUS. Not at all the same, you hairsplitter; the words
  are right.

DIONYSUS. How so? Tell me what you mean.

AESCHYLUS. A man who has a country and happens to arrive
  comes;
  An exile *comes* and *returns.*

DIONYSUS. Good, by Apollo. And what do you say, Euripides?

EURIPIDES. I say that Orestes never *returned.* He sneaked in,
  surreptitiously.

DIONYSUS. Good, by Hermes. —What it means I haven't a
  notion.

EURIPIDES. Continue with another line, please.

DIONYSUS. You, Aeschylus, continue at once. And you look for
  mistakes.

AESCHYLUS. *At the tomb's edge I invoke my father: hear,*
  hearken!

EURIPIDES. Again the same thing twice, most obviously: *hear,*
  hearken.

DIONYSUS. But it's to the dead he's speaking, rascal; they can't
  hear
  Even if we call them three times.

AESCHYLUS. And how do you make *your* prologues?

EURIPIDES. I'll tell you, and if you find repetition or padding,
  spit on me.

DIONYSUS. Speak, I'm eager to hear the perfection of your
  prologues.

EURIPIDES. *Oedipus was a lucky man at first.*

AESCHYLUS. Never, by Zeus, but most unlucky from the start.
  Before he was born
  Apollo predicted he'd murder his father. How could he be
  A lucky man at first?

EURIPIDES. *Then he became the wretchedest of mortals.*

AESCHYLUS. Zeus, no! He never stopped being. As a babe new-
  born, and in winter,

They put him out in a crock, not to grow up to murder his
    father;
Then with swollen feet he hobbles off to Polybus, then he
    marries
An old woman, and his mother to boot, then blinds himself.

DIONYSUS. Blindness would be lucky if he served with
    Erasinides.

EURIPIDES. Bosh! I make *good* prologues.

AESCHYLUS. I'll not maul your text word by word, but with
    heaven's help,
I'll smash them all with an oilcan.

EURIPIDES. My prologues with an oilcan?

AESCHYLUS. With just one. Such are your iambics that an
    afghan
Or reticule or oilcan can be fitted in.
I'll demonstrate.

EURIPIDES. You say you'll demonstrate?

AESCHYLUS. I do.

DIONYSUS. Time to speak.

EURIPIDES. *Aegyptus, according to the prevalent story,*
    Touching at Argos with fifty sons—

AESCHYLUS. Lost his oilcan.

EURIPIDES. What's that oilcan? Damn it!

DIONYSUS. Give him another prologue; the point will be
    clearer.

EURIPIDES. *Dionysus in fawn-skins clad, with Thyrsus and*
    torch
    Bounding and dancing—

AESCHYLUS. Lost his oilcan.

DIONYSUS. Ah, I am smitten once more—by the oilcan.

EURIPIDES. No matter. You'll not be able to fit your oilcan to
    this:
    No man is in all respects happy. One nobly poor is needy,
    Another, of low birth—

AESCHYLUS. Lost his oilcan.

DIONYSUS. Euripides!

EURIPIDES. What is it?

DIONYSUS. Better reef your sails; that little can will blow a
    gale.

EURIPIDES. I'm not worried, by Demeter. I'll smash it in his
    hand.

DIONYSUS. Recite another, then, but beware the oilcan.

EURIPIDES. *Upon leaving Sidon's town Agenor's son Cadmus—*

AESCHYLUS. Lost his oilcan.

DIONYSUS. Better buy that oilcan, friend: he'll chip away all
your prologues.

EURIPIDES. What, I buy of him?

DIONYSUS. If you take my advice.

EURIPIDES. Never. I can produce many prologues to which he
cannot fix his oilcan.
Tantalid Pelops faring to Pisa with swift mares—

AESCHYLUS. Lost his oilcan.

DIONYSUS. D'you see? He did tack the oilcan on. Buy it, do;
You can get it good as new for an obol.

EURIPIDES. Not yet; I still have plenty. *In his field one day
Oeneus—*

AESCHYLUS. Lost his oilcan.

EURIPIDES. Do let me finish the whole line. *In his field one day
Oeneus
After reaping an abundant harvest, while offering first
fruits—*

AESCHYLUS. Lost his oilcan.

DIONYSUS. In the midst of sacrifice? Who stole it?

EURIPIDES. Let be, mister. Let him try this one. *Zeus as Truth
hath said—*

DIONYSUS. He'll ruin you; he'll say *Lost his oilcan.* On your
prologues
That oilcan grows like sties on eyes. In heaven's name,
Turn now to his melodies.

EURIPIDES. I can prove he's a bad melody maker: he makes
them all alike.

CHORUS. What new action in this fray?
What charge, I wonder, can he lay
Against our age's master tragic,
Most melodious, most prolific?
How will he fault our Bacchic lord?
I tremble for the lesser bard.

EURIPIDES. Marvelous tunes indeed! You'll see through him
soon.
I'll cut all his lines down to one.

DIONYSUS. And I'll get some pebbles to keep score.
(Flute music offstage.)

EURIPIDES. *Phthian Achilles, why, hearing the man smiter
Hah, come you not to the rescue, striking?
Ancestor Hermes, whom we by the lakeside revere,
Hah, come you not to the rescue, striking?*

DIONYSUS. That's two strikes, Aeschylus.

AESCHYLUS. *Noblest of Achaeans, wide-ruling son of Atreus,*
   hear me:
   Hah, come you not to the rescue, striking?

DIONYSUS. Strike three, Aeschylus.

EURIPIDES. *Hush! Soon will the Bee keepers open Artemis'*
   house:
   Hah, come you not to the rescue, striking?
   Mine the right to utter the heroes' auspices:
   Hah, come you not to the rescue, striking?

DIONYSUS. Royal Zeus, what a heap of strikes; I must to the
   bath:
   Those strikes have inflamed my kidneys.

EURIPIDES. Not till you have heard the other sheaf,
   Worked from music for the lyre.

DIONYSUS. Go on, then; but not another strike, please.

EURIPIDES. *Twin-throned power of Achaeans, flower of Hellas,*
   Phlattothrattophlattothrat.
   Send baneful Sphinx, the presiding bitch
   Phlattothrattophlattothrat,
   With spear and avenging hand that stalwart bird
   Phlattothrattophlattothrat,
   Vouchsafes the stark air-faring fowl
   Phlattothrattophlattothrat,
   The onset against Ajax,
   Phlattothrattophlattothrat.

DIONYSUS. What's that *phlattothrattophlattothrat?* Where did
   you get that chanty?
   From Marathon? From rope twisters?

AESCHYLUS. From a noble source I took it and to noble use
   applied it;
   I would not be seen culling flowers like Phrynichus' in the
   Muses' meadow.
   He from all that's meretricious draws his ditties, catches
   Of Meletus, Carian flutings, dirges, dances. Proof is forth-
   coming;
   Bring a lyre, someone. But why a lyre for this—where's the
   tambourine girl
   With her castanets? Hither, Muse of Euripides! For such
   songs
   She is proper patroness.

   (*Enter a* WANTON, *swaying and clashing castanets.*)

DIONYSUS. The muse a Lesbian? No!

AESCHYLUS. *Halcyons ever twittering*
   By the billowing spume

With dewy droplets glittering
On every moistened plume.
Intricate, dainty webs of lace
Spiders weave with fingers nimble
In every nook and crannied place
Plying their shuttle like a cymbal.
Wantons the dolphin flute-loving
Before men-o'-war dark-prowed,
Oracular patterns proving
Or racing before a crowd.
Flowering spiral of fragrant vine,
Cluster of care-banishing grape:
Child, twine your arms in mine.
Do you see this foot's shape?

DIONYSUS. I do.

AESCHYLUS. So. And this one's?

DIONYSUS. I see it.

AESCHYLUS. Who writes knavery so prolix
Filled with a dozen whorish tricks,
Shall he dare my odes to spurn?
So much for odes. Now I turn
The fashion of his solos to transfix.
Darkness of shadowy Night,
What dire dream to affright
Sendest thou, Hades' queen,
From abyss unplumbed, unseen—
A horrible, shuddering sprite
In cerement's black bedight,
Portending slaughter in eye and maw
And in prodigious rending claw.
The lanterns, my maidens, be kindling,
Draw river-dew up in your pail;
The water boil till it's bubbling,
I'll slosh off that Vision's bale.
Busy at my task was I, poor soul,
My spindle full, making a hank
To sell at dawn at a market stall,
But up that rooster did soar and bank,
Spreading the tips of his agile wings,
To me bequeathing sorrow sore.
For the great grief disaster brings
I weep and shall weep forevermore.
Ye constables from Crete, Ida's band,
Limber your limbs, dance round the house,

Fly to the rescue, bows in hand.
Come too, Dictynna, your hounds arouse,
Maid Artemis come, the chambers rummage.
And you, O Hecate, child of Zeus,
Cast torches bright on Glyce's cottage,
Make the culprit pay back her dues.

DIONYSUS. Music enough, from both of you.

AESCHYLUS. Enough for me. I'd like now to bring him to the scales:

That's the only way to assay our poetry; that will
Prove whose verses are weightiest.

DIONYSUS. Step up, then, if I must apply the cheese-selling technique
To poetic operations.

(*A large pair of scales is brought in.*)

CHORUS. These clever men, how diligent!
Here's another brand-new portent,
Beyond the ordinary man's capacity;
If told I'd doubt the teller's veracity
And scorn the simpleton's naïveté.

DIONYSUS. Come, stand by the scales, both.

AESCHYLUS.⎱ Here!
EURIPIDES.⎰

DIONYSUS. Each hold it and recite a verse, and don't let go
Till I cry *Cuckoo!*

AESCHYLUS.⎱ We've got it.
EURIPIDES.⎰

DIONYSUS. Now speak your line into the scale.

EURIPIDES. *Would that Argo had never winged its way—*

AESCHYLUS. *River Spercheius, cattle-grazing haunts—*

DIONYSUS. Cuckoo! Let go! Aeschylus' sinks way down.

EURIPIDES. What's the reason?

DIONYSUS. Because he injected a river, like a wool merchant
Wetting his ware to make it weigh more. You put wings on yours.

EURIPIDES. Make him recite another verse and stand by it.

DIONYSUS. To the scales again!

AESCHYLUS.⎱ Here!
EURIPIDES.⎰

DIONYSUS. Speak.

EURIPIDES. *Persuasion's sole sanctuary is eloquence—*

AESCHYLUS. *Alone of the gods Death is no lover of gifts—*

DIONYSUS. Let go, let go! Again Aeschylus' is down.
He injected Death, the heaviest of all ills.

EURIPIDES. And I *Persuasion*, a word fine to speak.

DIONYSUS. Persuasion's a light and feather-brained thing. Think
Of something heavier to depress your scale, something big
and strong.

EURIPIDES. Where have I got one, where?

DIONYSUS. I'll tell you: *Achilles threw deuce and four.*
Speak up now; this is the last lap.

EURIPIDES. *An iron-studded club in his right hand he seized—*

AESCHYLUS. *Chariot upon chariot, and upon corpse corpse—*

DIONYSUS. He's foiled you again, Euripides.

EURIPIDES. How?

DIONYSUS. Two chariots and two corpses he heaved in.
A hundred gypsies couldn't hoist them.

AESCHYLUS. No more line for line. Let him get into the scale,
With his children, his wife, Cephisophon, and himself
Holding all his books; I need but two of my lines.

DIONYSUS. Both are my friends, and I cannot play judge.
Neither
Would I have my enemy. One I think clever, the other
delights me.

PLUTO. Then you won't accomplish your errand.

DIONYSUS. And if I decide?

PLUTO. You can take whichever you decide with you, and
your trip
Will not be footless.

DIONYSUS. Bless you! You know, it was for a poet I came.

PLUTO. With what motive?

DIONYSUS. So the city saved may keep its choral festivals.
Whichever is likely to advise the city well, him
I intend to take back. First about Alcibiades. What
Is your opinion? The city is still in heavy labor.

EURIPIDES. What is its feeling about Alcibiades?

DIONYSUS. What? Yearning, hatred, desire. But what of you
two?
Say what you think about him.

EURIPIDES. I hate a citizen slow to help his country, swift to
harm it.
Ingenious for himself, for the state feckless.

DIONYSUS. Well put, by Poseidon. And you, Aeschylus, what
is your opinion?

AESCHYLUS. Best it is never to rear a lion in the city; but if
reared
It has been, 'tis best to yield to its ways.

DIONYSUS. Savior Zeus, what a hard decision! One speaks cleverly,

The other clearly. Give us, each, one other response.

How think you the state may be saved?

EURIPIDES. Hitch wings to Cinesias and Cleocritus, so that breezes

Might waft them over the watery main.

DIONYSUS. A comical spectacle—but what's the idea?

EURIPIDES. In naval engagements supply vinegar to squirt in enemy eyes.

I know something I want to tell.

DIONYSUS. Say on.

EURIPIDES. When we hold the mistrusted trustworthy, and the trustworthy mistrust.

DIONYSUS. How's that? I don't understand. Less profundity, please,

And more clarity.

EURIPIDES. If citizens we now trust we mistrust, and employ those

We do not now employ, we shall be saved. If disastrous

Our present course, surely its opposite must bring salvation.

DIONYSUS. Well done, Palamedes! What a genius! This invention—

Is it yours or Cephisophon's?

EURIPIDES. All mine. The vinegar idea was Cephisophon's.

DIONYSUS. What about you, Aeschylus? What do you say?

AESCHYLUS. Tell me first whom the city employs. The good?

DIONYSUS. What a notion! It hates them worst of all.

AESCHYLUS. But likes the bad?

DIONYSUS. Not really, but uses them perforce.

AESCHYLUS. How save a city which likes neither cape nor coat?

DIONYSUS. Do find some solution if you go up again.

AESCHYLUS. There I may speak; here I will not.

DIONYSUS. No, please; send the good things up from here.

AESCHYLUS. When they come to regard enemy land as their own

And their own as the enemy's, their ships as true wealth

And their wealth a cipher.

DIONYSUS. Good enough, but the juries devour it all.

PLUTO. Make your decision.

DIONYSUS. As between these two, him I choose in whom my soul delights.

EURIPIDES. Remember the gods by whom you swore you'd take me

Home again; choose your friends!

DIONYSUS. *'Tis my tongue that swore—, 'tis Aeschylus I choose.*

EURIPIDES. What have you done, vile creature?

DIONYSUS. Me? Judged Aeschylus victor. Why not?

EURIPIDES. And after conduct so shameful you dare face me?

DIONYSUS. *What's shameful if spectators do not so regard it?*

EURIPIDES. Cruel! Will you ignore me when I'm dead?

DIONYSUS. Who knows whether to live is to die, to breathe to dine,
To sleep a fuzzy blanket?

PLUTO. Come inside now, Dionysus.

DIONYSUS. What for?

PLUTO. We'll entertain you two before you embark.

DIONYSUS. Thanks, by Zeus; it's no trouble at all.

(PLUTO *and* AESCHYLUS *withdraw*.)

CHORUS. Happy is the man of intellect keen—
In cases many is this principle seen.
Proven to possess an intelligent brain,
Aeschylus goes back home again,
To his fellow citizens to be a boon,
A boon likewise unto his own
Kith and kin—all for his sagacity.
Better it is to eschew loquacity,
Following in the Socratic train,
Rejecting music with high disdain,
Abandoning with foolish equanimity
Noble tragedy's lofty sublimity.
To make your study grandiloquence
And busy quibbling devoid of sense
Argues an empty mind and sick,
In point of fact a lunatic.

PLUTO. Fare you well, Aeschylus, go and save
Our hard-pressed city by your precepts grave.
School the silly; their kind is numerous.
This rope to Cleophon take, this to Nicomachus,
This to the gang that the revenue collects,
This to Archenomus, this to Myrmex.
Tell them all what I have to say:
Come to me here with no delay.
If they dawdle, I swear by Apollo,
Branded and fettered down they go
With Adeimantus, Leucolophus' son
To lowest darkness every one.

AESCHYLUS. Your bidding I'll do. To this my chair

I make genial Sophocles my heir,
Till I return to guard and possess,
For he comes second to my success.
Never shall *that* impostor base
Occupy my rightful place—
That lying rogue, that low buffoon,
Will he nill he, late or soon.

PLUTO. Light, mystic throng, his upward way
As your holy torches glitter and sway.
Escort him with his own sweet chants,
Glorify him with song and dance.

CHORUS. First, ye deities of the world below,
Grant a happy journey to the poet who will go
To the light above. Next to our nation
Grant counsels sound to work salvation,
Surcease swift from all that harms,
Respite from foul war's alarms.
Cleophon may fight, and others that will,
In distant fields which foreigners till.

(*Exeunt.*)

Ecclesiazusae

"Women in Parliament," as Mr. Lindsay aptly renders *Ecclesiazusae*, was presented in 392 B.C., when Athens was fallen and impoverished. Aristophanes' ebullience, like his city's, appears to be fading. The introduction of communism, which only an impossible assembly of women could enact, is symptomatic of despair in more orthodox measures for improvement. The parody of the communist ideas later to be set forth in the fifth book of Plato's *Republic* shows that these ideas, including a better position for women, were being discussed. Aristophanes' characteristic counter is that human nature is incapable of the necessary altruism. The absence of the old sparkle tends to reduce much of the humor to mere nastiness, as in the picture of the three hags who, following the new law that the least favored must come first, quarrel over and maul a young man who is trying to make his way to his sweetheart in a balcony, with whom he sings pretty duets.

CHARACTERS

PRAXAGORA
FIRST WOMAN
SECOND WOMAN
WOMAN CRIER
YOUNG GIRL
HAG
SECOND HAG
THIRD HAG

SERVANT TO PRAXAGORA
BLEPYROS
NEIGHBOR
HUSBAND OF SECOND WOMAN
CHREMES
CITIZEN
CHORUS OF WOMEN
EPIGENES

Translated by Jack Lindsay

(*Before dawn* PRAXAGORA, *wearing her husband's clothes, is seen apostrophizing the lantern which is to serve as signal to her friends.*)

PRAXAGORA. O glittering face of earth made into a lantern!
Fitly raised up to swing in this high place
And beacon them to me . . . fitly, I say,
As thy thumbed birth and fortunes soon disclose:
For when the scraping potter's wheel revolves
With thy last curve, then dost thou straight assume
With thy wick's spout the sun's flaming office—
So launch the symbol of conspiring fire!
Thou art our trust, and naturally art,
Since in our bedrooms thou alone stand'st by
While we try various means of tangling kisses
And then untying the sweet knot of flesh:
Umpire of our bodies suavely vying,
Sole eye that no one wants kickt out of doors,
Thou alone pokest light in secret places
Darkened with warmth, mysterious, when we singe
Hair that is amorously superfluous.
Thou art our help when furtively we go
To raid the cellars for their store of fruit
And bubbles of Bacchos. And thou wink'st at it,
And not one prattle of flame gives us away.
Therefore shalt thou be our confidante
In the conspiracy my friends and I
Hatched at the Festival of the Parasol.
But none of them is here although it's time,
And dawn is softening there already. Soon
The Assembly will have met; and we, my women,
Must squat in the seats Phyromachos allotted us
(Is the allusion too recondite?) looking discreet. . . .
What can have happened? Perhaps they find it hard
To stitch their beards on as our edict insisted.
Perhaps they couldn't get hold of their husbands' clothes
And abscond with them. . . . Ah ha, I spy a lamp
Floating this way. I had better stand aside
In case some man is straggling in the street.
(*A woman enters,* PRAXAGORA *goes to meet her.*)
WOMAN. It's time. Let's go. As I was coming along
I heard the herald's second cockadoodle.

PRAXAGORA. I have been waiting, I have been watching here
　　All of the night for you. But now you've come,
　　Let's wake my neighbor. See, I'll scratch with my nail,
　　Gently, on the door, gently, and so
　　Won't wake her husband.
　　(*As she is scratching, the door opens and another woman
　　appears.*)
SECOND WOMAN.　　　　　　　It's all right, Praxagora.
　　I caught your nail's soft screekle on the wood,
　　For I was up and almost ready, just
　　Knotting my shoes on, for my husband, you know,
　　Is a Salaminian, dear, and keeps on rowing
　　Even in his sleep—I simply can't stop him—
　　He thinks I'm a boat; and mixed up with the bedclothes,
　　It's a wonder I got off even as late as I did.
PRAXAGORA. Oh, here they are. There is Cleinarete,
　　And Sostrata too, and there's Philainite.
SEMICHORUS. Hurry, my girls, Glyke has made a vow
　　The last one that arrives shall pay as fine
　　One quart of chickpease and nine quarts of wine.
FIRST WOMAN. Look at Melistiche, Smicythion's wife,
　　She has managed to get her husband's shoes.
PRAXAGORA.　　　　　　　　　　　　　And looks
　　The only one untousled by pointed dreams.
SECOND WOMAN. And there's Geusistrata, the innkeeper's wife,
　　Waggling in her hand a—yes, a torch.
PRAXAGORA. Look, Philodoretos' wife, Chairetades',
　　And scores of others scampering along,
　　The finest women whose faces honor the town.
SEMICHORUS. O sweetheart, I have had such an awful time.
　　I couldn't get away, I'll tell you about it,
　　My husband stuffed himself up with anchovies
　　And tossed and wheezed and coughed over me all night.
PRAXAGORA. Well, take your seats that I may make inquiry
　　If you have done that which at Scira we
　　Determined we would do.
FIRST WOMAN.　　　　　　　　I have, and if
　　I lifted my arm you'd see it; in my armpits
　　Thick ringlets darkly shrubbed to fit our compact.
　　And when my husband lounged off to the Market place
　　I oiled my body and stood as long as I could
　　Tanned daily naked in the sweat of the sun.
SECOND WOMAN. And so have I. As soon as I reached home,
　　I went and pitched the razor out of the window

So that hairiness unfeminine should patch
My sprouting body.

PRAXAGORA.   But have you all got beards,
As we decided should be worn today?

FIRST WOMAN. By Hecate, I have, and such a sweet one.

SECOND WOMAN. And I have, one much prettier than Epi-
crates'.

PRAXAGORA. What of you others?

FIRST WOMAN.   They nod to say they have them.

PRAXAGORA. The other details are carried out, I see.
You have red Laconian shoes and walking sticks
And the men's overcoats as you were ordered.

FIRST WOMAN. Look at this fine stick that I stole from Lamias
As he was snoring.

PRAXAGORA.   O we've heard of that,
The club which Lamia fartingly doth wield.

FIRST WOMAN. By Savior Zeus, no better man than he
To don the leathern cloak heaven's herdsman wore
With all those hundred eyes, and sit on guard
Over the public hangman.

PRAXAGORA.   But now the time
Comes to conclude what we have all begun,
While yet the stars are ruffled in the sky—
For the Parliament for which we now prepare
Our going forth, must open with the dawn.

FIRST WOMAN. O yes, by Zeus, and we're to seat ourselves
Opposite the Prytanes, underneath the Bema.

SECOND WOMAN. See what I've brought with me, my dear. I
intend
To do some carding while they're mustering.

PRAXAGORA. Mustering, poor fool?

SECOND WOMAN.   Why not, by Artemis?
Can't I card wool and listen at the same time?
And I might tell you, my children badly need clothes.

PRAXAGORA. Carding indeed! you who must sit gravely
Displaying not one flush of nakedness!
We'd be in a nice mess, wouldn't we? if when
The place was crowded out, some woman came
Scrambling over the seats so that her cloak
Got twisted back and showed her sex's mat.
But if we push in first, in the front lines,
Safely wrapped up in our husband's clothes,
None will suspect us. And when we're sitting there,
Having attached our beards emphatically,

Who that looks at us will smell out what we are?
Did not Agyrrhios win masculinity
By putting on the beard of Pronomos?
And yet he who was a woman for the asking
Now struts a man, and more, a politician,
A strutting politician; and it's for that,
By yonder dawn burning softly over the roofs,
We dare to do this daring deed and see
If we can get our fingers in the affairs
Of the commonwealth and knead it to more health.
For otherwise wreck's certain—both oar and sail
Fail the stranded boat.

FIRST WOMAN.   But tell me this:
How can women, who are clearly feminine,
Harangue the Parliament?

PRAXAGORA.   Extremely well.
Boys who were girls whenever convenient
Are those from whom the best orators are recruited,
And so we've gossiped into natural speakers.

FIRST WOMAN. Perhaps you're right; but when a thing's so new
One's liable to make mistakes.

PRAXAGORA.   Of course.
Isn't that why this rehearsal was convened?
Now slip your beards on and grow hairy suddenly,
And all who have practiced talking, talk.

FIRST WOMAN. Who practiced? We don't need it, we knew
before.

PRAXAGORA. Come don your beard and bristle into a man.
I'll drop these garlands and also beard myself,
And probably add a few remarks of my own.

SECOND WOMAN. O isn't it funny, darling Praxagora?
It tickles, and it's funny, isn't it?

PRAXAGORA. What are you giggling at?

SECOND WOMAN.   All those half-tanned faces. . . .
They look just like cuttlefish browning by the fire
With big beards pinned on.

PRAXAGORA.   Here, O Purifier!
Begin at once and carry round the Pussy.
Enter the lustral line—Ariphrades,
Stop chattering—ho, enter and sit down.
Who wishes to address the Parliament?

FIRST WOMAN. I do.

PRAXAGORA. Good luck be yours then, and this garland.

FIRST WOMAN. Thank you.

PRAXAGORA. So speak.

FIRST WOMAN. But I haven't had a drink.

PRAXAGORA. Drink, did you say?

FIRST WOMAN. Well, what's the garland for?

PRAXAGORA. That's enough of you. Would you have spoken thus
In the real assembly?

FIRST WOMAN. Don't men drink in Parliament?

PRAXAGORA. Still with your drinking!

FIRST WOMAN. But I'm sure they do,
By Artemis, I am! and strong stuff too.
Only look at the laws they pass and it's obvious
They'd never pass such things unless very drunk.
And then they spill libations, don't they? or tell me
Why would they spend such a long time in prayers
Unless they had some wine bottles going round?
And then they're all as rowdy as squabbling drunkards,
And when one of them gets outrageously drunk
The rest call Order and the Archers lug him out.

PRAXAGORA. You are no use at all, go back to your seat.

FIRST WOMAN. Good Lord, I wish I'd never worn a beard.
I wouldn't have if I'd known there'd be nothing to drink—
I'm absolutely parched.

PRAXAGORA. Who else would speak?

SECOND WOMAN. I would.

PRAXAGORA. Then put this garland on your head,
Make a concise address, for time throbs nearer.
Now gruff your voice and hem just like a man
And lean convincingly upon your stick.

SECOND WOMAN. I wish some member of an older standing
Than I had risen on this serious matter
And spared me from personally taking up
The question of exposing this gross abuse,
Which, since no other has protested, I
Must raise my voice against. It must be stopped.
You know the tanks dug in the taverns? Well,
Some men have actually filled them up
With water. Shall this be allowed? By the Goddesses—

PRAXAGORA. By the Goddesses! Now, have you lost your head?

SECOND WOMAN. What's wrong? I didn't ask anyone for a drink.

PRAXAGORA. You're a fine man, swearing by the Goddesses!
Though, for the rest, you did it very well.

SECOND WOMAN. By Apollo, I meant.

PRAXAGORA.   Let this be understood:
  I shall withdraw from this Parliamentary Plot
  Unless each detail is studied and exact.
SECOND WOMAN. Give me the garland and another try.
  I have a good idea, and I'll take such care:
  Listen to me, all you assembled women—
PRAXAGORA. All wrong again. We're men and you say women.
SECOND WOMAN. I'm sorry, but it's all Epigonos' fault,
  He caught my eye and I thought I was lecturing women.
PRAXAGORA. That'll do now, go also to your seat
  And on my own head will I place the garland
  On behalf of your great cause; and now I pray
  The gods to add their voices to our voices.

  I am a citizen as deeply involved
  As any of you in this our country's fate,
  And I am sadly stricken to behold
  The darkness hurrying over our state.
  For I behold the city lifting up
  Base men to walk upon its broken face;
  And if one day a man advocates wisdom,
  The next ten times he leads you into disgrace.
  And then you try another, only to find
  One ten times worse. Ah, very hard it is
  To counsel men so rash . . . your wits desert you,
  Always suspecting those that most do love you,
  Always smiling on those that smile to hurt you.
  Once on a time we did not flock to assemblies—
  For Agyrrhios then we did not care a rap—
  But now we bustle along, because the man
  Whose palm takes money uses it to clap,
  And he who gets no dole we hear fiercely railing
  That those who got it deserve instant jailing.
FIRST WOMAN. By Aphrodite, isn't it a wonderful speech!
PRAXAGORA. By Aphrodite! you silly swearer, think
  How sweetly that would sound in Parliament.
FIRST WOMAN. O but I won't say it there.
PRAXAGORA.   Well, don't get the habit.
  When we deliberated in the League
  It was agreed that nothing else could save
  The ruining state; but once the pact was signed,
  It was the worst prick galling the state's flesh.
  The sponsor of the vote took to his heels,
  He had to. Then there are the navy-estimates:

We must have ships—the poorer classes assent
The capitalists and landowners disagree.
You used to hate Corinth, Corinth used to hate you. . . .
Now she is making overtures, be friendly.
Wisdom's a babbler, and the biggest fool
The state's philosopher . . . for then we saw
A peep of safety flutter past; but now
Thrasybulos' advice is no longer asked.

FIRST WOMAN. This is a very clever fellow.

PRAXAGORA.   That's right.
But you, people of Athens, are to blame.
You draw your doles out of the public store,
Yet each man's care for the state ends precisely
Where that salary ends; and so the city
Staggers shamefully, like Aisimos.
But trust my counsels and you may yet be saved,
For I propose this law: that we put at once
The city's entire rule in the women's hands.
Do they not manage households efficiently?

FIRST WOMAN. Hear, hear! by the Lord Zeus, speak on, my
      man!

PRAXAGORA. That they're superior in everything to us
I soon shall demonstrate to you. Now firstly:
They are wont to dye their wools in tinctures brought
To boiling—that's the old way, and the modern;
And you won't find them changing methods merely
To have a change, and wouldn't Athens yet
Boast the serene stones of her power
If she had kept to projects proved quite sound
Instead of any faddy substitute?
Just think of women's sound tradition of life:
They roast barley, sitting, as of old.
They carry baskets on their heads, as of old.
They keep the Thesmophoria, as of old.
They bake their honey-cheesecakes, as of old.
They nag their husbands biddable, as of old.
They hide lovers under their beds, as of old.
They buy sweets to eat on the sly, as of old.
They don't like wine in water, as of old.
They like being ravished kindly, as of old.
Consequently, sirs, let us abandon
The city up to their tenacious rule;
And not worry ourselves or ask a single question
Or be curious whatever they'll do with it,

But let them govern wholly, of one thing
Being certain: that the politician-mother
Will not be callous to the fate of her son
Gone off to be a soldier. And then the rations!
Who like the woman who bare the boy is fitted
To understand the commissariat?
For finding a way there's no one like a woman,
And there's no danger now that they'll be fooled
Once they're in charge, being adepts at that game
Themselves. No need for more words! merely pass
This law and lie back happy the rest of your lives.

FIRST WOMAN. O you're wonderful, you sweet Praxagora.
Where did you learn to talk so beautifully?

PRAXAGORA. When everyone fled into Athens, my husband
and I
Put up in the Pnyx and there heard the orators.

FIRST WOMAN. No wonder you know it so well, you sweet
smart thing.
And if we get that vote passed, then at once
We shall elect you dictatress of the city.
But what if Cephalos grows obstreperous?
How will you answer in front of all those men?

PRAXAGORA. I'll say he is demented.

FIRST WOMAN. But that's true.

PRAXAGORA. I'll say that he is broody-moody mad.

FIRST WOMAN. But everyone knows that too.

PRAXAGORA. That he's more suited
To solder the state up than a leaking pot.

FIRST WOMAN. And if Neocleides, the bleary-faced fool, insults you?

PRAXAGORA. I'll simply tell him to squint up a dog's behind.

FIRST WOMAN. What if they try to pull you down?

PRAXAGORA. Don't fret.
I'm used to that, it often happens to me,
So I know what to do.

FIRST WOMAN. But we've no precautions
In case the Archers try to throw you out.

PRAXAGORA. Once I get my arms akimbo thus, I'd like
To see the man who caught me in the middle.

SEMICHORUS. We'll help you too, we'll tell him not to be rude.

FIRST WOMAN. Then it is all arranged, and very neatly. . . .
But there's another point. We'll have to be careful.
One puts up arms to vote; if we don't think
We'll do the wrong thing—we're so much more used

To hold our legs up.

PRAXAGORA. An important point.

Let everyone remember the right procedure:
Lift up one arm, naked to the shoulder, thus.
Now catch your tunics up so they won't drag
And hurry into your Laconian shoes,
As you have seen your husbands dressing when
They meant to go out of doors, or to the assembly.
And then, when shoes and tunic don't flop loosely,
Gird on your beards, and see they are not attached
Askew or insecurely; the stolen cloaks
Take and throw on over the whole disguise,
And leaning negligently on your sticks
Off to Parliament! in a quavering whistle
Trying some old-man catch and gesturing
With rustic ways to hide any gawkiness.

FIRST WOMAN. Splendid! but let us go along ahead.
Other women, I know, will be coming straightaway
From outer suburbs to the Pnyx.

PRAXAGORA. O hasten!
Only early birds who reach the Pnyx by dawn
Make sure of seats and not slinking penniless off.

(*They go out.* CHORUS OF WOMEN *enter.*)

CHORUS. Move on, men—the more we use that word the better,
    or perplexed
In the Parliament we'll forget the way we're temporarily
    sexed—
For we'd be in a sad case if some shrewd-eyed fellow
    peered
And saw through our plans in darkness brewed and each
    impostor-beard.
Here move on, men, the meeting waits, and we must mind
    the magistrate's
            Stern utterance that
            The man who's unable to
            Tread flat the morning dew
            In the early light's pearly dust,
            Gobbling his breakfast snack
            Of garlick, and so comes late—
            Doleless must turn back,
            Turn back he must.

            So Charitemides,
            Smicythos, Draces, now

Hurry with us and please
See you allow
No word to escape you
The plot to betray,
But in everything ape you
Men's ways to-day.
So come on, be quick, it's
Time to rush away!
Let's get our tickets
And fill the front rows
And vote for whatever
Our sisters propose—
Our sisters! where do my wits stray?
Brothers, I meant to say.

Tread on their toes, and jostle too this irritating city-crew,
These men who of old
When a mere obol they,
All told, received for pay,
Lazily gazed time by—
Chatter and idle stare . . .
Nought else to do—
There in the Garland Fair
Useles they'd lie.
But when Myronides
Kept us so bravely afloat,
To have expected fees
For a mere vote
Would have been held a shame—
Eagerly then
To the assembly came
Each citizen,
And a goatskin of wine he
Brought—bread, two onions and
Three olives . . . tiny
Patriot feast.
But now they first demand
Three obols at least.
And ere they'll lift a hand
Their full price must understand.

(*Enter* BLEPYROS *dressed in his wife's petticoat and shoes.*)

BLEPYROS. What's wrong with the world? Where's my wife
disappeared?

It's almost morning and she's nowhere at all.
Here was I taken short in my own bed,
And I groped about to find my cloak and shoes
In the darkness, for I wanted to ease myself.
But I couldn't find a stitch, and all the while
The pain kept banging hard at my back door,
And so I wriggled into this chemise
And stuck my toes into these flapping slippers.
O where O where is a good nook? or is
Any spot in the dark a good enough one?
No man could see me if I squatted here,
I'm sure. O what a damned and utter fool
I was to go and get married in my old age;
I ought to be walloped, I ought. For it's not likely
She's gallivanting at this time of night
Out of pure goodness O but I can't wait!
(*The* NEIGHBOR *enters.*)

NEIGHBOR. Who is this here? Surely not neighbor Blepyros!
  Good Lord, it is. What's all this smeary yellow?
  Did Cinesias mistake you for an altar
  And start befouling you?

BLEPYROS.   No, I merely wanted
  To take the air and happened to put on
  This little yellow chemisette of my wife's.

NEIGHBOR. But where's your own shirt?

BLEPYROS.   That I cannot tell you.
  I looked for it, but it wasn't in the bedclothes.

NEIGHBOR. Didn't you ask your wife to look for it?

BLEPYROS. I didn't ask her and I'll tell you why.
  She wasn't there to ask. She's sliddered out,
  Somehow, I don't know how, I never saw her,
  And I'm afraid some revolution's muttering.

NEIGHBOR. Why, by Poseidon, exactly the same thing
  Has happened to me. My wife's flown out of the window;
  And so have the clothes I was wearing. And more than
    that:
  The plaguey wretch has vanished with my shoes.
  Anyhow, I looked for them and couldn't find them.

BLEPYROS. By Dionysus, it's the same with me.
  I couldn't find my Laconian shoes anywhere,
  And so as I was a bad case of the gripes
  I kicked her slippers on and out I tumbled.
  I didn't want to dirty the sheets, you see.
  They'd just been washt.

NEIGHBOR.   I wonder what's afoot.
   Can one of her friends have invited her to breakfast?
BLEPYROS. I think you're right, she's not a wicked girl. . . .
   At least, I think she isn't.
NEIGHBOR.   But good God,
   What's this? it's not a turd, man, it's a rope.
   But I must dash off to the assembly as soon
   As I have found the cloak I couldn't find—
   It's the only one I have.
BLEPYROS.   And I'll go with you
   As soon as I reach the end of this—O Lord,
   I think a prickly pear has blocked the way.
NEIGHBOR. The kind of wild pear that shut Thrasybulos up?
                                 (*Goes out.*)
BLEPYROS. By the Lord in Heaven, whatever kind it is,
   It's stuck for ever in my hinder parts.
   O what'll I do? the pain . . . it's hard as a brick.
   But I don't mind that so much; what worries me
   Is what will happen now to the food I eat.
   The bung-hole's stopped forever. What'll I do?
   I'll never dung again. This prickly slab
   Has plugged the venthole up, and nevermore
   Shall I evacuate deliciously.
   Bring me a doctor! . . . but what sort of doctor?
   Perhaps a pathic knows this business best
   And could dislodge it. Bring me a pathic then!
   Bring me Amynon! he knows . . . but perhaps
   He won't admit it . . . so fetch Antisthenes.
   O fetch Antisthenes that fellow sufferer.
   He'll understand and he'll know what to do.
   He knows well an insatiate itching breech.
   O midwife Ilythia, grant me ease—
   Deliver me of this tremendous turd!
   Don't let me burst or stay forever sealed
   A common night stool on the comic stage.

(CHREMES *enters.*)
CHREMES. Hullo there! What are you doing? Not diarrhea?
BLEPYROS. I? well, I was. But I have finished now.
CHREMES. And are you wearing your wife's chemise?
BLEPYROS.   You see,
   It was so dark inside I didn't know
   What I was taking; I picked it up in the dark.
   But where do you come from?

CHREMES.   I come from Parliament.

BLEPYROS. Is it dismissed already?

CHREMES.   Yes, today

It ended almost before it had begun.
And ha, my dear Zeus, you should have heard the laughter
And seen the way they lavished vermilion around.

BLEPYROS. Did you get your three obols?

CHREMES.   No, I didn't, damn it.

I arrived too late, and I'm ashamed to say
A bare wallet is my pay for the day.

BLEPYROS. How did that come about?

CHREMES.   It was like this:

You never saw such a crush about the Pnyx . . .
Pale-faced fellows all like shoemakers,
That's what we said: a pale blur of faces—
Queer it looked, a hubbub of white faces
Packing Parliament; so I and lots of us
Were turned away and didn't get our obols.

BLEPYROS. Do you think that I'd get mine if I did a sprint?

CHREMES. Not a hope. You couldn't have squeezed in
If you'd been there by the second crow of the morning.

BLEPYROS. Weep, weep, Antilochos, O weep for me
Who live to mourn, rather than weep for death,
The perished, lost three obols. The game's up.
But how was it such a mob got there so early?

CHREMES. I suppose it was because the Prytanes
Decided to have the assembled people vote
The best safety for the state. Out pushed Neocleides,
Trying to slip through and make the first speech.
Then what do you think? The people all bawled out:
Shame that this bleary-eyed idiot who can't see
Even the way that he is stumbling himself,
Should seek to guide the slippery fate of Athens!
And so he stopped, and glaring round roared out
What's to be done then?

BLEPYROS.   I'd have recommended

Some garlic pounded with verjuice and then mixed up
With some Laconian splurge: sore eyes to be
Anointed with it before going to bed.

CHREMES. Next that astute Euaion trotted out,
Quite naked, or so it looked to us from a distance,
But he insisted he was fully clad,
And made a loud speech in the popular style.
Look on me, citizens, he says, *and you'll see*

I too am in need of saving—to be precise,
Four staters. Yet I know the very way
To save the state and all its citizens.
Let every draper give thick woolen cloaks
To any man who wants one when the sun
Swings backward into winter. Immediately
There will be no more pleurisy anywhere.
And let those who have no blankets and no bed,
After they've had a good dinner, be permitted
To enter furriers' shops and make themselves snug.
And whoever shuts his door in chilly weather
Against them, shall be mulcted three blankets a time.

BLEPYROS. That was a good speech; and there's not a man
Who would have dared to raise one knuckle against him
If he'd gone on: Let those who trade in grain
Give three quarts gratis to the poor; or else
Be strung up. . . . Then that benefit at least
They'd wring from Nausicydes.

CHREMES.   And after him
Up skipped a spruce young fellow pale as Nicias
And made a speech declaring we should deliver
The state over to the control of women.
Then the whole wheyfaced pack of shoemakers
Cheered and cheered, while all the country people
Boohooed back at them.

BLEPYROS.   And very sensible.

CHREMES. But far too few, and so the boy continued
With an eloquent catalogue of women's virtues
And of your villainies.

BLEPYROS.   What's that?

CHREMES.   He said
First of all you were an abject scoundrel.

BLEPYROS. And you?

CHREMES.   I'll come to that soon. Next he called you
A thief.

BLEPYROS. And only me?

CHREMES.   And then he added
A sycophant.

BLEPYROS.   But only me?

CHREMES.   And added
The same remarks about the rest of us.

BLEPYROS. Well, I don't suppose anyone contradicted.

CHREMES. And then he went on saying how woman is
A witty and inventive piece of flesh,

Smiling mum over her Thesmaphorian secrets
While you and I blurt out anything about the state's.

BLEPYROS. Well, by Hermes, that is more or less true.

CHREMES. And women, he said, are always ready to lend
Dresses, jewelry, cash or drinking cups
To one another, when they're quite alone
And not a witness by; and yet they always
Redeem their word and make a full repayment.
But men are always quarreling over deals.

BLEPYROS. That's true enough . . . even though there were
witnesses.

CHREMES. Women don't inform, and they don't go to law,
Or suppress the people, but their own business
Quietly do; and a lot more, all praises.

BLEPYROS. What was the decision then?

CHREMES.   You're to surrender
The state to them. For this it was concluded
The only revolution not yet tried.

BLEPYROS. It was decreed then?

CHREMES.   It was.

BLEPYROS.   And now the women
Must be the administrating citizens?

CHREMES. Exactly.

BLEPYROS.   Then my wife's the dicast now,
Not I?

CHREMES. And she supports the house, not you.

BLEPYROS. Now she's the one to get grumbling up in the
morning?

CHREMES. Yes, from now on that is the woman's job.
You'll stay at home and surrender your morning grumble.

BLEPYROS. But it's just struck me, we'll have a hard time,
We older men, if now the women are over us
They decide to try to force us on to—

CHREMES.   What?

BLEPYROS. Fornicate.

CHREMES.   But if we can't?

BLEPYROS.   Well, then
They won't give us any breakfast.

CHREMES.   So it seems
We'll have to fornicate to earn our breakfast.

BLEPYROS. But forced! . . . I wouldn't.

CHREMES.   No, we must obey.
If it's concluded for the public good
That we should do it, do it like a man.

There is a saying blown from antique times
That all our silly and fantastic plans
Heaven warps awry to suit the public weal. . . .
So be it now, Lady Pallas and all you gods!
But I must go. Good-by.

BLEPYROS.   Chremes, good-by.

(*They part. The* CHORUS OF WOMEN *returning from the Pnyx come forward.*)

CHORUS.   Forward, step bolder. . . .
                 Look over your shoulder
                 Every now and then
                 To see if some men
                 Are following us.

          Hurry, but no flurry!
And take good care there's no one there who might unbare
Our sex by getting behind and upsetting our plot by pet-
    ting—I can't help fretting,
                 The rogues are so numerous.

                 Stamp on the ground
                 A flat-footed sound!
                 A pretty disgrace
                 We'd have to face
                 If the men found us out.

                 Look at ease if you please:
Hide your fright, tuck your clothes in tight, look to left and
    right,
Or some disaster will overmaster Praxagora and blast her
    . . . and so move faster,
                 And stare well round about.

                 In a moment or two
                 We'll have won through,
                 And be back once more
                 At the very door
From which we started when we departed
Courageous-hearted to Parliament.
This is the place full in your face
From which we proceeded on empire bent,
Where she dwells who pleaded our cause and succeeded,
    the leader we needed,
                 By heaven sent!

        It's dangerous
        Any longer for us
        To continue to wear
        This spurious hair.
Every idling minute has peril in it,
Some man that knows us may expose us. . . .
Closer I call!—beneath this wall—
Peep from side to side, and change dresses here. . . .
Ah, that head of pride, that beautiful stride, I am sure I
    spied our queen and guide,
        And lo! she comes near.

        Doff beards now—O dear,
        Didn't it feel queer!
        That fringe of tickles, these rays of prickles
        Smarting from ear to ear:
        I'm glad it's off my chin. . . .
        So, girls, we win.

PRAXAGORA. O women, you behold how happily
    Has fortune turned our hopes to acclaimed facts.
    Therefore before an eye betrays our game
    Off with your cloaks, kick your shoes off, undo
    The knotted rein of your Laconian shoes,
    Drop your sticks.
    (*To* LEADER OF CHORUS.)
                But no, I'll leave this section
    To you, my dear. See they do everything rightly,
    And I myself shall now tiptoe indoors
    And before my husband notices I'll lay
    His overcloak back where I found it thrown,
    And any other borrowed article.
CHORUS.   We have doffed our male array;
        And forever, from this day,
        Only speak—we obey.
        For sincerely I can say
        There's no woman in any way
        I admire so . . . none so gay
        And resourceful at bay.
PRAXAGORA. Then henceforth you'll stay
        At my side, and, I pray,
        The part of counselors play,
        For there in the fray
        Hullabalooing away

You proved yourself gay
Manly women at bay.

(As PRAXAGORA *is going in* BLEPYROS *comes out.*)

BLEPYROS. Hullo, Praxagora, where did you spring from?

PRAXAGORA. Sir,
What's that to you?

BLEPYROS. What's that to me? Are you mad?

PRAXAGORA. At any rate you can't say it's from a lover.

BLEPYROS. No, probably from more than one.

PRAXAGORA. Well, then
Test for yourself and find I'm innocent.

BLEPYROS. And how can I test it?

PRAXAGORA. Smell my hair, of course.
Is it scented?

BLEPYROS. Can't a woman be embraced
Unless there is some scent curling her hair?

PRAXAGORA. I don't choose to be, anyhow.

BLEPYROS. Then tell me why
You stole away so early in my overcloak.

PRAXAGORA. Before dawn I was summoned to a friend
Whose pangs had just begun.

BLEPYROS. Why didn't you tell me
Before you went off?

PRAXAGORA. And not hasten to her
To help her in her throes, my husband, eh?

BLEPYROS. Yes, after having told me. Why didn't you?
There's something underhand here.

PRAXAGORA. By the two goddesses!
I went straight off, just as I was; the girl
Who came for me, begged me not to dillydally.

BLEPYROS. And so that's why you left your chemise behind?
You threw it over my bed and took my cloak
And left me stretched out like a snoring corpse—
A corpse all but the wreath and bottle of oil.

PRAXAGORA. The early air was frosty; and I'm so delicate,
Only a weak little thing, and so I took
Your overcloak to snuggle me from the cold.
And you, my dear, I left cozily slumbering
Under rugs of huddled warmth.

BLEPYROS. Then will you inform me
How it was that my stick and my Laconians
Went out walking with you also?

PRAXAGORA. If you'll listen.
I put on your shoes to save your cloak, ungrateful!

Tramping like you, slapping with my feet
And sturdily clattering the stick on the stones.

BLEPYROS. It's all your fault that I've lost eight quarts of wheat,
Which I'd have got by going to the assembly.

PRAXAGORA. Well, cheer up. All went well, she was safely delivered.

BLEPYROS. Who was? the assembly was?

PRAXAGORA.   No, no, you blockhead;
My friend. But has the assembly met?

BLEPYROS.   Yes, blockhead.
I told you yesterday that it was to meet.

PRAXAGORA. O I remember.

BLEPYROS.   But you haven't heard
About the decree that was passed?

PRAXAGORA.   No, what was it?

BLEPYROS. O sit down munching cuttlefish with your friends!
This is the news: the state is in your hands.

PRAXAGORA. What for? weaving?

BLEPYROS.   That you may govern.

PRAXAGORA.   What?

BLEPYROS. All the executive business of the state.

PRAXAGORA. O what a happy state this is going to be!
By Aphrodite!

BLEPYROS. How? tell me.

PRAXAGORA.   For several reasons.
For instance, swaggerers shan't lord it now
Over the city's shame; and in a twinkling
There'll be no trade in witnesses; no longer
Shall the informers thrive.

BLEPYROS.   Don't go too far.
Don't rob me of my only livelihood.

CHREMES. Here, my good man, let the lady have her say.

PRAXAGORA. No stealing overcloaks, no coveting now,
No more poor and no more ragged people,
No more mud throwing, no distraining property—

CHREMES. By Poseidon, marvelous if it's truly true.

PRAXAGORA. It's true. I'll prove it so that I'll gain you over
And stop this foolish fellow's antagonism.

CHORUS. Gather your brave thoughts, let them shine,
And as you speak to these two,
Loose that clear lovely anger of yours
That never yet we knew
Fail when its strength was called to fight

For Athens and our dark distress.
Speak then, and all the torches light,
That darkness sweetly to bless.
Yes, speak your projects—now or never. . . .
To gain the populace we need
Some plan extravagantly clever;
And you must do the deed.
The audience is rather sick
Of plots antiquely patterned: so
Produce one new and striking—quick,
Before they go.

PRAXAGORA. I've a splendid conception, but feel rather scared
What my friends there would think of me if I once dared
To propound it. . . . I want to, but still fear to speak . . .
This new type of political dramatic technique.

BLEPYROS. If that's why you hesitate, don't get unnerved.
We've one steadfast principle, I have observed;
New things are good, old things bad.

PRAXAGORA.   Let no man
Interrupt the speaker till he's heard the whole plan.
Don't get excited and try to reply
Before you have grasped all the how, when, and why.
Briefly my scheme is: mankind should possess
In common the instruments of happiness.
Henceforth private property comes to an end—
It's all wrong for a man to have too much to spend,
While others moan, starving; another we see
Has acres of land tilled prosperously,
While this man has not enough earth for his grave.
You'll find men who haven't a single lean slave
While others have hundreds to run at their call. . . .
That's over: all things are owned henceforth by all.

BLEPYROS. But stop! . . . explain how that can be.

PRAXAGORA. You'll eat dung ahead of me!

BLEPYROS. Does your scheme then involve, to our indigestion,
A community of turds?

PRAXAGORA. No, you annoyed me intruding a question
To be answered in my next words.
All the titles to land being revoked, understand
Each equally now has a right to the land;
As to silver, to all things, the big things, the small things!
We'll declare there's no personal property first;
Then, taking charge of the wealth disembursed,

We'll maintain you by farming the whole vast estate
And working each branch at a sensible rate.

BLEPYROS. As to land it seems easy; but will you explain
What will happen where wealth is not tree, grass, or grain,
But bullion: not farms one can't put in one's pocket—
Can your scheme touch the man rich in coin? Can't he
block it?

PRAXAGORA. He must hand gold all in.

BLEPYROS.   But suppose that he lies,
And hoards it away from the state's prying eyes?
Lies and cheating! . . . Admitted; but what other feat
Gains money in commerce if not skill to cheat?

PRAXAGORA. You're right. So we take all the value from cash.

BLEPYROS. But how is that done?

PRAXAGORA.   Of itself it turns trash:
When all a man wants is set free to his hand,
What becomes of the law of supply and demand?
Cakes, barley loaves, chestnuts, warm clothes, wreaths,
wine, fish,
Blossom out of the air at his ripening wish. . . .
Why then should he cling to his ill-gotten gains?
Tell me why if you please?

BLEPYROS.   Those who take the most pains
To thieve money are those who already have most.

PRAXAGORA. That has been so till now; but I make it my
boast
That my scheme must destroy capitalistic morality.
Why cheat for a shadow? Here's free the reality.

BLEPYROS. But if a man's yearning to insinuate
His kisses abed with some wench, where's the bait?
He gets a mere share of the common estate. . . .
A fraction of kisses, a ration of legs
Deducted from breakfast—desire's dirty dregs!

PRAXAGORA. Don't forget how much easier henceforth to
mate is.
The whole city of girls are your wives now, and gratis!
Whoever's inclined to make mothers of any
Just catches them up, and it costs not a penny.

BLEPYROS. Then all you will see will be restless relays
Of lovers that stand in the long file for days
To get at the lovely ones . . . that's all you'll see.

PRAXAGORA. No, each beautiful girl, so runs my decree,
With a scraggy slut simpering flat-nosed is paired—
Rape the slut first, or else is the other not shared.

BLEPYROS. All very well for the lusty young men!
　Think of us elders—one trial, and then
　We'll be useless; don't make us make love, I beseech,
　To old hags to reach girls we can never once reach.
PRAXAGORA. They won't fight.
BLEPYROS. But what for ?
PRAXAGORA. Don't be scared or look blue.
　They won't fight.
BLEPYROS. But what for?
PRAXAGORA. For embraces from you.
　That's the point of the law: it is meant to exclude
　From the lovely ones' arms you old men who're still lewd.
BLEPYROS. I confess that there's sense in all that: a good trap
　For enclosing some man in each woman's wide lap.
　But won't it cut both ways? The girls, cuddled snugly,
　Will want all the nice men and none of the ugly.
PRAXAGORA. The uglier men shall all keep a good eye
　On their rivals, when rising from dinner, and spy
　How they chance to behave in the more public places;
　And if they once find them sprawled out in embraces
　They may stop them and take their turn first. The decree
　Says: Ugly men, little ones, first hugged must be.
BLEPYROS. Then Lysicrates now may carry his nose
　As high as the best, though so snubly it shows.
PRAXAGORA. Yes, by Apollo; and also please note
　How democratic the plan is, a fine antidote
　To false pride and snobbery, when a swell fellow
　Is stopped halfway through by a villainous bellow,
　Looks up, sees a hobnailed lout fumbling, and hears
　I'm first in; I'll lift you right off by the ears
　Unless you stand by. I am uglier than you,
　And so the first cut's mine, sir . . . howdoyedo?
BLEPYROS. But where love has run wild who will know his own
　child?
PRAXAGORA. He won't; and why should he? Now children will
　say
　Father to any man older than they.
BLEPYROS. And therefore will now very properly throttle
　Each old man, or hit his old head with a bottle,
　For henceforth they'll never know which one is he.
　Even now fathers kicked by their sons' feet we see;
　After this they will use him to piss on at least.
PRAXAGORA. You're mistaken. Such actions will not be in-
　creased.

For then those who stand near will all interfere,
Since he might be the father of anyone—now,
Shoulders they shrug, any conduct allow,
Because they are sure he's not theirs . . . but our plan
Makes your possible father every old man.

BLEPYROS. It sounds fairly well . . . but think of my shame
If Epicuros should rush to me, call on my name,
And assert I'm his father. Leucolophas too!
If they called me father, O what should I do!

CHREMES. I know something worse.

BLEPYROS. What?

CHREMES. If Aristyllos
Should kiss us as fathers and probably kill us.

BLEPYROS. I'd soon make him howl.

CHREMES. If you spanked him, I fear
Your fingers would smell most dis-as-trously queer.

PRAXAGORA. But, sirs, this is fooling. He was born long ago,
Ere this law; so you're safe.

BLEPYROS. Well, thank heavens, that's so.
But who is to cultivate land?

PRAXAGORA. That's the task
Of the slaves; the whole duty the state now will ask
From men such as you is to be well anointed
With oil, and then go, in the manner appointed,
When dials slant, ten-foot, the evening shade,
Sauntering to dinner.

BLEPYROS. But our clothes'll get frayed.

PRAXAGORA. There's the wardrobe you own, and when that is
worn out
We'll weave you another supply, don't you doubt.

BLEPYROS. A further point yet—if a man goes to law,
Where funds for expenses and fines will he draw?
Surely the exchequer won't pay for them too.

PRAXAGORA. A fine from a lawsuit! When things start anew,
There won't be any law.

BLEPYROS. O but isn't that wrong!
How earn money? what to do with oneself all day long?

CHREMES. That's true, there'll be many eyes tearful today.

PRAXAGORA. I know. But why go to law? Answer, I pray.

BLEPYROS. For hundreds of reasons. I'll give you one case:
If a man owing money refuses to pay?

PRAXAGORA. Won't pay! Will you tell me how in the first place
The creditor had money to lend—for we said
As the symbol of value the coin was quite dead.

The state makes all value, the state owns all coin. . . .
Before you are rooked, you must clearly purloin.

CHREMES. There's a well-turned dilemma.

BLEPYROS.   But then let's suppose
A fellow gets drunk, roaring drunk, and he goes
Knocking down all he sees in the street—what's the fine?
I've caught you with that one.

PRAXAGORA.   His food and his wine
Will be cut down awhile when he comes in to dine;
And I'm sure he'll remember his stomach's sharp pain
More than the old fine, and not do it again.

BLEPYROS. And won't there be thieves?

PRAXAGORA.   But why should you abstract
What is partly your own—a most imbecile act!

BLEPYROS. And so we won't meet in the streets late at night
A brigand who'll tweak off our cloaks and take flight?

PRAXAGORA. Not if you're sleeping at home . . . aye, not
  though
Down the streets after midnight you choose still to go.
Why take trouble to steal? there's enough now for all;
And if someone should try it, don't struggle or bawl.
What's the use of a fuss? you just go to the store,
Say: my cloak has been taken—they'll fetch you some more.

BLEPYROS. And shan't we now gamble?

PRAXAGORA.   What stakes will you give?

BLEPYROS. In what kind of a household henceforth will we
live?

PRAXAGORA. In one common to all—easy and free,
Mingling with beautiful liberty:
All family restrictions abolished.

BLEPYROS.   I see.
And where will the tables be laid?

PRAXAGORA.   I suggest
In the courts and arcades of the law would be best.
There shall we revel and banquet.

BLEPYROS.   That's grand.
But what of the pulpit where orators stand?

PRAXAGORA. That I shall turn to a buffet I think
For winecups and goblets, and from it we'll drink;
And a squad of young lads shall be grouped round the
  stone
Singing deeds of the heroes, the wild laughter blown
Through the clang of the swords, then the coward's pale
  shame,

So nobly, each coward will feel his own name
Cried in the music—hot-cheeked off he'll crawl—
BLEPYROS. Ho, very good! and each balloting stall?—
PRAXAGORA. I shall send to the top of the marketing square
To be stuck in a row ... and I'll govern from there,
By Harmodios' statue distributing round
Tickets assigning the feeding ground:
One for each person explaining what section's
Alloted to him, with his dining directions,
The man who draws A will be shown on the way
To Arcade A, to Portico P the P's, X's
Separated to go—
BLEPYROS.   Won't you mix up the sexes?
PRAXAGORA. Of course I will, fool.
BLEPYROS.   Well, it seems fairly good. . . .
But who misses his letter, is given no food.
PRAXAGORA. Don't brood over that. You'll have all you can
    swallow.
Luxurious plenty's the menu we'll follow.

> You'll totter home each night,
> Your belly warm and tight,
> Drunk and happy: that's our plan
> To send home a contented man.
> Get him drunk till he can't stand,
> Put a brave torch in his hand,
> Stick some flowers on his head,
> And so send him home to bed.
>
> And then as he on staggering feet
> Rollicks roundly down the street,
> Women will come mysteriously
> Hemming him in with whispers sweet. . . .
> *Come O come with me.*
>
> *Come to my lodgings,* they'll repeat,
> *I've a lovely girl for you.*
> *I've a lovelier softer one,*
> *Softly made for kisses, come*
> *And have a private view.*
>
> From each window, from each shadow,
> Whispers drifting break,
> *I've a girl who's white all over*
> *But before she takes a lover*
> *Love to me he must make.*

And then a squiny blunt-faced fellow
To his younger calls,
My pretty boy, hey, not so fast,
Your kisses climb in last;
My lot earlier falls.

This box of beauty it's my luck
To open first and find
What's warmly inside. Wait at the door,
Twiddle your thumbs, you can't do more.
I'm going in . . . d'ye mind?

So; what's your opinion now of my device?
BLEPYROS. Magnificent.
PRAXAGORA.   I must go to the market place,
Choosing some shrill-voiced girl as Crieress,
And there I'll stand as Public Receiver, taking
All of the confiscated property
As people bring it in. This is my office,
Since I have been elected Governess
To control the state and manage all the dinners,
That we may start our banqueting today.
BLEPYROS. What, are we all to eat at once?
PRAXAGORA.   You are.
And next I'll round in all the whores pellmell,
Thrown together in a flouncing babble of flesh.
BLEPYROS. But why?
PRAXAGORA.   Because it's clearly necessary
To have them out of the way and give us others
A decent chance in our communal lechery.
Till now they've taken the first freshness from
The tips of all our sprouting youth, and we
Have had but the mauled stalk. But now we're rulers
Nevermore shall these vendible gawds of flesh
With their poor flaunts of laughter tap the stores
Of running kisses broached for our delight.
No, let them lie with slaves, being slaves to them,
Their frizzled hair all shaved away to match.
BLEPYROS. Onward, my dear; and I'll come close behind you.
I want the men to point at me and murmur:
There goes the husband of our Governess.
CHREMES. And I'll collect and detail my belongings
And bring them along to surrender to the state.
                    [Chorus lost.]

(CHREMES *commences to bring out all his possessions and arrange them in processional order, mimicking the elements of the Panathenaic pageant.*)

CHREMES. Beloved bran sifter, lovelily appear!
Step forth the first of all my household chattels,
Neatly powdered like some young basket bearer—
Many a sackful of mine have you gobbled down.
Then where's the chair girl? Briskly forth, my pot.
You black-faced thing . . . you couldn't be blacker even
If you had boiled Lysicrates' hair dye.
Forth to your place by her. Ho, there, tire maiden!
And you, pitch bearer, pitch your pitcher there!
And you my trumpet squawker, halt you there!
Who with your screech have scratched me often awake
To get up cursing in time for the assembly.
You with the dish, move forward, take with you
The honeycombs, and put the olive branches
Beside them, and fetch out the bottle of oil,
And then the tripod—all of the burnt saucepans
And the rubbishy odds and ends you can leave behind.

(*Another citizen comes out of the neighboring house.*)

CITIZEN. Am I to dump my belongings out for anyone?
I would be a shiftless ninny if I did.
I won't. I won't, I say. No, by Poseidon.
I want to see how things are going first.
The others can test it; I'll join afterward.
I'm not the kind to throw away for nothing
What gains I've sweated from my thrifty pores.
No, I must get the hang of this thing first.
Hi, you! what's all this pile of furniture?
Are you moving out? or are you just hard up
And off to pawn them?

CHREMES.   Neither.

CITIZEN.   Then explain
Why they're all mustered if you do not mean
To march them off to Hiero the auctioneer.

CHREMES. Certainly. You find me sorting out
The contributions to the public stock;
That's the new law. Haven't you heard of it?

CITIZEN. You're going to give them up?

CHREMES.   I am.

CITIZEN.   By God,
What an unfortunate idiot you are.

CHREMES. How?

CITIZEN.   How? Look at yourself in the mirror.

CHREMES. But oughtn't I to obey the law?

CITIZEN.   The law!
You're mad. What law?

CHREMES.   The law that's just been made.

CITIZEN. That newfangled law! I thought that you were mad;
And you are.

CHREMES.   Mad?

CITIZEN.   Now, aren't you? answer frankly.
You happen to be the worst fool in Athens.

CHREMES. Because I obey the law?

CITIZEN.   Is it the part
Of a wise man to follow laws like a sheep?—

CHREMES. Yes, of course; isn't it?

CITIZEN.   Bah, no! you fool;
That's what fools do.

CHREMES.   Then you're not giving yours?

CITIZEN. I'm going to do nothing for a while.
I'll see how things go and what the others do.

CHREMES. What can they do except deliver up
Their property to the state?

CITIZEN.   When I see it done,
Then I'll believe it.

CHREMES.   Listen to them talking
Anywhere in the streets.

CITIZEN.   O I know they'll talk.

CHREMES. But they say they'll bring their goods.

CITIZEN.   O so they say.

CHREMES. Hell, you doubt everything.

CITIZEN.   Yes, they'll soon doubt.

CHREMES. God damn you.

CITIZEN.   O yes, they will soon be damning.
Surely you don't think men in their right senses
Will all so easily discard their goods?
No, that is not the way we are born—rather
To take than give is the way our hands are made. . . .
Just like the palms of the gods. Look at their statues,
Stretching out their inexorable hands;
And we pray up to them for prosperity,
And they are hollowing hands of greedy stone
Explaining that they mean to take not give.

CHREMES. Here now, my friend, let me be; I've work to do.
Where is that strap? I want to fasten these.

CITIZEN. You really intend to do it?

CHREMES. Therefore you see
That I am knotting these tripods here together.

CITIZEN. But this is lunatic. Why don't you wait
And see what all the other people will do.
And then—

CHREMES. And then?

CITIZEN. Then wait a little longer,
And look before you leap.

CHREMES. And why?

CITIZEN. Because
An earthquake might come splitting up the town,
Or else a shatter of lightning, or a cat
Might cross the street, and then there'd be bad luck,
And nobody bring anything more in—
You dotard!

CHREMES. And a pleasing jest it'd be
If I could find no room to bring my goods.

CITIZEN. To take away, you mean. Let two days pass
And then there will be time to cart them off.

CHREMES. But why?

CITIZEN. I know these fellows, their rash heads,
Voting for any measure when excited
And then forgetting it by the time they're home.

CHREMES. They'll fetch their things.

CITIZEN. And if they don't, what then?

CHREMES. O but they will.

CITIZEN. And if they don't, what then?

CHREMES. We'll force them.

CITIZEN. And if they're stronger than you, what then?

CHREMES. I'll run away.

CITIZEN. If they knock you down, what then?

CHREMES. Go and be hanged.

CITIZEN. And if I do, what then?

CHREMES. Why, then you'd do a charitable deed.

CITIZEN. You really intend to continue?

CHREMES. At last I find
You grasp my meaning. I see my neighbors taking
Their pots and pans along.

CITIZEN. And whom do you see?
Anisthenes, I bet. He'd rather sit
For thirty days acquiring piles on the stool.

CHREMES. Get out.

CITIZEN. Then it's Callimachos the poet.
What will he fetch?

CHREMES. Far more than Callias can.

CITIZEN. Well, there's a spendthrift silly prodigal.

CHREMES. You're a hard man.

CITIZEN. Hard! when every day
We see a hill of rocky resolutions
Reared up for citizens to bark their shins on.
Do you remember the vote on the salt question?

CHREMES. I do.

CITIZEN. And then the vote on the copper coinage?

CHREMES. I do; and it hit me badly, I can tell you.
I sold some grapes I had and stuffed my gob
With coppers and went off to buy some barley.
I got to the market and as far as holding
My sack out open, when up blurts a herald;
And what did he cry? All copper coins illegal,
Nothing but silver now must circulate.

CITIZEN. And what about the recent tax Euripides
Persuaded us to impose? He promised us
That two and a half per cent. would yield the state
Five hundred talents at the least; so we
Wanted one and all to gild the man
In flaming gold from head to foot, until
We started doing the arithmetic
And found the scheme a dunce's palace of clouds
Gone when the wind unpicks the mortised sun.
And then we all wanted to tar Euripides.

CHREMES. But things are not the same now, my good sir.
All that was during the men's empire; here
We enter on the women's.

CITIZEN. And by heaven!
I'll give them a wide berth, too. I won't have them
Piddling over me.

CHREMES. But this is balderdash.
Boy, there, take up the yoke.

(*A woman* CRIER *enters.*)

CRIER. O all you citizens,
Not a few chosen ones, but all of you
By the new ordinance, hurry to your Mistress.
There draw your lots, and luck will tell each one
What neighbors are his elbows to be given
At dinner time; for the tables are made ready.
With dainty luxury the food is heaped
Beside the couches softly rich with furs
And riotous cushions; and they're mixing wine.

The scent girls have been shown where they're to stand;
And slices brightly feed the sizzling fire,
The spits hold hares, and the ovens little cakes,
And girls are plaiting garlands for your head.
Sweetmeats are parching lusciously; more girls,
The youngest girls, are stirring the pea soup.
And Simous sidling in his riding suit
Licks all the women's platters he can find.
And Geron too, cloaked gallantly and shod
With dancing pumps, laughs with another lad,
Laughing loudly and preens about, forgetting now
His cracking shoes and his old tattered coat.
Come then, and quickly come—bread in his hand
The butler stands—and open wide your mouth!

CITIZEN. I'm going. Of course I am. Why linger here
When you have heard the state's decreed these things?

CHREMES. Where are you going? You've not sent in your
goods.

CITIZEN. To dinner.

CHREMES.   Not, if they have any sense,
Till you've contributed your property.

CITIZEN. O I'll give it up.

CHREMES.   And when?

CITIZEN.   What does it matter?
My being a bit late won't hold up the nation.

CHREMES. Why not?

CITIZEN.   Won't there be others later still?

CHREMES. And yet you're off to the dinner.

CITIZEN.   What am I to do?
Good citizens must all stand by the state
In such important matters loyally—
Good-by!

CHREMES.   But if they turn you back, what then?

CITIZEN. I'll go in headfirst.

CHREMES.   If they kick, what then?

CITIZEN. I'll summons them.

CHREMES.   And if they mock, what then?

CITIZEN. Ho, then I'll stand up by the door and—

CHREMES.   Eh?

CITIZEN. Snatch at the victuals as they're carried in.

CHREMES. Come later then. Here, Parmeno and Sicon,
Up with my goods on your shoulders and be off.

CITIZEN. I'll help you along with them.

CHREMES.   O no you won't.
I've a shrewd fear that if we so arrive
And you are helping the goods to find their places
You'll tell the Governess that they are yours.
(*Goes with his slaves.*)

CITIZEN. Now I must find some really good excuse
For stowing my things away and at the same time
Getting a share of these here public dinners....
Ho, ho, I've got it. That'll take them in,
So now we'll go and have a bit of dinner.

                                  (*Goes off.*)

[Chorus lost.]

(*An old woman appears loitering at the door of one of the houses next to* PRAXAGORA'S.)

HAG. What's keeping all the men? They're long since due,
And here I'm posturing most obviously.
My skin I've stained with beauty and thick ceruse
To seem the skin of roses: dressed in yellow,
Looking lazy, singing red-lipped to myself
Softly and lewdly, and shifting every time
Into a poise of more fidgetty desire
To catch the eye of someone, anyone.
O Muses, curl the redness of my mouth
Into some pretty, obscene Ionian song.
(*A young girl comes out of the same house.*)

GIRL. So for once, old Ugly, you've pushed in
Ahead of me, and put your face out first.
I know. You thought your face painted on the darkness
Would get a man, my man, if I was away.
Fancy! and murmuring songs like rustling kisses
As if you could suck a lover from the air.
Don't let me stop you, certainly not, sing on;
And I shall sing against you if you do—
For though our duet bores the audience
It's in the true tradition of stage humor.

HAG (*tossing her a phallus*). Here, talk to this, the best part of
    a man.
Go inside and converse with it. But, hey, you there,
My piper with a tone like honey melting,
Play up! a song that's worthy you, and me.

        Ah do you long at last to win
        Love's beautiful whimper of delight?

Then come in.
Ah do you long for love's smooth night
Of kisses dying endlessly?
Come to my arms, and come with me
To bed, to bed, to bed.

For there's not much that I don't know,
And sweet love is a difficult art,
Decidedly so.
The young girl doesn't know her part,
Gadding about, a fool of kisses;
No man can know the joy he misses
Till with us he's been to bed.

GIRL. Don't grudge the young their merriness.
Wondering in beauty each lies. . . .
And delicately the plump light
Dimples her long thighs,
And flowers drink with soft rich petals
Where her breasts rise.

But you, your eyebrows' hairiness
With tweezers you've attacked.
You've filled your faces' cracks with white
Where time has roughly hacked,
Until you look a plaster corpse,
Death's whore, in fact.

HAG. I hope the cords that hold your bed
Grow rotten, and you fall on your head.
I hope next time you love in bed,
The mattress tears and you fall through
Whack on the floor, and get up dead—
That's what I hope for you.

And if a lover ever you take
I hope he's frigid as a snake,
Only a snake that you can't wake,
Though stroked and tossed that way and this,
A boneless snake that will not wake,
Not even with the longest kiss.

GIRL. I am so sad, what shall I do?
My lover is not come. . . .

And lonely I, lonely,
Wait here at home.

My mother has gone out, my mother
Has left me lonely here
With no one to protect me. . . .
No one, I fear.

Ah nurse, take pity on your child,
Bring my lover to me
And happy for the rest of your life
I'll pray that you may be.

How may you my true love tell?
O he is so proud
And so erectly always standing
He towers over the crowd.

HAG. It's clear to me that you must be
An ordinary whore;
But not only do you haggle
As they use for a man—
From the manner that you waggle
Your posterior,
I think that you're more:
Yes, a Lesbian!

GIRL. All this abuse is not much use,
And I will tell you why.
It cannot render pale
One blush of the beauty here
And so must ever fail
To steal my lover—I
Merrily defy
Your sweetest leer.

HAG. Sing on, sing on until you choke yourself.
Stick out your face, you kitten, your cat's face,
It's only luring the men in for me.

GIRL. Why? You're not dead yet, and your funeral
Alone could bring them in to lay you out.
That is a new joke isn't it?

HAG.   No, old.

GIRL. Stale jokes then for stale ears.

HAG. O my old age
Won't distress *you.*

GIRL. What will then? unless you mean
Your cheeks embossed with rouge and flaking whitewash?

HAG. Why do you talk to me?

GIRL. Why are you peeping?

HAG. I? O I am singing to myself
A song of sighs to dear Epigenes.

GIRL. I thought old lecher Geres was your dear.

HAG. You'll soon observe your error. The dear lad
Will come to me. And here he is in person.

GIRL. Not wanting anything from you, old Shrivel.

HAG. O yes he is, you poor anemic thing.

GIRL. His acts will show. Now I am going in.

HAG. And so am I. You'll see that I spoke truly.
(*They go inside;* EPIGENES *enters.*)

EPIGENES. O that I could freely lie
Down by my darling's kisses in bed,
And not be cursed
To take a filthy bitch there first,
Some harridan with but one eye,
Or else already half-blowsy-dead. . . .
I won't submit. Why should I, why?
O I think I'd rather die.

HAG (*appearing in the background*). Ah my boy, you'll soon
discover
That there's no such scot-free lover;
Now no more
Can you idle with your whore,
Love's not set to a slow song
Warbling anyhow along:
No longer foolish fondling beauty—
Strenuous duty
Must you show. . . .
So I'll watch where it is you go.

EPIGENES. If I could only find her in alone,
To whom I hurry, all my body flushed
With a new skin of radiant love and wine.

GIRL (*appearing above*). Ah, I have fooled that nasty bad old
thing.
She thinks I'm safely shut indoors, and so
She's waddled off somewhere. O and now I see
The very one that we were squabbling about.

Here I am, my lover....
Look up and see
Where I bend warmly over,
And come, dear, to me.

I love you, I love you,
I shall love till the end,
And I bend here above you,
Toward kisses I bend.

Tonight naked beside me
Your body must lie
And with kisses hide me
Naked too, or I die.

Ah you hurt me, each dimple
Twists my mouth, my head whirls,
And I choke at each simple
Toss of your curls.

Strangely, slowly,
Love aches sigh by sigh
Through me till wholly
Love's I lie.

Ah I would not be dead!
Love, pitiful be....
Cold is my bed,
Send my lover to me.

EPIGENES.   Come down, come down, my lovely one,
Come down, I implore.
Jump from your bed and lovingly run
To open the door.

Do you refuse? Then I shall fall
And moan here in despite.
Ah let me come in after all
And lie on your breasts tonight.

Ah let me lie there sweetly attacking
Your embattled hips,
Besieging your slapped buttocks, and sacking
Surrendered lips.

O Cypris, why must you have me mad?
O Love, more kindly be. . . .
Show how her kisses may be had,
And send her down to me.

I have sung enough to show
How sadly I stand
Singing here below,
Singing my sorrow—
You must understand.

And if you do, you'll come,
I know, to me,
Leaving your dark room,
Coming downstairs through the gloom
Silently.

Open, open: I cry.
If you could feel
How sadly I sadly sigh
Down you would steal;
And Love, O Love, you statue of light
Swimming golden through the night,
Child of Venus, honeybee
Of the Muses, milkily
O the Graces suckled thee—
Those beauties open, please, to me!

Open, open: I cry.
If you could feel
How sadly I sadly sigh
Down you would steal.

HAG. Who's this knocking? Hey, is it me you want?
EPIGENES. How?
HAG.   Well, you were rapping on my door.
EPIGENES. Damned if I was.
HAG.   Then why that spluttering torch?
    What do you want?
EPIGENES.   An Anaphlystian burgher,
    A self-lover, hands-and-fist man, no use to you.
HAG. What's his name?

EPIGENES.   If Sebinos—

HAG.   O zebb in us!

EPIGENES. Not if I can help it anyway.

HAG. But you can't help it, you simply have to do it.

EPIGENES. There is no need to delve in cases which
   Reach sixty years back; they're not to be entered.
   They are adjourned indefinitely. The only
   Ones we are probing are those under twenty.

HAG. That's how it was before the revolution.
   But now you have to put us through the first.

EPIGENES. Yes, if I want to. Appetite has no law.

HAG. And did you take your dinner by that law?

EPIGENES. I don't understand you. There's the girl I want.

HAG. Yes, but you must enter through my door
   To get at her.

EPIGENES.   But I have no desire
   To try a big bag lined with moldy linen.

HAG. I know I'm loved. I suppose you're wondering
   How a weak little thing like me is here unprotected....
   So kiss me quick.

EPIGENES.   I'm afraid of your lover. I won't.

HAG. Who's that?

EPIGENES.   The finest of our painters.

HAG.   Who?

EPIGENES. He paints life studies from the bottles of the dead.
   So go away, stand at the door that he may see you.

HAG. You can't fool me, I know what you're after.

EPIGENES. And that's exactly what I know of you.

HAG. By Aphrodite, my spirit's angel, I
   Will never let you go.

EPIGENES.   You rave, old lady.

HAG. You babble. So I am taking you to bed.

EPIGENES. O why do we waste our money buying hooks
   When this damned hag, let neatly upside down
   Into a well, could claw the buckets up,
   Using her crooked fingers for grappling irons.

HAG. Sarcasm's no good. I am taking you to bed.

EPIGENES. It's not your privilege unless you've paid
   Your taxes to the state: a fifth per cent.
   Of all your years.

HAG.   I am taking you to bed,
   Because I like a cozy lad like you
   For bedclothes.

EPIGENES.   I object peremptorily
To being bedclothes for a hag like you.
I won't.

HAG.   O yes you will. This says you will.

EPIGENES. What is it?

HAG.   The decree that makes you mine.

EPIGENES. Well, read it out.

HAG.   Then listen to me, dearie.
We lady legislators here enact:
If a boy wishes for a girl's embraces,
Ere he's permitted to perform the act
He must exercise himself, rehearse his paces
In an old woman; and if he refuses
To do so and essays with the girl to lie,
The old woman can do with him whatever she chooses,
Catching him by the best lever she can spy.

EPIGENES. Procrustean law! to procreate for a crust
Of measly after-kisses, racked to fit—

HAG. Now don't get agitated, you must obey.

EPIGENES. But couldn't some other man, a friend who knows me,
Come and bail me from your arms?

HAG. What's that? A man!
Man's credit is not worth one bushel now.

EPIGENES. Won't any pleas hold?

HAG.   No chicanery!

EPIGENES. I'll say that I'm a merchant, exempt from service.

HAG. Do so and be sorry.

EPIGENES.   Then must I come?

HAG. You must.

EPIGENES.   It's absolutely necessary?

HAG. Diomedean! a rape of destiny.

EPIGENES. Then sprinkle dittany about your bed
And break some vine twigs off and put them under,
Tie on the fillets, get a bottle of oil,
And place the water jar beside the door.

HAG. O you will buy me a garland yet, my sweetie.

EPIGENES. Yes, one of wax to smoke upon your death,
For I am sure that you're so crackly old
You'll be pitchforked into bits of flying flesh.
(*The* GIRL *comes out.*)

GIRL. Where are you pulling him?

HAG.   To bed. He's mine.

GIRL. I think you're wrong; he's far too young, just look!

He couldn't do a thing, no, not an inch;
And you are old enough to be his mother,
Not his woman. If this law's to work,
There'll be an Oedipus under every sheet.

HAG. You horrid vicious little thing! you thought
That argument out only from spite and envy.
I'll pay you for it.   (*Rushes away.*)

EPIGENES.   O by Zeus the Savior,
How can I speak my gratitude, my darling,
For being rescued from that ancient maw.
Tonight you'll find how large, how thick and pressing
And how recurrent are my piercing thanks.
(*Another* OLD WOMAN *enters.*)

SECOND HAG. Hullo, young woman, what's this you've got
    there?
Haven't you any respect for law? you know
That you can't have him till I've done with him.

EPIGENES. My God, damnation, O where did you pop from?
You horrible old woman, go to hell.
She's worse than the other, worse by a hundred wrinkles!

SECOND HAG. Come quietly, my lamb.

EPIGENES.   Dear girl, please help me!
Can you stand by and see me ravished, help!

SECOND HAG. It's not me, it's the law, that leads you in.

EPIGENES. She's a vampire belched from hell and clothed with
    blood
And festering blisters.

SECOND HAG.   Come on, duckie, come;
And don't have so much to say for yourself either.

EPIGENES. O let me go to a privy for a while
If you have any pity; if you refuse
There'll be an addition of yellow to the landscape.
I am so frightened.

SECOND HAG.   Come quietly along.
You can do it with me inside if you still wish.

EPIGENES. More than I wish, I fear. But let me go.
I'll give you two good sureties as bail.

SECOND HAG. Bail me no bails.
    (*Another* OLD WOMAN *appears.*)

THIRD HAG. Hullo, where are you going,
Boy, with that woman?

EPIGENES.   Going? I'm being dragged.
But heaven bless you whosoever you are
For stepping thus between me and my death.

(He turns.) O Heracles, O all you Pans, and O
You Corybantes and you Dioscuri!
She's worse again, worse trebly, worse than worse.
What is she? Language can't exude such horror.
A monkey clotted with cosmetics? or
A dirty ghost coughed up from hell's vast stench?

THIRD HAG. No funny business there; come quietly.

SECOND HAG. No, this way!

THIRD HAG.   I shall never let you go.

SECOND HAG. Nor I.

EPIGENES.   You bitches, stop, you'll have me in halves.

SECOND HAG. Obey the law and come into my bed.

THIRD HAG. I'm older, and I'm uglier; consequently
This boy belongs to me.

EPIGENES.   And if I die
Between the pits of your decaying loves
How shall I come to her that I adore?

SECOND HAG. That's for you to discover. This you must do.

EPIGENES. Well, then the quicker the better. Let's get it over.
Which first?

SECOND HAG.   You know, come here.

EPIGENES.   Then make her release me.

THIRD HAG. No, come with me.

EPIGENES.   I will if she'll let go.

SECOND HAG. Ho, but I won't.

THIRD HAG.   And that's my answer also.

EPIGENES. You'd do a lot of damage as ferrymen.

SECOND HAG. And why?

EPIGENES.   You'd tear the passengers to pieces
If this is how you compete.

SECOND HAG.   Shut up, come here.

THIRD HAG. Come here, I tell you.

EPIGENES.   O this game reminds me
Of that Canonos law: the way I'm fettered
With ropes of women skinnily hanging round me.
Can a man embrace two women when in halves?
Can I row the pair of you doubled-handed?

SECOND HAG. Eat onions, they'll make you strong enough.

EPIGENES.   Good Lord,
I've been dragged to the very door.

THIRD HAG.   But it's no use,
I'll come in too and wrestle abed for him.

EPIGENES. Heaven forbid! it's better far to grapple
With but one squirming evil than with two.

THIRD HAG. Yet now you will, by Hecate, and willy-nilly.
EPIGENES. O thrice unhappy am I who must lie
　　Upon an animated corpse all night
　　And all next day; and when at last shook off,
　　Will find another Phryne grinning at me,
　　A bottle of oil beside her deathy jaw.
　　Aren't I unlucky? O by God I am,
　　By Savior Zeus, a miserable man,
　　Who must swim through such a choppy stretch of flesh
　　Such a dank weedy ocean—very like
　　I shall go under and be drowned therein.
　　Ah if my sturdy breast stroke fails me at last
　　When I am forced to wade out of my depth
　　And swim through flotsam of love t'ward receding shores
　　Of beauty, and I sink sucked out of sight,
　　Bury my body at the harbor's mouth,
　　And take the upper hag, the sole survivor,
　　Black her with pitch and clamp her to the spot
　　With lead poured molten round her ankles: let
　　Her carcass stand memorial on my tomb,
　　A grimy substitute for the bottle of oil.
　　(*They pull him inside. Enter a* SERVANT GIRL, *drunk.*)
SERVANT. O all the blessed people and blessed myself
　　And my mistress the most blessed of us all
　　And O you blessed citizens who lounge
　　About our doors and all you blessed neighbors
　　And the whole town in short, in me you see
　　The blessed servant girl whose head just now
　　Was in a drench of precious unguents scented,
　　But the best perfume's certainly the wine,
　　Fragrant flagons full of Thasian vintage,
　　Yes, wine's the finest scent, the way it fumes
　　Inside instead of out with wreathing sweetness,
　　But all the others stalely evaporate
　　And thin away sickly, while the wine inside
　　Churns up a smoke of warmth and keeps on doing it.
　　It's the best thing in the world, easily the best,
　　O gods, isn't it? I'll tell you how:
　　Take the biggest jar and mix it neat without water,
　　Then pour it carefully down your throat and then
　　It makes you feel chirpy and snugglish all the night.
　　But, ladies, can you tell me where my master is?
　　The husband of my mistress of course I mean.
CHORUS. Wait here, he'll be along now any time.

SERVANT. Yes, here he comes. He's going off to dine.
O master, O you lucky man, aren't you happy?
BLEPYROS. Me?
SERVANT. Yes, you, by Zeus, you should be happy.
What greater luck could pinnacle a man
High on a crag of bliss than that he only
Out of city of some thirty thousand
Should go without his dinner?
CHORUS.   Felicitously
You phrase a happy man.
SERVANT.   Here, where are you going?
BLEPYROS. I'm off to have my dinner.
SERVANT.   The last of all,
By Aphrodite! Still, your wife's instructions
Were that I was to find you and fetch you in,
You and these little girls. And I can promise
There are gallons of Chian wine there yet undrunk,
And other dainties not yet guzzled. Come,
Don't waste more time; and let the audience
(That is, those of them who think our play's a good one)
And any judge who's going to vote for us,
Come along too. There's room enough for all.
BLEPYROS. No, let's have no omissions. Ask them all,
Be generously rash, invite the whole crowd,
Grandfather, lad, and child; freely proclaim
That every one of them will find a table
Provided with the sustenance they need,
In their own homes. But ah, it's time I went.
I must rush away, and here's a handy torch.
CHORUS. Then why do you keep delaying on and on?
Your daughters there are famished. Take them along,
We'll make a din and sing a dinner song.
While you are going. But you judges, first
I want a word with you, to put you all right—
Let the serious wiseheads choose me because of my serious
side,
The jokes being mere additions not too profuse for them.
Let the wags also choose me for the witticisms I provide,
The other part being but a mere excuse for them.
Then clearly I must win the suffrages of one and all.
Don't let the impression made by us begin at length to pall
Because our play is acted first and others get between
That seem better plays for no other reason than that they
were later seen.

But keep your oaths and judge the plays as justly as you
can:

> Don't be like harlots who can't tell
> Very well
> Which lover truly is the man
> They want, because they always cast
> Their vote of kisses on the last.

> But ho! ho!
> It's time to go.

Stop your song and come along: if you mean to come be
dumb.

> Dinner's ready, left right left!
> Here steady, clumsy, take more care.
> First your right leg: put it there,
> Then the left leg, stuck out so. . . .
> Time to go!
> A Cretan measure.

BLEPYROS. Yes, with pleasure.

CHORUS. Come swing your bellies
Not yet filled with lazy jellies,
Give your legs to the rhythm, show
Appetite twisting head and toe
To and fro.
Soon there will appear a dish
Smoking with oysters and saltfish shark and lark and little
bits in a jar with vinegar on sharp spits and leeks with
honey thrush blackbird dove pigeons roasted with cock's
brain above throstle jostling cushat flush at top with hare
in wine stewed fine hued syrupy and fricassee—

> Chirruping we'll eat it quick
> Until we're sick.

> So now you know your way about,
> Snatch an omelet and get out,
> Find a corner where you can sit
> And immediately swallow it.

BLEPYROS. They're at it now already, hark!

CHORUS. Then up and off, away, hooray!
Iai, euai,
Dinner! euoi, euai, euai
And may our play be the winner!
Euai, euai, euai, euai!

(Exeunt.)

Plutus

Plutus (388 B.C.) is so different from its predecessors that it must be counted with the new genre of Middle Comedy, of which it is, indeed, our only specimen. It attacks no contemporary situation or person but is rather a travesty of myth which has general application. No individual or institution could take exception to the notion that good men are afflicted with poverty because Plutus (Wealth) is blind. When his blindness is healed things are made right, but we can see that they will not remain so, because of human avarice and ambition. Because it is easy and edifying and requires little commentary *Plutus* was the most widely read of all Aristophanes' plays in the Byzantine period. Instead of choral lyrics there is now merely the mark *chorou*, indicating where a choral interlude was to be provided, as there was to be in New Comedy also. So Cario is the forerunner of the contriving slave of New Comedy.

CHARACTERS

CARIO, SERVANT OF
    CHREMYLUS
CHREMYLUS
PLUTUS, GOD OF WEALTH
BLEPSIDEMUS
POVERTY
WIFE OF CHREMYLUS
A GOOD MAN

AN INFORMER
AN OLD LADY
A YOUTH
HERMES
A PRIEST OF ZEUS
CHORUS OF NEEDY
    AGRICULTURISTS

Translated by B. B. Rogers

(Blind PLUTUS *is seen groping his way on an Athenian street, followed by* CHREMYLUS *and his slave* CARIO.)

CARIO. How hard it is, O Zeus and all ye gods,
To be the slave of a demented master!
For though the servant give the best advice,
Yet if his owner otherwise decide,
The servant needs must share the ill results.
For a man's body, such is fate, belongs
Not to himself, but to whoe'er has bought it.
So much for that. But now with Loxias,
Who from his golden tripod chants his high
Oracular strains, I've got a bone to pick.
A wise Physician-seer they call him, yet
He has sent my master off so moody-mad,
That now he's following a poor blind old man,
Just the reverse of what he ought to do.
For we who see should go *before* the blind,
But he goes *after* (and constrains me too)
One who won't answer even with a gr-r-r.
I won't keep silence, master, no I won't,
Unless you tell me why you're following *him.*
I'll plague you, sir; I know you won't chastise me
So long as I've this sacred chaplet on.

CHREMYLUS. I'll pluck it off, that you may smart the more,
If you keep bothering.

CARIO.   Humbug! I won't stop
Until you have told me who the fellow is.
You know I ask it out of love for you.

CHREMYLUS. I'll tell you, for of all my servants you
I count the truest and most constant—thief.
—I've been a virtuous and religious man
Yet always poor and luckless.

CARIO.   So you have.

CHREMYLUS. While Temple breakers, orators, informers,
And knaves grow rich and prosper.

CARIO.   So they do.

CHREMYLUS. So then I went to question of the god—
Not for myself, the quiver of my life
Is well-nigh emptied of its arrows now,—
But for my son, my only son, to ask

If, changing all his habits, he should turn
A rogue, dishonest, rotten to the core.
For such as they, methinks, succeed the best.

CARIO. And what droned Phoebus from his wreaths of bay?

CHREMYLUS. He told me plainly that with whomsoe'er
I first forgathered as I left the shrine,
Of him I never should leave go again,
But win him back, in friendship, to my home.

CARIO. With whom then did you first forgather?

CHREMYLUS.   Him.

CARIO. And can't you see the meaning of the god,
Your ignoramus, who so plainly tells you
Your son should follow the prevailing fashion?

CHREMYLUS. Why think you that?

CARIO.   He means that even the blind
Can see 'tis better for our present life
To be a rascal, rotten to the core.

CHREMYLUS. 'Tis not that way the oracle inclines,
It cannot be. 'Tis something more than that.
Now if this fellow told us who he is,
And why and wherefore he has come here now,
We'd soon discover what the god intended.

CARIO (to PLUTUS). Hallo, you sirrah, tell me who you are,
Or take the consequence! Out with it, quick!

PLUTUS. Go and be hanged!

CARIO.   O master, did you hear
The name he gave?

CHREMYLUS.   'Twas meant for you, not me.
You ask in such a rude and vulgar way.
(To PLUTUS). Friend, if you love an honest gentleman,
Tell me your name.

PLUTUS.   Get out, you vagabond!

CARIO. O! O! Accept the omen, and the man.

CHREMYLUS. O, by Demeter, you shall smart for this.
Answer this instant or you die the death.

PLUTUS. Men, men, depart and leave me.

CHREMYLUS.   Wouldn't you like it?

CARIO. O master, what I say is far the best:
I'll make him die a miserable death.
I'll set him on some precipice, and leave him,
So then he'll topple down and break his neck.

CHREMYLUS. Up with him!

PLUTUS.   O pray don't.

CHREMYLUS. Do you mean to answer?

PLUTUS. And if I do, I'm absolutely sure
You'll treat me ill: you'll never let me go.

CHREMYLUS. I vow we will, at least if you desire it.

PLUTUS. Then first unhand me.

CHREMYLUS. There, we both unhand you.

PLUTUS. Then listen, both: for I, it seems, must needs
Reveal the secret I proposed to keep.
Know then, I'm Wealth!

CHREMYLUS. You most abominable.
Of all mankind, you, Plutus, and keep it snug!

CARIO. You, Plutus, in such a miserable plight!

CHREMYLUS. O King Apollo! O ye gods and daemons!
O Zeus! what mean you? are you really *he?*

PLUTUS. I am.

CHREMYLUS. Himself?

PLUTUS. His own self's self.

CHREMYLUS. Whence come you
So grimed with dirt?

PLUTUS. From Patrocles's house,
A man who never washed in all his life.

CHREMYLUS. And this, your sad affliction, how came this?

PLUTUS. 'Twas Zeus that caused it, jealous of mankind.
For, when a little chap, I used to brag
I'd visit none except the wise and good
And orderly; he therefore made me blind,
That I might ne'er distinguish which was which,
So jealous is he always of the good!

CHREMYLUS. And yet 'tis only from the just and good
His worship comes.

PLUTUS. I grant you that.

CHREMYLUS. Then tell me,
If you could see again as once you could,
Would you avoid the wicked?

PLUTUS. Yes, I would.

CHREMYLUS. And visit all the good?

PLUTUS. Yes; more by token
I have not seen the good for many a day.

CHREMYLUS. No more have I, although I've got my eyes.

PLUTUS. Come, let me go; you know my story now.

CHREMYLUS. And therefore, truly, hold we on the more.

PLUTUS. I told you so: you vowed you'd let me go.
I knew you wouldn't.

CHREMYLUS.   O be guided, pray,
And don't desert me. Search where'er you will
You'll never find a better man than I.

CARIO. No more there is, by Zeus—except myself.

PLUTUS. They all say that; but when in sober earnest
They find they've got me, and are wealthy men,
They place no limit on their evil ways.

CHREMYLUS. Too true! And yet not every one is bad.

PLUTUS. Yes, every single one.

CARIO (aside).   You'll smart for that.

CHREMYLUS. Nay, nay, but hear what benefits you'll get
If you're persuaded to abide with us.
For well I trust—I trust, with God to aid,
That I shall rid you of this eye disease,
And make you see.

PLUTUS.   For mercy's sake, forbear.
I do not wish to see again.

CHREMYLUS.   Eh? what?

CARIO. O why, the man's a born unfortunate!

PLUTUS. Let Zeus but hear their follies, and I know
He'll pay me out.

CHREMYLUS.   And doesn't he do that now;
Letting you wander stumbling through the world?

PLUTUS. Eh, but I'm horribly afraid of Zeus!

CHREMYLUS. Aye, say you so, you cowardliest God alive?
What! do you think the imperial power of Zeus
And all his thunderbolts were worth one farthing,
Could you but see, for ever so short a time?

PLUTUS. Ah, don't say that, you wretches!

CHREMYLUS.   Don't be frightened!
I'll prove that you're far stronger, mightier far
Than Zeus.

PLUTUS.   You'll prove that I am?

CHREMYLUS.   Easily.
Come, what makes Zeus the Ruler of the Gods?

CARIO. His silver. He's the wealthiest of them.

CHREMYLUS.   Well,
Who gives him all his riches?

CARIO.   Our friend here.

CHREMYLUS. And for whose sake do mortals sacrifice
To Zeus?

CARIO.   For his: and pray straight out for wealth.

CHREMYLUS. 'Tis all his doing: and 'tis he can quickly
Undo it if he will.

PLUTUS. How mean you that?

CHREMYLUS. I mean that nevermore will mortal man
    Bring ox, or cake, or any sacrifice,
    If such your will.

PLUTUS. How so?

CHREMYLUS. How can he buy
    A gift to offer, if your power deny
    The needful silver? Singlehanded, you,
    If Zeus prove troublesome, can crush his power.

PLUTUS. Men sacrifice to Zeus for *me?*

CHREMYLUS. They do.
    And whatsoever in the world is bright,
    And fair, and graceful, all is done for you.
    For every mortal thing subserves to Wealth.

CARIO. Hence for a little filthy lucre I'm
    A slave, forsooth, because I've got no wealth.

CHREMYLUS. And those Corinthian hussies, so they say,
    If he who sues them for their love is poor,
    Turn up their noses at the man; but grant
    A wealthy suitor more than he desires.

CARIO. So too the boy-loves; just to get some money,
    And not at all because they love their lovers.

CHREMYLUS. Those are the baser, not the nobler sort,
    These never ask for money.

CARIO. No? what then?

CHREMYLUS. O one a hunter, one a pack of hounds.

CARIO. Ah, they're ashamed, I warrant, of their vice,
    And seek to crust it over with a name.

CHREMYLUS. And every art existing in the world,
    And every craft, was for your sake invented.
    For you one sits and cobbles all the day,
    One works in bronze, another works in wood,
    One fuses gold—the gold derived from you—

CARIO. One plies the footpad's, one the burglar's trade,

CHREMYLUS. One is a fuller, one a sheepskin washer,
    One is a tanner, one an onion seller,
    Through you the nabbed adulterer gets off plucked.

PLUTUS. O, and all this I never knew before!

CHREMYLUS. Aye, 'tis on him the Great King plumes himself;
    And our Assemblies all are held for him;
    Do you not man our triremes? Answer that.
    Does he not feed the foreign troop at Corinth?
    Won't Pamphilus be brought to grief for him?

CARIO. Won't Pamphilus and the needle seller too?
   Does not Agyrrhius flout us all for him?
CHREMYLUS. Does not Philepsius tell his tales for you?
   Do you not make the Egyptians our allies?
   And Laïs love the uncouth Philonides?
CARIO. Timotheus' tower—
CHREMYLUS.   Pray Heaven it fall and crush you!
   Aye, everything that's done is done for you.
   You are alone, yourself alone, the source
   Of all our fortunes, good and bad alike.
   'Tis so in war; wherever *he* alights,
   That side is safe the victory to win.
PLUTUS. Can I, unaided, do such feats as these?
CHREMYLUS. O yes, by Zeus, and many more than these.
   So that none ever has enough of you.
   Of all things else a man may have too much,
   Of love,
CARIO.   Of loaves,
CHREMYLUS.   Of literature,
CARIO.   Of sweets,
CHREMYLUS. Of honor,
CARIO.   Cheesecakes,
CHREMYLUS.   Manliness,
CARIO.   Dried figs,
CHREMYLUS. Ambition,
CARIO.   Barley meal,
CHREMYLUS.   Command,
CARIO.   Pea soup.
CHREMYLUS. But no man ever has enough of you.
   For give a man a sum of thirteen talents,
   And all the more he hungers for sixteen;
   Give him sixteen, and he must needs have forty,
   Or life's not worth his living, so he says.
PLUTUS. Ye seem to me to speak extremely well,
   Yet on one point I'm fearful.
CHREMYLUS.   What is that?
PLUTUS. This mighty power which ye ascribe to me,
   I can't imagine how I'm going to wield it.
CHREMYLUS. O this it is that all the people say,
   Wealth is the cowardliest thing.
PLUTUS.   It is not true.
   That is some burglar's slander; breaking into
   A wealthy house, he found that everything

Was under lock and key, and so got nothing:
Wherefore he called my forethought, cowardliness.

CHREMYLUS. Well, never mind; assist us in the work
And play the man; and very soon I'll make you
Of keener sight than ever Lynceus was.

PLUTUS. Why, how can you, a mortal man, do that?

CHREMYLUS. Good hope have I from that which Phoebus told
me,
Shaking the Pythian laurel as he spoke.

PLUTUS. Is Phoebus privy to your plan?

CHREMYLUS.   He is.

PLUTUS. Take heed!

CHREMYLUS.   Don't fret yourself, my worthy friend.
I am the man: I'll work the matter through,
Though I should die for it.

CARIO.   And so will I.

CHREMYLUS. And many other bold allies will come,
Good virtuous men without a grain of—barley.

PLUTUS. Bless me! a set of rather poor allies.

CHREMYLUS. Not when you've made them wealthy men once
more.
Hi, Cario, run your fastest, and

CARIO.   Do what?

CHREMYLUS. Summon my farm companions from the fields
(You'll find them there, poor fellows, hard at work),
And fetch them hither; so that each and all
May have, with me, an equal share in Wealth.

CARIO. Here goes! I'm off. Come out there, somebody,
And carry in my little piece of meat.

CHREMYLUS. I'll see to that: you, run away directly.
But you, dear Wealth, the mightiest power of all,
Come underneath my roof. Here stands the house,
Which you are going evermore to fill
With wealth and plenty, by fair means or foul.

PLUTUS. And yet it irks me, I protest it does,
To enter in beneath a stranger's roof.
I never got the slightest good from that.
Was it a miser's house; the miser straight
Would dig a hole and pop me underground;
And if some worthy neighbor came to beg
A little silver for his urgent needs,
Would vow he'd never seen me in his life.
Or was it some young madcap's: in a jiffy

Squandered and lost amongst his drabs and dice
I'm bundled, naked, out of house and home.

CHREMYLUS. You never chanced upon a moderate man,
But now you have; for such a man am I.
For much I joy in saving, no man more,
And much in spending when 'tis right to spend.
So go we in; I long to introduce
My wife and only son whom most I love—
After yourself of course.

PLUTUS.   That I believe.

CHREMYLUS. Why should one say what is not true to you?

CARIO. O ye who many a day have chewed a root of thyme
    with master,
  My labor-loving village friends be pleased to step out
    faster;
  Be staunch and strong, and stride along, let nothing now
    delay you,
  Your fortunes lie upon the die, come save them quick, I
    pray you.

CHORUS. Now don't you see we're bustling, we, as fast as we
    can go, sir?
  We're not so young as once we were, and Age is somewhat
    slow, sir.
  You'd think it fun to see us run, and that before you've
    told us
  The reason why your master seems so anxious to be-
    hold us.

CARIO. Why, I've been telling long ago; 'tis you are not at-
    tending!
  He bade me call and fetch you all that you, forever ending
  This chill ungenial life of yours, might lead a life luxurious.

CHORUS. Explain to me how that can be; i' faith I'm rather
    curious.

CARIO. He's got a man, an ancient man, of sorriest form and
    feature,
  Bald, toothless, squalid, wrinkled, bent, a very loathsome
    creature.
  I really should not be surprised to hear the wretch is
    circumcised.

CHORUS. O Messenger of golden news, you thrill my heart with
    pleasure.
  I do believe the man has come with quite a heap of
    treasure!

CARIO. O aye, he's got a heap, I guess, a heap of woes and
  wretchedness.

CHORUS. You think, I see, you think you're free to gull me with
  impunity.

  No, no; my stick I've got and quick I'll get my opportunity.

CARIO. What, think you I'm the sort of man such things as that
  to do, sirs?

  Am I a man a tale to tell wherein there's nothing true, sirs?

CHORUS. How absolute the knave has grown! your shins, my
  boy, are bawling

  Ah! Ah! with all their might and main, for gyves and fetters
  calling.

CARIO. You've drawn your lot; the grave you've got to judge
  in; why delay now?

  Old Charon gives the ticket there; why don't you pass away
  now?

CHORUS. Go hang yourself, you peevish elf, you born buffoon
  and scoffer.

  You love to tantalize and tease, nor condescend to offer

  A word of explanation why we're summoned here so hur-
  riedly.

  I had to shirk some urgent work, and here so quickly
  hasted,

  That many a tempting root of thyme I passed, and left
  untasted.

CARIO. I'll hide it not: 'tis Wealth we've got; the god of wealth
  we've captured,

  You'll all be rich and wealthy now. Ha, don't you look
  enraptured?

CHORUS. He says we'll all be wealthy now; upon my word this
  passes, sirs.

CARIO. O yes, you'll all be Midases, if only you've the asses'
  ears.

CHORUS. O I'm so happy, I'm so glad, I needs must dance for
  jollity,

  If what you say is really true, and not your own frivolity.

CARIO. And I before your ranks will go, *Threttanelo! Threttanelo!*

  And I, the Cyclops, heel and toe, will dance the sailor's
  hornpipe,—sol

  Come up, come up, my little ones all, come raise your
  multitudinous squall,

   Come bleating loudly the tuneful notes
   Of sheep and of rankly odorous goats.

Come follow along on your loves intent; come goats, 'tis
time to your meal ye went.

CHORUS. And you we'll seek where'er you go, *Threttanelo!*
Threttanelo!

And you, the Cyclops, will we find in dirty, drunken sleep
reclined,

Your well-stuffed wallet beside you too, with many a pot-
herb bathed in dew.

And then from out of the fire we'll take
A sharply pointed and burning stake,

And whirling it round till our shoulders ache, its flame in
your hissing eyeball slake.

CARIO. And now I'll change to Circe's part, who mixed her
drugs with baleful art;

Who late in Corinth, as I've learned, Philonides's comrades
turned
To loathsome swine in a loathsome sty,

And fed them all on kneaded dung which, kneading, she
among them flung.

And turn you all into swine will I.
And then ye'll grunt in your bestial glee
Wee! wee! wee!
Follow your mother, pigs, quoth she.

CHORUS. We'll catch you, Circe dear, we will; who mix your
drugs with baleful skill;

Who with enchantments strange and vile ensnare our comrades and defile;
We'll hang you up as you erst were hung

By bold Odysseus, lady fair; and then as if a goat you were
We'll rub your nose in the kneaded dung.
Like Aristyllus you'll gape with glee
Wee! wee! wee!
Follow your mother, pigs, quoth he.

CARIO. But now, old mates, break off, break off; no longer may
we jest and scoff;
No longer play the fool today.
And ye must sail on another tack,
While I, behind my master's back,
Rummage for meat and bread to eat,

And then, while yet the food I chew, I'll join the work we
are going to do.

CHREMYLUS. To bid you "welcome," fellow burghers, now
Is old and musty; so I—"clasp" you all.

Ye who have come in this stouthearted way,
This strenuous way, this unrelaxing way,
Stand by me now, and prove yourselves today
In very truth the Saviors of the god.

CHORUS. Fear not: I'll bear me like the god of War.
What, shall we push and hustle in the Assembly
To gain our three poor obols, and today
Let Wealth be wrested from our grasp?

CHREMYLUS. And here, I see, comes Blepsidemus too.
Look! by his speed and bearing you can tell
He has heard a rumor of what's happening here.
(*Enter* BLEPSIDEMUS.)

BLEPSIDEMUS. What can it mean? Old Chremylus grown
wealthy!
Then whence and how? I don't believe that story.
And yet by Heracles 'twas bruited wide
Among the loungers in the barbers' shops
That Chremylus had all at once grown rich.
And if he has, 'tis passing wonderful
That he should call his neighbors in to share.
That's not our country's fashion, anyhow.

CHREMYLUS. I'll tell him everything. O Blepsidemus,
We're better off today than yesterday.
You are my friend, and you shall share in all.

BLEPSIDEMUS. What, are you really wealthy, as men say?

CHREMYLUS. Well, if God will, I shall be presently.
But there's some risk, some risk, about it yet.

BLEPSIDEMUS. What sort of risk?

CHREMYLUS.   Such as—

BLEPSIDEMUS.   Pray, pray go on.

CHREMYLUS. If we succeed, we're prosperous all our lives:
But if we fail, we perish utterly.

BLEPSIDEMUS. I like not this; there's something wrong behind,
Some evil venture. To become, offhand,
So overwealthy, and to fear such risks,
Smacks of a man who has done some rotten thing.

CHREMYLUS. Rotten! what mean you?

BLEPSIDEMUS.   If you've stolen aught,
Or gold or silver, from the God out there,
And now perchance repent you of your sin—

CHREMYLUS. Apollo shield us! no, I've not done that.

BLEPSIDEMUS. O don't tell *me*. I see it plainly now.

CHREMYLUS. Pray don't suspect me of such crimes.

BLEPSIDEMUS. Alas!
There's nothing sound or honest in the world,
The love of money overcomes us all.

CHREMYLUS. Now by Demeter, friend, you have lost your wits.

BLEPSIDEMUS. O how unlike the man he used to be!

CHREMYLUS. Poor chap, you're moody-mad: I vow you are.

BLEPSIDEMUS. His very eye's grown shifty: he can't look you
Straight in the face: I warrant he's turned rogue.

CHREMYLUS. I understand. You think I've stolen something,
And want a share.

BLEPSIDEMUS. I want a share? in what?

CHREMYLUS. But 'tis not so: the thing's quite otherwise.

BLEPSIDEMUS. Not stol'n, but robbed outright?

CHREMYLUS. The man's possessed.

BLEPSIDEMUS. Have you embezzled someone else's cash?

CHREMYLUS. I haven't: no.

BLEPSIDEMUS. O Heracles, where now
Can a man turn! you won't confess the truth.

CHREMYLUS. You bring your charge before you have heard the
facts.

BLEPSIDEMUS. Now prithee let me hush the matter up
For a mere trifle, ere it all leaks out.
A few small coins will stop the speakers' mouths.

CHREMYLUS. You'd like, I warrant, in your friendly way,
To spend three minas, and to charge me twelve.

BLEPSIDEMUS. I see an old man pleading for his life
With olive branch in hand, and at his side
His weeping wife and children, shrewdly like
The suppliant Heracleids of Pamphilus.

CHREMYLUS. Nay, luckless idiot, 'tis the good alone
And right- and sober-minded that I'm going
At once to make so wealthy.

BLEPSIDEMUS. Heaven and earth!
What, have you stol'n so largely?

CHREMYLUS. O confound it,
You'll be my death.

BLEPSIDEMUS. You'll be your own, I fancy.

CHREMYLUS. Not so, you reprobate; 'tis *Wealth* I've got.

BLEPSIDEMUS. You, wealth! What sort of wealth?

CHREMYLUS. The god himself.

BLEPSIDEMUS. Where? where?

CHREMYLUS. Within.

BLEPSIDEMUS. Where?

CHREMYLUS. In my house.

BLEPSIDEMUS. In yours?

CHREMYLUS. Yes.

BLEPSIDEMUS. You be hanged! Plutus in your house?

CHREMYLUS. I swear it.

BLEPSIDEMUS. Is this the truth?

CHREMYLUS. It is.

BLEPSIDEMUS. By Hestia?

CHREMYLUS. Aye; by Poseidon.

BLEPSIDEMUS. Him that rules the sea?

CHREMYLUS. If there's another, by that other too.

BLEPSIDEMUS. Then don't you send him round for friends to share?

CHREMYLUS. Not yet; things haven't reached that stage.

BLEPSIDEMUS. What stage? The stage of sharing?

CHREMYLUS. Aye, we've first to—

BLEPSIDEMUS. What?

CHREMYLUS. Restore the sight—

BLEPSIDEMUS. Restore the sight of whom?

CHREMYLUS. The sight of Plutus, by any means we can.

BLEPSIDEMUS. What, is he really blind?

CHREMYLUS. He really is.

BLEPSIDEMUS. O that is why he never came to me.

CHREMYLUS. But now he'll come, if such the will of Heaven.

BLEPSIDEMUS. Had we not better call a doctor in?

CHREMYLUS. Is there a doctor now in all the town? There are no fees, and therefore there's no skill.

BLEPSIDEMUS. Let's think awhile.

CHREMYLUS. There's none.

BLEPSIDEMUS. No more there is.

CHREMYLUS. Why then, 'tis best to do what I intended, To let him lie inside Asclepius' temple A whole night long.

BLEPSIDEMUS. That's far the best, I swear it. So don't be dawdling: quick; get something done.

CHREMYLUS. I'm going.

BLEPSIDEMUS. Make you haste.

CHREMYLUS. I'm doing that.

POVERTY. You pair of luckless manikins who dare A rash, unholy, lawless deed to do— Where! What! Why flee ye? Tarry?

BLEPSIDEMUS. Heracles!

POVERTY. I'll make you die a miserable death. For ye have dared a deed intolerable

Which no one else has ever dared to do,
Or god or man! Now therefore ye must die.

CHREMYLUS. But who are you that look so pale and wan?

BLEPSIDEMUS. Belike some Fury from a tragic play.
She has a wild and tragic sort of look.

CHREMYLUS. No, for she bears no torch.

BLEPSIDEMUS. The worse for her.

POVERTY. What do you take me for?

CHREMYLUS. Some pothouse girl
Or omelette seller: else you would not bawl
At us so loudly ere you're harmed at all.

POVERTY. Not harmed! Why, is it not a shameful thing
That you should seek to drive me from the land?

CHREMYLUS. At all events you've got the Deadman's Pit.
But tell us quickly who and what you are.

POVERTY. One who is going to pay you out today
Because ye seek to banish me from hence.

BLEPSIDEMUS. Is it the barmaid from the neighboring tap
Who always cheats me with her swindling pint pots?

POVERTY. It's *Poverty*, your mate for many a year!

BLEPSIDEMUS. O King Apollo and ye gods, I'm off.

CHREMYLUS. Hi! What are you at? Stop, stop, you coward you,
Stop, can't you?

BLEPSIDEMUS. Anything but that.

CHREMYLUS. Pray stop.
What! shall one woman scare away two men?

BLEPSIDEMUS. But this is Poverty herself, you rogue,
The most destructive pest in all the world.

CHREMYLUS. Stay, I implore you, stay.

BLEPSIDEMUS. Not I, by Zeus.

CHREMYLUS. Why, this, I tell you, were the cowardliest deed
That ere was heard of, did we leave the god
Deserted here, and flee away ourselves
Too scared to strike one blow in his defense.

BLEPSIDEMUS. O, on what arms, what force, can we rely?
Is there a shield, a corselet, anywhere
Which this vile creature has not put in pawn?

CHREMYLUS. Courage! the god will, singlehanded, rear
A trophy o'er this atrophied assailant.

POVERTY. What! dare you mutter, you two outcasts you,
Caught in the act, doing such dreadful deeds?

CHREMYLUS. O, you accursed jade, why come you here
Abusing us? We never did you wrong.

POVERTY. No wrong, forsooth! O by the heavenly Powers
 No wrong to *me*, your trying to restore
 Plutus' sight again?

CHREMYLUS. How can it injure *you*,
 If we are trying to confer a blessing
 On all mankind?

POVERTY. Blessing! what blessing?

CHREMYLUS. What?
 Expelling *you* from Hellas, first of all.

POVERTY. Expelling *me* from Hellas! Could you do
 A greater injury to mankind than that?

CHREMYLUS. A greater? Yes; by *not* expelling you.

POVERTY. Now that's a question I am quite prepared
 To argue out at once; and if I prove
 That I'm the source of every good to men,
 And that by me ye live—but if I fail,
 Then do thereafter whatsoe'er ye list.

CHREMYLUS. You dare to offer this, you vixen you?

POVERTY. And you, accept it: easily enough
 Methinks I'll show you altogether wrong
 Making the good men rich, as you propose.

BLEPSIDEMUS. O clubs and pillories! To the rescue! Help!

POVERTY. Don't shout and storm before you have heard the facts.

BLEPSIDEMUS. Who can help shouting, when he hears such wild
 Extravagant notions?

POVERTY. Any man of sense.

CHREMYLUS. And what's the penalty you'll bear, in case
 You lose the day?

POVERTY. Whate'er you please.

CHREMYLUS. 'Tis well.

POVERTY. But, if ye are worsted, ye must bear the same.

BLEPSIDEMUS (*to* CHREMYLUS). Think you that twenty deaths
 are fine enough?

CHREMYLUS. Enough for *her*; but two will do for us.

POVERTY. Well then, be quick about it; for, indeed,
 How can my statements be with truth gainsaid?

CHORUS. Find something, I pray, philosophic to say, whereby
 you may vanquish and rout her.
 No thought of retreat; but her arguments meet with arguments stronger and stouter.

CHREMYLUS. All people with me, I am sure, will agree, for to
 all men alike it is clear,

That the honest and true should enjoy, as their due, a
    successful and happy career,
Whilst the lot of the godless and wicked shall fall in exactly
    the opposite sphere.
'Twas to compass this end that myself and my friend have
    been thinking as hard as we can,
And have hit on a nice beneficial device, a truly magnificent
    plan.
For if Plutus should attain to his eyesight again, nor among
    us so aimlessly roam,
To the dwellings I know of the good he would go, nor ever
    depart from their home.
The unjust and profane with disgust and disdain he is cer-
    tain thereafter to shun,
Till all shall be honest and wealthy at last, to virtue and
    opulence won.
Is there any design more effective than mine a blessing on
    men to confer?

BLEPSIDEMUS. No, nothing, that's flat; I will answer for that;
    so don't be inquiring of *her*.

CHREMYLUS. For our life of today were a man to survey and
    consider its chances aright,
He might fancy, I ween, it were madness or e'en the sport
    of some mischievous sprite.
So often the best of the world is possessed by the most
    undeserving of men,
Who have gotten their pile of money by vile injustice; so
    often again
The righteous are seen to be famished and lean, yea, with
    you as their comrade to dwell.
Now if Wealth were tonight to recover his sight, and her
    from among us expel,
Can you tell me, I pray, a more excellent way of bestowing
    a boon on mankind?

POVERTY. O men on the least provocation prepared to be crazy
    and out of your mind,
Men bearded and old, yet companions enrolled in the
    Order of zanies and fools,
O what is the gain that the world would obtain were it
    governed by you and your rules?
Why, if Wealth should allot himself equally out (assume
    that his sight you restore),
Then none would to science his talents devote or practice a
    craft any more.

Yet if science and art from the world should depart, pray
  whom would ye get for the future

To build you a ship, or your leather to snip, or to make you
  a wheel or a suture?

Do ye think that a man will be likely to tan, or a smithy or
  laundry to keep,

Or to break up the soil with his plowshare, and toil the
  fruits of Demeter to reap,

If regardless of these he can dwell at his ease, a life without
  labor enjoying?

CHREMYLUS. Absurd! why the troubles and tasks you describe
  we of course shall our servants employ in.

POVERTY. Your servants! But how will you get any now? I
  pray you the secret to tell.

CHREMYLUS. With the silver we've got we can purchase a lot.

POVERTY.   But who is the man that will sell?

CHREMYLUS. Some merchant from Thessaly coming, belike,
  where most of the kidnapers dwell.

Who still, for the sake of the gain he will make, with the
  slaves that we want will provide us.

POVERTY. But first let me say, if we walk in the way wherein
  ye are seeking to guide us,

There'll be never a kidnaper left in the world. No merchant
  of course (can ye doubt it?)

His life would expose to such perils as those had he plenty
  of money without it.

No, no; I'm afraid you must handle the spade and follow
  the plowtail in person,

Your life will have double the toil and the trouble it used to.

CHREMYLUS.   Yourself be your curse on!

POVERTY. No more on a bed will you pillow your head, for
  there won't be a bed in the land,

Nor carpets; for whom will you find at the loom, when he's
  plenty of money in hand?

Rich perfumes no more will ye sprinkle and pour as home
  you are bringing the bride,

Or apparel the fair in habiliments rare so cunningly fash-
  ioned and dyed.

Yet of little avail is your wealth if it fail such enjoyments as
  these to procure you.

You fools, it is I who alone a supply of the goods which you
  covet ensure you.

I sit like a mistress, by Poverty's lash constraining the
  needy mechanic;

When I raise it, to earn his living he'll turn, and work in a terrible panic.

CHREMYLUS. Why, what have *you* got to bestow but a lot of burns from the bathing-room station

And a hollow-cheeked rabble of destitute hags, and brats on the verge of starvation?

And the lice, if you please, and the gnats and the fleas whom I can't even count for their numbers,

Who around you all night will buzz and will bite, and arouse you betimes from your slumbers.

> *Up! up! they will shrill, 'tis to hunger, but still up! up! to your pain and privation.*

For a robe but a rag, for a bed but a bag of rushes which harbor a nation

Of bugs whose envenomed and tireless attacks would the soundest of sleepers awaken.

And then for a carpet a sodden old mat, which is falling to bits, must be taken.

And a jolly hard stone for a pillow you'll own; and, for griddle cakes barley and wheaten,

Must leaves dry and lean of the radish or e'en sour stalks of the mallow be eaten.

And the head of a barrel, stove in, for a chair; and, instead of a trough, for your kneading

A stave of a vat you must borrow, and that all broken. So great and exceeding

Are the blessings which Poverty brings in her train on the children of men to bestow!

POVERTY. The life you define with such skill is not mine: 'tis the life of a beggar, I trow.

CHREMYLUS. Well, Poverty, Beggary, truly the twain to be sisters we always declare.

POVERTY. Aye, *you!* who to good Thrasybulus forsooth Dionysius the Tyrant compare!

But the life I allot to my people is not, nor shall be, so full of distresses.

'Tis a beggar alone who has nought of his own, nor even an obol possesses.

My *poor* man, 'tis true, has to scrape and to screw and his work he must never be slack in;

There'll be no superfluity found in his cot; but then there will nothing be lacking.

CHREMYLUS. Damater! a life of the Blessed you give: forever to toil and to slave

At Poverty's call, and to leave after all not even enough for
a grave.

POVERTY. You are all for your jeers and your comedy sneers,
and you can't be in earnest a minute,

Nor observe that alike in their bodily frame and the spirit
residing within it,

My people are better than Wealth's; for by *him*, men
bloated and gross are presented,

Fat rogues with big bellies and dropsical legs, whose toes
by the gout are tormented;

But mine are the lean and the wasplike and keen, who
strike at their foemen and sting them.

CHREMYLUS. Ah, yes; to a wasplike condition, no doubt, by
the pinch of starvation you bring them.

POVERTY. I can show you besides that Decorum abides with
those whom I visit; that mine

Are the modest and orderly folk, and that Wealth's are *with
insolence flushed and with wine*.

CHREMYLUS. 'Tis an orderly job, then, to thieve and to rob
and to break into houses by night.

BLEPSIDEMUS. Such modesty too! In whatever they do they are
careful to keep out of sight.

POVERTY. Behold in the cities the Orator tribe; when poor in
their early career

How faithful and just to the popular trust, how true to the
State they appear.

When wealth at the City's expense they have gained, they
are worsened at once by the pelf,

Intriguing the popular cause to defeat, attacking the People itself.

CHREMYLUS. That is perfectly true though 'tis spoken by you,
you spiteful malevolent witch!

But still you shall squall for contending that all had better
be poor than be rich.

So don't be elate; for a terrible fate shall your steps over-
take before long.

POVERTY. Why, I haven't yet heard the ghost of a word to
prove my contention is wrong.

You splutter and try to flutter and fly: but of argument
never a letter.

CHREMYLUS. Pray why do all people abhor you and shun?

POVERTY.   Because I'm for making them better.

So children, we see, from their parents will flee who would
teach them the way they should go.

So hardly we learn what is right to discern; so few what is
    best for them know.

CHREMYLUS. Then Zeus, I suppose, is mistaken, nor knows
    what most for his comfort and bliss is,

Since money and pelf he acquires for himself.

BLEPSIDEMUS.   And *her* to the earth he dismisses.

POVERTY. O dullards and blind! full of sties is your mind;
    there are tumors titantic within it.

Zeus wealthy! Not he: he's as poor as can be: and this I
    can prove in a minute.

If Zeus be so wealthy, how came it of yore that out of his
    riches abounding

He could find but a wreath of wild olive for those who
    should win at the games he was founding,

By all the Hellenes in each fourth year on Olympia's plains
    to be holden?

If Zeus were as wealthy and rich as you say, the wreath
    should at least have been golden.

CHREMYLUS. It is plain, I should think, 'tis from love of the
    chink that the conduct you mention arises;

The god is unwilling to lavish a doit of the money he loves
    upon prizes.

The rubbish may go to the victors below; the gold he re-
    tains in his coffers.

POVERTY. How dare you produce such a libel on Zeus, you
    couple of ignorant scoffers?

'Twere better, I'm sure, to be honest and poor, than rich
    and so stingy and screwing.

CHREMYLUS. Zeus crown you, I pray, with the wild olive spray,
    and send you away to your ruin!

POVERTY. To think that you dare to persist and declare that
    Poverty does not present you

With all that is noblest and best in your lives!

CHREMYLUS.   Will Hecate's judgment content you?

If you question her which are the better, the rich or the
    poor, she will say, I opine,

Each month do the wealthy a supper provide, to be used
    in my service divine,

But the poor lie in wait for a snatch at the plate, or e'er it
    is placed on my shrine.

      So away, nor retort with a g-r-r, you degraded
      Importunate scold!

Persuade me you may, but I won't be persuaded.

POVERTY. O Argos, behold!

CHREMYLUS. Nay Pauson, your messmate, to aid you invite.

POVERTY. O woe upon woe!

CHREMYLUS. Be off to the ravens; get out of my sight.

POVERTY. O where shall I go?

CHREMYLUS. Go? Go to the pillory; don't be so slack,
Nor longer delay.

POVERTY. Ah me, but ye'll speedily send for me back,
Who scout me today!

CHREMYLUS. When we send for you, come; not before. So
farewell!
With Wealth as my comrade 'tis better to dwell.
Get you gone, and bemoan your misfortunes alone.

BLEPSIDEMUS. I too have a mind for an opulent life
Of reveal and mirth with my children and wife,
Untroubled by Poverty's panics.
And then as I'm passing, all shiny and bright,
From my bath to my supper, what joy and delight
My fingers to snap in disdain at the sight
Of herself and her frowsy mechanics.

CHREMYLUS. That cursed witch, thank Heaven, has gone and
left us.
But you and I will take the god at once
To spend the night inside Asclepius' temple.

BLEPSIDEMUS. And don't delay one instant, lest there come
Some other hindrance to the work in hand.

CHREMYLUS. Hi! boy there, Cario, fetch me out the blankets,
And bring the god himself, with due observance,
And whatsoever is prepared within.

CARIO. Here's joy, here's happiness, old friends, for you
Who, at the feast of Theseus, many a time
Have ladled up small sops of barley broth!
Here's joy for you and all good folk besides.

CHREMYLUS. How now, you best of all your fellow knaves?
You seem to come a messenger of good.

CARIO. With happiest fortune has my master sped,
Or rather Plutus himself; no longer blind,
He hath relumed the brightness of his eyes,
So kind a healer hath Asclepius proved.

CHORUS (singing). Joy for the news you bring.
                                Joy! Joy! with shouts I sing.

CARIO. Aye, will you, nill you, it is joy indeed.

CHORUS (singing). Sing we with all our might Asclepius first
and best,
To men a glorious light, sire in his offspring blest.

WIFE. What means this shouting? Has good news arrived?
  For I've been sitting till I'm tired within
  Waiting for *him*, and longing for good news.

CARIO. Bring wine, bring wine, my mistress; quaff yourself
  The flowing bowl (you like it passing well).
  I bring you here all blessings in a lump.

WIFE. Where?

CARIO.   That you'll learn from what I am going to say.

WIFE. Be pleased to tell me with what speed you can.

CARIO. Listen. I'll tell you all this striking business
  Up from the foot on to the very head.

WIFE. Not on *my* head, I pray you.

CARIO.   Not the blessings
  We have all got?

WIFE.   Not all that striking business.

CARIO. Soon as we reached the temple of the god
  Bringing the man, most miserable then,
  But who so happy, who so prosperous now?
  Without delay we took him to the sea
  And bathed him there.

WIFE   O what a happy man,
  The poor old fellow bathed in the cold sea!

CARIO. Then to the precincts of the god we went.
  There on the altar honey cakes and bakemeats
  Were offered, food for the Hephaestian flame.
  There laid we Plutus as custom bids; and we
  Each for himself stitched up a pallet near.

WIFE. Were there no others waiting to be healed?

CARIO. Neocleides was, for one; the purblind man,
  Who in his thefts outshoots the keenest-eyed.
  And many others, sick with every form
  Of ailment. Soon the temple servitor
  Put out the lights, and bade us fall asleep,
  Nor stir, nor speak, whatever noise we heard.
  So down we lay in orderly repose.
  And I could catch no slumber, not one wink,
  Struck by a nice tureen of broth which stood
  A little distance from an old wife's head,
  Whereto I marvelously longed to creep.
  Then, glancing upward, I behold the priest
  Whipping the cheesecakes and the figs from off
  The holy table; thence he coasted round
  To every altar, spying what was left.
  And everything he found he consecrated

Into a sort of sack; so I, concluding
This was the right and proper thing to do,
Arose at once to tackle that tureen.

WIFE. Unhappy man! Did you not fear the god?

CARIO. Indeed I did, lest he should cut in first,
Garlands and all, and capture my tureen.
For so the priest forewarned me he might do.
Then the old lady when my steps she heard
Reached out a stealthy hand; I gave a hiss,
And mouthed it gently like a sacred snake.
Back flies her hand; she draws her coverlets
More tightly round her, and, beneath them, lies
In deadly terror like a frightened cat.
Then of the broth I gobbled down a lot
Till I could eat no more, and then I stopped.

WIFE. Did not the god approach you?

CARIO.   Not till later.
And then I did a thing will make you laugh.
For as he neared me, by some dire mishap
My wind exploded like a thunderclap.

WIFE. I guess the god was awfully disgusted.

CARIO. No, but Iaso blushed a rosy red
And Panacea turned away her head
Holding her nose: my wind's not frankincense.

WIFE. But he himself?

CARIO.   Observed it not, nor cared.

WIFE. O why, you're making out the god a clown!

CARIO. No, no; an ordure taster.

WIFE.   Oh! you wretch.

CARIO. So then, alarmed, I muffled up my head,
While *he* went round, with calm and quiet tread,
To every patient, scanning each disease.
Then by his side a servant placed a stone
Pestle and mortar; and a medicine chest.

WIFE. A stone one?

CARIO.   Hang it, not the medicine chest.

WIFE. How saw you this, you villain, when your head,
You said just now, was muffled?

CARIO.   Through my cloak.
Full many a peephole has that cloak, I trow.
Well, first he set himself to mix a plaster
For Neocleides, throwing in three cloves
Of Tenian garlic; and with these he mingled
Verjuice and squills; and brayed them up together

Then drenched the mass with Sphettian vinegar,
And turning up the eyelids of the man
Plastered their inner sides, to make the smart
More painful. Up he springs with yells and roars
In act to flee; then laughed the god, and said,
Nay, sit thou there, beplastered; I'll restrain thee,
Thou reckless swearer, from the Assembly now.

WIFE. O what a clever, patriotic god!

CARIO. Then, after this, he sat him down by Plutus,
And first he felt the patient's head, and next
Taking a linen napkin, clean and white,
Wiped both his lips, and all around them, dry.
Then Panacea with a scarlet cloth
Covered his face and head; then the god clucked,
And out there issued from the holy shrine
Two great enormous serpents.

WIFE.   O good heavens!

CARIO. And underneath the scarlet cloth they crept
And licked his eyelids, as it seemed to me;
And, mistress dear, before you could have drunk
Of wine ten goblets, Plutus arose and saw.
O then for joy I clapped my hands together
And woke my master, and, hey presto! both
The god and serpents vanished in the shrine.
And those who lay by Plutus, imagine how
They blessed and greeted him, nor closed their eyes
The whole night long till daylight did appear.
And I could never praise the god enough
For both his deeds, enabling Plutus to see,
And making Neocleides still more blind.

WIFE. O Lord and King, what mighty power is thine!
But prithee where is Plutus?

CARIO.   He's coming here,
With such a crowd collected at his heels.
For all the honest fellows, who before
Had scanty means of living, flocked round,
Welcomed the God and clasped his hand for joy.
—Though others, wealthy rascals, who had gained
Their pile of money by unrighteous means,
Wore scowling faces, knitted up in frowns—
But those went following on, begarlanded,
With smiles and blessings; and the old men's shoes
Rang out in rhythmic progress as they marched.
Now therefore all, arise with one accord,

And skip, and bound, and dance the choral dance,
For nevermore, returning home, ye'll hear
Those fatal words, *No barley in the bin!*

WIFE. By Hecate, for this good news you bring
I've half a mind to crown you with a wreath
Of barley loaves.

CARIO.   Well, don't be loitering now.
The men, by this, are nearly at your gates.

WIFE. Then I will in, and fetch the welcoming gifts
Wherewith to greet these newly purchased—eyes.
                                        (*Exit* WIFE.)

CARIO. And I will out, and meet them as they come.—
                                        (*Exit* CARIO.)

(PLUTUS *enters*.)

PLUTUS. And first I make obeisance to you sun;
Then to august Athene's famous plain,
And all this hospitable land of Cecrops.
Shame on my past career! I blush to think
With whom I long consorted, unawares,
While those who my companionship deserved
I shunned, not knowing. O unhappy me!
In neither this nor that I acted rightly.
But now, reversing all my former ways,
I'll show mankind 'twas through no wish of mine
I used to give myself to rogues and knaves.

(CHREMYLUS *enters, a crowd at his heels*.)

CHREMYLUS. Hang you, be off! The nuisance these friends are,
Emerging suddenly when fortune smiles.
Tcha! How they nudge your ribs, and punch your shins,
Displaying each some token of good will.
What man addressed me not? What aged group
Failed to enwreathe me in the market place?

(WIFE *enters*.)

WIFE. Dearest of men, O welcome you and you.
Come now, I'll take these welcoming gifts and pour them
O'er *you*, as custom bids.

PLUTUS.   Excuse me, no.
When first I'm entering with my sight restored
Into a house, 'twere meeter far that I
Confer a largess rather than receive.

WIFE. Then won't you take the welcoming gifts I bring?

PLUTUS. Aye, by the hearth within, as custom bids.
So too we 'scape the vulgar tricks of farce.
It is not meet, with such a Bard as ours,

To fling a shower of figs and comfits out
Among the audience, just to make them laugh.

WIFE. Well said indeed: for Dexinicus there
Is rising up, to scramble for the figs.

(*They all go into the house.*)

(CARIO *and* CHREMYLUS *come out by turns; they are never
on the stage together. An interval elapses before* CARIO's
first entrance.)

CARIO. How pleasant 'tis to lead a prosperous life,
And that, expending nothing of one's own.
Into this house a heap of golden joys
Has hurled itself though nothing wrong we've done.
Truly a sweet and pleasant thing is wealth.
With good white barley is our garner filled
And all our casks with red and fragrant wine.
And every vessel in the house is crammed
With gold and silver, wonderful to see.
The tank o'erflows with oil; the oil flasks teem
With precious unguents; and the loft with figs.
And every cruet, pitcher, pannikin,
Is turned to bronze; the moldy trencherlets
That held the fish are all of silver now.
Our lantern, all at once, is ivory-framed.
And we the servants, play at odd-or-even
With golden staters; and to cleanse us, use
Not stones, but garlic leaves, so nice we are.
And master now, with garlands round his brow,
Is offering up hog, goat, and ram within.
But me the smoke drove out. I could not bear
To stay within; it bit my eyelids so.

(*A prosperous and well-dressed citizen enters with an attendant carrying a tattered gaberdine and a disreputable
pair of shoes.*)

GOOD MAN. Now then, young fellow, come along with me
To find the god.

CARIO. Eh? Who comes here, I wonder.

GOOD MAN. A man once wretched, but so happy now.

CARIO. One of the honest sort, I dare aver.

GOOD MAN. Aye, aye.

CARIO. What want you now?

GOOD MAN. I am come to thank
The god: great blessings hath he wrought for me.
For I, inheriting a fair estate,

Used it to help my comrades in their need,
Esteeming that the wisest thing to do.

CARIO. I guess your money soon began to fail.

GOOD MAN. Aye, that it did!

CARIO. And then you came to grief.

GOOD MAN. Aye, that I did! And I supposed that they
Whom I had succored in their need, would now
Be glad to help me when in need myself.
But all slipped off as though they saw me not.

CARIO. And jeered you, I'll be bound.

GOOD MAN. Aye, that they did!
The drought in all my vessels proved my ruin.

CARIO. But not so now.

GOOD MAN. Therefore with right good cause
I come with thankfulness to praise the god.

CARIO. But what's the meaning, by the Powers, of that,
That ancient gaberdine your boy is bearing?

GOOD MAN. This too I bring, an offering to the god.

(INFORMER *enters, with witness.*)

CARIO. That's not the robe you were initiate in?

GOOD MAN. No, but I shivered thirteen years therein.

CARIO. Those shoes?

GOOD MAN. Have weathered many a storm with me.

CARIO. And them you bring as votive offerings?

GOOD MAN. Yes.

CARIO. What charming presents to the god you bring!

INFORMER. O me unlucky! O my hard, hard fate!
O thrice unlucky, four times, five times, yea
Twelve times, ten thousand times! O woe is me,
So strong the spirit of ill luck that swamps me.

CARIO. Apollo shield us and ye gracious gods,
What dreadful misery has this poor wretch suffered?

INFORMER. What misery quotha? Shameful, scandalous wrong.
Why, all my goods are spirited away
Through this same god, who shall be blind again
If any justice can be found in Hellas.

GOOD MAN. Methinks I've got a glimmering of the truth.
This is some wretched fellow, come to grief;
Belike he is metal of the baser sort.

CARIO. Then well done he to come to wrack and ruin.

INFORMER. Where, where is he who promised he would make
All of us wealthy in a trice, if only
He could regain his sight? Some of us truly
He has brought to ruin rather than to wealth.

CARIO. Whom has he brought to ruin?

INFORMER. Me, this chap.

CARIO. One of the rogues and housebreakers perchance?

INFORMER. O aye, by Zeus, and you're quite rotten too.
'Tis you have got my goods, I do believe.

CARIO. How bold, Damater, has the Informing rogue
Come blustering in! 'Tis plain he's hunger-mad.

INFORMER. You, sirrah, come to the market place at once,
There to be broken on the wheel, and forced
To tell your misdemeanors.

CARIO. You be hanged!

GOOD MAN. O, if the God would extirpate the whole
Informer brood, right well would he deserve,
O Savior Zeus, of all the Hellenic race!

INFORMER. You jeer me too? Alack, you shared the spoil,
Or whence that brand new cloak? I'll take my oath
I saw you yesterday in a gaberdine.

GOOD MAN. I fear you not. I wear an antidote,
A ring Eudemus sold me for a drachma.

CARIO. 'Tis not inscribed For an Informer's bite.

INFORMER. Is not this insolence? You jest and jeer,
And have not told me what you are doing here.
'Tis for no good you two are here, I'm thinking.

CARIO. Not for your good, you may be sure of that.

INFORMER. For off my goods you are going to dine, I trow.

CARIO. O that in very truth you'd burst asunder,
You and your witness, crammed with nothingness.

INFORMER. Dare you deny it? In your house they are cooking
A jolly lot of flesh and fish, you miscreants.

(*The* INFORMER *gives five double sniffs.*)

CARIO. Smell you aught, lackpurse?

GOOD MAN. Maybe 'tis the cold,
Look what a wretched gaberdine he's wearing.

INFORMER. O Zeus and gods, can such affronts be borne
From rogues like these? O me, how vexed I am
That I, a virtuous patriot, get such treatment.

CARIO. What, you a virtuous patriot?

INFORMER. No man more so.

CARIO. Come then, I'll ask you—answer me.

INFORMER. Well.

CARIO. Are you
A farmer?

INFORMER. Do you take me for a fool?

CARIO. A merchant?

INFORMER.   Aye, I feign so, on occasion.

CARIO. Have you learned *any* trade?

INFORMER.   No, none by Zeus.

CARIO. Then how and whence do you earn your livelihood?

INFORMER. All public matters and all private too
   Are in any charge.

CARIO.   How so?

INFORMER.   'Tis I *who will*.

CARIO. *You* virtuous, housebreaker? When all men hate you
   Meddling with matters which concern you not.

INFORMER. What, think you, booby, it concerns me not
   To aid the State with all my might and main?

CARIO. To aid the State! Does that mean mischief making?

INFORMER. It means upholding the established laws
   And punishing the rogues who break the same.

CARIO. I thought the State appointed Justices
   For this one task.

INFORMER.   And who's to prosecute?

CARIO. Whoever will.

INFORMER.   I am that *man who will*.
   Therefore, at last, the State depends on me.

CARIO. 'Fore Zeus, a worthless leader it has got.
   Come, *will* you this, to lead a quiet life
   And peaceful?

INFORMER.   That's a sheep's life you're describing,
   Living with nothing in the world to do.

CARIO. Then you won't change?

INFORMER.   Not if you gave me all
   Battus's silphium, aye and Wealth to boot.

CARIO. Put off your cloak!

GOOD MAN.   Fellow, to *you* he's speaking.

CARIO. And then your shoes.

GOOD MAN.   All this to *you* he's speaking.

INFORMER. I dare you all. Come on and tackle me
   Whoever will.

CARIO.   I am that *man who will*.

INFORMER. O me, they are stripping me in open day.

CARIO. You choose to live by mischief making, do you?

INFORMER. What are you at? I call you, friend, to witness.

CARIO. Methinks the witness that you brought has cut it.

INFORMER. O me! I am trapped alone.

CARIO.   Aye, now you are roaring.

INFORMER. O me! once more.

CARIO (*to* GOOD MAN).   Hand me your garberdine,
  I'll wrap this rogue of an Informer in it.

GOOD MAN. Nay, that long since is dedicate to Plutus.

CARIO. Where can it then more aptly be suspended
  Than on a rogue and housebreaker like this?
  Plutus we will decorate with nobler robes.

GOOD MAN. How shall we manage with my cast-off shoes?

CARIO. Those on his forehead, as upon the stock
  Of a wild olive, will I nail at once.

INFORMER. I'll stay no longer; for, alone, I am weaker,
  I know, than you; but give me once a comrade,
  A *willing* one, and ere the day is spent
  I'll bring this lusty god of yours to justice,
  For that, being only one, he is overthrowing
  Our great democracy; nor seeks to gain
  The Council's sanction, or the Assembly's either.

                                               (*Exit*)

GOOD MAN. Aye run you off, accoutered as you are
  In all my panoply, and take the station
  I held erewhile beside the bathroom fire,
  The Coryphaeus of the starvelings there.

CARIO. Nay, but the keeper of the baths will drag him
  Out by the ears; for he'll at once perceive
  The man is metal of the baser sort.
  But go we in that you may pray the god.

  (*The* GOOD MAN *and* CARIO *enter the house. An* OLD LADY
*enters with attendant, carrying cakes and sweetmeats on
a tray.*)

OLD LADY. Pray, have we really reached, you dear old men,
  The very dwelling where this new god dwells?
  Or have we altogether missed the way?

CHORUS. No, you have really reached his very door,
  You dear young girl; for girllike is your speech.

OLD LADY. O, then, I'll summon one of those within.
  (CHREMYLUS *enters.*)

CHREMYLUS. Nay, for, unsummoned, I have just come out.
  So tell me freely what has brought you here.

OLD LADY. O, sad, my dear, and anguished is my lot,
  For ever since this god began to see
  My life's been not worth living; all through him.

CHREMYLUS. What, were you too a she informer then
  Among the women?

OLD LADY.   No indeed, not I.

CHREMYLUS. Or, not elected, sat you judging—wine?

OLD LADY. You jest; but I, poor soul, am misery-stung.

CHREMYLUS. What kind of misery stings you? tell me quick.

OLD LADY. Then listen. I'd a lad that loved me well,
Poor, but so handsome, and so fair to see,
Quite virtuous too; whate'er I wished, he did
In such a nice and gentlemanly way;
And what he wanted, I in turn supplied.

CHREMYLUS. What were the things he asked you to supply?

OLD LADY. Not many: so prodigious the respect
In which he held me. 'Twould be twenty drachmas
To buy a cloak and, maybe, eight for shoes;
Then for his sisters he would want a gown,
And just one mantle for his mother's use,
And twice twelve bushels of good wheat perchance.

CHREMYLUS. Not many truly were the gifts he asked!
'Tis plain he held you in immense respect.

OLD LADY. And these he wanted not for greed, he swore,
But for love's sake, that when my robe he wore,
He might, by that, remember me the more.

CHREMYLUS. A man prodigiously in love indeed!

OLD LADY. Aye, but the scamp's quite other-minded now.
He's altogether changed from what he was.
So when I sent him this delicious cake,
And all these bonbons here upon the tray,
Adding a whispered message that I hoped
To come at even—

CHREMYLUS. Tell me what he did?

OLD LADY. He sent them back, and sent this cream-cake too,
Upon condition that I come no more;
And said withal, *Long since, in war's alarms
Were the Milesians lusty men-at-arms.*

CHREMYLUS. O, then the lad's not vicious; now he's rich
He cares for broth no longer, though before,
When he was poor, he snapped up anything.

OLD LADY. O, by the Twain, and every day before,
He used to come, a suppliant, to my door.

CHREMYLUS. What, for your funeral?

OLD LADY. No, he was but fain
My voice to hear.

CHREMYLUS. Your bounty to obtain.

OLD LADY. When in the dumps, he'd smother me with love,
Calling me *little duck* and *little dove.*

CHREMYLUS. And then begged something for a pair of shoes.

OLD LADY. And if perchance, when riding in my coach
  At the Great Mysteries, some gallant threw
  A glance my way, he'd beat me black and blue,
  So very jealous had the young man grown.

CHREMYLUS. Aye, aye, he liked to eat his cake alone.

OLD LADY. He vowed my hands were passing fair and white.

CHREMYLUS. With twenty drachmas in them—well he might.

OLD LADY. And much he praised the fragrance of my skin.

CHREMYLUS. No doubt, no doubt, if Thasian you poured in.

OLD LADY. And then he swore my glance was soft and sweet.

CHREMYLUS. He was no fool: he knew the way to eat
  The goodly substance of a fond old dame.

OLD LADY. O then, my dear, the god is much to blame.
  He said he'd right the injured, every one.

CHREMYLUS. What shall he do? speak, and the thing is done.

OLD LADY. He should, by Zeus, this graceless youth compel
  To recompense the love that loved him well;
  Or no good fortune on the lad should light.

CHREMYLUS. Did he not then repay you every night?

OLD LADY. He'd never leave me all my life, he said.

CHREMYLUS. And rightly too; but now he counts you dead.

OLD LADY. My dear, with love's fierce pangs I've pined away.

CHREMYLUS. Nay rather, grown quite rotten, I should say.

OLD LADY. O, you could draw me through a ring, I know.

CHREMYLUS. A ring? A hoop that round a sieve could go.

OLD LADY. O, here comes he of whom I've been complaining
  All this long while; this is that very lad!
  Bound to some revel surely.

CHREMYLUS.   So it seems.
  At least, he has got the chaplets and the torch.
  (YOUTH enters.)

YOUTH. Friends, I salute you.

OLD LADY.   Eh?

YOUTH.   Mine ancient flame,
  How very suddenly you've got gray hair.

OLD LADY. O me, the insults I am forced to bear.

CHREMYLUS. 'Tis years since last he saw you, I dare say.

OLD LADY. What years, you wretch? He saw me yesterday!

CHREMYLUS. Why then, his case is different from the rest;
  When in his cups, methinks, he sees the best.

OLD LADY. No, this is just his naughty, saucy way.

YOUTH. O gods of old! Poseidon of the Main!
  What countless wrinkles does her face contain!

OLD LADY. O! O!

Keep your torch off me, do.

CHREMYLUS. In that she's right.

For if one spark upon her skin should light,

'Twould set her blazing, like a shriveled wreath.

YOUTH. Come, shall we play together?

OLD LADY. Where? for shame!

YOUTH. Here with some nuts.

OLD LADY. And what's your little game?

YOUTH. How many teeth you've got.

CHREMYLUS. How many teeth?

I'll make a guess at that. She's three, no, four.

YOUTH. Pay up; you've lost: one grinder, and no more.

OLD LADY. Wretch, are you crazy that you make your friend

A washing pot before so many men?

YOUTH. Were you well washed, 'twould do you good belike.

CHREMYLUS. No, no, she's got up for the market now.

But if her white-lead paint were washed away,

Too plain you'd see the tatters of her face.

OLD LADY. So old and saucy! Are you crazy too?

YOUTH. What, is he trying to corrupt you, love,

Toying and fondling you when I'm not looking?

OLD LADY. By Aphrodite, no, you villain you!

CHREMYLUS. No, no, by Hecate, I'm not so daft.

But come, my boy, I really can't allow you

To hate the girl.

YOUTH. Hate her? I love her dearly.

CHREMYLUS. Yet she complains of—

YOUTH. What?

CHREMYLUS. Your flouts and jeers,

Sending her word *Long since, in war's alarms*

Were the Milesian's lusty men-at-arms.

YOUTH. Well, I won't fight you for her sake.

CHREMYLUS. How mean you?

YOUTH. For I respect your age, since be you sure

It is not everybody I'd permit

To take my girl. You, take her and begone.

CHREMYLUS. I know, I know your drift; no longer now

You'd keep her company.

OLD LADY. Who'll permit *that?*

YOUTH. I won't have anything to do with one

Who has been the sport of thirteen thousand—suns.

CHREMYLUS. But, howsoever, as you drank the wine,

You should, in justice, also drink the dregs.

YOUTH. Phew! they're such very old and fusty dregs!

CHREMYLUS. Won't a dreg strainer remedy all that?

YOUTH. Well, go ye in. I want to dedicate
The wreaths I am wearing to this gracious god.

OLD LADY. Aye then, I want to tell him something too.

YOUTH. Aye then, I'll not go in.

CHREMYLUS.   Come, don't be frightened.
Why, she won't ravish you.

YOUTH.   I'm glad to hear it.
I've had enough of her in days gone by.

OLD LADY. Come, go you on; I'll follow close behind.

CHREMYLUS. O Zeus and King, the ancient woman sticks
Tight as a limpet to her poor young man.

(They all go into the house and shut the door.)
(HERMES enters, knocks, and hides himself.)

CARIO *(opening the door)*. Who's knocking at the door? Hallo,
    what's this!
'Twas nobody it seems. The door shall smart,
Making that row for nothing.

*(He comes out bearing a pot containing tripe and dirty
water.)*

HERMES.   Hoi, you sir,
Stop, Cario! don't go in.

CARIO.   Hallo, you fellow,
Was that you banging at the door so loudly?

HERMES. No, I was going to when you flung it open.
But run you in and call your master out,
And then his wife, and then his little ones,
And then the serving men, and then the dog,
And then yourself, and then the sow,

CARIO *(severely)*.   Now tell me
What all this means.

HERMES.   It means that Zeus is going
To mix you up, you rascal, in one dish,
And hurl you all into the Deadman's Pit!

CARIO. Now for this herald must the tongue be cut.
But what's the reason that he is going to do us
Such a bad turn?

HERMES.   Because you have done the basest
And worst of deeds. Since Plutus began to see,
No laurel, meal cake, victim, frankincense,
Has any man on any altar laid
Or aught beside.

CARIO.   Or ever will; for scant
  Your care for us in the evil days gone by.

HERMES. And for the other gods I'm less concerned,
  But I myself am smashed and ruined.

CARIO.   Good.

HERMES. For until now the tavern wives would bring
  From early dawn figs, honey, tipsy cake,
  Titbits for Hermes, such as Hermes loved;
  But now I idly cross my legs and starve.

CARIO. And rightly too who, though such gifts you got,
  Would wrong the givers.

HERMES.   O, my hapless lot!
  O me, the Fourth-day cake in days gone by!

CARIO. You want the absent; nought avails your cry.

HERMES. O me, the gammon which was erst my fare!

CARIO. Here play your game on bladders, in the air.

HERMES. O me, the innards which I ate so hot!

CARIO. In your own innards now a pain you've got.

HERMES. O me, the tankard, brimmed with half and half!
  (*Offers the dirty water in his pot.*)

CARIO. Begone your quickest, taking this to quaff.

HERMES. Will you not help a fellow knave to live?

CARIO. If anything you want is mine to give.

HERMES. O, could you get me but one toothsome loaf,
  Or from the sacrifice you make within
  One slice of lusty meat?

CARIO.   No exports here.

HERMES. O, whensoe'er your master's goods you stole,
  'Twas I that caused you to escape detection.

CARIO. Upon condition, ruffian, that you shared
  The spoils. A toothsome cake would go to you.

HERMES. And then you ate it every bit yourself.

CARIO. But you, remember, never shared the kicks
  Were I perchance detected at my tricks.

HERMES. Well, don't bear malice, if you've Phyle got,
  But take me in to share your happy lot.

CARIO. What, leave the gods, and settle here below?

HERMES. For things look better here than there, I trow.

CARIO. Think you Desertion is a name so grand?

HERMES. Where most I prosper, there's my fatherland.

CARIO. How could we use you if we took you in?

HERMES. Install me here, the Turn-god by the door.

CARIO. The Turn-god? Turns and twists we want no more.

HERMES. The god of Commerce?

CARIO. Wealth we've got, nor need
A petty-huckstering Hermes now to feed.

HERMES. The god of Craft?

CARIO. Craft? quite the other way.
Not craft, but Honesty, we need today.

HERMES. The god of guidance?

CARIO. Plutus can see, my boy!
A guide no more 'tis needful to employ.

HERMES. The god of games? Aha, I've caught you there.
For Plutus is always highly sympathetic
With literary games, and games athletic.

CARIO. How lucky 'tis to have a lot of names!
He has gained a living by that "god of games."
Not without cause our Justices contrive
Their names to enter in more lists than one.

HERMES. Then on these terms I enter?

CARIO. Aye, come in.
And so, at once, be Hermes, Ministrant.
(*Enter* PRIEST.)

PRIEST. O tell me, where may Chremylus be found?

CHREMYLUS. What cheer, my worthy fellow?

PRIEST. What but ill?
For ever since this Plutus began to see,
I'm downright famished, I've got nought to eat,
And that, although I'm Zeus the Savior's priest.

CHREMYLUS. O, by the Powers, and what's the cause of that?

PRIEST. No man will slay a victim now.

CHREMYLUS. Why not?

PRIEST. Because they all are wealthy; yet before,
When men had nothing, one, a merchant saved
From voyage perils, one, escaped from law,
Would come and sacrifice; or else at home
Perform his vows, and summon me, the priest.
But not a soul comes now, or body either,
Except a lot of chaps to do their needs.

CHREMYLUS. Then don't you take your wonted toll of that?

PRIEST. So I've myself a mind to cut the service
Of Zeus the Savior now, and settle here.

CHREMYLUS. Courage! God willing, all will yet be well.
For Zeus the Savior is himself within,
Coming unasked.

PRIEST. O, excellent good news!

CHREMYLUS. So we'll at once install—but bide awhile—
Plutus in the place where he was erst installed,

Guarding the Treasury in Athene's Temple.
Hi! bring me lighted candles. Take them, you,
And march before the god.

PRIEST.   With all my heart.

CHREMYLUS. Call Plutus out, somebody.

OLD LADY.   And I?

CHREMYLUS.   O, you.
Here, balance me these installation pots
Upon your head, and march along in state.
You've got your festive robes at all events.

OLD LADY. But what I came for?

CHREMYLUS.   Everything is right.
The lad you love shall visit you tonight.

OLD LADY. O, if you pledge your honor that my boy
Will come tonight, I'll bear the pots with joy.

CHREMYLUS. These pots are not like other pots at all.
In other pots the mother is atop,
But here the mother's underneath the pot.

CHORUS. 'Tis the end of the Play, and we too must delay
    our departure no longer, but hasten away,
And follow along at the rear of the throng, rejoicing and
    singing our festival song.

                                        (*Exeunt.*)

THE NAMES THAT SPELL
GREAT LITERATURE

Choose from today's most renowned world authors—every one
an important addition to your personal library.

Hermann Hesse

☐	2906	KNULP	$1.95
☐	11916	MAGISTER LUDI	$2.25
☐	2944	DEMIAN	$1.75
☐	10060	GERTRUDE	$1.95
☐	11978	THE JOURNEY TO THE EAST	$1.95
☐	11796	SIDDHARTHA	$1.95
☐	10352	BENEATH THE WHEEL	$1.95
☐	10466	NARCISSUS AND GOLDMUND	$1.95
☐	11289	STEPPENWOLF	$1.95
☐	11510	ROSSHALDE	$1.95

Alexander Solzhenitsyn

☐	10111	THE FIRST CIRCLE	$2.50
☐	11712	ONE DAY IN THE LIFE OF IVAN DENISOVICH	$1.95
☐	2997	AUGUST 1914	$2.50
☐	11300	CANCER WARD	$2.50
☐	12079	LENIN IN ZURICH	$2.95

Jerzy Kosinski

☐	11100	STEPS	$1.75
☐	11407	THE PAINTED BIRD	$1.95
☐	2613	COCKPIT	$2.25

Doris Lessing

☐	11870	THE SUMMER BEFORE THE DARK	$2.25
☐	10425	THE GOLDEN NOTEBOOK	$2.25
☐	7937	THE FOUR-GATED CITY	$1.95
☐	11717	BRIEFING FOR A DESCENT INTO HELL	$2.25

André Schwarz-Bart

☐	10469	THE LAST OF THE JUST	$1.95

Buy them at your local bookstore or use this handy coupon for ordering: